The Aeneid

Old Western Culture Reader
Volume 5

The Aeneid

Old Western Culture Reader
Volume 5

Companion to Old Western Culture,
a great books curriculum by Roman Roads Press

ROMAN ROADS PRESS

MOSCOW, IDAHO

The Aeneid: Old Western Culture Reader, Volume 5

Published by Roman Roads Press
Moscow, Idaho 83843
romanroadspress.com

Series Editor: Daniel Foucachon
Illustrations: E. Gunn Wilson
Interior Layout: E. Gunn Wilson, Summer Stokes, and Carissa Hale

The Aeneid: Old Western Culture Reader, Volume 5
Roman Roads Media, LLC
ISBN: 978-1-944482-45-9

Version 1.2.0 May 2022

This is a companion reader for the *Old Western Culture* curriculum by Roman Roads Press. To find out more about this course, visit www.romanroadspress.com.

OLD WESTERN CULTURE

Great Books Reader Series

THE GREEKS

VOLUME 1 *The Epics*
VOLUME 2 *Drama & Lyric*
VOLUME 3 *The Histories*
VOLUME 4 *The Philosophies*

THE ROMANS

VOLUME 5 *The Aeneid*
VOLUME 6 *The Historians*
VOLUME 7 *Early Christianity*
VOLUME 8 *Nicene Christianity*

CHRISTENDOM

VOLUME 9 *Early Medievals*
VOLUME 10 *Defense of the Faith*
VOLUME 11 *The Medieval Mind*
VOLUME 12 *The Reformation*

EARLY MODERNS

VOLUME 13 *Rise of England*
VOLUME 14 *Politics and Poetry*
VOLUME 15 *The Enlightenment*
VOLUME 16 *The Novels*

NOTE ABOUT LINE NUMBERS

The line numbers in this text match the English translation, which in most cases lines up closely with the original Greek line numbers. We also include the original Greek line numbers, indicated by italics and slightly more indented than the other numbers. Below is an example.

This allows readers to find their way in original texts or to compare with other editions which also indicate Greek line numbers.

ORESTEIA • AGAMEMNON

And slumbrous incense o'er the altars glowed
In fragrance. And for thee, what need to tell
Thy further tale? My lord himself shall well
Instruct me. Yet, to give my lord and king
All reverent greeting at his homecoming—
What dearer dawn on woman's eyes can flame
Than this, which casteth wide her gate to acclaim
The husband whom God leadeth safe from war?—
Go, bear my lord this prayer: That fast and far
He haste him to this town which loves his name;
And in his castle may he find the same
Wife that he left, a watchdog of the hall,
True to one voice and fierce to others all;
A body and soul unchanged, no seal of his
Broke in the waiting years.—No thought of ease
Nor joy from other men hath touched my soul,
Nor shall touch, until bronze be dyed like wool.
A boast so faithful and so plain, I wot,
Spoke by a royal Queen doth shame her not.

Contents

THE AENEID

VERGIL

Translated by John Dryden

VERGIL

Book I

The Trojans, after a seven years' voyage, set sail for Italy, but are overtaken by a dreadful storm, which Æolus raises at Juno's request. The tempest sinks one ship, and scatters the rest. Neptune drives off the winds, and calms the sea. Æneas, with his own ship, and six more, arrives safe at an African port. Venus complains to Jupiter of her son's misfortunes. Jupiter comforts her, and sends Mercury to procure him a kind reception among the Carthaginians. Æneas, going out to discover the country, meets his mother in the shape of a huntress, who conveys him in a cloud to Carthage, where he sees his friends whom he thought lost, and receives a kind entertainment from the queen. Dido, by a device of Venus, begins to have a passion for him, and, after some discourse with him, desires the history of his adventures since the siege of Troy, which is the subject of the two following books.

Arms, and the man I sing, who, forc'd by fate,
And haughty Juno's unrelenting hate,
Expell'd and exil'd, left the Trojan shore.
Long labors, both by sea and land, he bore,
And in the doubtful war, before he won
The Latian realm, and built the destin'd town;
His banish'd gods restor'd to rites divine,
And settled sure succession in his line,
From whence the race of Alban fathers come,
And the long glories of majestic Rome.

O Muse! the causes and the crimes relate;
What goddess was provok'd, and whence her hate;
For what offense the Queen of Heav'n began

To persecute so brave, so just a man;
Involv'd his anxious life in endless cares,
Expos'd to wants, and hurried into wars!
Can heav'nly minds such high resentment show,
Or exercise their spite in human woe?

Against the Tiber's mouth, but far away,
An ancient town was seated on the sea;
A Tyrian colony; the people made
Stout for the war, and studious of their trade:
Carthage the name; belov'd by Juno more
Than her own Argos, or the Samian shore.
Here stood her chariot; here, if Heav'n were kind,
The seat of awful empire she design'd.
Yet she had heard an ancient rumor fly,
(Long cited by the people of the sky,)
That times to come should see the Trojan race
Her Carthage ruin, and her tow'rs deface;
Nor thus confin'd, the yoke of sov'reign sway
Should on the necks of all the nations lay.
She ponder'd this, and fear'd it was in fate;
Nor could forget the war she wag'd of late
For conqu'ring Greece against the Trojan state.
Besides, long causes working in her mind,
And secret seeds of envy, lay behind;
Deep graven in her heart the doom remain'd
Of partial Paris, and her form disdain'd;
The grace bestow'd on ravish'd Ganymed,
Electra's glories, and her injur'd bed.
Each was a cause alone; and all combin'd
To kindle vengeance in her haughty mind.
For this, far distant from the Latian coast
She drove the remnants of the Trojan host;
And sev'n long years th' unhappy wand'ring train
Were toss'd by storms, and scatter'd thro' the main.
Such time, such toil, requir'd the Roman name,
Such length of labor for so vast a frame.

Now scarce the Trojan fleet, with sails and oars,
Had left behind the fair Sicilian shores,
Ent'ring with cheerful shouts the wat'ry reign,
And plowing frothy furrows in the main;
When, lab'ring still with endless discontent,
The Queen of Heav'n did thus her fury vent:

"Then am I vanquish'd? must I yield?" said she,
"And must the Trojans reign in Italy?
So Fate will have it, and Jove adds his force;
Nor can my pow'r divert their happy course.
Could angry Pallas, with revengeful spleen,
The Grecian navy burn, and drown the men?
She, for the fault of one offending foe,
The bolts of Jove himself presum'd to throw:
With whirlwinds from beneath she toss'd the ship,
And bare expos'd the bosom of the deep;
Then, as an eagle gripes the trembling game,
The wretch, yet hissing with her father's flame,
She strongly seiz'd, and with a burning wound
Transfix'd, and naked, on a rock she bound.
But I, who walk in awful state above,
The majesty of heav'n, the sister wife of Jove,
For length of years my fruitless force employ
Against the thin remains of ruin'd Troy!
What nations now to Juno's pow'r will pray,
Or off'rings on my slighted altars lay?"

Thus rag'd the goddess; and, with fury fraught.
The restless regions of the storms she sought,
Where, in a spacious cave of living stone,
The tyrant Æolus, from his airy throne,
With pow'r imperial curbs the struggling winds,
And sounding tempests in dark prisons binds.
This way and that th' impatient captives tend,
And, pressing for release, the mountains rend.
High in his hall th' undaunted monarch stands,

And shakes his scepter, and their rage commands;
Which did he not, their unresisted sway
Would sweep the world before them in their way;
Earth, air, and seas thro' empty space would roll,
And heav'n would fly before the driving soul.
In fear of this, the Father of the Gods
Confin'd their fury to those dark abodes,
And lock'd 'em safe within, oppress'd with
mountain loads;
Impos'd a king, with arbitrary sway,
To loose their fetters, or their force allay.
To whom the suppliant queen her pray'rs address'd,
And thus the tenor of her suit express'd:
"O Æolus! for to thee the King of Heav'n
The pow'r of tempests and of winds has giv'n;
Thy force alone their fury can restrain,
And smooth the waves, or swell the troubled main—
A race of wand'ring slaves, abhorr'd by me,
With prosp'rous passage cut the Tuscan sea;
To fruitful Italy their course they steer,
And for their vanquish'd gods design new temples there.
Raise all thy winds; with night involve the skies;
Sink or disperse my fatal enemies.
Twice sev'n, the charming daughters of the main,
Around my person wait, and bear my train:
Succeed my wish, and second my design;
The fairest, Deiopeia, shall be thine,
And make thee father of a happy line."

To this the god: "'Tis yours, O queen, to will
The work which duty binds me to fulfill.
These airy kingdoms, and this wide command,
Are all the presents of your bounteous hand:
Yours is my sov'reign's grace; and, as your guest,
I sit with gods at their celestial feast;
Raise tempests at your pleasure, or subdue;
Dispose of empire, which I hold from you."

He said, and hurl'd against the mountain side
His quiv'ring spear, and all the god applied.
The raging winds rush thro' the hollow wound,
And dance aloft in air, and skim along the ground;
Then, settling on the sea, the surges sweep,
Raise liquid mountains, and disclose the deep.
South, East, and West with mix'd confusion roar,
And roll the foaming billows to the shore.
The cables crack; the sailors' fearful cries
Ascend; and sable night involves the skies;
And heav'n itself is ravish'd from their eyes.
Loud peals of thunder from the poles ensue;
Then flashing fires the transient light renew;
The face of things a frightful image bears,
And present death in various forms appears.
Struck with unusual fright, the Trojan chief,
With lifted hands and eyes, invokes relief;
And, "Thrice and four times happy those," he cried,
"That under Ilian walls before their parents died!
Tydides, bravest of the Grecian train!
Why could not I by that strong arm be slain,
And lie by noble Hector on the plain,
Or great Sarpedon, in those bloody fields
Where Simoïs rolls the bodies and the shields
Of heroes, whose dismember'd hands yet bear
The dart aloft, and clench the pointed spear!"

Thus while the pious prince his fate bewails,
Fierce Boreas drove against his flying sails,
And rent the sheets; the raging billows rise,
And mount the tossing vessels to the skies:
Nor can the shiv'ring oars sustain the blow;
The galley gives her side, and turns her prow;
While those astern, descending down the steep,
Thro' gaping waves behold the boiling deep.
Three ships were hurried by the southern blast,
And on the secret shelves with fury cast.

Those hidden rocks th' Ausonian sailors knew:
They call'd them Altars, when they rose in view,
And show'd their spacious backs above the flood.
Three more fierce Eurus, in his angry mood,
Dash'd on the shallows of the moving sand,
And in mid ocean left them moor'd aland.
Orontes' bark, that bore the Lycian crew,
(A horrid sight!) ev'n in the hero's view,
From stem to stern by waves was overborne:
The trembling pilot, from his rudder torn,
Was headlong hurl'd; thrice round the ship was toss'd,
Then bulg'd at once, and in the deep was lost;
And here and there above the waves were seen
Arms, pictures, precious goods, and floating men.
The stoutest vessel to the storm gave way,
And suck'd thro' loosen'd planks the rushing sea.
Ilioneus was her chief: Alethes old,
Achates faithful, Abas young and bold,
Endur'd not less; their ships, with gaping seams,
Admit the deluge of the briny streams.

Meantime imperial Neptune heard the sound
Of raging billows breaking on the ground.
Displeas'd, and fearing for his wat'ry reign,
He rear'd his awful head above the main,
Serene in majesty; then roll'd his eyes
Around the space of earth, and seas, and skies.
He saw the Trojan fleet dispers'd, distress'd,
By stormy winds and wintry heav'n oppress'd.
Full well the god his sister's envy knew,
And what her aims and what her arts pursue.
He summon'd Eurus and the western blast,
And first an angry glance on both he cast;
Then thus rebuk'd: "Audacious winds! from whence
This bold attempt, this rebel insolence?
Is it for you to ravage seas and land,
Unauthoriz'd by my supreme command?

To raise such mountains on the troubled main?
Whom I—but first 'tis fit the billows to restrain;
And then you shall be taught obedience to my reign.
Hence! to your lord my royal mandate bear—
The realms of ocean and the fields of air
Are mine, not his. By fatal lot to me
The liquid empire fell, and trident of the sea.
His pow'r to hollow caverns is confin'd:
There let him reign, the jailer of the wind,
With hoarse commands his breathing subjects call,
And boast and bluster in his empty hall."
He spoke; and, while he spoke, he smooth'd the sea,
Dispell'd the darkness, and restor'd the day.
Cymothœ, Triton, and the sea-green train
Of beauteous nymphs, the daughters of the main,
Clear from the rocks the vessels with their hands:
The god himself with ready trident stands,
And opes the deep, and spreads the moving sands;
Then heaves them off the shoals. Where'er he guides
His finny coursers and in triumph rides,
The waves unruffle and the sea subsides.
As, when in tumults rise th' ignoble crowd,
Mad are their motions, and their tongues are loud;
And stones and brands in rattling volleys fly,
And all the rustic arms that fury can supply:
If then some grave and pious man appear,
They hush their noise, and lend a list'ning ear;
He soothes with sober words their angry mood,
And quenches their innate desire of blood:
So, when the Father of the Flood appears,
And o'er the seas his sov'reign trident rears,
Their fury falls: he skims the liquid plains,
High on his chariot, and, with loosen'd reins,
Majestic moves along, and awful peace maintains.
The weary Trojans ply their shatter'd oars
To nearest land, and make the Libyan shores.

Within a long recess there lies a bay:
An island shades it from the rolling sea,
And forms a port secure for ships to ride;
Broke by the jutting land, on either side,
In double streams the briny waters glide.
Betwixt two rows of rocks a sylvan scene
Appears above, and groves for ever green:
A grot is form'd beneath, with mossy seats,
To rest the Nereids, and exclude the heats.
Down thro' the crannies of the living walls
The crystal streams descend in murm'ring falls:
No haulsers need to bind the vessels here,
Nor bearded anchors; for no storms they fear.
Sev'n ships within this happy harbor meet,
The thin remainders of the scatter'd fleet.
The Trojans, worn with toils, and spent with woes,
Leap on the welcome land, and seek their
wish'd repose.

First, good Achates, with repeated strokes
Of clashing flints, their hidden fire provokes:
Short flame succeeds; a bed of wither'd leaves
The dying sparkles in their fall receives:
Caught into life, in fiery fumes they rise,
And, fed with stronger food, invade the skies.
The Trojans, dropping wet, or stand around
The cheerful blaze, or lie along the ground:
Some dry their corn, infected with the brine,
Then grind with marbles, and prepare to dine.
Æneas climbs the mountain's airy brow,
And takes a prospect of the seas below,
If Capys thence, or Antheus he could spy,
Or see the streamers of Caïcus fly.
No vessels were in view; but, on the plain,
Three beamy stags command a lordly train
Of branching heads: the more ignoble throng
Attend their stately steps, and slowly graze along.

He stood; and, while secure they fed below,
He took the quiver and the trusty bow
Achates us'd to bear: the leaders first
He laid along, and then the vulgar pierc'd;
Nor ceas'd his arrows, till the shady plain
Sev'n mighty bodies with their blood distain.
For the sev'n ships he made an equal share,
And to the port return'd, triumphant from the war.
The jars of gen'rous wine (Acestes' gift,
When his Trinacrian shores the navy left)
He set abroach, and for the feast prepar'd,
In equal portions with the ven'son shar'd.
Thus while he dealt it round, the pious chief
With cheerful words allay'd the common grief:
"Endure, and conquer! Jove will soon dispose
To future good our past and present woes.
With me, the rocks of Scylla you have tried;
Th' inhuman Cyclops and his den defied.
What greater ills hereafter can you bear?
Resume your courage and dismiss your care,
An hour will come, with pleasure to relate
Your sorrows past, as benefits of Fate.
Thro' various hazards and events, we move
To Latium and the realms foredoom'd by Jove.
Call'd to the seat (the promise of the skies)
Where Trojan kingdoms once again may rise,
Endure the hardships of your present state;
Live, and reserve yourselves for better fate."

These words he spoke, but spoke not from his heart;
His outward smiles conceal'd his inward smart.
The jolly crew, unmindful of the past,
The quarry share, their plenteous dinner haste.
Some strip the skin; some portion out the spoil;
The limbs, yet trembling, in the cauldrons boil;
Some on the fire the reeking entrails broil.
Stretch'd on the grassy turf, at ease they dine,

Restore their strength with meat, and cheer
  their souls with wine.
Their hunger thus appeas'd, their care attends
The doubtful fortune of their absent friends:
Alternate hopes and fears their minds possess,
Whether to deem 'em dead, or in distress.
Above the rest, Æneas mourns the fate
Of brave Orontes, and th' uncertain state
Of Gyas, Lycus, and of Amycus.
The day, but not their sorrows, ended thus.

When, from aloft, almighty Jove surveys
Earth, air, and shores, and navigable seas,
At length on Libyan realms he fix'd his eyes—
Whom, pond'ring thus on human miseries,
When Venus saw, she with a lowly look,
Not free from tears, her heav'nly sire bespoke:

"O King of Gods and Men! whose awful hand
Disperses thunder on the seas and land,
Disposing all with absolute command;
How could my pious son thy pow'r incense?
Or what, alas! is vanish'd Troy's offense?
Our hope of Italy not only lost,
On various seas by various tempests toss'd,
But shut from ev'ry shore, and barr'd from ev'ry coast.
You promis'd once, a progeny divine
Of Romans, rising from the Trojan line,
In after times should hold the world in awe,
And to the land and ocean give the law.
How is your doom revers'd, which eas'd my care
When Troy was ruin'd in that cruel war?
Then fates to fates I could oppose; but now,
When Fortune still pursues her former blow,
What can I hope? What worse can still succeed?
What end of labors has your will decreed?
Antenor, from the midst of Grecian hosts,

Could pass secure, and pierce th' Illyrian coasts,
Where, rolling down the steep, Timavus raves
And thro' nine channels disembogues his waves.
At length he founded Padua's happy seat,
And gave his Trojans a secure retreat;
There fix'd their arms, and there renew'd their name,
And there in quiet rules, and crown'd with fame.
But we, descended from your sacred line,
Entitled to your heav'n and rites divine,
Are banish'd earth; and, for the wrath of one,
Remov'd from Latium and the promis'd throne.
Are these our scepters? these our due rewards?
And is it thus that Jove his plighted faith regards?"

To whom the Father of th' immortal race,
Smiling with that serene indulgent face,
With which he drives the clouds and clears the skies,
First gave a holy kiss; then thus replies:

"Daughter, dismiss thy fears; to thy desire
The fates of thine are fix'd, and stand entire.
Thou shalt behold thy wish'd Lavinian walls;
And, ripe for heav'n, when fate Æneas calls,
Then shalt thou bear him up, sublime, to me:
No councils have revers'd my firm decree.
And, lest new fears disturb thy happy state,
Know, I have search'd the mystic rolls of Fate:
Thy son (nor is th' appointed season far)
In Italy shall wage successful war,
Shall tame fierce nations in the bloody field,
And sov'reign laws impose, and cities build,
Till, after ev'ry foe subdued, the sun
Thrice thro' the signs his annual race shall run:
This is his time prefix'd. Ascanius then,
Now call'd Iulus, shall begin his reign.
He thirty rolling years the crown shall wear,
Then from Lavinium shall the seat transfer,

And, with hard labor, Alba Longa build.
The throne with his succession shall be fill'd
Three hundred circuits more: then shall be seen
Ilia the fair, a priestess and a queen,
Who, full of Mars, in time, with kindly throes,
Shall at a birth two goodly boys disclose.
The royal babes a tawny wolf shall drain:
Then Romulus his grandsire's throne shall gain,
Of martial tow'rs the founder shall become,
The people Romans call, the city Rome.
To them no bounds of empire I assign,
Nor term of years to their immortal line.
Ev'n haughty Juno, who, with endless broils,
Earth, seas, and heav'n, and Jove himself turmoils;
At length aton'd, her friendly pow'r shall join,
To cherish and advance the Trojan line.
The subject world shall Rome's dominion own,
And, prostrate, shall adore the nation of the gown.
An age is ripening in revolving fate
When Troy shall overturn the Grecian state,
And sweet revenge her conqu'ring sons shall call,
To crush the people that conspir'd her fall.
Then Cæsar from the Julian stock shall rise,
Whose empire ocean, and whose fame the skies
Alone shall bound; whom, fraught with eastern spoils,
Our heav'n, the just reward of human toils,
Securely shall repay with rites divine;
And incense shall ascend before his sacred shrine.
Then dire debate and impious war shall cease,
And the stern age be soften'd into peace:
Then banish'd Faith shall once again return,
And Vestal fires in hallow'd temples burn;
And Remus with Quirinus shall sustain
The righteous laws, and fraud and force restrain.
Janus himself before his fane shall wait,

And keep the dreadful issues of his gate,
With bolts and iron bars: within remains
Imprison'd Fury, bound in brazen chains;
High on a trophy rais'd, of useless arms,
He sits, and threats the world with vain alarms."

He said, and sent Cyllenius with command
To free the ports, and ope the Punic land
To Trojan guests; lest, ignorant of fate,
The queen might force them from her town and state.
Down from the steep of heav'n Cyllenius flies,
And cleaves with all his wings the yielding skies.
Soon on the Libyan shore descends the god,
Performs his message, and displays his rod:
The surly murmurs of the people cease;
And, as the fates requir'd, they give the peace:
The queen herself suspends the rigid laws,
The Trojans pities, and protects their cause.

Meantime, in shades of night Æneas lies:
Care seiz'd his soul, and sleep forsook his eyes.
But, when the sun restor'd the cheerful day,
He rose, the coast and country to survey,
Anxious and eager to discover more.
It look'd a wild uncultivated shore;
But, whether humankind, or beasts alone
Possess'd the new-found region, was unknown.
Beneath a ledge of rocks his fleet he hides:
Tall trees surround the mountain's shady sides;
The bending brow above a safe retreat provides.
Arm'd with two pointed darts, he leaves his friends,
And true Achates on his steps attends.
Lo! in the deep recesses of the wood,
Before his eyes his goddess mother stood:
A huntress in her habit and her mien;

Her dress a maid, her air confess'd a queen.
Bare were her knees, and knots her garments bind;
Loose was her hair, and wanton'd in the wind;
Her hand sustain'd a bow; her quiver hung behind.
She seem'd a virgin of the Spartan blood:
With such array Harpalyce bestrode
Her Thracian courser and outstripp'd the
rapid flood.
"Ho, strangers! have you lately seen," she said,
"One of my sisters, like myself array'd,
Who cross'd the lawn, or in the forest stray'd?
A painted quiver at her back she bore;
Varied with spots, a lynx's hide she wore;
And at full cry pursued the tusky boar."

Thus Venus: thus her son replied again:
"None of your sisters have we heard or seen,
O virgin! or what other name you bear
Above that style—O more than mortal fair!
Your voice and mien celestial birth betray!
If, as you seem, the sister of the day,
Or one at least of chaste Diana's train,
Let not an humble suppliant sue in vain;
But tell a stranger, long in tempests toss'd,
What earth we tread, and who commands
the coast?
Then on your name shall wretched mortals call,
And offer'd victims at your altars fall."
"I dare not," she replied, "assume the name
Of goddess, or celestial honors claim:
For Tyrian virgins bows and quivers bear,
And purple buskins o'er their ankles wear.
Know, gentle youth, in Libyan lands you are—
A people rude in peace, and rough in war.
The rising city, which from far you see,
Is Carthage, and a Tyrian colony.
Phœnician Dido rules the growing state,

Who fled from Tyre, to shun her brother's hate.
Great were her wrongs, her story full of fate;
Which I will sum in short. Sichæus, known
For wealth, and brother to the Punic throne,
Possess'd fair Dido's bed; and either heart
At once was wounded with an equal dart.
Her father gave her, yet a spotless maid;
Pygmalion then the Tyrian scepter sway'd:
One who condemn'd divine and human laws.
Then strife ensued, and cursed gold the cause.
The monarch, blinded with desire of wealth,
With steel invades his brother's life by stealth;
Before the sacred altar made him bleed,
And long from her conceal'd the cruel deed.
Some tale, some new pretense, he daily coin'd,
To soothe his sister, and delude her mind.
At length, in dead of night, the ghost appears
Of her unhappy lord: the specter stares,
And, with erected eyes, his bloody bosom bares.
The cruel altars and his fate he tells,
And the dire secret of his house reveals,
Then warns the widow, with her household gods,
To seek a refuge in remote abodes.
Last, to support her in so long a way,
He shows her where his hidden treasure lay.
Admonish'd thus, and seiz'd with mortal fright,
The queen provides companions of her flight:
They meet, and all combine to leave the state,
Who hate the tyrant, or who fear his hate.
They seize a fleet, which ready rigg'd they find;
Nor is Pygmalion's treasure left behind.
The vessels, heavy laden, put to sea
With prosp'rous winds; a woman leads the way.
I know not, if by stress of weather driv'n,
Or was their fatal course dispos'd by Heav'n;
At last they landed, where from far your eyes
May view the turrets of new Carthage rise;

There bought a space of ground, which (Byrsa call'd,
From the bull's hide) they first enclos'd, and wall'd.
But whence are you? what country claims your birth?
What seek you, strangers, on our Libyan earth?"

To whom, with sorrow streaming from his eyes,
And deeply sighing, thus her son replies:
"Could you with patience hear, or I relate,
O nymph, the tedious annals of our fate!
Thro' such a train of woes if I should run,
The day would sooner than the tale be done!
From ancient Troy, by force expell'd, we came—
If you by chance have heard the Trojan name.
On various seas by various tempests toss'd,
At length we landed on your Libyan coast.
The good Æneas am I call'd—a name,
While Fortune favor'd, not unknown to fame.
My household gods, companions of my woes,
With pious care I rescued from our foes.
To fruitful Italy my course was bent;
And from the King of Heav'n is my descent.
With twice ten sail I cross'd the Phrygian sea;
Fate and my mother goddess led my way.
Scarce sev'n, the thin remainders of my fleet,
From storms preserv'd, within your harbor meet.
Myself distress'd, an exile, and unknown,
Debarr'd from Europe, and from Asia thrown,
In Libyan deserts wander thus alone."

His tender parent could no longer bear;
But, interposing, sought to soothe his care.
"Whoe'er you are—not unbelov'd by Heav'n,
Since on our friendly shore your ships are driv'n—
Have courage: to the gods permit the rest,

And to the queen expose your just request.
Now take this earnest of success, for more:
Your scatter'd fleet is join'd upon the shore;
The winds are chang'd, your friends from danger free;
Or I renounce my skill in augury.
Twelve swans behold in beauteous order move,
And stoop with closing pinions from above;
Whom late the bird of Jove had driv'n along,
And thro' the clouds pursued the scatt'ring throng:
Now, all united in a goodly team,
They skim the ground, and seek the quiet stream.
As they, with joy returning, clap their wings,
And ride the circuit of the skies in rings;
Not otherwise your ships, and ev'ry friend,
Already hold the port, or with swift sails descend.
No more advice is needful; but pursue
The path before you, and the town in view."

Thus having said, she turn'd, and made appear
Her neck refulgent, and dishevel'd hair,
Which, flowing from her shoulders, reach'd the ground.
And widely spread ambrosial scents around:
In length of train descends her sweeping gown;
And, by her graceful walk, the Queen of Love is known.
The prince pursued the parting deity
With words like these: "Ah! whither do you fly?
Unkind and cruel! to deceive your son
In borrow'd shapes, and his embrace to shun;
Never to bless my sight, but thus unknown;
And still to speak in accents not your own."
Against the goddess these complaints he made,
But took the path, and her commands obey'd.
They march, obscure; for Venus kindly shrouds
With mists their persons, and involves in clouds,

That, thus unseen, their passage none might stay,
Or force to tell the causes of their way.
This part perform'd, the goddess flies sublime
To visit Paphos and her native clime;
Where garlands, ever green and ever fair,
With vows are offer'd, and with solemn pray'r:
A hundred altars in her temple smoke;
A thousand bleeding hearts her pow'r invoke.

They climb the next ascent, and, looking down,
Now at a nearer distance view the town.
The prince with wonder sees the stately tow'rs,
Which late were huts and shepherds' homely bow'rs,
The gates and streets; and hears, from ev'ry part,
The noise and busy concourse of the mart.
The toiling Tyrians on each other call
To ply their labor: some extend the wall;
Some build the citadel; the brawny throng
Or dig, or push unwieldy stones along.
Some for their dwellings choose a spot of ground,
Which, first design'd, with ditches they surround.
Some laws ordain; and some attend the choice
Of holy senates, and elect by voice.
Here some design a mole, while others there
Lay deep foundations for a theater;
From marble quarries mighty columns hew,
For ornaments of scenes, and future view.
Such is their toil, and such their busy pains,
As exercise the bees in flow'ry plains,
When winter past, and summer scarce begun,
Invites them forth to labor in the sun;
Some lead their youth abroad, while some condense
Their liquid store, and some in cells dispense;
Some at the gate stand ready to receive
The golden burthen, and their friends relieve;
All with united force, combine to drive
The lazy drones from the laborious hive:

With envy stung, they view each other's deeds;
The fragrant work with diligence proceeds.
"Thrice happy you, whose walls already rise!"
Æneas said, and view'd, with lifted eyes,
Their lofty tow'rs; then, entering at the gate,
Conceal'd in clouds (prodigious to relate)
He mix'd, unmark'd, among the busy throng,
Borne by the tide, and pass'd unseen along.

Full in the center of the town there stood,
Thick set with trees, a venerable wood.
The Tyrians, landing near this holy ground,
And digging here, a prosp'rous omen found:
From under earth a courser's head they drew,
Their growth and future fortune to foreshew.
This fated sign their foundress Juno gave,
Of a soil fruitful, and a people brave.
Sidonian Dido here with solemn state
Did Juno's temple build, and consecrate,
Enrich'd with gifts, and with a golden shrine;
But more the goddess made the place divine.
On brazen steps the marble threshold rose,
And brazen plates the cedar beams enclose:
The rafters are with brazen cov'rings crown'd;
The lofty doors on brazen hinges sound.
What first Æneas this place beheld,
Reviv'd his courage, and his fear expell'd.
For while, expecting there the queen, he rais'd
His wond'ring eyes, and round the temple gaz'd,
Admir'd the fortune of the rising town,
The striving artists, and their arts' renown;
He saw, in order painted on the wall,
Whatever did unhappy Troy befall:
The wars that fame around the world had blown,
All to the life, and ev'ry leader known.
There Agamemnon, Priam here, he spies,
And fierce Achilles, who both kings defies.

He stopp'd, and weeping said: "O friend! ev'n here
The monuments of Trojan woes appear!
Our known disasters fill ev'n foreign lands:
See there, where old unhappy Priam stands!
Ev'n the mute walls relate the warrior's fame,
And Trojan griefs the Tyrians' pity claim."
He said (his tears a ready passage find),
Devouring what he saw so well design'd,
And with an empty picture fed his mind:
For there he saw the fainting Grecians yield,
And here the trembling Trojans quit the field,
Pursued by fierce Achilles thro' the plain,
On his high chariot driving o'er the slain.
The tents of Rhesus next his grief renew,
By their white sails betray'd to nightly view;
And wakeful Diomede, whose cruel sword
The sentries slew, nor spar'd their slumb'ring lord,
Then took the fiery steeds, ere yet the food
Of Troy they taste, or drink the Xanthian flood.
Elsewhere he saw where Troilus defied
Achilles, and unequal combat tried;
Then, where the boy disarm'd, with loosen'd reins,
Was by his horses hurried o'er the plains,
Hung by the neck and hair, and dragg'd around:
The hostile spear, yet sticking in his wound,
With tracks of blood inscrib'd the dusty ground.
Meantime the Trojan dames, oppress'd with woe,
To Pallas' fane in long procession go,
In hopes to reconcile their heav'nly foe.
They weep, they beat their breasts, they rend
their hair,
And rich embroider'd vests for presents bear;
But the stern goddess stands unmov'd with pray'r.
Thrice round the Trojan walls Achilles drew
The corpse of Hector, whom in fight he slew.
Here Priam sues; and there, for sums of gold,
The lifeless body of his son is sold.

So sad an object, and so well express'd,
Drew sighs and groans from the griev'd
hero's breast,
To see the figure of his lifeless friend,
And his old sire his helpless hand extend.
Himself he saw amidst the Grecian train,
Mix'd in the bloody battle on the plain;
And swarthy Memnon in his arms he knew,
His pompous ensigns, and his Indian crew.
Penthisilea there, with haughty grace,
Leads to the wars an Amazonian race:
In their right hands a pointed dart they wield;
The left, for ward, sustains the lunar shield.
Athwart her breast a golden belt she throws,
Amidst the press alone provokes a thousand foes,
And dares her maiden arms to manly force oppose.

Thus while the Trojan prince employs his eyes,
Fix'd on the walls with wonder and surprise,
The beauteous Dido, with a num'rous train
And pomp of guards, ascends the sacred fane.
Such on Eurotas' banks, or Cynthus' height,
Diana seems; and so she charms the sight,
When in the dance the graceful goddess leads
The choir of nymphs, and overtops their heads:
Known by her quiver, and her lofty mien,
She walks majestic, and she looks their queen;
Latona sees her shine above the rest,
And feeds with secret joy her silent breast.
Such Dido was; with such becoming state,
Amidst the crowd, she walks serenely great.
Their labor to her future sway she speeds,
And passing with a gracious glance proceeds;
Then mounts the throne, high plac'd before
the shrine:
In crowds around, the swarming people join.
She takes petitions, and dispenses laws,

Hears and determines ev'ry private cause;
Their tasks in equal portions she divides,
And, where unequal, there by lots decides.
Another way by chance Æneas bends
His eyes, and unexpected sees his friends,
Antheus, Sergestus grave, Cloanthus strong,
And at their backs a mighty Trojan throng,
Whom late the tempest on the billows toss'd,
And widely scatter'd on another coast.
The prince, unseen, surpris'd with wonder stands,
And longs, with joyful haste, to join their hands;
But, doubtful of the wish'd event, he stays,
And from the hollow cloud his friends surveys,
Impatient till they told their present state,
And where they left their ships, and what their fate,
And why they came, and what was their request;
For these were sent, commission'd by the rest,
To sue for leave to land their sickly men,
And gain admission to the gracious queen.
Ent'ring, with cries they fill'd the holy fane;
Then thus, with lowly voice, Ilioneus began:

"O queen! indulg'd by favor of the gods
To found an empire in these new abodes,
To build a town, with statutes to restrain
The wild inhabitants beneath thy reign,
We wretched Trojans, toss'd on ev'ry shore,
From sea to sea, thy clemency implore.
Forbid the fires our shipping to deface!
Receive th' unhappy fugitives to grace,
And spare the remnant of a pious race!
We come not with design of wasteful prey,
To drive the country, force the swains away:
Nor such our strength, nor such is our desire;
The vanquish'd dare not to such thoughts aspire.
A land there is, Hesperia nam'd of old;
The soil is fruitful, and the men are bold—

Th' Œnotrians held it once—by common fame
Now call'd Italia, from the leader's name.
To that sweet region was our voyage bent,
When winds and ev'ry warring element
Disturb'd our course, and, far from sight of land,
Cast our torn vessels on the moving sand:
The sea came on; the South, with mighty roar,
Dispers'd and dash'd the rest upon the rocky shore.
Those few you see escap'd the Storm, and fear,
Unless you interpose, a shipwreck here.
What men, what monsters, what inhuman race,
What laws, what barb'rous customs of the place,
Shut up a desert shore to drowning men,
And drive us to the cruel seas again?
If our hard fortune no compassion draws,
Nor hospitable rights, nor human laws,
The gods are just, and will revenge our cause.
Æneas was our prince: a juster lord,
Or nobler warrior, never drew a sword;
Observant of the right, religious of his word.
If yet he lives, and draws this vital air,
Nor we, his friends, of safety shall despair;
Nor you, great queen, these offices repent,
Which he will equal, and perhaps augment.
We want not cities, nor Sicilian coasts,
Where King Acestes Trojan lineage boasts.
Permit our ships a shelter on your shores,
Refitted from your woods with planks and oars,
That, if our prince be safe, we may renew
Our destin'd course, and Italy pursue.
But if, O best of men, the Fates ordain
That thou art swallow'd in the Libyan main,
And if our young Iulus be no more,
Dismiss our navy from your friendly shore,
That we to good Acestes may return,
And with our friends our common losses mourn."
Thus spoke Ilioneus: the Trojan crew
With cries and clamors his request renew.

The modest queen a while, with downcast eyes,
Ponder'd the speech; then briefly thus replies:
"Trojans, dismiss your fears; my cruel fate,
And doubts attending an unsettled state,
Force me to guard my coast from foreign foes.
Who has not heard the story of your woes,
The name and fortune of your native place,
The fame and valor of the Phrygian race?
We Tyrians are not so devoid of sense,
Nor so remote from Phœbus' influence.
Whether to Latian shores your course is bent,
Or, driv'n by tempests from your first intent,
You seek the good Acestes' government,
Your men shall be receiv'd, your fleet repair'd,
And sail, with ships of convoy for your guard:
Or, would you stay, and join your friendly pow'rs
To raise and to defend the Tyrian tow'rs,
My wealth, my city, and myself are yours.
And would to Heav'n, the Storm, you felt, would bring
On Carthaginian coasts your wand'ring king.
My people shall, by my command, explore
The ports and creeks of ev'ry winding shore,
And towns, and wilds, and shady woods, in quest
Of so renown'd and so desir'd a guest."

Rais'd in his mind the Trojan hero stood,
And long'd to break from out his ambient cloud:
Achates found it, and thus urg'd his way:
"From whence, O goddess-born, this long delay?
What more can you desire, your welcome sure,
Your fleet in safety, and your friends secure?
One only wants; and him we saw in vain
Oppose the Storm, and swallow'd in the main.
Orontes in his fate our forfeit paid;
The rest agrees with what your mother said."
Scarce had he spoken, when the cloud gave way,
The mists flew upward and disolv'd in day.

The Trojan chief appear'd in open sight,
August in visage, and serenely bright.
His mother goddess, with her hands divine,
Had form'd his curling locks, and made his temples shine,
And giv'n his rolling eyes a sparkling grace,
And breath'd a youthful vigor on his face;
Like polish'd ivory, beauteous to behold,
Or Parian marble, when encas'd in gold:
Thus radiant from the circling cloud he broke,
And thus with manly modesty he spoke:

"He whom you seek am I; by tempests toss'd,
And sav'd from shipwreck on your Libyan coast;
Presenting, gracious queen, before your throne,
A prince that owes his life to you alone.
Fair majesty, the refuge and redress
Of those whom fate pursues, and wants oppress,
You, who your pious offices employ
To save the relics of abandon'd Troy;
Receive the shipwreck'd on your friendly shore,
With hospitable rites relieve the poor;
Associate in your town a wand'ring train,
And strangers in your palace entertain:
What thanks can wretched fugitives return,
Who, scatter'd thro' the world, in exile mourn?
The gods, if gods to goodness are inclin'd;
If acts of mercy touch their heav'nly mind,
And, more than all the gods, your gen'rous heart.
Conscious of worth, requite its own desert!
In you this age is happy, and this earth,
And parents more than mortal gave you birth.
While rolling rivers into seas shall run,
And round the space of heav'n the radiant sun;
While trees the mountain tops with shades supply,
Your honor, name, and praise shall never die.
Whate'er abode my fortune has assign'd,
Your image shall be present in my mind."

Thus having said, he turn'd with pious haste,
And joyful his expecting friends embrac'd:
With his right hand Ilioneus was grac'd,
Serestus with his left; then to his breast
Cloanthus and the noble Gyas press'd;
And so by turns descended to the rest.

The Tyrian queen stood fix'd upon his face,
Pleas'd with his motions, ravish'd with his grace;
Admir'd his fortunes, more admir'd the man;
Then recollected stood, and thus began:
"What fate, O goddess-born; what angry pow'rs
Have cast you shipwreck'd on our barren shores?
Are you the great Æneas, known to fame,
Who from celestial seed your lineage claim?

The same Æneas whom fair Venus bore
To fam'd Anchises on th' Idæan shore?
It calls into my mind, tho' then a child,
When Teucer came, from Salamis exil'd,
And sought my father's aid, to be restor'd:
My father Belus then with fire and sword
Invaded Cyprus, made the region bare,
And, conqu'ring, finish'd the successful war.
From him the Trojan siege I understood,
The Grecian chiefs, and your illustrious blood.
Your foe himself the Dardan valor prais'd,
And his own ancestry from Trojans rais'd.
Enter, my noble guest, and you shall find,
If not a costly welcome, yet a kind:
For I myself, like you, have been distress'd,
Till Heav'n afforded me this place of rest;
Like you, an alien in a land unknown,
I learn to pity woes so like my own."
She said, and to the palace led her guest;
Then offer'd incense, and proclaim'd a feast.
Nor yet less careful for her absent friends,

Twice ten fat oxen to the ships she sends;
Besides a hundred boars, a hundred lambs,
With bleating cries, attend their milky dams;
And jars of gen'rous wine and spacious bowls
She gives, to cheer the sailors' drooping souls.
Now purple hangings clothe the palace walls,
And sumptuous feasts are made in splendid halls:
On Tyrian carpets, richly wrought, they dine;
With loads of massy plate the sideboards shine,
And antique vases, all of gold emboss'd
(The gold itself inferior to the cost),
Of curious work, where on the sides were seen
The fights and figures of illustrious men,
From their first founder to the present queen.

The good Æneas, whose paternal care
Iülus' absence could no longer bear,
Dispatch'd Achates to the ships in haste,
To give a glad relation of the past,
And, fraught with precious gifts, to bring the boy,
Snatch'd from the ruins of unhappy Troy:
A robe of tissue, stiff with golden wire;
An upper vest, once Helen's rich attire,
From Argos by the fam'd adult'ress brought,
With golden flow'rs and winding foliage wrought,
Her mother Leda's present, when she came
To ruin Troy and set the world on flame;
The scepter Priam's eldest daughter bore,
Her orient necklace, and the crown she wore
Of double texture, glorious to behold,
One order set with gems, and one with gold.
Instructed thus, the wise Achates goes,
And in his diligence his duty shows.

But Venus, anxious for her son's affairs,
New counsels tries, and new designs prepares:
That Cupid should assume the shape and face

Of sweet Ascanius, and the sprightly grace;
Should bring the presents, in her nephew's stead,
And in Eliza's veins the gentle poison shed:
For much she fear'd the Tyrians, double-tongued,
And knew the town to Juno's care belong'd.
These thoughts by night her golden slumbers broke,
And thus alarm'd, to winged Love she spoke:
"My son, my strength, whose mighty pow'r alone
Controls the Thund'rer on his awful throne,
To thee thy much-afflicted mother flies,
And on thy succor and thy faith relies.
Thou know'st, my son, how Jove's revengeful wife,
By force and fraud, attempts thy brother's life;
And often hast thou mourn'd with me his pains.
Him Dido now with blandishment detains;
But I suspect the town where Juno reigns.
For this 'tis needful to prevent her art,
And fire with love the proud Phœnician's heart:
A love so violent, so strong, so sure,
As neither age can change, nor art can cure.
How this may be perform'd, now take my mind:
Ascanius by his father is design'd
To come, with presents laden, from the port,
To gratify the queen, and gain the court.
I mean to plunge the boy in pleasing sleep,
And, ravish'd, in Idalian bow'rs to keep,
Or high Cythera, that the sweet deceit
May pass unseen, and none prevent the cheat.
Take thou his form and shape. I beg the grace
But only for a night's revolving space:
Thyself a boy, assume a boy's dissembled face;
That when, amidst the fervor of the feast,
The Tyrian hugs and fonds thee on her breast,
And with sweet kisses in her arms constrains,
Thou may'st infuse thy venom in her veins."
The God of Love obeys, and sets aside
His bow and quiver, and his plumy pride;

He walks Iülus in his mother's sight,
And in the sweet resemblance takes delight.

The goddess then to young Ascanius flies,
And in a pleasing slumber seals his eyes:
Lull'd in her lap, amidst a train of Loves,
She gently bears him to her blissful groves,
Then with a wreath of myrtle crowns his head,
And softly lays him on a flow'ry bed.
Cupid meantime assum'd his form and face,
Foll'wing Achates with a shorter pace,
And brought the gifts. The queen already sate
Amidst the Trojan lords, in shining state,
High on a golden bed: her princely guest
Was next her side; in order sate the rest.
Then canisters with bread are heap'd on high;
Th' attendants water for their hands supply,
And, having wash'd, with silken towels dry.
Next fifty handmaids in long order bore
The censers, and with fumes the gods adore:
Then youths, and virgins twice as many, join
To place the dishes, and to serve the wine.
The Tyrian train, admitted to the feast,
Approach, and on the painted couches rest.
All on the Trojan gifts with wonder gaze,
But view the beauteous boy with more amaze,
His rosy-color'd cheeks, his radiant eyes,
His motions, voice, and shape, and all the god's disguise;
Nor pass unprais'd the vest and veil divine,
Which wand'ring foliage and rich flow'rs entwine.
But, far above the rest, the royal dame,
(Already doom'd to love's disastrous flame,)
With eyes insatiate, and tumultuous joy,
Beholds the presents, and admires the boy.
The guileful god about the hero long,
With children's play, and false embraces, hung;

Then sought the queen: she took him to her arms
With greedy pleasure, and devour'd his charms.
Unhappy Dido little thought what guest,
How dire a god, she drew so near her breast;
But he, not mindless of his mother's pray'r,
Works in the pliant bosom of the fair,
And molds her heart anew, and blots her former care.
The dead is to the living love resign'd;
And all Æneas enters in her mind.

Now, when the rage of hunger was appeas'd,
The meat remov'd, and ev'ry guest was pleas'd,
The golden bowls with sparkling wine are crown'd,
And thro' the palace cheerful cries resound.
From gilded roofs depending lamps display
Nocturnal beams, that emulate the day.
A golden bowl, that shone with gems divine,
The queen commanded to be crown'd with wine:
The bowl that Belus us'd, and all the Tyrian line.
Then, silence thro' the hall proclaim'd, she spoke:
"O hospitable Jove! we thus invoke,
With solemn rites, thy sacred name and pow'r;
Bless to both nations this auspicious hour!
So may the Trojan and the Tyrian line
In lasting concord from this day combine.
Thou, Bacchus, god of joys and friendly cheer,
And gracious Juno, both be present here!
And you, my lords of Tyre, your vows address
To Heav'n with mine, to ratify the peace."
The goblet then she took, with nectar crown'd
(Sprinkling the first libations on the ground,)
And rais'd it to her mouth with sober grace;
Then, sipping, offer'd to the next in place.
'Twas Bitias whom she call'd, a thirsty soul;
He took challenge, and embrac'd the bowl,
With pleasure swill'd the gold, nor ceas'd to draw,
Till he the bottom of the brimmer saw.

The goblet goes around: Iopas brought
His golden lyre, and sung what ancient Atlas taught:
The various labors of the wand'ring moon,
And whence proceed th' eclipses of the sun;
Th' original of men and beasts; and whence
The rains arise, and fires their warmth dispense,
And fix'd and erring stars dispose their influence;
What shakes the solid earth; what cause delays
The summer nights and shortens winter days.
With peals of shouts the Tyrians praise the song:
Those peals are echo'd by the Trojan throng.
Th' unhappy queen with talk prolong'd the night,
And drank large draughts of love with vast delight;
Of Priam much inquir'd, of Hector more;
Then ask'd what arms the swarthy Memnon wore,
What troops he landed on the Trojan shore;
The steeds of Diomede varied the discourse,
And fierce Achilles, with his matchless force;
At length, as fate and her ill stars requir'd,
To hear the series of the war desir'd.
"Relate at large, my godlike guest," she said,
"The Grecian stratagems, the town betray'd:
The fatal issue of so long a war,
Your flight, your wand'rings, and your woes, declare;
For, since on ev'ry sea, on ev'ry coast,
Your men have been distress'd, your navy toss'd,
Sev'n times the sun has either tropic view'd,
The winter banish'd, and the spring renew'd."

Book II

Æneas relates how the city of Troy was taken, after a ten years' siege, by the treachery of Sinon, and the strategem of a wooden horse. He declares the fixed resolution he had taken not to survive the ruins of his country, and the various adventures he met with in the defense of it. At last, having been before advised by Hector's ghost, and now by the appearance of his mother Venus, he is prevailed upon to leave the town, and settle his household gods in another country. In order to do this, he carries off his father on his shoulders, and leads his little son by the hand, his wife following him behind. When he comes to the place appointed for the general rendezvous, he finds a great confluence of people, but misses his wife whose ghost afterwards appears to him, and tells him the land which was designed for him.

All were attentive to the godlike man,
When from his lofty couch he thus began:
"Great queen, what you command me to relate
Renews the sad remembrance of our fate:
An empire from its old foundations rent,
And ev'ry woe the Trojans underwent;
A peopled city made a desert place;
All that I saw, and part of which I was:
Not ev'n the hardest of our foes could hear,
Nor stern Ulysses tell without a tear.
And now the latter watch of wasting night,
And setting stars, to kindly rest invite;
But, since you take such int'rest in our woe,
And Troy's disastrous end desire to know,
I will restrain my tears, and briefly tell
What in our last and fatal night befell.

"By destiny compell'd, and in despair,
The Greeks grew weary of the tedious war,
And by Minerva's aid a fabric rear'd,
Which like a steed of monstrous height appear'd:
The sides were plank'd with pine; they feign'd it made
For their return, and this the vow they paid.
Thus they pretend, but in the hollow side
Selected numbers of their soldiers hide:
With inward arms the dire machine they load,
And iron bowels stuff the dark abode.
In sight of Troy lies Tenedos, an isle
(While Fortune did on Priam's empire smile)
Renown'd for wealth; but, since, a faithless bay,
Where ships expos'd to wind and weather lay.
There was their fleet conceal'd. We thought, for Greece
Their sails were hoisted, and our fears release.
The Trojans, coop'd within their walls so long,
Unbar their gates, and issue in a throng,
Like swarming bees, and with delight survey
The camp deserted, where the Grecians lay:
The quarters of the sev'ral chiefs they show'd;
Here Phœnix, here Achilles, made abode;
Here join'd the battles; there the navy rode.
Part on the pile their wond'ring eyes employ:
The pile by Pallas rais'd to ruin Troy.
Thymœtes first ('tis doubtful whether hir'd,
Or so the Trojan destiny requir'd)
Mov'd that the ramparts might be broken down,
To lodge the monster fabric in the town.
But Capys, and the rest of sounder mind,
The fatal present to the flames designed,
Or to the wat'ry deep; at least to bore
The hollow sides, and hidden frauds explore.
The giddy vulgar, as their fancies guide,
With noise say nothing, and in parts divide.

Laocoon, follow'd by a num'rous crowd,
Ran from the fort, and cried, from far, aloud:
'O wretched countrymen! what fury reigns?
What more than madness has possess'd
your brains?
Think you the Grecians from your coasts
are gone?
And are Ulysses' arts no better known?
This hollow fabric either must enclose,
Within its blind recess, our secret foes;
Or 'tis an engine rais'd above the town,
T' o'erlook the walls, and then to batter down.
Somewhat is sure design'd, by fraud or force:
Trust not their presents, nor admit the horse.'
Thus having said, against the steed he threw
His forceful spear, which, hissing as flew,
Pierc'd thro' the yielding planks of jointed wood,
And trembling in the hollow belly stood.
The sides, transpierc'd, return a rattling sound,
And groans of Greeks enclos'd
come issuing thro' the wound
And, had not Heav'n the fall of Troy design'd,
Or had not men been fated to be blind,
Enough was said and done t' inspire
a better mind.
Then had our lances pierc'd the
treach'rous wood,
And Ilian tow'rs and Priam's empire stood.
Meantime, with shouts, the Trojan
shepherds bring
A captive Greek, in bands, before the king;
Taken to take; who made himself their prey,
T' impose on their belief, and Troy betray;
Fix'd on his aim, and obstinately bent
To die undaunted, or to circumvent.
About the captive, tides of Trojans flow;
All press to see, and some insult the foe.

Now hear how well the Greeks their
wiles disguis'd;
Behold a nation in a man compris'd.
Trembling the miscreant stood,
unarm'd and bound;
He star'd, and roll'd his haggard eyes around,
Then said: 'Alas! what earth remains, what sea
Is open to receive unhappy me?
What fate a wretched fugitive attends,
Scorn'd by my foes, abandon'd by my friends?'
He said, and sigh'd, and cast a rueful eye:
Our pity kindles, and our passions die.
We cheer youth to make his own defense,
And freely tell us what he was, and whence:
What news he could impart, we long to know,
And what to credit from a captive foe.

"His fear at length dismiss'd, he said: 'Whate'er
My fate ordains, my words shall be sincere:
I neither can nor dare my birth disclaim;
Greece is my country, Sinon is my name.
Tho' plung'd by Fortune's pow'r in misery,
'Tis not in Fortune's pow'r to make me lie.
If any chance has hither brought the name
Of Palamedes, not unknown to fame,
Who suffer'd from the malice of the times,
Accus'd and sentenc'd for pretended crimes,
Because these fatal wars he would prevent;
Whose death the wretched Greeks
too late lament—
Me, then a boy, my father, poor and bare
Of other means, committed to his care,
His kinsman and companion in the war.
While Fortune favor'd, while his arms support
The cause, and rul'd the counsels, of the court,
I made some figure there; nor was my name
Obscure, nor I without my share of fame.

But when Ulysses, with fallacious arts,
Had made impression in the people's hearts,
And forg'd a treason in my patron's name
(I speak of things too far divulg'd by fame),
My kinsman fell. Then I, without support,
In private mourn'd his loss, and left the court.
Mad as I was, I could not bear his fate
With silent grief, but loudly blam'd the state,
And curs'd the direful author of my woes.
'Twas told again; and hence my ruin rose.
I threaten'd, if indulgent Heav'n once more
Would land me safely on my native shore,
His death with double vengeance to restore.
This mov'd the murderer's hate;
and soon ensued
Th' effects of malice from a man so proud.
Ambiguous rumors thro' the camp he spread,
And sought, by treason, my devoted head;
New crimes invented; left unturn'd no stone,
To make my guilt appear, and hide his own;
Till Calchas was by force and
threat'ning wrought—
But why—why dwell I on that anxious thought?
If on my nation just revenge you seek,
And 'tis t' appear a foe, t' appear a Greek;
Already you my name and country know;
Assuage your thirst of blood, and strike the blow:
My death will both the kingly brothers please,
And set insatiate Ithacus at ease.'
This fair unfinish'd tale, these broken starts,
Rais'd expectations in our longing hearts:
Unknowing as we were in Grecian arts.
His former trembling once again renew'd,
With acted fear, the villain thus pursued:

"'Long had the Grecians (tir'd with fruitless care,
And wearied with an unsuccessful war)

Resolv'd to raise the siege, and leave the town;
And, had the gods permitted, they had gone;
But oft the wintry seas and southern winds
Withstood their passage home,
and chang'd their minds.
Portents and prodigies their souls amaz'd;
But most, when this stupendous pile was rais'd:
Then flaming meteors, hung in air, were seen,
And thunders rattled thro' a sky serene.
Dismay'd, and fearful of some dire event,
Eurypylus t' inquire their fate was sent.
He from the gods this dreadful answer brought:
"O Grecians, when the Trojan shores you sought,
Your passage with a virgin's blood was bought:
So must your safe return be bought again,
And Grecian blood once more atone the main."
The spreading rumor round the people ran;
All fear'd, and each believ'd himself the man.
Ulysses took th' advantage of their fright;
Call'd Calchas, and produc'd in open sight:
Then bade him name the wretch, ordain'd by fate
The public victim, to redeem the state.
Already some presag'd the dire event,
And saw what sacrifice Ulysses meant.
For twice five days the good old seer withstood
Th' intended treason, and was dumb to blood,
Till, tir'd, with endless clamors and pursuit
Of Ithacus, he stood no longer mute;
But, as it was agreed, pronounc'd that I
Was destin'd by the wrathful gods to die.
All prais'd the sentence, pleas'd the storm
should fall
On one alone, whose fury threaten'd all.
The dismal day was come; the priests prepare
Their leaven'd cakes, and fillets for my hair.
I follow'd nature's laws, and must avow
I broke my bonds and fled the fatal blow.

Hid in a weedy lake all night I lay,
Secure of safety when they sail'd away.
But now what further hopes for me remain,
To see my friends, or native soil, again;
My tender infants, or my careful sire,
Whom they returning will to death require;
Will perpetrate on them their first design,
And take the forfeit of their heads for mine?
Which, O! if pity mortal minds can move,
If there be faith below, or gods above,
If innocence and truth can claim desert,
Ye Trojans, from an injur'd wretch avert.'

"False tears true pity move; the king commands
To loose his fetters, and unbind his hands:
Then adds these friendly words:
'Dismiss thy fears;
Forget the Greeks; be mine as thou wert theirs.
But truly tell, was it for force or guile,
Or some religious end, you rais'd the pile?'
Thus said the king. He, full of fraudful arts,
This well-invented tale for truth imparts:
'Ye lamps of heav'n!' he said, and lifted high
His hands now free, 'thou venerable sky!
Inviolable pow'rs, ador'd with dread!
Ye fatal fillets, that once bound this head!
Ye sacred altars, from whose flames I fled!
Be all of you adjur'd; and grant I may,
Without a crime, th' ungrateful Greeks betray,
Reveal the secrets of the guilty state,
And justly punish whom I justly hate!
But you, O king, preserve the faith you gave,
If I, to save myself, your empire save.
The Grecian hopes, and all th' attempts they made,
Were only founded on Minerva's aid.
But from the time when impious Diomede,
And false Ulysses, that inventive head,

Her fatal image from the temple drew,
The sleeping guardians of the castle slew,
Her virgin statue with their bloody hands
Polluted, and profan'd her holy bands;
From thence the tide of fortune left their shore,
And ebb'd much faster than it flow'd before:
Their courage languish'd, as their hopes decay'd;
And Pallas, now averse, refus'd her aid.
Nor did the goddess doubtfully declare
Her alter'd mind and alienated care.
When first her fatal image touch'd the ground,
She sternly cast her glaring eyes around,
That sparkled as they roll'd, and seem'd to threat:
Her heav'nly limbs distill'd a briny sweat.
Thrice from the ground she leap'd, was seen to wield
Her brandish'd lance, and shake her horrid shield.
Then Calchas bade our host for flight
And hope no conquest from the tedious war,
Till first they sail'd for Greece; with pray'rs besought
Her injur'd pow'r, and better omens brought.
And now their navy plows the wat'ry main,
Yet soon expect it on your shores again,
With Pallas pleas'd; as Calchas did ordain.
But first, to reconcile the blue-ey'd maid
For her stol'n statue and her tow'r betray'd,
Warn'd by the seer, to her offended name
We rais'd and dedicate this wondrous frame,
So lofty, lest thro' your forbidden gates
It pass, and intercept our better fates:
For, once admitted there, our hopes are lost;
And Troy may then a new Palladium boast;
For so religion and the gods ordain,
That, if you violate with hands profane

Minerva's gift, your town in flames shall burn,
(Which omen, O ye gods, on Græcia turn!)
But if it climb, with your assisting hands,
The Trojan walls, and in the city stands;
Then Troy shall Argos and Mycenæ burn,
And the reverse of fate on us return.'

"With such deceits he gain'd their easy hearts,
Too prone to credit his perfidious arts.
What Diomede, nor Thetis' greater son,
A thousand ships, nor ten years' siege, had done—
False tears and fawning words the city won.

"A greater omen, and of worse portent,
Did our unwary minds with fear torment,
Concurring to produce the dire event.
Laocoon, Neptune's priest by lot that year,
With solemn pomp then sacrific'd a steer;
When, dreadful to behold, from sea we spied
Two serpents, rank'd abreast, the seas divide,
And smoothly sweep along the swelling tide.
Their flaming crests above the waves they show;
Their bellies seem to burn the seas below;
Their speckled tails advance to steer their course,
And on the sounding shore the flying billows force.
And now the strand, and now the plain they held;
Their ardent eyes with bloody streaks were fill'd;
Their nimble tongues they brandish'd as they came,
And lick'd their hissing jaws, that sputter'd flame.
We fled amaz'd; their destin'd way they take,

And to Laocoon and his children make;
And first around the tender boys they wind,
Then with their sharpen'd fangs
their limbs and bodies grind.
The wretched father, running to their aid
With pious haste, but vain, they next invade;
Twice round his waist their winding
volumes roll'd;
And twice about his gasping throat
they fold.
The priest thus doubly chok'd,
their crests divide,
And tow'ring o'er his head in triumph ride.
With both his hands he labors at the knots;
His holy fillets the blue venom blots;
His roaring fills the flitting air around.
Thus, when an ox receives a glancing wound,
He breaks his bands, the fatal altar flies,
And with loud bellowings breaks the
yielding skies.
Their tasks perform'd, the serpents quit
their prey,
And to the tow'r of Pallas make their way:
Couch'd at her feet, they lie protected there
By her large buckler and protended spear.
Amazement seizes all; the gen'ral cry
Proclaims Laocoon justly doom'd to die,
Whose hand the will of Pallas had withstood,
And dared to violate the sacred wood.
All vote t' admit the steed, that vows be paid
And incense offer'd to th' offended maid.
A spacious breach is made; the town lies bare;
Some hoisting-levers, some the wheels prepare
And fasten to the horse's feet; the rest
With cables haul along th' unwieldy beast.
Each on his fellow for assistance calls;

At length the fatal fabric mounts the walls,
Big with destruction. Boys with chaplets crown'd,
And choirs of virgins, sing and dance around.
Thus rais'd aloft, and then descending down,
It enters o'er our heads, and threats the town.
O sacred city, built by hands divine!
O valiant heroes of the Trojan line!
Four times he struck: as oft the clashing sound
Of arms was heard, and inward groans rebound.
Yet, mad with zeal, and blinded with our fate,
We haul along the horse in solemn state;
Then place the dire portent within the tow'r.
Cassandra cried, and curs'd th' unhappy hour;
Foretold our fate; but, by the god's decree,
All heard, and none believ'd the prophecy.
With branches we the fanes adorn, and waste,
In jollity, the day ordain'd to be the last.
Meantime the rapid heav'ns roll'd down the light,
And on the shaded ocean rush'd the night;
Our men, secure, nor guards nor sentries held,
But easy sleep their weary limbs compell'd.
The Grecians had embark'd their naval pow'rs
From Tenedos, and sought our well-known shores,
Safe under covert of the silent night,
And guided by th' imperial galley's light;
When Sinon, favor'd by the partial gods,
Unlock'd the horse, and op'd his dark abodes;
Restor'd to vital air our hidden foes,
Who joyful from their long confinement rose.
Tysander bold, and Sthenelus their guide,
And dire Ulysses down the cable slide:
Then Thoas, Athamas, and Pyrrhus haste;
Nor was the Podalirian hero last,
Nor injur'd Menelaüs, nor the fam'd
Epeüs, who the fatal engine fram'd.
A nameless crowd succeed; their forces join

T' invade the town, oppress'd with sleep and wine.
Those few they find awake first meet their fate;
Then to their fellows they unbar the gate.

"'Twas in the dead of night, when sleep repairs
Our bodies worn with toils, our minds with cares,
When Hector's ghost before my sight appears:
A bloody shroud he seem'd, and bath'd in tears;
Such as he was, when, by Pelides slain,
Thessalian coursers dragg'd him o'er the plain.
Swoln were his feet, as when the thongs were thrust
Thro' the bor'd holes; his body black with dust;
Unlike that Hector who return'd from toils
Of war, triumphant, in Æacian spoils,
Or him who made the fainting Greeks retire,
And launch'd against their navy Phrygian fire.
His hair and beard stood stiffen'd with his gore;
And all the wounds he for his country bore
Now stream'd afresh, and with new purple ran.
I wept to see the visionary man,
And, while my trance continued, thus began:
'O light of Trojans, and support of Troy,
Thy father's champion, and thy country's joy!
O, long expected by thy friends! from whence
Art thou so late return'd for our defense?
Do we behold thee, wearied as we are
With length of labors, and with toils of war?
After so many fun'rals of thy own
Art thou restor'd to thy declining town?
But say, what wounds are these?
What new disgrace
Deforms the manly features of thy face?'

"To this the specter no reply did frame,
But answer'd to the cause for which he came,
And, groaning from the bottom of his breast,
This warning in these mournful words express'd:

'O goddess-born! escape, by timely flight,
The flames and horrors of this fatal night.
The foes already have possess'd the wall;
Troy nods from high, and totters to her fall.
Enough is paid to Priam's royal name,
More than enough to duty and to fame.
If by a mortal hand my father's throne
Could be defended, 'twas by mine alone.
Now Troy to thee commends her future state,
And gives her gods companions of thy fate:
From their assistance walls expect,
Which, wand'ring long, at last thou shalt erect.'
He said, and brought me, from their blest abodes,
The venerable statues of the gods,
With ancient Vesta from the sacred choir,
The wreaths and relics of th' immortal fire.

"Now peals of shouts come thund'ring from afar,
Cries, threats, and loud laments, and mingled war:
The noise approaches, tho' our palace stood
Aloof from streets, encompass'd with a wood.
Louder, and yet more loud, I hear th' alarms
Of human cries distinct, and clashing arms.
Fear broke my slumbers; I no longer stay,
But mount the terrace, thence the town survey,
And hearken what the frightful sounds convey.
Thus, when a flood of fire by wind is borne,
Crackling it rolls, and mows the standing corn;
Or deluges, descending on the plains,
Sweep o'er the yellow year, destroy the pains
Of lab'ring oxen and the peasant's gains;
Unroot the forest oaks, and bear away
Flocks, folds, and trees, and undistinguish'd prey:

The shepherd climbs the cliff, and sees from far
The wasteful ravage of the wat'ry war.
Then Hector's faith was manifestly clear'd,
And Grecian frauds in open light appear'd.
The palace of Deïphobus ascends
In smoky flames, and catches on his friends.
Ucalegon burns next: the seas are bright
With splendor not their own,
    and shine with Trojan light.
New clamors and new clangors now arise,
The sound of trumpets mix'd with fighting cries.
With frenzy seiz'd, I run to meet th' alarms,
Resolv'd on death, resolv'd to die in arms,
But first to gather friends, with them t' oppose
(If fortune favor'd) and repel the foes;
Spurr'd by my courage, by my country fir'd,
With sense of honor and revenge inspir'd.

"Pantheus, Apollo's priest, a sacred name,
Had scap'd the Grecian swords, and pass'd
    the flame:
With relics laden, to my doors he fled,
And by the hand his tender grandson led.
'What hope, O Pantheus? whither can we run?
Where make a stand? and what may yet be done?'
Scarce had I said, when Pantheus, with a groan:
'Troy is no more, and Ilium was a town!
The fatal day, th' appointed hour, is come,
When wrathful Jove's irrevocable doom
Transfers the Trojan state to Grecian hands.
The fire consumes the town, the foe commands;
And armed hosts, an unexpected force,
Break from the bowels of the fatal horse.
Within the gates, proud Sinon throws about
The flames; and foes for entrance press without,
With thousand others, whom I fear to name,
More than from Argos or Mycenæ came.

To sev'ral posts their parties they divide;
Some block the narrow streets, some scour
the wide:
The bold they kill, th' unwary they surprise;
Who fights finds death, and death finds
him who flies.
The warders of the gate but scarce maintain
Th' unequal combat, and resist in vain.'

"I heard; and Heav'n, that well-born souls inspires,
Prompts me thro' lifted swords and rising fires
To run where clashing arms and clamor calls,
And rush undaunted to defend the walls.
Ripheus and Iph'itus by my side engage,
For valor one renown'd, and one for age.
Dymas and Hypanis by moonlight knew
My motions and my mien, and to my party drew;
With young Corœbus, who by love was led
To win renown and fair Cassandra's bed,
And lately brought his troops to Priam's aid,
Forewarn'd in vain by the prophetic maid.
Whom when I saw resolv'd in arms to fall,
And that one spirit animated all:
'Brave souls!' said I,—'but brave, alas! in vain—
Come, finish what our cruel fates ordain.
You see the desp'rate state of our affairs,
And heav'n's protecting pow'rs are deaf to pray'rs.
The passive gods behold the Greeks defile
Their temples, and abandon to the spoil
Their own abodes: we, feeble few, conspire
To save a sinking town, involv'd in fire.
Then let us fall, but fall amidst our foes:
Despair of life the means of living shows.'
So bold a speech encourag'd their desire
Of death, and added fuel to their fire.

"As hungry wolves, with raging appetite,
Scour thro' the fields, nor fear the stormy night—

Their whelps at home expect the promis'd food,
And long to temper their dry chaps in blood—
So rush'd we forth at once; resolv'd to die,
Resolv'd, in death, the last extremes to try.
We leave the narrow lanes behind, and dare
Th' unequal combat in the public square:
Night was our friend; our leader was despair.
What tongue can tell the slaughter of that night?
What eyes can weep the sorrows and affright?
An ancient and imperial city falls:
The streets are fill'd with frequent funerals;
Houses and holy temples float in blood,
And hostile nations make a common flood.
Not only Trojans fall; but, in their turn,
The vanquish'd triumph, and the victors mourn.
Ours take new courage from despair and night:
Confus'd the fortune is, confus'd the fight.
All parts resound with tumults, plaints, and fears;
And grisly Death in sundry shapes appears.
Androgeos fell among us, with his band,
Who thought us Grecians newly come to land.
'From whence,' said he, 'my friends,
this long delay?
You loiter, while the spoils are borne away:
Our ships are laden with the Trojan store;
And you, like truants, come too late ashore.'
He said, but soon corrected his mistake,
Found, by the doubtful answers which we make:
Amaz'd, he would have shunn'd th' unequal fight;
But we, more num'rous, intercept his flight.
As when some peasant, in a bushy brake,
Has with unwary footing press'd a snake;
He starts aside, astonish'd, when he spies
His rising crest, blue neck, and rolling eyes;
So from our arms surpris'd Androgeos flies.
In vain; for him and his we compass'd round,
Possess'd with fear, unknowing of the ground,

And of their lives an easy conquest found.
Thus Fortune on our first endeavor smil'd.
Corœbus then, with youthful hopes beguil'd,
Swoln with success, and a daring mind,
This new invention fatally design'd.
'My friends,' said he, 'since Fortune shows the way,
'Tis fit we should th' auspicious guide obey.
For what has she these Grecian arms bestow'd,
But their destruction, and the Trojans' good?
Then change we shields, and their devices bear:
Let fraud supply the want of force in war.
They find us arms.' This said, himself he dress'd
In dead Androgeos' spoils, his upper vest,
His painted buckler, and his plumy crest.
Thus Ripheus, Dymas, all the Trojan train,
Lay down their own attire, and strip the slain.
Mix'd with the Greeks, we go with ill presage,
Flatter'd with hopes to glut our greedy rage;
Unknown, assaulting whom we blindly meet,
And strew with Grecian carcasses the street.
Thus while their straggling parties we defeat,
Some to the shore and safer ships retreat;
And some, oppress'd with more ignoble fear,
Remount the hollow horse, and pant in secret there.

"But, ah! what use of valor can be made,
When heav'n's propitious pow'rs refuse their aid!
Behold the royal prophetess, the fair
Cassandra, dragg'd by her dishevel'd hair,
Whom not Minerva's shrine, nor sacred bands,
In safety could protect from sacrilegious hands:
On heav'n she cast her eyes, she sigh'd, she cried—
'Twas all she could—her tender arms were tied.
So sad a sight Corœbus could not bear;
But, fir'd with rage, distracted with despair,

Amid the barb'rous ravishers he flew:
Our leader's rash example we pursue.
But storms of stones, from the proud
temple's height,
Pour down, and on our batter'd helms alight:
We from our friends receiv'd this fatal blow,
Who thought us Grecians, as we seem'd in show.
They aim at the mistaken crests, from high;
And ours beneath the pond'rous ruin lie.
Then, mov'd with anger and disdain, to see
Their troops dispers'd, the royal virgin free,
The Grecians rally, and their pow'rs unite,
With fury charge us, and renew the fight.
The brother kings with Ajax join their force,
And the whole squadron of Thessalian horse.

"Thus, when the rival winds their quarrel try,
Contending for the kingdom of the sky,
South, east, and west, on airy coursers borne;
The whirlwind gathers, and the woods are torn:
Then Nereus strikes the deep; the billows rise,
And, mix'd with ooze and sand, pollute the skies.
The troops we squander'd first again appear
From several quarters, and enclose the rear.
They first observe, and to the rest betray,
Our diff'rent speech; our borrow'd arms survey.
Oppress'd with odds, we fall; Corœbus first,
At Pallas' altar, by Peneleus pierc'd.
Then Ripheus follow'd, in th' unequal fight;
Just of his word, observant of the right:
Heav'n thought not so. Dymas their fate attends,
With Hypanis, mistaken by their friends.
Nor, Pantheus, thee, thy miter, nor the bands
Of awful Phœbus, sav'd from impious hands.
Ye Trojan flames, your testimony bear,
What I perform'd, and what I suffer'd there;
No sword avoiding in the fatal strife,

Expos'd to death, and prodigal of life;
Witness, ye heavens! I live not by my fault:
I strove to have deserv'd the death I sought.
But, when I could not fight, and would have died,
Borne off to distance by the growing tide,
Old Iphitus and I were hurried thence,
With Pelias wounded, and without defense.
New clamors from th' invested palace ring:
We run to die, or disengage the king.
So hot th' assault, so high the tumult rose,
While ours defend, and while the Greeks oppose
As all the Dardan and Argolic race
Had been contracted in that narrow space;
Or as all Ilium else were void of fear,
And tumult, war, and slaughter, only there.
Their targets in a tortoise cast, the foes,
Secure advancing, to the turrets rose:
Some mount the scaling ladders; some, more bold,
Swerve upwards, and by posts and pillars hold;
Their left hand gripes their bucklers in th' ascent,
While with their right they seize the battlement.
From their demolish'd tow'rs the Trojans throw
Huge heaps of stones, that, falling, crush the foe;
And heavy beams and rafters from the sides
(Such arms their last necessity provides)
And gilded roofs, come tumbling from on high,
The marks of state and ancient royalty.
The guards below, fix'd in the pass, attend
The charge undaunted, and the gate defend.
Renew'd in courage with recover'd breath,
A second time we ran to tempt our death,
To clear the palace from the foe, succeed
The weary living, and revenge the dead.

"A postern door, yet unobserv'd and free,
Join'd by the length of a blind gallery,
To the king's closet led: a way well known

To Hector's wife, while Priam held the throne,
Thro' which she brought Astyanax, unseen,
To cheer his grandsire and his grandsire's queen.
Thro' this we pass, and mount the tow'r,
from whence
With unavailing arms the Trojans make defense.
From this the trembling king had oft descried
The Grecian camp, and saw their navy ride.
Beams from its lofty height with swords we hew,
Then, wrenching with our hands,
th' assault renew;
And, where the rafters on the columns meet,
We push them headlong with our arms and feet.
The lightning flies not swifter than the fall,
Nor thunder louder than the ruin'd wall:
Down goes the top at once; the Greeks beneath
Are piecemeal torn, or pounded into death.
Yet more succeed, and more to death are sent;
We cease not from above, nor they below relent.
Before the gate stood Pyrrhus, threat'ning loud,
With glitt'ring arms conspicuous in the crowd.
So shines, renew'd in youth, the crested snake,
Who slept the winter in a thorny brake,
And, casting off his slough when spring returns,
Now looks aloft, and with new glory burns;
Restor'd with poisonous herbs, his ardent sides
Reflect the sun; and rais'd on spires he rides;
High o'er the grass, hissing he rolls along,
And brandishes by fits his forky tongue.
Proud Periphas, and fierce Automedon,
His father's charioteer, together run
To force the gate; the Scyrian infantry
Rush on in crowds, and the barr'd passage free.
Ent'ring the court, with shouts the skies they rend;
And flaming firebrands to the roofs ascend.
Himself, among the foremost, deals his blows,
And with his ax repeated strokes bestows

On the strong doors; then all their shoulders ply,
Till from the posts the brazen hinges fly.
He hews apace; the double bars at length
Yield to his ax and unresisted strength.
A mighty breach is made: the rooms conceal'd
Appear, and all the palace is reveal'd;
The halls of audience, and of public state,
And where the lonely queen in secret sate.
Arm'd soldiers now by trembling maids are seen,
With not a door, and scarce a space, between.
The house is fill'd with loud laments and cries,
And shrieks of women rend the vaulted skies;
The fearful matrons run from place to place,
And kiss the thresholds, and the posts embrace.
The fatal work inhuman Pyrrhus plies,
And all his father sparkles in his eyes;
Nor bars, nor fighting guards, his force sustain:
The bars are broken, and the guards are slain.
In rush the Greeks, and all the apartments fill;
Those few defendants whom they find, they kill.
Not with so fierce a rage the foaming flood
Roars, when he finds his rapid course withstood;
Bears down the dams with unresisted sway,
And sweeps the cattle and the cots away.
These eyes beheld him when he march'd between
The brother kings: I saw th' unhappy queen,
The hundred wives, and where old Priam stood,
To stain his hallow'd altar with his brood.
The fifty nuptial beds (such hopes had he,
So large a promise, of a progeny),
The posts, of plated gold, and hung with spoils,
Fell the reward of the proud victor's toils.
Where'er the raging fire had left a space,
The Grecians enter and possess the place.

"Perhaps you may of Priam's fate inquire.
He, when he saw his regal town on fire,
His ruin'd palace, and his ent'ring foes,
On ev'ry side inevitable woes,
In arms, disus'd, invests his limbs, decay'd,
Like them, with age; a late and useless aid.
His feeble shoulders scarce the weight sustain;
Loaded, not arm'd, he creeps along with pain,
Despairing of success, ambitious to be slain!
Uncover'd but by heav'n, there stood in view
An altar; near the hearth a laurel grew,
Dodder'd with age, whose boughs encompass round
The household gods, and shade the holy ground.
Here Hecuba, with all her helpless train
Of dames, for shelter sought, but sought in vain.
Driv'n like a flock of doves along the sky,
Their images they hug, and to their altars fly.
The Queen, when she beheld her trembling lord,
And hanging by his side a heavy sword,
'What rage,' she cried, 'has seiz'd my husband's mind?
What arms are these, and to what use design'd?
These times want other aids! Were Hector here,
Ev'n Hector now in vain, like Priam, would appear.
With us, one common shelter thou shalt find,
Or in one common fate with us be join'd.'
She said, and with a last salute embrac'd
The poor old man, and by the laurel plac'd.
Behold! Polites, one of Priam's sons,
Pursued by Pyrrhus, there for safety runs.
Thro' swords and foes, amaz'd and hurt, he flies
Thro' empty courts and open galleries.
Him Pyrrhus, urging with his lance, pursues,
And often reaches, and his thrusts renews.
The youth, transfix'd, with lamentable cries,
Expires before his wretched parent's eyes:
Whom gasping at his feet when Priam saw,

The fear of death gave place to nature's law;
And, shaking more with anger than with age,
'The gods,' said he, 'requite thy brutal rage!
As sure they will, barbarian, sure they must,
If there be gods in heav'n, and gods be just—
Who tak'st in wrongs an insolent delight;
With a son's death t' infect a father's sight.
Not he, whom thou and lying fame conspire
To call thee his—not he, thy vaunted sire,
Thus us'd my wretched age: the gods he fear'd,
The laws of nature and of nations heard.
He cheer'd my sorrows, and, for sums of gold,
The bloodless carcass of my Hector sold;
Pitied the woes a parent underwent,
And sent me back in safety from his tent.'

"This said, his feeble hand a javelin threw,
Which, flutt'ring, seem'd to loiter as it flew:
Just, and but barely, to the mark it held,
And faintly tinkled on the brazen shield.

"Then Pyrrhus thus: 'Go thou from me to fate,
And to my father my foul deeds relate.
Now die!' With that he dragg'd the trembling sire,
Slidd'ring thro' clotter'd blood and holy mire,
(The mingled paste his murder'd son had made,)
Haul'd from beneath the violated shade,
And on the sacred pile the royal victim laid.
His right hand held his bloody falchion bare,
His left he twisted in his hoary hair;
Then, with a speeding thrust, his heart he found:
The lukewarm blood came rushing thro' the wound,
And sanguine streams distain'd the sacred ground.
Thus Priam fell, and shar'd one common fate
With Troy in ashes, and his ruin'd state:
He, who the scepter of all Asia sway'd,
Whom monarchs like domestic slaves obey'd.

On the bleak shore now lies th' abandon'd king,
A headless carcass, and a nameless thing.

"Then, not before, I felt my curdled blood
Congeal with fear, my hair with horror stood:
My father's image fill'd my pious mind,
Lest equal years might equal fortune find.
Again I thought on my forsaken wife,
And trembled for my son's abandon'd life.
I look'd about, but found myself alone,
Deserted at my need! My friends were gone.
Some spent with toil, some with despair oppress'd,
Leap'd headlong from the heights;
the flames consum'd the rest.
Thus, wand'ring in my way, without a guide,
The graceless Helen in the porch I spied
Of Vesta's temple; there she lurk'd alone;
Muffled she sate, and, what she could, unknown:
But, by the flames that cast their blaze around,
That common bane of Greece and Troy I found.
For Ilium burnt, she dreads the Trojan sword;
More dreads the vengeance of her injur'd lord;
Ev'n by those gods who refug'd her abhorr'd.
Trembling with rage, the strumpet I regard,
Resolv'd to give her guilt the due reward:
'Shall she triumphant sail before the wind,
And leave in flames unhappy Troy behind?
Shall she her kingdom and her friends review,
In state attended with a captive crew,
While unreveng'd the good old Priam falls,
And Grecian fires consume the Trojan walls?
For this the Phrygian fields and Xanthian flood
Were swell'd with bodies, and were drunk
with blood?
'Tis true, a soldier can small honor gain,
And boast no conquest, from a woman slain:
Yet shall the fact not pass without applause,

Of vengeance taken in so just a cause;
The punish'd crime shall set my soul at ease,
And murm'ring manes of my friends appease.'
Thus while I rave, a gleam of pleasing light
Spread o'er the place; and, shining heav'nly bright,
My mother stood reveal'd before my sight
Never so radiant did her eyes appear;
Not her own star confess'd a light so clear:
Great in her charms, as when on gods above
She looks, and breathes herself into their love.
She held my hand, the destin'd blow to break;
Then from her rosy lips began to speak:
'My son, from whence this madness, this neglect
Of my commands, and those whom I protect?
Why this unmanly rage? Recall to mind
Whom you forsake, what pledges leave behind.
Look if your helpless father yet survive,
Or if Ascanius or Creüsa live.
Around your house the greedy Grecians err;
And these had perish'd in the nightly war,
But for my presence and protecting care.
Not Helen's face, nor Paris, was in fault;
But by the gods was this destruction brought.
Now cast your eyes around, while I dissolve
The mists and films that mortal eyes involve,
Purge from your sight the dross, and make you see
The shape of each avenging deity.
Enlighten'd thus, my just commands fulfill,
Nor fear obedience to your mother's will.
Where yon disorder'd heap of ruin lies,
Stones rent from stones; where clouds of dust arise—
Amid that smother Neptune holds his place,
Below the wall's foundation drives his mace,

And heaves the building from the solid base.
Look where, in arms, imperial Juno stands
Full in the Scæan gate, with loud commands,
Urging on shore the tardy Grecian bands.
See! Pallas, of her snaky buckler proud,
Bestrides the tow'r, refulgent thro' the cloud:
See! Jove new courage to the foe supplies,
And arms against the town the partial deities.
Haste hence, my son; this fruitless labor end:
Haste, where your trembling spouse
 and sire attend:
Haste; and a mother's care your passage
 shall befriend.'
She said, and swiftly vanish'd from my sight,
Obscure in clouds and gloomy shades of night.
I look'd, I listen'd; dreadful sounds I hear;
And the dire forms of hostile gods appear.
Troy sunk in flames I saw (nor could prevent),
And Ilium from its old foundations rent;
Rent like a mountain ash, which dar'd the winds,
And stood the sturdy strokes of lab'ring hinds.
About the roots the cruel ax resounds;
The stumps are pierc'd with oft-repeated wounds:
The war is felt on high; the nodding crown
Now threats a fall, and throws the leafy
 honors down.
To their united force it yields, tho' late,
And mourns with mortal groans th'
 approaching fate:
The roots no more their upper load sustain;
But down she falls, and spreads a ruin thro'
 the plain.

"Descending thence, I scape thro' foes and fire:
Before the goddess, foes and flames retire.
Arriv'd at home, he, for whose only sake,
Or most for his, such toils I undertake,

The good Anchises, whom, by timely flight,
I purpos'd to secure on Ida's height,
Refus'd the journey, resolute to die
And add his fun'rals to the fate of Troy,
Rather than exile and old age sustain.
'Go you, whose blood runs warm in ev'ry vein.
Had Heav'n decreed that I should life enjoy,
Heav'n had decreed to save unhappy Troy.
'Tis, sure, enough, if not too much, for one,
Twice to have seen our Ilium overthrown.
Make haste to save the poor remaining crew,
And give this useless corpse a long adieu.
These weak old hands suffice to stop my breath;
At least the pitying foes will aid my death,
To take my spoils, and leave my body bare:
As for my sepulcher, let Heav'n take care.
'Tis long since I, for my celestial wife
Loath'd by the gods, have dragg'd a ling'ring life;
Since ev'ry hour and moment I expire,
Blasted from heav'n by Jove's avenging fire.'
This oft repeated, he stood fix'd to die:
Myself, my wife, my son, my family,
Entreat, pray, beg, and raise a doleful cry—
'What, will he still persist, on death resolve,
And in his ruin all his house involve!'
He still persists his reasons to maintain;
Our pray'rs, our tears, our loud laments, are vain.

"Urg'd by despair, again I go to try
The fate of arms, resolv'd in fight to die:
'What hope remains, but what my death must give?
Can I, without so dear a father, live?
You term it prudence, what I baseness call:
Could such a word from such a parent fall?
If Fortune please, and so the gods ordain,
That nothing should of ruin'd Troy remain,
And you conspire with Fortune to be slain,

The way to death is wide, th' approaches near:
For soon relentless Pyrrhus will appear,
Reeking with Priam's blood—the wretch who slew
The son (inhuman) in the father's view,
And then the sire himself to the dire altar drew.
O goddess mother, give me back to Fate;
Your gift was undesir'd, and came too late!
Did you, for this, unhappy me convey
Thro' foes and fires, to see my house a prey?
Shall I my father, wife, and son behold,
Welt'ring in blood, each other's arms enfold?
Haste! gird my sword, tho' spent and overcome:
'Tis the last summons to receive our doom.
I hear thee, Fate; and I obey thy call!
Not unreveng'd the foe shall see my fall.
Restore me to the yet unfinish'd fight:
My death is wanting to conclude the night.'
Arm'd once again, my glitt'ring sword I wield,
While th' other hand sustains my weighty shield,
And forth I rush to seek th' abandon'd field.
I went; but sad Creüsa stopp'd my way,
And cross the threshold in my passage lay,
Embrac'd my knees, and, when I would have gone,
Shew'd me my feeble sire and tender son:
'If death be your design, at least,' said she,
'Take us along to share your destiny.
If any farther hopes in arms remain,
This place, these pledges of your love, maintain.
To whom do you expose your father's life,
Your son's, and mine, your now forgotten wife!'
While thus she fills the house with clam'rous cries,
Our hearing is diverted by our eyes:
For, while I held my son, in the short space
Betwixt our kisses and our last embrace;
Strange to relate, from young Iülus' head
A lambent flame arose, which gently spread
Around his brows, and on his temples fed.

Amaz'd, with running water we prepare
To quench the sacred fire, and slake his hair;
But old Anchises, vers'd in omens, rear'd
His hands to heav'n, and this request preferr'd:
'If any vows, almighty Jove, can bend
Thy will; if piety can pray'rs commend,
Confirm the glad presage which thou art
    pleas'd to send.'
Scarce had he said, when, on our left, we hear
A peal of rattling thunder roll in air:
There shot a streaming lamp along the sky,
Which on the winged lightning seem'd to fly;
From o'er the roof the blaze began to move,
And, trailing, vanish'd in th' Idæan grove.
It swept a path in heav'n, and shone a guide,
Then in a steaming stench of sulphur died

"The good old man with suppliant hands implor'd
The gods' protection, and their star ador'd.
'Now, now,' said he, 'my son, no more delay!
I yield, I follow where Heav'n shews the way.
Keep, O my country gods, our dwelling place,
And guard this relic of the Trojan race,
This tender child! These omens are your own,
And you can yet restore the ruin'd town.
At least accomplish what your signs foreshow:
I stand resign'd, and am prepar'd to go.'

"He said. The crackling flames appear on high.
And driving sparkles dance along the sky.
With Vulcan's rage the rising winds conspire,
And near our palace roll the flood of fire.
'Haste, my dear father, ('tis no time to wait,)
And load my shoulders with a willing freight.
Whate'er befalls, your life shall be my care;
One death, or one deliv'rance, we will share.
My hand shall lead our little son; and you,

My faithful consort, shall our steps pursue.
Next, you, my servants, heed my strict commands:
Without the walls a ruin'd temple stands,
To Ceres hallow'd once; a cypress nigh
Shoots up her venerable head on high,
By long religion kept; there bend your feet,
And in divided parties let us meet.
Our country gods, the relics, and the bands,
Hold you, my father, in your guiltless hands:
In me 'tis impious holy things to bear,
Red as I am with slaughter, new from war,
Till in some living stream I cleanse the guilt
Of dire debate, and blood in battle spilt.'
Thus, ord'ring all that prudence could provide,
I clothe my shoulders with a lion's hide
And yellow spoils; then, on my bending back,
The welcome load of my dear father take;
While on my better hand Ascanius hung,
And with unequal paces tripp'd along.
Creüsa kept behind; by choice we stray
Thro' ev'ry dark and ev'ry devious way.
I, who so bold and dauntless, just before,
The Grecian darts and shock of lances bore,
At ev'ry shadow now am seiz'd with fear,
Not for myself, but for the charge I bear;
Till, near the ruin'd gate arriv'd at last,
Secure, and deeming all the danger past,
A frightful noise of trampling feet we hear.
My father, looking thro' the shades, with fear,
Cried out: 'Haste, haste, my son, the foes are nigh;
Their swords and shining armor I descry.'
Some hostile god, for some unknown offense,
Had sure bereft my mind of better sense;
For, while thro' winding ways I took my flight,
And sought the shelter of the gloomy night,
Alas! I lost Creüsa: hard to tell
If by her fatal destiny she fell,

Or weary sate, or wander'd with affright;
But she was lost for ever to my sight.
I knew not, or reflected, till I meet
My friends, at Ceres' now deserted seat.
We met: not one was wanting; only she
Deceiv'd her friends, her son, and wretched me.

"What mad expressions did my tongue refuse!
Whom did I not, of gods or men, accuse!
This was the fatal blow, that pain'd me more
Than all I felt from ruin'd Troy before.
Stung with my loss, and raving with despair,
Abandoning my now forgotten care,
Of counsel, comfort, and of hope bereft,
My sire, my son, my country gods I left.
In shining armor once again I sheathe
My limbs, not feeling wounds, nor fearing death.
Then headlong to the burning walls I run,
And seek the danger I was forc'd to shun.
I tread my former tracks; thro' night explore
Each passage, ev'ry street I cross'd before.
All things were full of horror and affright,
And dreadful ev'n the silence of the night.
Then to my father's house I make repair,
With some small glimpse of hope to find her there.
Instead of her, the cruel Greeks I met;
The house was fill'd with foes, with flames beset.
Driv'n on the wings of winds, whole sheets of fire,
Thro' air transported, to the roofs aspire.
From thence to Priam's palace I resort,
And search the citadel and desert court.
Then, unobserv'd, I pass by Juno's church:
A guard of Grecians had possess'd the porch;
There Phœnix and Ulysses watch prey,

And thither all the wealth of Troy convey:
The spoils which they from ransack'd
    houses brought,
And golden bowls from burning altars caught,
The tables of the gods, the purple vests,
The people's treasure, and the pomp of priests.
A rank of wretched youths, with pinion'd hands,
And captive matrons, in long order stands.
Then, with ungovern'd madness, I proclaim,
Thro' all the silent street, Creüsa's name:
Creüsa still I call; at length she hears,
And sudden thro' the shades of night appears—
Appears, no more Creüsa, nor my wife,
But a pale specter, larger than the life.
Aghast, astonish'd, and struck dumb with fear,
I stood; like bristles rose my stiffen'd hair.
Then thus the ghost began to soothe my grief
'Nor tears, nor cries, can give the dead relief.
Desist, my much-lov'd lord, to indulge your pain;
You bear no more than what the gods ordain.
My fates permit me not from hence to fly;
Nor he, the great controller of the sky.
Long wand'ring ways for you the pow'rs decree;
On land hard labors, and a length of sea.
Then, after many painful years are past,
On Latium's happy shore you shall be cast,
Where gentle Tiber from his bed beholds
The flow'ry meadows, and the feeding folds.
There end your toils; and there your fates provide
A quiet kingdom, and a royal bride:
There fortune shall the Trojan line restore,
And you for lost Creüsa weep no more.
Fear not that I shall watch, with servile shame,
Th' imperious looks of some proud Grecian dame;
Or, stooping to the victor's lust, disgrace
My goddess mother, or my royal race.
And now, farewell! The parent of the gods

Restrains my fleeting soul in her abodes:
I trust our common issue to your care.'
She said, and gliding pass'd unseen in air.
I strove to speak: but horror tied my tongue;
And thrice about her neck my arms I flung,
And, thrice deceiv'd, on vain embraces hung.
Light as an empty dream at break of day,
Or as a blast of wind, she rush'd away.

"Thus having pass'd the night in fruitless pain,
I to my longing friends return again,
Amaz'd th' augmented number to behold,
Of men and matrons mix'd, of young and old;
A wretched exil'd crew together brought,
With arms appointed, and with treasure fraught,
Resolv'd, and willing, under my command,
To run all hazards both of sea and land.
The Morn began, from Ida, to display
Her rosy cheeks; and Phosphor led the day:
Before the gates the Grecians took their post,
And all pretense of late relief was lost.
I yield to Fate, unwillingly retire,
And, loaded, up the hill convey my sire."

Book III

Æneas proceeds with his story: he gives an account of the fleet with which he sailed, and the success of his first voyage to Thrace. From thence he directs his course to Delos, and asks the oracle what place the gods had appointed for his habitation. By a mistake of the oracle's answer, he settles in Crete; his household gods give him the true sense of the oracle, in a dream. He follows their advice, and makes the best of his way to Italy. He is cast on several shores, and meets with very surprising adventures, till at length he lands on Sicily, where his father Anchises dies. This is the place which he was sailing from, when the tempest rose, and threw him upon the Carthaginian coast.

"When Heav'n had overturn'd the Trojan state
And Priam's throne, by too severe a fate;
When ruin'd Troy became the Grecians' prey,
And Ilium's lofty tow'rs in ashes lay;
Warn'd by celestial omens, we retreat,
To seek in foreign lands a happier seat.
Near old Antandros, and at Ida's foot,
The timber of the sacred groves we cut,
And build our fleet; uncertain yet to find
What place the gods for our repose assign'd.
Friends daily flock; and scarce the kindly spring
Began to clothe the ground, and birds to sing,
When old Anchises summon'd all to sea:
The crew my father and the Fates obey.
With sighs and tears I leave my native shore,
And empty fields, where Ilium stood before.
My sire, my son, our less and greater gods,
All sail at once, and cleave the briny floods.

"Against our coast appears a spacious land,
Which once the fierce Lycurgus did command,
(Thracia the name—the people bold in war;
Vast are their fields, and tillage is their care,)
A hospitable realm while Fate was kind,
With Troy in friendship and religion join'd.
I land; with luckless omens then adore
Their gods, and draw a line along the shore;
I lay the deep foundations of a wall,
And Ænos, nam'd from me, the city call.
To Dionæan Venus vows are paid,
And all the pow'rs that rising labors aid;
A bull on Jove's imperial altar laid.
Not far, a rising hillock stood in view;
Sharp myrtles on the sides, and cornels grew.
There, while I went to crop the sylvan scenes,
And shade our altar with their leafy greens,
I pull'd a plant—with horror I relate
A prodigy so strange and full of fate.
The rooted fibers rose, and from the wound
Black bloody drops distill'd upon the ground.
Mute and amaz'd, my hair with terror stood;
Fear shrunk my sinews, and congeal'd my blood.
Mann'd once again, another plant I try:
That other gush'd with the same sanguine dye.
Then, fearing guilt for some offense unknown,
With pray'rs and vows the Dryads I atone,
With all the sisters of the woods, and most
The God of Arms, who rules the Thracian coast,
That they, or he, these omens would avert,
Release our fears, and better signs impart.
Clear'd, as I thought, and fully fix'd at length
To learn the cause, I tugged with all my strength:
I bent my knees against the ground; once more
The violated myrtle ran with gore.
Scarce dare I tell the sequel: from the womb

Of wounded earth, and caverns of the tomb,
A groan, as of a troubled ghost, renew'd
My fright, and then these dreadful words ensued:
'Why dost thou thus my buried body rend?
O spare the corpse of thy unhappy friend!
Spare to pollute thy pious hands with blood:
The tears distill not from the wounded wood;
But ev'ry drop this living tree contains
Is kindred blood, and ran in Trojan veins.
O fly from this unhospitable shore,
Warn'd by my fate; for I am Polydore!
Here loads of lances, in my blood embrued,
Again shoot upward, by my blood renew'd.'

"My falt'ring tongue and shiv'ring limbs declare
My horror, and in bristles rose my hair.
When Troy with Grecian arms was closely pent,
Old Priam, fearful of the war's event,
This hapless Polydore to Thracia sent:
Loaded with gold, he sent his darling, far
From noise and tumults, and destructive war,
Committed to the faithless tyrant's care;
Who, when he saw the pow'r of Troy decline,
Forsook the weaker, with the strong to join;
Broke ev'ry bond of nature and of truth,
And murder'd, for his wealth, the royal youth.
O sacred hunger of pernicious gold!
What bands of faith can impious lucre hold?
Now, when my soul had shaken off her fears,
I call my father and the Trojan peers;
Relate the prodigies of Heav'n, require
What he commands, and their advice desire.
All vote to leave that execrable shore,
Polluted with the blood of Polydore;
But, ere we sail, his fun'ral rites prepare,
Then, to his ghost, a tomb and altars rear.

In mournful pomp the matrons walk the round,
With baleful cypress and blue fillets crown'd,
With eyes dejected, and with hair unbound.
Then bowls of tepid milk and blood we pour,
And thrice invoke the soul of Polydore.

"Now, when the raging storms no longer reign,
But southern gales invite us to the main,
We launch our vessels, with a prosp'rous wind,
And leave the cities and the shores behind.

"An island in th' Ægæan main appears;
Neptune and wat'ry Doris claim it theirs.
It floated once, till Phœbus fix'd the sides
To rooted earth, and now it braves the tides.
Here, borne by friendly winds, we come ashore,
With needful ease our weary limbs restore,
And the Sun's temple and his town adore.

"Anius, the priest and king, with laurel crown'd,
His hoary locks with purple fillets bound,
Who saw my sire the Delian shore ascend,
Came forth with eager haste to meet his friend;
Invites him to his palace; and, in sign
Of ancient love, their plighted hands they join.
Then to the temple of the god I went,
And thus, before the shrine, my vows present:
'Give, O Thymbræus, give a resting place
To the sad relics of the Trojan race;
A seat secure, a region of their own,
A lasting empire, and a happier town.
Where shall we fix? where shall our labors end?
Whom shall we follow, and what fate attend?
Let not my pray'rs a doubtful answer find;
But in clear auguries unveil thy mind.'
Scarce had I said: he shook the holy ground,
The laurels, and the lofty hills around;

And from the tripos rush'd a bellowing sound.
Prostrate we fell; confess'd the present god,
Who gave this answer from his dark abode:
'Undaunted youths, go, seek that mother earth
From which your ancestors derive their birth.
The soil that sent you forth, her ancient race
In her old bosom shall again embrace.
Thro' the wide world th' Æneian house shall reign,
And children's children shall the crown sustain.'
Thus Phœbus did our future fates disclose:
A mighty tumult, mix'd with joy, arose.

"All are concern'd to know what place the god
Assign'd, and where determin'd our abode.
My father, long revolving in his mind
The race and lineage of the Trojan kind,
Thus answer'd their demands: 'Ye princes, hear
Your pleasing fortune, and dispel your fear.
The fruitful isle of Crete, well known to fame,
Sacred of old to Jove's imperial name,
In the mid ocean lies, with large command,
And on its plains a hundred cities stand.
Another Ida rises there, and we
From thence derive our Trojan ancestry.
From thence, as 'tis divulg'd by certain fame,
To the Rhœtean shores old Teucrus came;
There fix'd, and there the seat of empire chose,
Ere Ilium and the Trojan tow'rs arose.
In humble vales they built their soft abodes,
Till Cybele, the mother of the gods,
With tinkling cymbals charm'd th' Idæan woods,
She secret rites and ceremonies taught,
And to the yoke the savage lions brought.
Let us the land which Heav'n appoints, explore;
Appease the winds, and seek the Gnossian shore.
If Jove assists the passage of our fleet,

The third propitious dawn discovers Crete.'
Thus having said, the sacrifices, laid
On smoking altars, to the gods he paid:
A bull, to Neptune an oblation due,
Another bull to bright Apollo slew;
A milk-white ewe, the western winds to please,
And one coal-black, to calm the stormy seas.
Ere this, a flying rumor had been spread
That fierce Idomeneus from Crete was fled,
Expell'd and exil'd; that the coast was free
From foreign or domestic enemy.

"We leave the Delian ports, and put to sea;
By Naxos, fam'd for vintage, make our way;
Then green Donysa pass; and sail in sight
Of Paros' isle, with marble quarries white.
We pass the scatter'd isles of Cyclades,
That, scarce distinguish'd, seem to stud the seas.
The shouts of sailors double near the shores;
They stretch their canvas, and they ply their oars.
'All hands aloft! for Crete! for Crete!' they cry,
And swiftly thro' the foamy billows fly.
Full on the promis'd land at length we bore,
With joy descending on the Cretan shore.
With eager haste a rising town I frame,
Which from the Trojan Pergamus I name:
The name itself was grateful; I exhort
To found their houses, and erect a fort.
Our ships are haul'd upon the yellow strand;
The youth begin to till the labor'd land;
And I myself new marriages promote,
Give laws, and dwellings I divide by lot;
When rising vapors choke the wholesome air,
And blasts of noisome winds corrupt the year;
The trees devouring caterpillars burn;
Parch'd was the grass, and blighted was the corn:

Nor 'scape the beasts; for Sirius, from on high,
With pestilential heat infects the sky:
My men—some fall, the rest in fevers fry.
Again my father bids me seek the shore
Of sacred Delos, and the god implore,
To learn what end of woes we might expect,
And to what clime our weary course direct.

"'Twas night, when ev'ry creature, void of cares,
The common gift of balmy slumber shares:
The statues of my gods (for such they seem'd),
Those gods whom I from flaming Troy redeem'd,
Before me stood, majestically bright,
Full in the beams of Phœbe's ent'ring light.
Then thus they spoke, and eas'd my troubled mind:
'What from the Delian god thou go'st to find,
He tells thee here, and sends us to relate.
Those pow'rs are we, companions of thy fate,
Who from the burning town by thee were brought,
Thy fortune follow'd, and thy safety wrought.
Thro' seas and lands as we thy steps attend,
So shall our care thy glorious race befriend.
An ample realm for thee thy fates ordain,
A town that o'er the conquer'd world shall reign.
Thou, mighty walls for mighty nations build;
Nor let thy weary mind to labors yield:
But change thy seat; for not the Delian god,
Nor we, have giv'n thee Crete for our abode.
A land there is, Hesperia call'd of old,
(The soil is fruitful, and the natives bold—
Th' Œnotrians held it once,) by later fame
Now call'd Italia, from the leader's name.
Iasius there and Dardanus were born;
From thence we came, and thither must return.

Rise, and thy sire with these glad tidings greet.
Search Italy; for Jove denies thee Crete.'

"Astonish'd at their voices and their sight,
(Nor were they dreams, but visions of the night;
I saw, I knew their faces, and descried,
In perfect view, their hair with fillets tied;)
I started from my couch; a clammy sweat
On all my limbs and shiv'ring body sate.
To heav'n I lift my hands with pious haste,
And sacred incense in the flames I cast.
Thus to the gods their perfect honors done,
More cheerful, to my good old sire I run,
And tell the pleasing news. In little space
He found his error of the double race;
Not, as before he deem'd, deriv'd from Crete;
No more deluded by the doubtful seat:
Then said: 'O son, turmoil'd in Trojan fate!
Such things as these Cassandra did relate.
This day revives within my mind what she
Foretold of Troy renew'd in Italy,
And Latian lands; but who could then
have thought
That Phrygian gods to Latium should
be brought,
Or who believ'd what mad Cassandra taught?
Now let us go where Phœbus leads the way.'

"He said; and we with glad consent obey,
Forsake the seat, and, leaving few behind,
We spread our sails before the willing wind.
Now from the sight of land our galleys move,
With only seas around and skies above;
When o'er our heads descends a burst of rain,
And night with sable clouds involves the main;
The ruffling winds the foamy billows raise;
The scatter'd fleet is forc'd to sev'ral ways;

The face of heav'n is ravish'd from our eyes,
And in redoubled peals the roaring thunder flies.
Cast from our course, we wander in the dark.
No stars to guide, no point of land to mark.
Ev'n Palinurus no distinction found
Betwixt the night and day; such darkness reign'd around.
Three starless nights the doubtful navy strays,
Without distinction, and three sunless days;
The fourth renews the light, and, from our shrouds,
We view a rising land, like distant clouds;
The mountain-tops confirm the pleasing sight,
And curling smoke ascending from their height.
The canvas falls; their oars the sailors ply;
From the rude strokes the whirling waters fly.
At length I land upon the Strophades,
Safe from the danger of the stormy seas.
Those isles are compass'd by th' Ionian main,
The dire abode where the foul Harpies reign,
Forc'd by the winged warriors to repair
To their old homes, and leave their costly fare.
Monsters more fierce offended Heav'n ne'er sent
From hell's abyss, for human punishment:
With virgin faces, but with wombs obscene,
Foul paunches, and with ordure still unclean;
With claws for hands, and looks for ever lean.

"We landed at the port, and soon beheld
Fat herds of oxen graze the flow'ry field,
And wanton goats without a keeper stray'd.
With weapons we the welcome prey invade,
Then call the gods for partners of our feast,
And Jove himself, the chief invited guest.
We spread the tables on the greensward ground;
We feed with hunger, and the bowls go round;

When from the mountain-tops, with hideous cry,
And clatt'ring wings, the hungry Harpies fly;
They snatch the meat, defiling all they find,
And, parting, leave a loathsome stench behind.
Close by a hollow rock, again we sit,
New dress the dinner, and the beds refit,
Secure from sight, beneath a pleasing shade,
Where tufted trees a native arbor made.
Again the holy fires on altars burn;
And once again the rav'nous birds return,
Or from the dark recesses where they lie,
Or from another quarter of the sky;
With filthy claws their odious meal repeat,
And mix their loathsome ordures with their meat.
I bid my friends for vengeance then prepare,
And with the hellish nation wage the war.
They, as commanded, for the fight provide,
And in the grass their glitt'ring weapons hide;
Then, when along the crooked shore we hear
Their clatt'ring wings, and saw the foes appear,
Misenus sounds a charge: we take th' alarm,
And our strong hands with swords and
bucklers arm.
In this new kind of combat all employ
Their utmost force, the monsters to destroy.
In vain—the fated skin is proof to wounds;
And from their plumes the shining
sword rebounds.
At length rebuff'd, they leave their mangled prey,
And their stretch'd pinions to the skies display.
Yet one remain'd—the messenger of Fate:
High on a craggy cliff Celæno sate,
And thus her dismal errand did relate:
'What! not contented with our oxen slain,
Dare you with Heav'n an impious war maintain,
And drive the Harpies from their native reign?
Heed therefore what I say; and keep in mind

What Jove decrees, what Phœbus has design'd,
And I, the Furies' queen, from both relate—
You seek th' Italian shores, foredoom'd by fate:
Th' Italian shores are granted you to find,
And a safe passage to the port assign'd.
But know, that ere your promis'd walls you build,
My curses shall severely be fulfill'd.
Fierce famine is your lot for this misdeed,
Reduc'd to grind the plates on which you feed.'
She said, and to the neighb'ring forest flew.
Our courage fails us, and our fears renew.
Hopeless to win by war, to pray'rs we fall,
And on th' offended Harpies humbly call,
And whether gods or birds obscene they were,
Our vows for pardon and for peace prefer.
But old Anchises, off'ring sacrifice,
And lifting up to heav'n his hands and eyes,
Ador'd the greater gods: 'Avert,' said he,
'These omens; render vain this prophecy,
And from th' impending curse a pious
people free!'

"Thus having said, he bids us put to sea;
We loose from shore our haulsers, and obey,
And soon with swelling sails pursue
the wat'ry way.
Amidst our course, Zacynthian woods appear;
And next by rocky Neritos we steer:
We fly from Ithaca's detested shore,
And curse the land which dire Ulysses bore.
At length Leucate's cloudy top appears,
And the Sun's temple, which the sailor fears.
Resolv'd to breathe a while from labor past,
Our crooked anchors from the prow we cast,
And joyful to the little city haste.
Here, safe beyond our hopes, our vows we pay
To Jove, the guide and patron of our way.

The customs of our country we pursue,
And Trojan games on Actian shores renew.
Our youth their naked limbs besmear with oil,
And exercise the wrastlers' noble toil;
Pleas'd to have sail'd so long before the wind,
And left so many Grecian towns behind.
The sun had now fulfill'd his annual course,
And Boreas on the seas display'd his force:
I fix'd upon the temple's lofty door
The brazen shield which vanquish'd Abas bore;
The verse beneath my name and action speaks:
'These arms Æneas took from conqu'ring Greeks.'
Then I command to weigh; the seamen ply
Their sweeping oars; the smoking billows fly.
The sight of high Phæacia soon we lost,
And skimm'd along Epirus' rocky coast.

"Then to Chaonia's port our course we bend,
And, landed, to Buthrotus' heights ascend.
Here wondrous things were loudly blaz'd fame:
How Helenus reviv'd the Trojan name,
And reign'd in Greece; that Priam's captive son
Succeeded Pyrrhus in his bed and throne;
And fair Andromache, restor'd by fate,
Once more was happy in a Trojan mate.
I leave my galleys riding in the port,
And long to see the new Dardanian court.
By chance, the mournful queen, before the gate,
Then solemnis'd her former husband's fate.
Green altars, rais'd of turf, with gifts she crown'd,
And sacred priests in order stand around,
And thrice the name of hapless Hector sound.
The grove itself resembles Ida's wood;
And Simoïs seem'd the well-dissembled flood.
But when at nearer distance she beheld
My shining armor and my Trojan shield,
Astonish'd at the sight, the vital heat

Forsakes her limbs; her veins no longer beat:
She faints, she falls, and scarce recov'ring strength,
Thus, with a falt'ring tongue, she speaks at length:

"'Are you alive, O goddess-born ?' she said,
'Or if a ghost, then where is Hector's shade?'
At this, she cast a loud and frightful cry.
With broken words I made this brief reply:
'All of me that remains appears in sight;
I live, if living be to loathe the light.
No phantom; but I drag a wretched life,
My fate resembling that of Hector's wife.
What have you suffer'd since you lost your lord?
By what strange blessing are you now restor'd?
Still are you Hector's? or is Hector fled,
And his remembrance lost in Pyrrhus' bed?'
With eyes dejected, in a lowly tone,
After a modest pause she thus begun:

"'O only happy maid of Priam's race,
Whom death deliver'd from the foes' embrace!
Commanded on Achilles' tomb to die,
Not forc'd, like us, to hard captivity,
Or in a haughty master's arms to lie.
In Grecian ships unhappy we were borne,
Endur'd the victor's lust, sustain'd the scorn:
Thus I submitted to the lawless pride
Of Pyrrhus, more a handmaid than a bride.
Cloy'd with possession, he forsook my bed,
And Helen's lovely daughter sought to wed;
Then me to Trojan Helenus resign'd,
And his two slaves in equal marriage join'd;
Till young Orestes, pierc'd with deep despair,
And longing to redeem the promis'd fair,
Before Apollo's altar slew the ravisher.
By Pyrrhus' death the kingdom we regain'd:
At least one half with Helenus remain'd.

Our part, from Chaon, he Chaonia calls,
And names from Pergamus his rising walls.
But you, what fates have landed on our coast?
What gods have sent you, or what storms have toss'd?
Does young Ascanius life and health enjoy,
Sav'd from the ruins of unhappy Troy?
O tell me how his mother's loss he bears,
What hopes are promis'd from his blooming years,
How much of Hector in his face appears?'
She spoke; and mix'd her speech with mournful cries,
And fruitless tears came trickling from her eyes.

"At length her lord descends upon the plain,
In pomp, attended with a num'rous train;
Receives his friends, and to the city leads,
And tears of joy amidst his welcome sheds.
Proceeding on, another Troy I see,
Or, in less compass, Troy's epitome.
A riv'let by the name of Xanthus ran,
And I embrace the Scæan gate again.
My friends in porticoes were entertain'd,
And feasts and pleasures thro' the city reign'd.
The tables fill'd the spacious hall around,
And golden bowls with sparkling wine were crown'd.
Two days we pass'd in mirth, till friendly gales,
Blown from the supplied our swelling sails.
Then to the royal seer I thus began:
'O thou, who know'st, beyond the reach of man,
The laws of heav'n, and what the stars decree;
Whom Phœbus taught unerring prophecy,
From his own tripod, and his holy tree;
Skill'd in the wing'd inhabitants of air,
What auspices their notes and flights declare:

O say—for all religious rites portend
A happy voyage, and a prosp'rous end;
And ev'ry power and omen of the sky
Direct my course for destin'd Italy;
But only dire Celæno, from the gods,
A dismal famine fatally forebodes—
O say what dangers I am first to shun,
What toils vanquish, and what course to run.'

"The prophet first with sacrifice adores
The greater gods; their pardon then implores;
Unbinds the fillet from his holy head;
To Phœbus, next, my trembling steps he led,
Full of religious doubts and awful dread.
Then, with his god possess'd, before the shrine,
These words proceeded from his mouth divine:
'O goddess-born, (for Heav'n's appointed will,
With greater auspices of good than ill,
Foreshows thy voyage, and thy course directs;
Thy fates conspire, and Jove himself protects,)
Of many things some few I shall explain,
Teach thee to shun the dangers of the main,
And how at length the promis'd shore to gain.
The rest the fates from Helenus conceal,
And Juno's angry pow'r forbids to tell.
First, then, that happy shore, that seems so nigh,
Will far from your deluded wishes fly;
Long tracts of seas divide your hopes from Italy:
For you must cruise along Sicilian shores,
And stem the currents with your struggling oars;
Then round th' Italian coast your navy steer;
And, after this, to Circe's island veer;
And, last, before your new foundations rise,
Must pass the Stygian lake, and view the
nether skies.
Now mark the signs of future ease and rest,
And bear them safely treasur'd in thy breast.

When, in the shady shelter of a wood,
And near the margin of a gentle flood,
Thou shalt behold a sow upon the ground,
With thirty sucking young encompass'd round;
The dam and offspring white as falling snow—
These on thy city shall their name bestow,
And there shall end thy labors and thy woe.
Nor let the threaten'd famine fright thy mind,
For Phœbus will assist, and Fate the way will find.
Let not thy course to that ill coast be bent,
Which fronts from far th' Epirian continent:
Those parts are all by Grecian foes possess'd;
The salvage Locrians here the shores infest;
There fierce Idomeneus his city builds,
And guards with arms the Salentinian fields;
And on the mountain's brow Petilia stands,
Which Philoctetes with his troops commands.
Ev'n when thy fleet is landed on the shore,
And priests with holy vows the gods adore,
Then with a purple veil involve your eyes,
Lest hostile faces blast the sacrifice.
These rites and customs to the rest commend,
That to your pious race they may descend.

"'When, parted hence, the wind, that ready waits
For Sicily, shall bear you to the straits
Where proud Pelorus opes a wider way,
Tack to the larboard, and stand off to sea:
Veer starboard sea and land. Th' Italian shore
And fair Sicilia's coast were one, before
An earthquake caus'd the flaw: the roaring tides
The passage broke that land from land divides;
And where the lands retir'd, the rushing
 ocean rides.
Distinguish'd by the straits, on either hand,
Now rising cities in long order stand,
And fruitful fields: so much can time invade

The mold'ring work that beauteous Nature made.
Far on the right, her dogs foul Scylla hides:
Charybdis roaring on the left presides,
And in her greedy whirlpool sucks the tides;
Then spouts them from below: with
fury driv'n,
The waves mount up and wash the face
of heav'n.
But Scylla from her den, with open jaws,
The sinking vessel in her eddy draws,
Then dashes on the rocks. A human face,
And virgin bosom, hides her tail's disgrace:
Her parts obscene below the waves descend,
With dogs enclos'd, and in a dolphin end.
'Tis safer, then, to bear aloof to sea,
And coast Pachynus, tho' with more delay,
Than once to view misshapen Scylla near,
And the loud yell of wat'ry wolves to hear.

"'Besides, if faith to Helenus be due,
And if prophetic Phœbus tell me true,
Do not this precept of your friend forget,
Which therefore more than once I must repeat:
Above the rest, great Juno's name adore;
Pay vows to Juno; Juno's aid implore.
Let gifts be to the mighty queen design'd,
And mollify with pray'rs her haughty mind.
Thus, at the length, your passage shall be free,
And you shall safe descend on Italy.
Arriv'd at Cumæ, when you view the flood
Of black Avernus, and the sounding wood,
The mad prophetic Sibyl you shall find,
Dark in a cave, and on a rock reclin'd.
She sings the fates, and, in her frantic fits,
The notes and names, inscrib'd, to leafs commits.
What she commits to leafs, in order laid,
Before the cavern's entrance are display'd:

Unmov'd they lie; but, if a blast of wind
Without, or vapors issue from behind,
The leafs are borne aloft in liquid air,
And she resumes no more her museful care,
Nor gathers from the rocks her scatter'd verse,
Nor sets in order what the winds disperse.
Thus, many not succeeding, most upbraid
The madness of the visionary maid,
And with loud curses leave the mystic shade.
"'Think it not loss of time a while to stay,
Tho' thy companions chide thy long delay;
Tho' summon'd to the seas, tho' pleasing gales
Invite thy course, and stretch thy swelling sails:
But beg the sacred priestess to relate
With willing words, and not to write thy fate.
The fierce Italian people she will show,
And all thy wars, and all thy future woe,
And what thou may'st avoid, and what
    must undergo.
She shall direct thy course, instruct thy mind,
And teach thee how the happy shores to find.
This is what Heav'n allows me to relate:
Now part in peace; pursue thy better fate,
And raise, by strength of arms, the Trojan state.'

"This when the priest with friendly voice declar'd,
He gave me license, and rich gifts prepar'd:
Bounteous of treasure, he supplied my want
With heavy gold, and polish'd elephant;
Then Dodonæan cauldrons put on board,
And ev'ry ship with sums of silver stor'd.
A trusty coat of mail to me he sent,
Thrice chain'd with gold, for use and ornament;
The helm of Pyrrhus added to the rest,
That flourish'd with a plume and waving crest.
Nor was my sire forgotten, nor my friends;
And large recruits he to my navy sends:

Men, horses, captains, arms, and warlike stores;
Supplies new pilots, and new sweeping oars.
Meantime, my sire commands to hoist our sails,
Lest we should lose the first auspicious gales.

"The prophet bless'd the parting crew, and last,
With words like these, his ancient friend embrac'd:
'Old happy man, the care of gods above,
Whom heav'nly Venus honor'd with her love,
And twice preserv'd thy life, when Troy was lost,
Behold from far the wish'd Ausonian coast:
There land; but take a larger compass round,
For that before is all forbidden ground.
The shore that Phœbus has design'd for you,
At farther distance lies, conceal'd from view.
Go happy hence, and seek your new abodes,
Blest in a son, and favor'd by the gods:
For I with useless words prolong your stay,
When southern gales have summon'd you away.'

"Nor less the queen our parting thence deplor'd,
Nor was less bounteous than her Trojan lord.
A noble present to my son she brought,
A robe with flow'rs on golden tissue wrought,
A Phrygian vest; and loads with gifts beside
Of precious texture, and of Asian pride.
'Accept,' she said, 'these monuments of love,
Which in my youth with happier hands I wove:
Regard these trifles for the giver's sake;
'Tis the last present Hector's wife can make.
Thou call'st my lost Astyanax to mind;
In thee his features and his form I find:
His eyes so sparkled with a lively flame;
Such were his motions; such was all his frame;
And ah! had Heav'n so pleas'd,
his years had been the same.'

"With tears I took my last adieu, and said:
'Your fortune, happy pair, already made,
Leaves you no farther wish. My diff'rent state,
Avoiding one, incurs another fate.
To you a quiet seat the gods allow:
You have no shores to search, no seas to plow,
Nor fields of flying Italy to chase:
(Deluding visions, and a vain embrace!)
You see another Simoïs, and enjoy
The labor of your hands, another Troy,
With better auspice than her ancient tow'rs,
And less obnoxious to the Grecian pow'rs.
If e'er the gods, whom I with vows adore,
Conduct my steps to Tiber's happy shore;
If ever I ascend the Latian throne,
And build a city I may call my own;
As both of us our birth from Troy derive,
So let our kindred lines in concord live,
And both in acts of equal friendship strive.
Our fortunes, good or bad, shall be the same:
The double Troy shall differ but in name;
That what we now begin may never end,
But long to late posterity descend.'

"Near the Ceraunian rocks our course we bore;
The shortest passage to th' Italian shore.
Now had the sun withdrawn his radiant light,
And hills were hid in dusky shades of night:
We land, and, on the bosom of the ground,
A safe retreat and a bare lodging found.
Close by the shore we lay; the sailors keep
Their watches, and the rest securely sleep.
The night, proceeding on with silent pace,
Stood in her noon, and view'd with equal face
Her steepy rise and her declining race.
Then wakeful Palinurus rose, to spy
The face of heav'n, and the nocturnal sky;

And listen'd ev'ry breath of air to try;
Observes the stars, and notes their sliding course,
The Pleiads, Hyads, and their wat'ry force;
And both the Bears is careful to behold,
And bright Orion, arm'd with burnish'd gold.
Then, when he saw no threat'ning tempest nigh,
But a sure promise of a settled sky,
He gave the sign to weigh; we break our sleep,
Forsake the pleasing shore, and plow the deep.

"And now the rising morn with rosy light
Adorns the skies, and puts the stars to flight;
When we from far, like bluish mists, descry
The hills, and then the plains, of Italy.
Achates first pronounc'd the joyful sound;
Then, 'Italy!' the cheerful crew rebound.
My sire Anchises crown'd a cup with wine,
And, off'ring, thus implor'd the pow'rs divine:
'Ye gods, presiding over lands and seas,
And you who raging winds and waves appease,
Breathe on our swelling sails a prosp'rous wind,
And smooth our passage to the port assign'd!'
The gentle gales their flagging force renew,
And now the happy harbor is in view.
Minerva's temple then salutes our sight,
Plac'd, as a landmark, on the mountain's height.
We furl our sails, and turn the prows to shore;
The curling waters round the galleys roar.
The land lies open to the raging east,
Then, bending like a bow, with rocks compress'd,
Shuts out the storms; the winds and
waves complain,
And vent their malice on the cliffs in vain.
The port lies hid within; on either side
Two tow'ring rocks the narrow mouth divide.
The temple, which aloft we view'd before,
To distance flies, and seems to shun the shore.

Scarce landed, the first omens I beheld
Were four white steeds that cropp'd
the flow'ry field.
'War, war is threaten'd from this foreign ground,'
My father cried, 'where warlike steeds are found.
Yet, since reclaim'd to chariots they submit,
And bend to stubborn yokes, and champ the bit,
Peace may succeed to war.' Our way we bend
To Pallas, and the sacred hill ascend;
There prostrate to the fierce virago pray,
Whose temple was the landmark of our way.
Each with a Phrygian mantle veil'd his head,
And all commands of Helenus obey'd,
And pious rites to Grecian Juno paid.
These dues perform'd, we stretch our sails,
and stand
To sea, forsaking that suspected land.

"From hence Tarentum's bay appears in view,
For Hercules renown'd, if fame be true.
Just opposite, Lacinian Juno stands;
Caulonian tow'rs, and Scylacæan strands,
For shipwrecks fear'd. Mount Ætna thence we spy,
Known by the smoky flames which cloud the sky.
Far off we hear the waves with surly sound
Invade the rocks, the rocks their groans rebound.
The billows break upon the sounding strand,
And roll the rising tide, impure with sand.
Then thus Anchises, in experience old:
''Tis that Charybdis which the seer foretold,
And those the promis'd rocks! Bear off to sea!'
With haste the frighted mariners obey.
First Palinurus to the larboard veer'd;
Then all the fleet by his example steer'd.
To heav'n aloft on ridgy waves we ride,
Then down to hell descend, when they divide;
And thrice our galleys knock'd the stony ground,

And thrice the hollow rocks return'd the sound,
And thrice we saw the stars, that stood
with dews around.
The flagging winds forsook us, with the sun;
And, wearied, on Cyclopian shores we run.
The port capacious, and secure from wind,
Is to the foot of thund'ring Ætna join'd.
By turns a pitchy cloud she rolls on high;
By turns hot embers from her entrails fly,
And flakes of mounting flames, that lick the sky.
Oft from her bowels massy rocks are thrown,
And, shiver'd by the force, come piecemeal down.
Oft liquid lakes of burning sulphur flow,
Fed from the fiery springs that boil below.
Enceladus, they say, transfix'd by Jove,
With blasted limbs came tumbling from above;
And, where he fell, th' avenging father drew
This flaming hill, and on his body threw.
As often as he turns his weary sides,
He shakes the solid isle, and smoke
the heavens hides.
In shady woods we pass the tedious night,
Where bellowing sounds and groans
our souls affright,
Of which no cause is offer'd to the sight;
For not one star was kindled in the sky,
Nor could the moon her borrow'd light supply;
For misty clouds involv'd the firmament,
The stars were muffled, and the moon was pent.

"Scarce had the rising sun the day reveal'd,
Scarce had his heat the pearly dews dispell'd,
When from the woods there bolts,
before our sight,
Somewhat betwixt a mortal and a sprite,
So thin, so ghastly meager, and so wan,
So bare of flesh, he scarce resembled man.

This thing, all tatter'd, seem'd from far t' implore
Our pious aid, and pointed to the shore.
We look behind, then view his shaggy beard;
His clothes were tagg'd with thorns, and filth his limbs besmear'd;
The rest, in mien, in habit, and in face,
Appear'd a Greek, and such indeed he was.
He cast on us, from far, a frightful view,
Whom soon for Trojans and for foes he knew;
Stood still, and paus'd; then all at once began
To stretch his limbs, and trembled as he ran.
Soon as approach'd, upon his knees he falls,
And thus with tears and sighs for pity calls:
'Now, by the pow'rs above, and what we share
From Nature's common gift, this vital air,
O Trojans, take me hence! I beg no more;
But bear me far from this unhappy shore.
'Tis true, I am a Greek, and farther own,
Among your foes besieg'd th' imperial town.
For such demerits if my death be due,
No more for this abandon'd life I sue;
This only favor let my tears obtain,
To throw me headlong in the rapid main:
Since nothing more than death my crime demands,
I die content, to die by human hands.'
He said, and on his knees my knees embrac'd:
I bade him boldly tell his fortune past,
His present state, his lineage, and his name,
Th' occasion of his fears, and whence he came.
The good Anchises rais'd him with his hand;
Who, thus encourag'd, answer'd our demand:
'From Ithaca, my native soil, I came
To Troy; and Achæmenides my name.
Me my poor father with Ulysses sent;
(O had I stay'd, with poverty content!)
But, fearful for themselves, my countrymen

Left me forsaken in the Cyclops' den.
The cave, tho' large, was dark; the dismal floor
Was pav'd with mangled limbs and putrid gore.
Our monstrous host, of more than human size,
Erects his head, and stares within the skies;
Bellowing his voice, and horrid is his hue.
Ye gods, remove this plague from mortal view!
The joints of slaughter'd wretches are his food;
And for his wine he quaffs the streaming blood.
These eyes beheld, when with his spacious hand
He seiz'd two captives of our Grecian band;
Stretch'd on his back, he dash'd against the stones
Their broken bodies, and their crackling bones:
With spouting blood the purple pavement swims,
While the dire glutton grinds the trembling limbs.

"'Not unreveng'd Ulysses bore their fate,
Nor thoughtless of his own unhappy state;
For, gorg'd with flesh, and drunk with human wine
While fast asleep the giant lay supine,
Snoring aloud, and belching from his maw
His indigested foam, and morsels raw;
We pray; we cast the lots, and then surround
The monstrous body, stretch'd along the ground:
Each, as he could approach him, lends a hand
To bore his eyeball with a flaming brand.
Beneath his frowning forehead lay his eye;
For only one did the vast frame supply—
But that a globe so large, his front it fill'd,
Like the sun's disk or like a Grecian shield.
The stroke succeeds; and down the pupil bends:
This vengeance follow'd for our slaughter'd friends.
But haste, unhappy wretches, haste to fly!
Your cables cut, and on your oars rely!

Such, and so vast as Polypheme appears,
A hundred more this hated island bears:
Like him, in caves they shut their woolly sheep;
Like him, their herds on tops of mountains keep;
Like him, with mighty strides, they stalk
from steep to steep
And now three moons their sharpen'd
horns renew,
Since thus, in woods and wilds, obscure
from view,
I drag my loathsome days with mortal fright,
And in deserted caverns lodge by night;
Oft from the rocks a dreadful prospect see
Of the huge Cyclops, like a walking tree:
From far I hear his thund'ring voice resound,
And trampling feet that shake the
solid ground.
Cornels and salvage berries of the wood,
And roots and herbs, have been my
meager food.
While all around my longing eyes I cast,
I saw your happy ships appear at last.
On those I fix'd my hopes, to these I run;
'Tis all I ask, this cruel race to shun;
What other death you please,
yourselves bestow.'

"Scarce had he said, when on the mountain's brow
We saw the giant shepherd stalk before
His following flock, and leading to the shore:
A monstrous bulk, deform'd, depriv'd
of sight;
His staff a trunk of pine, to guide his
steps aright.
His pond'rous whistle from his neck descends;
His woolly care their pensive lord attends:
This only solace his hard fortune sends.

Soon as he reach'd the shore and touch'd
the waves,
From his bor'd eye the gutt'ring blood he laves:
He gnash'd his teeth, and groan'd;
thro' seas he strides,
And scarce the topmost billows touch'd
his sides.

"Seiz'd with a sudden fear, we run to sea,
The cables cut, and silent haste away;
The well-deserving stranger entertain;
Then, buckling to the work, our oars divide
the main.
The giant harken'd to the dashing sound:
But, when our vessels out of reach he found,
He strided onward, and in vain essay'd
Th' Ionian deep, and durst no farther wade.
With that he roar'd aloud: the dreadful cry
Shakes earth, and air, and seas; the billows fly
Before the bellowing noise to distant Italy.
The neighb'ring Ætna trembling all around,
The winding caverns echo to the sound.
His brother Cyclops hear the yelling roar,
And, rushing down the mountains,
crowd the shore.
We saw their stern distorted looks, from far,
And one-eyed glance, that vainly threaten'd war:
A dreadful council, with their heads on high;
(The misty clouds about their foreheads fly;)
Not yielding to the tow'ring tree of Jove,
Or tallest cypress of Diana's grove.
New pangs of mortal fear our minds assail;
We tug at ev'ry oar, and hoist up ev'ry sail,
And take th' advantage of the friendly gale.
Forewarn'd by Helenus, we strive to shun
Charybdis' gulf, nor dare to Scylla run.
An equal fate on either side appears:

We, tacking to the left, are free from fears;
For, from Pelorus' point, the North arose,
And drove us back where swift Pantagias flows.
His rocky mouth we pass, and make our way
By Thapsus and Megara's winding bay.
This passage Achæmenides had shown,
Tracing the course which he before had run.

"Right o'er against Plemmyrium's wat'ry strand,
There lies an isle once call'd th' Ortygian land.
Alpheus, as old fame reports, has found
From Greece a secret passage under ground,
By love to beauteous Arethusa led;
And, mingling here, they roll in the same
sacred bed.
As Helenus enjoin'd, we next adore
Diana's name, protectress of the shore.
With prosp'rous gales we pass the quiet sounds
Of still Elorus, and his fruitful bounds.
Then, doubling Cape Pachynus, we survey
The rocky shore extended to the sea.
The town of Camarine from far we see,
And fenny lake, undrain'd by fate's decree.
In sight of the Geloan fields we pass,
And the large walls, where mighty Gela was;
Then Agragas, with lofty summits crown'd,
Long for the race of warlike steeds renown'd.
We pass'd Selinus, and the palmy land,
And widely shun the Lilybæan strand,
Unsafe, for secret rocks and moving sand.
At length on shore the weary fleet arriv'd,
Which Drepanum's unhappy port receiv'd.
Here, after endless labors, often toss'd
By raging storms, and driv'n on ev'ry coast,
My dear, dear father, spent with age, I lost:
Ease of my cares, and solace of my pain,
Sav'd thro' a thousand toils, but sav'd in vain

The prophet, who my future woes reveal'd,
Yet this, the greatest and the worst, conceal'd;
And dire Celæno, whose foreboding skill
Denounc'd all else, was silent of the ill.
This my last labor was. Some friendly god
From thence convey'd us to your blest abode."

Thus, to the list'ning queen, the royal guest
His wand'ring course and all his toils express'd;
And here concluding, he retir'd to rest.

Book IV

Dido reveals to her sister her passion for Æneas, and her thoughts of marrying him. She prepares a hunting match for his entertainment. Juno, by Venus's consent, raises a storm, which separates the hunters, and drives Æneas and Dido into the same cave, where their marriage is supposed to be completed. Jupiter dispatches Mercury to Æneas, to warn him from Carthage. Æneas secretly prepares for his voyage. Dido finds out his design, and, to put a stop to it, makes use of her own and her sister's entreaties, and reveals all the variety of passions that are incident to a neglected lover. When nothing would prevail upon him, she contrives her own death, with which this book concludes.

But anxious cares already seiz'd the queen:
She fed within her veins a flame unseen;
The hero's valor, acts, and birth inspire
Her soul with love, and fan the secret fire.
His words, his looks, imprinted in her heart,
Improve the passion, and increase the smart.
Now, when the purple morn had chas'd away
The dewy shadows, and restor'd the day,
Her sister first with early care she sought,
And thus in mournful accents eas'd her thought:

"My dearest Anna, what new dreams affright
My lab'ring soul! what visions of the night
Disturb my quiet, and distract my breast
With strange ideas of our Trojan guest!
His worth, his actions, and majestic air,
A man descended from the gods declare.
Fear ever argues a degenerate kind;

His birth is well asserted by his mind.
Then, what he suffer'd, when by Fate betray'd!
What brave attempts for falling Troy he made!
Such were his looks, so gracefully he spoke,
That, were I not resolv'd against the yoke
Of hapless marriage, never to be curst
With second love, so fatal was my first,
To this one error I might yield again;
For, since Sichæus was untimely slain,
This only man is able to subvert
The fix'd foundations of my stubborn heart.
And, to confess my frailty, to my shame,
Somewhat I find within, if not the same,
Too like the sparkles of my former flame.
But first let yawning earth a passage rend,
And let me thro' the dark abyss descend;
First let avenging Jove, with flames from high,
Drive down this body to the nether sky,
Condemn'd with ghosts in endless night to lie,
Before I break the plighted faith I gave!
No! he who had my vows shall ever have;
For, whom I lov'd on earth, I worship in the grave."

She said: the tears ran gushing from her eyes,
And stopp'd her speech. Her sister thus replies:
"O dearer than the vital air I breathe,
Will you to grief your blooming years bequeath,
Condemn'd to waste in woes your lonely life,
Without the joys of mother or of wife?
Think you these tears, this pompous train of woe,
Are known or valued by the ghosts below?
I grant that, while your sorrows yet were green,
It well became a woman, and a queen,
The vows of Tyrian princes to neglect,
To scorn Hyarbas, and his love reject,
With all the Libyan lords of mighty name;
But will you fight against a pleasing flame!

This little spot of land, which Heav'n bestows,
On ev'ry side is hemm'd with warlike foes;
Gætulian cities here are spread around,
And fierce Numidians there your frontiers bound;
Here lies a barren waste of thirsty land,
And there the Syrtes raise the moving sand;
Barcæan troops besiege the narrow shore,
And from the sea Pygmalion threatens more.
Propitious Heav'n, and gracious Juno, lead
This wand'ring navy to your needful aid:
How will your empire spread, your city rise,
From such a union, and with such allies?
Implore the favor of the pow'rs above,
And leave the conduct of the rest to love.
Continue still your hospitable way,
And still invent occasions of their stay,
Till storms and winter winds shall cease to threat,
And planks and oars repair their shatter'd fleet."

These words, which from a friend and sister came,
With ease resolv'd the scruples of her fame,
And added fury to the kindled flame.
Inspir'd with hope, the project they pursue;
On ev'ry altar sacrifice renew:
A chosen ewe of two years old they pay
To Ceres, Bacchus, and the God of Day;
Preferring Juno's pow'r, for Juno ties
The nuptial knot and makes the marriage joys.
The beauteous queen before her altar stands,
And holds the golden goblet in her hands.
A milk-white heifer she with flow'rs adorns,
And pours the ruddy wine betwixt her horns;
And, while the priests with pray'r the gods invoke,
She feeds their altars with Sabæan smoke,
With hourly care the sacrifice renews,
And anxiously the panting entrails views.
What priestly rites, alas! what pious art,

What vows avail to cure a bleeding heart!
A gentle fire she feeds within her veins,
Where the soft god secure in silence reigns.

Sick with desire, and seeking him she loves,
From street to street the raving Dido roves.
So when the watchful shepherd, from the blind,
Wounds with a random shaft the careless hind,
Distracted with her pain she flies the woods,
Bounds o'er the lawn, and seeks the silent floods,
With fruitless care; for still the fatal dart
Sticks in her side, and rankles in her heart.
And now she leads the Trojan chief along
The lofty walls, amidst the busy throng;
Displays her Tyrian wealth, and rising town,
Which love, without his labor, makes his own.
This pomp she shows, to tempt her wand'ring guest;
Her falt'ring tongue forbids to speak the rest.
When day declines, and feasts renew the night,
Still on his face she feeds her famish'd sight;
She longs again to hear the prince relate
His own adventures and the Trojan fate.
He tells it o'er and o'er; but still in vain,
For still she begs to hear it once again.
The hearer on the speaker's mouth depends,
And thus the tragic story never ends.

Then, when they part, when Phœbe's paler light
Withdraws, and falling stars to sleep invite,
She last remains, when ev'ry guest is gone,
Sits on the bed he press'd, and sighs alone;
Absent, her absent hero sees and hears;
Or in her bosom young Ascanius bears,
And seeks the father's image in the child,
If love by likeness might be so beguil'd.

Meantime the rising tow'rs are at a stand;
No labors exercise the youthful band,
Nor use of arts, nor toils of arms they know;
The mole is left unfinish'd to the foe;
The mounds, the works, the walls, neglected lie,
Short of their promis'd heighth,
 that seem'd to threat the sky.

But when imperial Juno, from above,
Saw Dido fetter'd in the chains of love,
Hot with the venom which her veins inflam'd,
And by no sense of shame to be reclaim'd,
With soothing words to Venus she begun:
"High praises, endless honors, you have won,
And mighty trophies, with your worthy son!
Two gods a silly woman have undone!
Nor am I ignorant, you both suspect
This rising city, which my hands erect:
But shall celestial discord never cease?
'Tis better ended in a lasting peace.
You stand possess'd of all your soul desir'd:
Poor Dido with consuming love is fir'd.
Your Trojan with my Tyrian let us join;
So Dido shall be yours, Æneas mine:
One common kingdom, one united line.
Eliza shall a Dardan lord obey,
And lofty Carthage for a dow'r convey."
Then Venus, who her hidden fraud descried,
Which would the scepter of the world misguide
To Libyan shores, thus artfully replied:
"Who, but a fool, would wars with Juno choose,
And such alliance and such gifts refuse,
If Fortune with our joint desires comply?
The doubt is all from Jove and destiny;
Lest he forbid, with absolute command,
To mix the people in one common land—
Or will the Trojan and the Tyrian line

In lasting leagues and sure succession join?
But you, the partner of his bed and throne,
May move his mind; my wishes are your own."

"Mine," said imperial Juno, "be the care;
Time urges, now, to perfect this affair:
Attend my counsel, and the secret share.
When next the Sun his rising light displays,
And gilds the world below with purple rays,
The queen, Æneas, and the Tyrian court
Shall to the shady woods, for sylvan game, resort.
There, while the huntsmen pitch their toils around,
And cheerful horns from side to side resound,
A pitchy cloud shall cover all the plain
With hail, and thunder, and tempestuous rain;
The fearful train shall take their speedy flight,
Dispers'd, and all involv'd in gloomy night;
One cave a grateful shelter shall afford
To the fair princess and the Trojan lord.
I will myself the bridal bed prepare,
If you, to bless the nuptials, will be there:
So shall their loves be crown'd with due delights,
And Hymen shall be present at the rites."
The Queen of Love consents, and closely smiles
At her vain project, and discover'd wiles.

The rosy morn was risen from the main,
And horns and hounds awake the princely train:
They issue early thro' the city gate,
Where the more wakeful huntsmen ready wait,
With nets, and toils, and darts, beside the force
Of Spartan dogs, and swift Massylian horse.
The Tyrian peers and officers of state
For the slow queen in antechambers wait;
Her lofty courser, in the court below,
Who his majestic rider seems to know,
Proud of his purple trappings, paws the ground,

And champs the golden bit, and spreads the
foam around.
The queen at length appears; on either hand
The brawny guards in martial order stand.
A flow'r'd simar with golden fringe she wore,
And at her back a golden quiver bore;
Her flowing hair a golden caul restrains,
A golden clasp the Tyrian robe sustains.
Then young Ascanius, with a sprightly grace,
Leads on the Trojan youth to view the chase.
But far above the rest in beauty shines
The great Æneas, the troop he joins;
Like fair Apollo, when he leaves the frost
Of wint'ry Xanthus, and the Lycian coast,
When to his native Delos he resorts,
Ordains the dances, and renews the sports;
Where painted Scythians, mix'd with
Cretan bands,
Before the joyful altars join their hands:
Himself, on Cynthus walking, sees below
The merry madness of the sacred show.
Green wreaths of bays his length of
hair enclose;
A golden fillet binds his awful brows;
His quiver sounds: not less the prince is seen
In manly presence, or in lofty mien.

Now had they reach'd the hills, and storm'd
the seat
Of salvage beasts, in dens, their last retreat.
The cry pursues the mountain goats: they bound
From rock to rock, and keep the craggy ground;
Quite otherwise the stags, a trembling train,
In herds unsingled, scour the dusty plain,
And a long chase in open view maintain.
The glad Ascanius, as his courser guides,
Spurs thro' the vale, and these and those outrides.

His horse's flanks and sides are forc'd to feel
The clanking lash, and goring of the steel.
Impatiently he views the feeble prey,
Wishing some nobler beast to cross his way,
And rather would the tusky boar attend,
Or see the tawny lion downward bend.

Meantime, the gath'ring clouds obscure the skies:
From pole to pole the forky lightning flies;
The rattling thunders roll; and Juno pours
A wint'ry deluge down, and sounding show'rs.
The company, dispers'd, to converts ride,
And seek the homely cots, or mountain's
hollow side.
The rapid rains, descending from the hills,
To rolling torrents raise the creeping rills.
The queen and prince, as love or fortune guides,
One common cavern in her bosom hides.
Then first the trembling earth the signal gave,
And flashing fires enlighten all the cave;
Hell from below, and Juno from above,
And howling nymphs, were conscious of
their love.
From this ill-omen'd hour in time arose
Debate and death, and all succeeding woes.

The queen, whom sense of honor could not move,
No longer made a secret of her love,
But call'd it marriage, by that specious name
To veil the crime and sanctify the shame.

The loud report thro' Libyan cities goes.
Fame, the great ill, from small beginnings grows:
Swift from the first; and ev'ry moment brings
New vigor to her flights, new pinions to her wings.
Soon grows the pigmy to gigantic size;
Her feet on earth, her forehead in the skies.

Enrag'd against the gods, revengeful Earth
Produc'd her last of the Titanian birth.
Swift is her walk, more swift her winged haste:
A monstrous phantom, horrible and vast.
As many plumes as raise her lofty flight,
So many piercing eyes enlarge her sight;
Millions of opening mouths to Fame belong,
And ev'ry mouth is furnish'd with a tongue,
And round with list'ning ears the flying plague is hung.
She fills the peaceful universe with cries;
No slumbers ever close her wakeful eyes;
By day, from lofty tow'rs her head she shews,
And spreads thro' trembling crowds disastrous news;
With court informers haunts, and royal spies;
Things done relates, not done she feigns, and mingles truth with lies.
Talk is her business, and her chief delight
To tell of prodigies and cause affright.
She fills the people's ears with Dido's name,
Who, lost to honor and the sense of shame,
Admits into her throne and nuptial bed
A wand'ring guest, who from his country fled:
Whole days with him she passes in delights,
And wastes in luxury long winter nights,
Forgetful of her fame and royal trust,
Dissolv'd in ease, abandon'd to her lust.

The goddess widely spreads the loud report,
And flies at length to King Hyarba's court.
When first possess'd with this unwelcome news
Whom did he not of men and gods accuse?
This prince, from ravish'd Garamantis born,
A hundred temples did with spoils adorn,
In Ammon's honor, his celestial sire;
A hundred altars fed with wakeful fire;

And, thro' his vast dominions, priests ordain'd,
Whose watchful care these holy rites maintain'd.
The gates and columns were with garlands crown'd,
And blood of victim beasts enrich'd the ground.

He, when he heard a fugitive could move
The Tyrian princess, who disdain'd his love,
His breast with fury burn'd, his eyes with fire,
Mad with despair, impatient with desire;
Then on the sacred altars pouring wine,
He thus with pray'rs implor'd his sire divine:
"Great Jove! propitious to the Moorish race,
Who feast on painted beds, with off'rings grace
Thy temples, and adore thy pow'r divine
With blood of victims, and with sparkling wine,
Seest thou not this? or do we fear in vain
Thy boasted thunder, and thy thoughtless reign?
Do thy broad hands the forky lightnings lance?
Thine are the bolts, or the blind work of chance?
A wand'ring woman builds, within our state,
A little town, bought at an easy rate;
She pays me homage, and my grants allow
A narrow space of Libyan lands to plow;
Yet, scorning me, by passion blindly led,
Admits a banish'd Trojan to her bed!
And now this other Paris, with his train
Of conquer'd cowards, must in Afric reign!
(Whom, what they are, their looks and garb confess,
Their locks with oil perfum'd, their Lydian dress.)
He takes the spoil, enjoys the princely dame;
And I, rejected I, adore an empty name."

His vows, in haughty terms, he thus preferr'd,
And held his altar's horns. The mighty
Thund'rer heard;
Then cast his eyes on Carthage, where he found
The lustful pair in lawless pleasure drown'd,

Lost in their loves, insensible of shame,
And both forgetful of their better fame.
He calls Cyllenius, and the god attends,
By whom his menacing command he sends:
"Go, mount the western winds, and cleave the sky;
Then, with a swift descent, to Carthage fly:
There find the Trojan chief, who wastes his days
In slothful riot and inglorious ease,
Nor minds the future city, giv'n by fate.
To him this message from my mouth relate:
'Not so fair Venus hop'd, when twice she won
Thy life with pray'rs, nor promis'd such a son.
Hers was a hero, destin'd to command
A martial race, and rule the Latian land,
Who should his ancient line from Teucer draw,
And on the conquer'd world impose the law.'
If glory cannot move a mind so mean,
Nor future praise from fading pleasure wean,
Yet why should he defraud his son of fame,
And grudge the Romans their immortal name!
What are his vain designs! what hopes he more
From his long ling'ring on a hostile shore,
Regardless to redeem his honor lost,
And for his race to gain th' Ausonian coast!
Bid him with speed the Tyrian court forsake;
With this command the slumb'ring warrior wake."

Hermes obeys; with golden pinions binds
His flying feet, and mounts the western winds:
And, whether o'er the seas or earth he flies,
With rapid force they bear him down the skies.
But first he grasps within his awful hand
The mark of sov'reign pow'r, his magic wand;
With this he draws the ghosts from hollow graves;
With this he drives them down the Stygian waves;
With this he seals in sleep the wakeful sight,
And eyes, tho' clos'd in death, restores to light.

Thus arm'd, the god begins his airy race,
And drives the racking clouds along the
liquid space;
Now sees the tops of Atlas, as he flies,
Whose brawny back supports the starry skies;
Atlas, whose head, with piny forests crown'd,
Is beaten by the winds, with foggy vapors bound.
Snows hide his shoulders; from beneath his chin
The founts of rolling streams their race begin;
A beard of ice on his large breast depends.
Here, pois'd upon his wings, the god descends:
Then, rested thus, he from the tow'ring height
Plung'd downward, with precipitated flight,
Lights on the seas, and skims along the flood.
As waterfowl, who seek their fishy food,
Less, and yet less, to distant prospect show;
By turns they dance aloft, and dive below:
Like these, the steerage of his wings he plies,
And near the surface of the water flies,
Till, having pass'd the seas, and cross'd
the sands,
He clos'd his wings, and stoop'd on
Libyan lands:
Where shepherds once were hous'd
in homely sheds,
Now tow'rs within the clouds advance
their heads.
Arriving there, he found the Trojan prince
New ramparts raising for the town's defense.
A purple scarf, with gold embroider'd o'er,
(Queen Dido's gift,) about his waist he wore;
A sword, with glitt'ring gems diversified,
For ornament, not use, hung idly by his side.

Then thus, with winged words, the god began,
Resuming his own shape: "Degenerate man,
Thou woman's property, what mak'st thou here,

These foreign walls and Tyrian tow'rs to rear,
Forgetful of thy own? All-pow'rful Jove,
Who sways the world below and heav'n above,
Has sent me down with this severe command:
What means thy ling'ring in the Libyan land?
If glory cannot move a mind so mean,
Nor future praise from flitting pleasure wean,
Regard the fortunes of thy rising heir:
The promis'd crown let young Ascanius wear,
To whom th' Ausonian scepter, and the state
Of Rome's imperial name is ow'd by fate."
So spoke the god; and, speaking, took his flight,
Involv'd in clouds, and vanish'd out of sight.

The pious prince was seiz'd with sudden fear;
Mute was his tongue, and upright stood his hair.
Revolving in his mind the stern command,
He longs to fly, and loathes the charming land.
What should he say? or how should he begin?
What course, alas! remains to steer between
Th' offended lover and the pow'rful queen?
This way and that he turns his anxious mind,
And all expedients tries, and none can find.
Fix'd on the deed, but doubtful of the means,
After long thought, to this advice he leans:
Three chiefs he calls, commands them to repair
The fleet, and ship their men with silent care;
Some plausible pretense he bids them find,
To color what in secret he design'd.
Himself, meantime, the softest hours would choose,
Before the love-sick lady heard the news;
And move her tender mind, by slow degrees,
To suffer what the sov'reign pow'r decrees:
Jove will inspire him, when, and what to say.
They hear with pleasure, and with haste obey.

But soon the queen perceives the thin disguise:

(What arts can blind a jealous woman's eyes!)
She was the first to find the secret fraud,
Before the fatal news was blaz'd abroad.
Love the first motions of the lover hears,
Quick to presage, and ev'n in safety fears.
Nor impious Fame was wanting to report
The ships repair'd, the Trojans' thick resort,
And purpose to forsake the Tyrian court.
Frantic with fear, impatient of the wound,
And impotent of mind, she roves the city round.
Less wild the Bacchanalian dames appear,
When, from afar, their nightly god they hear,
And howl about the hills, and shake the wreathy spear.
At length she finds the dear perfidious man;
Prevents his form'd excuse, and thus began:
"Base and ungrateful! could you hope to fly,
And undiscover'd scape a lover's eye?
Nor could my kindness your compassion move.
Nor plighted vows, nor dearer bands of love?
Or is the death of a despairing queen
Not worth preventing, tho' too well foreseen?
Ev'n when the wintry winds command your stay,
You dare the tempests, and defy the sea.
False as you are, suppose you were not bound
To lands unknown, and foreign coasts to sound;
Were Troy restor'd, and Priam's happy reign,
Now durst you tempt, for Troy, the raging main?
See whom you fly! am I the foe you shun?
Now, by those holy vows, so late begun,
By this right hand, (since I have nothing more
To challenge, but the faith you gave before;)
I beg you by these tears too truly shed,
By the new pleasures of our nuptial bed;
If ever Dido, when you most were kind,
Were pleasing in your eyes, or touch'd your mind;
By these my pray'rs, if pray'rs may yet have place,

Pity the fortunes of a falling race.
For you I have provok'd a tyrant's hate,
Incens'd the Libyan and the Tyrian state;
For you alone I suffer in my fame,
Bereft of honor, and expos'd to shame.
Whom have I now to trust, ungrateful guest?
(That only name remains of all the rest!)
What have I left? or whither can I fly?
Must I attend Pygmalion's cruelty,
Or till Hyarba shall in triumph lead
A queen that proudly scorn'd his proffer'd bed?
Had you deferr'd, at least, your hasty flight,
And left behind some pledge of our delight,
Some babe to bless the mother's mournful sight,
Some young Æneas, to supply your place,
Whose features might express his father's face;
I should not then complain to live bereft
Of all my husband, or be wholly left."

Here paus'd the queen. Unmov'd he holds his eyes,
By Jove's command; nor suffer'd love to rise,
Tho' heaving in his heart; and thus at length replies:
"Fair queen, you never can enough repeat
Your boundless favors, or I own my debt;
Nor can my mind forget Eliza's name,
While vital breath inspires this mortal frame.
This only let me speak in my defense:
I never hop'd a secret flight from hence,
Much less pretended to the lawful claim
Of sacred nuptials, or a husband's name.
For, if indulgent Heav'n would leave me free,
And not submit my life to fate's decree,
My choice would lead me to the Trojan shore,
Those relics to review, their dust adore,
And Priam's ruin'd palace to restore.
But now the Delphian oracle commands,
And fate invites me to the Latian lands.

That is the promis'd place to which I steer,
And all my vows are terminated there.
If you, a Tyrian, and a stranger born,
With walls and tow'rs a Libyan town adorn,
Why may not we—like you, a foreign race—
Like you, seek shelter in a foreign place?
As often as the night obscures the skies
With humid shades, or twinkling stars arise,
Anchises' angry ghost in dreams appears,
Chides my delay, and fills my soul with fears;
And young Ascanius justly may complain
Of his defrauded and destin'd reign.
Ev'n now the herald of the gods appear'd:
Waking I saw him, and his message heard.
From Jove he came commission'd, heav'nly bright
With radiant beams, and manifest to sight
(The sender and the sent I both attest)
These walls he enter'd, and those words express'd.
Fair queen, oppose not what the gods command;
Forc'd by my fate, I leave your happy land."

Thus while he spoke, already she began,
With sparkling eyes, to view the guilty man;
From head to foot survey'd his person o'er,
Nor longer these outrageous threats forebore:
"False as thou art, and, more than false, forsworn!
Not sprung from noble blood, nor goddess-born,
But hewn from harden'd entrails of a rock!
And rough Hyrcanian tigers gave thee suck!
Why should I fawn? what have I worse to fear?
Did he once look, or lent a list'ning ear,
Sigh'd when I sobb'd, or shed one kindly tear?—
All symptoms of a base ungrateful mind,
So foul, that, which is worse, 'tis hard to find.
Of man's injustice why should I complain?
The gods, and Jove himself, behold in vain
Triumphant treason; yet no thunder flies,

Nor Juno views my wrongs with equal eyes;
Faithless is earth, and faithless are the skies!
Justice is fled, and Truth is now no more!
I sav'd the shipwreck'd exile on my shore;
With needful food his hungry Trojans fed;
I took the traitor to my throne and bed:
Fool that I was—'tis little to repeat
The rest—I stor'd and rigg'd his ruin'd fleet.
I rave, I rave! A god's command he pleads,
And makes Heav'n accessary to his deeds.
Now Lycian lots, and now the Delian god,
Now Hermes is employ'd from Jove's abode,
To warn him hence; as if the peaceful state
Of heav'nly pow'rs were touch'd with human fate!
But go! thy flight no longer I detain—
Go seek thy promis'd kingdom thro' the main!
Yet, if the heav'ns will hear my pious vow,
The faithless waves, not half so false as thou,
Or secret sands, shall sepulchers afford
To thy proud vessels, and their perjur'd lord.
Then shalt thou call on injur'd Dido's name:
Dido shall come in a black sulph'ry flame,
When death has once dissolv'd her mortal frame;
Shall smile to see the traitor vainly weep:
Her angry ghost, arising from the deep,
Shall haunt thee waking, and disturb thy sleep.
At least my shade thy punishment shall know,
And Fame shall spread the pleasing news below."

Abruptly here she stops; then turns away
Her loathing eyes, and shuns the sight of day.
Amaz'd he stood, revolving in his mind
What speech to frame, and what excuse to find.
Her fearful maids their fainting mistress led,
And softly laid her on her ivory bed.

But good Æneas, tho' he much desir'd
To give that pity which her grief requir'd;

Tho' much he mourn'd, and labor'd with his love,
Resolv'd at length, obeys the will of Jove;
Reviews his forces: they with early care
Unmoor their vessels, and for sea prepare.
The fleet is soon afloat, in all its pride,
And well-calk'd galleys in the harbor ride.
Then oaks for oars they fell'd; or, as they stood,
Of its green arms despoil'd the growing wood,
Studious of flight. The beach is cover'd o'er
With Trojan bands, that blacken all the shore:
On ev'ry side are seen, descending down,
Thick swarms of soldiers, loaden from the town.
Thus, in battalia, march embodied ants,
Fearful of winter, and of future wants,
T' invade the corn, and to their cells convey
The plunder'd forage of their yellow prey.
The sable troops, along the narrow tracks,
Scarce bear the weighty burthen on their backs:
Some set their shoulders to the pond'rous grain;
Some guard the spoil; some lash the lagging train;
All ply their sev'ral tasks, and equal toil sustain.

What pangs the tender breast of Dido tore,
When, from the tow'r, she saw the cover'd shore,
And heard the shouts of sailors from afar,
Mix'd with the murmurs of the wat'ry war!
All-pow'rful Love! what changes canst thou cause
In human hearts, subjected to thy laws!
Once more her haughty soul the tyrant bends:
To pray'rs and mean submissions she descends.
No female arts or aids she left untried,
Nor counsels unexplor'd, before she died.
"Look, Anna! look! the Trojans crowd to sea;
They spread their canvas, and their anchors weigh.
The shouting crew their ships with garlands bind,
Invoke the sea gods, and invite the wind.
Could I have thought this threat'ning blow so near,
My tender soul had been forewarn'd to bear.

But do not you my last request deny;
With yon perfidious man your int'rest try,
And bring me news, if I must live or die.
You are his fav'rite; you alone can find
The dark recesses of his inmost mind:
In all his trusted secrets you have part,
And know the soft approaches to his heart.
Haste then, and humbly seek my haughty foe;
Tell him, I did not with the Grecians go,
Nor did my fleet against his friends employ,
Nor swore the ruin of unhappy Troy,
Nor mov'd with hands profane his father's dust:
Why should he then reject a just!
Whom does he shun, and whither would he fly!
Can he this last, this only pray'r deny!
Let him at least his dang'rous flight delay,
Wait better winds, and hope a calmer sea.
The nuptials he disclaims I urge no more:
Let him pursue the promis'd Latian shore.
A short delay is all I ask him now;
A pause of grief, an interval from woe,
Till my soft soul be temper'd to sustain
Accustom'd sorrows, and inur'd to pain.
If you in pity grant this one request,
My death shall glut the hatred of his breast."
This mournful message pious Anna bears,
And seconds with her own her sister's tears:
But all her arts are still employ'd in vain;
Again she comes, and is refus'd again.
His harden'd heart nor pray'rs nor
threat'nings move;
Fate, and the god, had stopp'd his ears to love.

As, when the winds their airy quarrel try,
Justling from ev'ry quarter of the sky,
This way and that the mountain oak they bend,
His boughs they shatter, and his branches rend;

With leaves and falling mast they spread
the ground;
The hollow valleys echo to the sound:
Unmov'd, the royal plant their fury mocks,
Or, shaken, clings more closely to the rocks;
Far as he shoots his tow'ring head on high,
So deep in earth his fix'd foundations lie.
No less a storm the Trojan hero bears;
Thick messages and loud complaints he hears,
And bandied words, still beating on his ears.
Sighs, groans, and tears proclaim his inward pains;
But the firm purpose of his heart remains.

The wretched queen, pursued by cruel fate,
Begins at length the light of heav'n to hate,
And loathes to live. Then dire portents she sees,
To hasten on the death her soul decrees:
Strange to relate! for when, before the shrine,
She pours in sacrifice the purple wine,
The purple wine is turn'd to putrid blood,
And the white offer'd milk converts to mud.
This dire presage, to her alone reveal'd,
From all, and ev'n her sister, she conceal'd.
A marble temple stood within the grove,
Sacred to death, and to her murther'd love;
That honor'd chapel she had hung around
With snowy fleeces, and with garlands crown'd:
Oft, when she visited this lonely dome,
Strange voices issued from her husband's tomb;
She thought she heard him summon her away,
Invite her to his grave, and chide her stay.
Hourly 'tis heard, when with a boding note
The solitary screech owl strains her throat,
And, on a chimney's top, or turret's height,
With songs obscene disturbs the silence
of the night.
Besides, old prophecies augment her fears;

And stern Æneas in her dreams appears,
Disdainful as by day: she seems, alone,
To wander in her sleep, thro' ways unknown,
Guideless and dark; or, in a desert plain,
To seek her subjects, and to seek in vain:
Like Pentheus, when, distracted with his fear,
He saw two suns, and double Thebes, appear;
Or mad Orestes, when his mother's ghost
Full in his face infernal torches toss'd,
And shook her snaky locks: he shuns the sight,
Flies o'er the stage, surpris'd with mortal fright;
The Furies guard the door and intercept his flight.

Now, sinking underneath a load of grief,
From death alone she seeks her last relief;
The time and means resolv'd within her breast,
She to her mournful sister thus address'd
(Dissembling hope, her cloudy front she clears,
And a false vigor in her eyes appears):
"Rejoice!" she said. "Instructed from above,
My lover I shall gain, or lose my love.
Nigh rising Atlas, next the falling sun,
Long tracts of Ethiopian climates run:
There a Massylian priestess I have found,
Honor'd for age, for magic arts renown'd:
Th' Hesperian temple was her trusted care;
'Twas she supplied the wakeful dragon's fare.
She poppy seeds in honey taught to steep,
Reclaim'd his rage, and sooth'd him into sleep.
She watch'd the golden fruit; her charms unbind
The chains of love, or fix them on the mind:
She stops the torrents, leaves the channel dry,
Repels the stars, and backward bears the sky.
The yawning earth rebellows to her call,

Pale ghosts ascend, and mountain ashes fall.
Witness, ye gods, and thou my better part,
How loth I am to try this impious art!
Within the secret court, with silent care,
Erect a lofty pile, expos'd in air:
Hang on the topmost part the Trojan vest,
Spoils, arms, and presents, of my faithless guest.
Next, under these, the bridal bed be plac'd,
Where I my ruin in his arms embrac'd:
All relics of the wretch are doom'd to fire;
For so the priestess and her charms require."

Thus far she said, and farther speech forbears;
A mortal paleness in her face appears:
Yet the mistrustless Anna could not find
The secret fun'ral in these rites design'd;
Nor thought so dire a rage possess'd her mind.
Unknowing of a train conceal'd so well,
She fear'd no worse than when Sichæus fell;
Therefore obeys. The fatal pile they rear,
Within the secret court, expos'd in air.
The cloven holms and pines are heap'd on high,
And garlands on the hollow spaces lie.
Sad cypress, vervain, yew, compose the wreath,
And ev'ry baleful green denoting death.
The queen, determin'd to the fatal deed,
The spoils and sword he left, in order spread,
And the man's image on the nuptial bed.

And now (the sacred altars plac'd around)
The priestess enters, with her hair unbound,
And thrice invokes the pow'rs below the ground.
Night, Erebus, and Chaos she proclaims,
And threefold Hecate, with her hundred names,
And three Dianas: next, she sprinkles round
With feign'd Avernian drops the hallow'd ground;
Culls hoary simples, found by Phœbe's light,

With brazen sickles reap'd at noon of night;
Then mixes baleful juices in the bowl,
And cuts the forehead of a newborn foal,
Robbing the mother's love. The destin'd queen
Observes, assisting at the rites obscene;
A leaven'd cake in her devoted hands
She holds, and next the highest altar stands:
One tender foot was shod, her other bare;
Girt was her gather'd gown, and loose her hair.
Thus dress'd, she summon'd, with her dying breath,
The heav'ns and planets conscious of her death,
And ev'ry pow'r, if any rules above,
Who minds, or who revenges, injur'd love.

"'Twas dead of night, when weary bodies close
Their eyes in balmy sleep and soft repose:
The winds no longer whisper thro' the woods,
Nor murm'ring tides disturb the gentle floods.
The stars in silent order mov'd around;
And Peace, with downy wings, was brooding on the ground
The flocks and herds, and party-color'd fowl,
Which haunt the woods, or swim the weedy pool,
Stretch'd on the quiet earth, securely lay,
Forgetting the past labors of the day.
All else of nature's common gift partake:
Unhappy Dido was alone awake.
Nor sleep nor ease the furious queen can find;
Sleep fled her eyes, as quiet fled her mind.
Despair, and rage, and love divide her heart;
Despair and rage had some, but love the greater part.

Then thus she said within her secret mind:
"What shall I do? what succor can I find?
Become a suppliant to Hyarba's pride,

And take my turn, to court and be denied?
Shall I with this ungrateful Trojan go,
Forsake an empire, and attend a foe?
Himself I refug'd, and his train reliev'd—
'Tis true—but am I sure to be receiv'd?
Can gratitude in Trojan souls have place!
Laomedon still lives in all his race!
Then, shall I seek alone the churlish crew,
Or with my fleet their flying sails pursue?
What force have I but those whom scarce before
I drew reluctant from their native shore?
Will they again embark at my desire,
Once more sustain the seas, and quit their second Tyre?
Rather with steel thy guilty breast invade,
And take the fortune thou thyself hast made.
Your pity, sister, first seduc'd my mind,
Or seconded too well what I design'd.
These dear-bought pleasures had I never known,
Had I continued free, and still my own;
Avoiding love, I had not found despair,
But shar'd with salvage beasts the common air.
Like them, a lonely life I might have led,
Not mourn'd the living, nor disturb'd the dead."
These thoughts she brooded in hera nxious breast.
On board, the Trojan found more easy rest.
Resolv'd to sail, in sleep he pass'd the night;
And order'd all things for his early flight.

To whom once more the winged god appears;
His former youthful mien and shape he wears,
And with this new alarm invades his ears:
"Sleep'st thou, O goddess-born! and canst thou drown
Thy needful cares, so near a hostile town,
Beset with foes; nor hear'st the western gales

Invite thy passage, and inspire thy sails?
She harbors in her heart a furious hate,
And thou shalt find the dire effects too late;
Fix'd on revenge, and obstinate to die.
Haste swiftly hence, while thou hast pow'r to fly.
The sea with ships will soon be cover'd o'er,
And blazing firebrands kindle all the shore.
Prevent her rage, while night obscures the skies,
And sail before the purple morn arise.
Who knows what hazards thy delay may bring?
Woman's a various and a changeful thing."
Thus Hermes in the dream; then took his flight
Aloft in air unseen, and mix'd with night.

Twice warn'd by the celestial messenger,
The pious prince arose with hasty fear;
Then rous'd his drowsy train without delay:
"Haste to your banks; your crooked anchors weigh,
And spread your flying sails, and stand to sea.
A god commands: he stood before my sight,
And urg'd us once again to speedy flight.
O sacred pow'r, what pow'r soe'er thou art,
To thy blest orders I resign my heart.
Lead thou the way; protect thy Trojan bands,
And prosper the design thy will commands."
He said: and, drawing forth his flaming sword,
His thund'ring arm divides the many-twisted cord.
An emulating zeal inspires his train:
They run; they snatch; they rush into the main.
With headlong haste they leave the desert shores,
And brush the liquid seas with lab'ring oars.

Aurora now had left her saffron bed,
And beams of early light the heav'ns o'erspread,
When, from a tow'r, the queen, with wakeful eyes,
Saw day point upward from the rosy skies.
She look'd to seaward; but the sea was void,

And scarce in ken the sailing ships descried.
Stung with despite, and furious with despair,
She struck her trembling breast, and tore her hair.
"And shall th' ungrateful traitor go," she said,
"My land forsaken, and my love betray'd?
Shall we not arm? not rush from ev'ry street,
To follow, sink, and burn his perjur'd fleet?
Haste, haul my galleys out! pursue the foe!
Bring flaming brands! set sail, and swiftly row!
What have I said? where am I? Fury turns
My brain; and my distemper'd bosom burns.
Then, when I gave my person and my throne,
This hate, this rage, had been more timely shown.
See now the promis'd faith, the vaunted name,
The pious man, who, rushing thro' the flame,
Preserv'd his gods, and to the Phrygian shore
The burthen of his feeble father bore!
I should have torn him piecemeal; strow'd in floods
His scatter'd limbs, or left expos'd in woods;
Destroy'd his friends and son; and, from the fire,
Have set the reeking boy before the sire.
Events are doubtful, which on battles wait:
Yet where's the doubt, to souls secure of fate?
My Tyrians, at their injur'd queen's command,
Had toss'd their fires amid the Trojan band;
At once extinguish'd all the faithless name;
And I myself, in vengeance of my shame,
Had fall'n upon the pile, to mend the fun'ral flame.
Thou Sun, who view'st at once the world below;
Thou Juno, guardian of the nuptial vow;
Thou Hecate hearken from thy dark abodes!
Ye Furies, fiends, and violated gods,
All pow'rs invok'd with Dido's dying breath,
Attend her curses and avenge her death!
If so the Fates ordain, Jove commands,

Th' ungrateful wretch should find the
Latian lands,
Yet let a race untam'd, and haughty foes,
His peaceful entrance with dire arms oppose:
Oppress'd with numbers in th' unequal field,
His men discourag'd, and himself expell'd,
Let him for succor sue from place to place,
Torn from his subjects, and his son's embrace.
First, let him see his friends in battle slain,
And their untimely fate lament in vain;
And when, at length, the cruel war shall cease,
On hard conditions may he buy his peace:
Nor let him then enjoy supreme command;
But fall, untimely, by some hostile hand,
And lie unburied on the barren sand!
These are my pray'rs, and this my dying will;
And you, my Tyrians, ev'ry curse fulfill.
Perpetual hate and mortal wars proclaim,
Against the prince, the people, and the name.
These grateful off'rings on my grave bestow;
Nor league, nor love, the hostile nations know!
Now, and from hence, in ev'ry future age,
When rage excites your arms,
and strength supplies the rage
Rise some avenger of our Libyan blood,
With fire and sword pursue the perjur'd brood;
Our arms, our seas, our shores, oppos'd to theirs;
And the same hate descend on all our heirs!"

This said, within her anxious mind she weighs
The means of cutting short her odious days.
Then to Sichæus' nurse she briefly said
(For, when she left her country, hers was dead):
"Go, Barce, call my sister. Let her care
The solemn rites of sacrifice prepare;
The sheep, and all th' atoning off'rings bring,
Sprinkling her body from the crystal spring

With living drops; then let her come, and thou
With sacred fillets bind thy hoary brow.
Thus will I pay my vows to Stygian Jove,
And end the cares of my disastrous love;
Then cast the Trojan image on the fire,
And, as that burns, my passions shall expire."

The nurse moves onward, with officious care,
And all the speed her aged limbs can bear.
But furious Dido, with dark thoughts involv'd,
Shook at the mighty mischief she resolv'd.
With livid spots distinguish'd was her face;
Red were her rolling eyes, and discompos'd
her pace;
Ghastly she gaz'd, with pain she drew
her breath,
And nature shiver'd at approaching death.

Then swiftly to the fatal place she pass'd,
And mounts the fun'ral pile with furious haste;
Unsheathes the sword the Trojan left behind
(Not for so dire an enterprise design'd).
But when she view'd the garments loosely spread,
Which once he wore, and saw the conscious bed,
She paus'd, and with a sigh the robes embrac'd;
Then on the couch her trembling body cast,
Repress'd the ready tears, and spoke her last:
"Dear pledges of my love, while Heav'n
so pleas'd,
Receive a soul, of mortal anguish eas'd:
My fatal course is finish'd; and I go,
A glorious name, among the ghosts below.
A lofty city by my hands is rais'd,
Pygmalion punish'd, and my lord appeas'd.
What could my fortune have afforded more,
Had the false Trojan never touch'd my shore!"
Then kiss'd the couch; and, "Must I die,"
she said,

"And unreveng'd? 'Tis doubly to be dead!
Yet ev'n this death with pleasure I receive:
On any terms, 'tis better than to live.
These flames, from far, may the false
Trojan view;
These boding omens his base flight pursue!"

She said, and struck; deep enter'd in her side
The piercing steel, with reeking purple dyed:
Clogg'd in the wound the cruel weapon stands;
The spouting blood came streaming on
her hands.
Her sad attendants saw the deadly stroke,
And with loud cries the sounding palace shook.
Distracted, from the fatal sight they fled,
And thro' the town the dismal rumor spread.
First from the frighted court the yell began;
Redoubled, thence from house to house it ran:
The groans of men, with shrieks, laments,
and cries
Of mixing women, mount the vaulted skies.
Not less the clamor, than if—ancient Tyre,
Or the new Carthage, set by foes on fire—
The rolling ruin, with their lov'd abodes,
Involv'd the blazing temples of their gods.

Her sister hears; and, furious with despair,
She beats her breast, and rends her yellow hair,
And, calling on Eliza's name aloud,
Runs breathless to the place, and breaks
the crowd.
"Was all that pomp of woe for this prepar'd;
These fires, this fun'ral pile, these altars rear'd?
Was all this train of plots contriv'd," said she,
"All only to deceive unhappy me?
Which is the worst? Didst thou in death pretend
To scorn thy sister, or delude thy friend?

Thy summon'd sister, and thy friend, had come;
One sword had serv'd us both, one common tomb:
Was I to raise the pile, the pow'rs invoke,
Not to be present at the fatal stroke?
At once thou hast destroy'd thyself and me,
Thy town, thy senate, and thy colony!
Bring water; bathe the wound; while I in death
Lay close my lips to hers, and catch the flying breath."
This said, she mounts the pile with eager haste,
And in her arms the gasping queen embrac'd;
Her temples chaf'd; and her own garments tore,
To stanch the streaming blood, and cleanse the gore.
Thrice Dido tried to raise her drooping head,
And, fainting thrice, fell grov'ling on the bed;
Thrice op'd her heavy eyes, and sought the light,
But, having found it, sicken'd at the sight,
And clos'd her lids at last in endless night.

Then Juno, grieving that she should sustain
A death so ling'ring, and so full of pain,
Sent Iris down, to free her from the strife
Of lab'ring nature, and dissolve her life.
For since she died, not doom'd by Heav'n's decree,
Or her own crime, but human casualty,
And rage of love, that plung'd her in despair,
The Sisters had not cut the topmost hair,
Which Proserpine and they can only know;
Nor made her sacred to the shades below.
Downward the various goddess took her flight,
And drew a thousand colors from the light;
Then stood above the dying lover's head,
And said: "I thus devote thee to the dead.

This off'ring to th' infernal gods I bear."
Thus while she spoke, she cut the fatal hair:
The struggling soul was loos'd, and life
 dissolv'd in air.

Book V

Æneas, setting sail from Africa, is driven by a storm on the coasts of Sicily, where he is hospitably received by his friend Acestes, king of part of the island, and born of Trojan parentage. He applies himself to celebrate the memory of his father with divine honors, and accordingly institutes funeral games, and appoints prizes for those who should conquer in them. While the ceremonies were performing, Juno sends Iris to persuade the Trojan women to burn the ships, who, upon her instigation, set fie to them; which burnt four, and would have consumed the rest, had not Jupiter, by a miraculous shower, extinguished it. Upon this, Æneas, by the advice of one of his generals, and a vision of his father, builds a city for the women, old men, and others, who were either unfit for war, or weary of the voyage, and sails for Italy. Venus procures from Neptune a safe voyage for him and all his men, excepting only his pilot Palilnurus, who is unfortunately lost.

Meantime the Trojan cuts his wat'ry way,
Fix'd on his voyage, thro' the curling sea;
Then, casting back his eyes, with dire amaze,
Sees on the Punic shore the mounting blaze.
The cause unknown; yet his presaging mind
The fate of Dido from the fire divin'd;
He knew the stormy souls of womankind,
What secret springs their eager passions move,
How capable of death for injur'd love.
Dire auguries from hence the Trojans draw;
Till neither fires nor shining shores they saw.
Now seas and skies their prospect only bound;
An empty space above, a floating field around.
But soon the heav'ns with shadows were o'erspread;
A swelling cloud hung hov'ring o'er their head:

Livid it look'd, the threat'ning of a storm:
Then night and horror ocean's face deform.
The pilot, Palinurus, cried aloud:
"What gusts of weather from that gath'ring cloud
My thoughts presage! Ere yet the tempest roars,
Stand to your tackle, mates, and stretch your oars;
Contract your swelling sails, and luff to wind."
The frighted crew perform the task assign'd.
Then, to his fearless chief: "Not Heav'n," said he,
"Tho' Jove himself should promise Italy,
Can stem the torrent of this raging sea.
Mark how the shifting winds from west arise,
And what collected night involves the skies!
Nor can our shaken vessels live at sea,
Much less against the tempest force their way.
'Tis fate diverts our course, and fate we must obey.
Not far from hence, if I observ'd aright
The southing of the stars, and polar light,
Sicilia lies, whose hospitable shores
In safety we may reach with struggling oars."
Æneas then replied: "Too sure I find
We strive in vain against the seas and wind:
Now shift your sails; what place can please me more
Than what you promise, the Sicilian shore,
Whose hallow'd earth Anchises' bones contains,
And where a prince of Trojan lineage reigns?"
The course resolv'd, before the western wind
They scud amain, and make the port assign'd.

Meantime Acestes, from a lofty stand,
Beheld the fleet descending on the land;
And, not unmindful of his ancient race,
Down from the cliff he ran with eager pace,
And held the hero in a strict embrace.

Of a rough Libyan bear the spoils he wore,
And either hand a pointed jav'lin bore.
His mother was a dame of Dardan blood;
His sire Crinisus, a Sicilian flood.
He welcomes his returning friends ashore
With plenteous country cates and homely store.

Now, when the following morn had chas'd away
The flying stars, and light restor'd the day,
Æneas call'd the Trojan troops around,
And thus bespoke them from a rising ground:
"Offspring of heav'n, divine Dardanian race!
The sun, revolving thro' th' ethereal space,
The shining circle of the year has fill'd,
Since first this isle my father's ashes held:
And now the rising day renews the year;
A day for ever sad, for ever dear.
This would I celebrate with annual games,
With gifts on altars pil'd, and holy flames,
Tho' banish'd to Gætulia's barren sands,
Caught on the Grecian seas, or hostile lands:
But since this happy storm our fleet has driv'n
(Not, as I deem, without the will of Heav'n)
Upon these friendly shores and flow'ry plains,
Which hide Anchises and his blest remains,
Let us with joy perform his honors due,
And pray for prosp'rous winds, our voyage to renew;
Pray, that in towns and temples of our own,
The name of great Anchises may be known,
And yearly games may spread the gods' renown.
Our sports Acestes, of the Trojan race,
With royal gifts ordain'd, is pleas'd to grace:
Two steers on ev'ry ship the king bestows;
His gods and ours shall share your equal vows.
Besides, if, nine days hence, the rosy morn
Shall with unclouded light the skies adorn,
That day with solemn sports I mean to grace:

Light galleys on the seas shall run a wat'ry race;
Some shall in swiftness for the goal contend,
And others try the twanging bow to bend;
The strong, with iron gauntlets arm'd, shall stand
Oppos'd in combat on the yellow sand.
Let all be present at the games prepar'd,
And joyful victors wait the just reward.
But now assist the rites, with garlands crown'd."
He said, and first his brows with myrtle bound.
Then Helymus, by his example led,
And old Acestes, each adorn'd his head;
Thus young Ascanius, with a sprightly grace,
His temples tied, and all the Trojan race.

Æneas then advanc'd amidst the train,
By thousands follow'd thro' the flow'ry plain,
To great Anchises' tomb; which when he found,
He pour'd to Bacchus, on the hallow'd ground,
Two bowls of sparkling wine, of milk two more,
And two (from offer'd bulls) of purple gore,
With roses then the sepulcher he strow'd
And thus his father's ghost bespoke aloud:
"Hail, O ye holy manes! hail again,
Paternal ashes, now review'd in vain!
The gods permitted not, that you, with me,
Should reach the promis'd shores of Italy,
Or Tiber's flood, what flood soe'er it be."
Scarce had he finish'd, when, with speckled pride,
A serpent from the tomb began to glide;
His hugy bulk on sev'n high volumes roll'd;
Blue was his breadth of back, but streak'd
with scaly gold:
Thus riding on his curls, he seem'd to pass
A rolling fire along, and singe the grass.
More various colors thro' his body run,
Than Iris when her bow imbibes the sun.
Betwixt the rising altars, and around,

The sacred monster shot along the ground;
With harmless play amidst the bowls he pass'd,
And with his lolling tongue assay'd the taste:
Thus fed with holy food, the wondrous guest
Within the hollow tomb retir'd to rest.
The pious prince, surpris'd at what he view'd,
The fun'ral honors with more zeal renew'd,
Doubtful if this place's genius were,
Or guardian of his father's sepulcher.
Five sheep, according to the rites, he slew;
As many swine, and steers of sable hue;
New gen'rous wine he from the goblets pour'd.
And call'd his father's ghost, from hell restor'd.
The glad attendants in long order come,
Off'ring their gifts at great Anchises' tomb:
Some add more oxen: some divide the spoil;
Some place the chargers on the grassy soil;
Some blow the fires, and offer'd entrails broil.

Now came the day desir'd. The skies were bright
With rosy luster of the rising light:
The bord'ring people, rous'd by sounding fame
Of Trojan feasts and great Acestes' name,
The crowded shore with acclamations fill,
Part to behold, and part to prove their skill.
And first the gifts in public view they place,
Green laurel wreaths, and palm, the victors' grace:
Within the circle, arms and tripods lie,
Ingots of gold and silver, heap'd on high,
And vests embroider'd, of the Tyrian dye.
The trumpet's clangor then the feast proclaims,
And all prepare for their appointed games.
Four galleys first, which equal rowers bear,
Advancing, in the wat'ry lists appear.
The speedy Dolphin, that outstrips the wind,
Bore Mnestheus, author of the Memmian kind:
Gyas the vast Chimæra's bulk commands,

Which rising, like a tow'ring city stands;
Three Trojans tug at ev'ry lab'ring oar;
Three banks in three degrees the sailors bore;
Beneath their sturdy strokes the billows roar.
Sergesthus, who began the Sergian race,
In the great Centaur took the leading place;
Cloanthus on the sea-green Scylla stood,
From whom Cluentius draws his Trojan blood.

Far in the sea, against the foaming shore,
There stands a rock: the raging billows roar
Above his head in storms; but, when 'tis clear,
Uncurl their ridgy backs, and at his foot appear.
In peace below the gentle waters run;
The cormorants above lie basking in the sun.
On this the hero fix'd an oak in sight,
The mark to guide the mariners aright.
To bear with this, the seamen stretch their oars;
Then round the rock they steer,
and seek the former shores.
The lots decide their place. Above the rest,
Each leader shining in his Tyrian vest;
The common crew with wreaths of poplar boughs
Their temples crown, and shade their sweaty brows:
Besmear'd with oil, their naked shoulders shine.
All take their seats, and wait the sounding sign:
They gripe their oars; and ev'ry panting breast
Is rais'd by turns with hope,
by turns with fear depress'd.
The clangor of the trumpet gives the sign;
At once they start, advancing in a line:
With shouts the sailors rend the starry skies;
Lash'd with their oars, the smoky billows rise;
Sparkles the briny main, and the vex'd ocean fries.
Exact in time, with equal strokes they row:
At once the brushing oars and brazen prow

Dash up the sandy waves, and ope the
depths below.
Not fiery coursers, in a chariot race,
Invade the field with half so swift a pace;
Not the fierce driver with more fury lends
The sounding lash, and, ere the stroke descends,
Low to the wheels his pliant body bends.
The partial crowd their hopes and fears divide,
And aid with eager shouts the favor'd side.
Cries, murmurs, clamors, with a mixing sound,
From woods to woods, from hills to hills rebound.

Amidst the loud applauses of the shore,
Gyas outstripp'd the rest, and sprung before:
Cloanthus, better mann'd, pursued him fast,
But his o'er-masted galley check'd his haste.
The Centaur and the Dolphin brush the brine
With equal oars, advancing in a line;
And now the mighty Centaur seems to lead,
And now the speedy Dolphin gets ahead;
Now board to board the rival vessels row,
The billows lave the skies, and ocean
groans below.
They reach'd the mark. Proud Gyas and his train
In triumph rode, the victors of the main;
But, steering round, he charg'd his pilot stand
More close to shore, and skim along the sand—
"Let others bear to sea!" Menœtes heard;
But secret shelves too cautiously he fear'd,
And, fearing, sought the deep;
and still aloof he steer'd.
With louder cries the captain call'd again:
"Bear to the rocky shore, and shun the main."
He spoke, and, speaking, at his stern he saw
The bold Cloanthus near the shelvings draw.
Betwixt the mark and him the Scylla stood,
And in a closer compass plow'd the flood.

He pass'd the mark; and, wheeling, got before:
Gyas blasphem'd the gods, devoutly swore,
Cried out for anger, and his hair he tore.
Mindless of others' lives (so high was grown
His rising rage) and careless of his own,
The trembling dotard to the deck he drew;
Then hoisted up, and overboard he threw:
This done, he seiz'd the helm; his fellows cheer'd,
Turn'd short upon the shelfs, and madly steer'd.

Hardly his head the plunging pilot rears,
Clogg'd with his clothes, and cumber'd with his years:
Now dropping wet, he climbs the cliff with pain.
The crowd, that saw him fall and float again,
Shout from the distant shore; and loudly laugh'd,
To see his heaving breast disgorge the briny draught.
The following Centaur, and the Dolphin's crew,
Their vanish'd hopes of victory renew;
While Gyas lags, they kindle in the race,
To reach the mark. Sergesthus takes the place;
Mnestheus pursues; and while around they wind,
Comes up, not half his galley's length behind;
Then, on the deck, amidst his mates appear'd,
And thus their drooping courage he cheer'd:
"My friends, and Hector's followers heretofore,
Exert your vigor; tug the lab'ring oar;
Stretch to your strokes, my still unconquer'd crew,
Whom from the flaming walls of Troy I drew.
In this, our common int'rest, let me find
That strength of hand, that courage of the mind,
As when you stemm'd the strong Malean flood,
And o'er the Syrtes' broken billows row'd.
I seek not now the foremost palm to gain;
Tho' yet—but, ah! that haughty wish is vain!
Let those enjoy it whom the gods ordain.

But to be last, the lags of all the race!—
Redeem yourselves and me from that disgrace."
Now, one and all, they tug amain; they row
At the full stretch, and shake the brazen prow.
The sea beneath 'em sinks; their lab'ring sides
Are swell'd, and sweat runs gutt'ring down in tides.
Chance aids their daring with unhop'd success;
Sergesthus, eager with his beak to press
Betwixt the rival galley and the rock,
Shuts up th' unwieldy Centaur in the lock.
The vessel struck; and, with the dreadful shock,
Her oars she shiver'd, and her head she broke.
The trembling rowers from their banks arise,
And, anxious for themselves, renounce the prize.
With iron poles they heave her off the shores,
And gather from the sea their floating oars.
The crew of Mnestheus, with elated minds,
Urge their success, and call the willing winds;
Then ply their oars, and cut their liquid way
In larger compass on the roomy sea.
As, when the dove her rocky hold forsakes,
Rous'd in a fright, her sounding wings she shakes;
The cavern rings with clatt'ring; out she flies,
And leaves her callow care, and cleaves the skies:
At first she flutters; but at length she springs
To smoother flight, and shoots upon her wings:
So Mnestheus in the Dolphin cuts the sea;
And, flying with a force, that force assists his way.
Sergesthus in the Centaur soon he pass'd,
Wedg'd in the rocky shoals, and sticking fast.
In vain the victor he with cries implores,
And practices to row with shatter'd oars.
Then Mnestheus bears with Gyas, and outflies:
The ship, without a pilot, yields the prize.
Unvanquish'd Scylla now alone remains;
Her he pursues, and all his vigor strains.

Shouts from the fav'ring multitude arise;
Applauding Echo to the shouts replies;
Shouts, wishes, and applause run rattling
thro' the skies.
These clamors with disdain the Scylla heard,
Much grudg'd the praise, but more the
robb'd reward:
Resolv'd to hold their own, they mend their pace,
All obstinate to die, or gain the race.
Rais'd with success, the Dolphin swiftly ran;
For they can conquer, who believe they can.
Both urge their oars, and fortune both supplies,
And both perhaps had shar'd an equal prize;
When to the seas Cloanthus holds his hands,
And succor from the wat'ry pow'rs demands:
"Gods of the liquid realms, on which I row!
If, giv'n by you, the laurel bind my brow,
Assist to make me guilty of my vow!
A snow-white bull shall on your shore be slain;
His offer'd entrails cast into the main,
And ruddy wine, from golden goblets thrown,
Your grateful gift and my return shall own."
The choir of nymphs, and Phorcus, from below,
With virgin Panopea, heard his vow;
And old Portunus, with his breadth of hand,
Push'd on, and sped the galley to the land.
Swift as a shaft, or winged wind, she flies,
And, darting to the port, obtains the prize.

The herald summons all, and then proclaims
Cloanthus conqu'ror of the naval games.
The prince with laurel crowns the victor's head,
And three fat steers are to his vessel led,
The ship's reward; with gen'rous wine beside,
And sums of silver, which the crew divide.
The leaders are distinguish'd from the rest;
The victor honor'd with a nobler vest,

Where gold and purple strive in equal rows,
And needlework its happy cost bestows.
There Ganymede is wrought with living art,
Chasing thro' Ida's groves the trembling hart:
Breathless he seems, yet eager to pursue;
When from aloft descends, in open view,
The bird of Jove, and, sousing on his prey,
With crooked talons bears the boy away.
In vain, with lifted hands and gazing eyes,
His guards behold him soaring thro' the skies,
And dogs pursue his flight with imitated cries.

Mnestheus the second victor was declar'd;
And, summon'd there, the second prize he shar'd.
A coat of mail, brave Demoleus bore,
More brave Æneas from his shoulders tore,
In single combat on the Trojan shore:
This was ordain'd for Mnestheus to possess;
In war for his defense, for ornament in peace.
Rich was the gift, and glorious to behold,
But yet so pond'rous with its plates of gold,
That scarce two servants could the weight sustain;
Yet, loaded thus, Demoleus o'er the plain
Pursued and lightly seiz'd the Trojan train.
The third, succeeding to the last reward,
Two goodly bowls of massy silver shar'd,
With figures prominent, and richly wrought,
And two brass cauldrons from Dodona brought.

Thus all, rewarded by the hero's hands,
Their conqu'ring temples bound with purple bands;
And now Sergesthus, clearing from the rock,
Brought back his galley shatter'd with the shock.
Forlorn she look'd, without an aiding oar,
And, houted by the vulgar, made to shore.
As when a snake, surpris'd upon the road,
Is crush'd athwart her body by the load

Of heavy wheels; or with a mortal wound
Her belly bruis'd, and trodden to the ground:
In vain, with loosen'd curls, she crawls along;
Yet, fierce above, she brandishes her tongue;
Glares with her eyes, and bristles with her scales;
But, groveling in the dust, her parts unsound
she trails:
So slowly to the port the Centaur tends,
But, what she wants in oars, with sails amends.
Yet, for his galley sav'd, the grateful prince
Is pleas'd th' unhappy chief to recompense.
Pholœ, the Cretan slave, rewards his care,
Beauteous herself, with lovely twins as fair.

From thence his way the Trojan hero bent
Into the neighb'ring plain, with mountains pent,
Whose sides were shaded with surrounding wood.
Full in the midst of this fair valley stood
A native theater, which, rising slow
By just degrees, o'erlook'd the ground below.
High on a sylvan throne the leader sate;
A num'rous train attend in solemn state.
Here those that in the rapid course delight,
Desire of honor and the prize invite.
The rival runners without order stand;
The Trojans mix'd with the Sicilian band.
First Nisus, with Euryalus, appears;
Euryalus a boy of blooming years,
With sprightly grace and equal beauty crown'd;
Nisus, for friendship to the youth renown'd.
Diores next, of Priam's royal race,
Then Salius joined with Patron, took their place;
(But Patron in Arcadia had his birth,
And Salius his from Arcananian earth;)
Then two Sicilian youths—the names of these,
Swift Helymus, and lovely Panopes:
Both jolly huntsmen, both in forest bred,

And owning old Acestes for their head;
With sev'ral others of ignobler name,
Whom time has not deliver'd o'er to fame.

To these the hero thus his thoughts explain'd,
In words which gen'ral approbation gain'd:
"One common largess is for all design'd,
(The vanquish'd and the victor shall be join'd,)
Two darts of polish'd steel and Gnosian wood,
A silver-studded ax, alike bestow'd.
The foremost three have olive wreaths decreed:
The first of these obtains a stately steed,
Adorn'd with trappings; and the next in fame,
The quiver of an Amazonian dame,
With feather'd Thracian arrows well supplied:
A golden belt shall gird his manly side,
Which with a sparkling diamond shall be tied.
The third this Grecian helmet shall content."
He said. To their appointed base they went;
With beating hearts th' expected sign receive,
And, starting all at once, the barrier leave.
Spread out, as on the winged winds, they flew,
And seiz'd the distant goal with greedy view.
Shot from the crowd, swift Nisus all o'erpass'd;
Nor storms, nor thunder, equal half his haste.
The next, but tho' the next, yet far disjoin'd,
Came Salius, and Euryalus behind;
Then Helymus, whom young Diores plied,
Step after step, and almost side by side,
His shoulders pressing; and, in longer space,
Had won, or left at least a dubious race.

Now, spent, the goal they almost reach at last,
When eager Nisus, hapless in his haste,
Slipp'd first, and, slipping, fell upon the plain,
Soak'd with the blood of oxen newly slain.
The careless victor had not mark'd his way;

But, treading where the treach'rous puddle lay,
His heels flew up; and on the grassy floor
He fell, besmear'd with filth and holy gore.
Not mindless then, Euryalus, of thee,
Nor of the sacred bonds of amity,
He strove th' immediate rival's hope to cross,
And caught the foot of Salius as he rose.
So Salius lay extended on the plain;
Euryalus springs out, the prize to gain,
And leaves the crowd: applauding peals attend
The victor to the goal, who vanquish'd
by his friend.
Next Helymus; and then Diores came,
By two misfortunes made the third in fame.

But Salius enters, and, exclaiming loud
For justice, deafens and disturbs the crowd;
Urges his cause may in the court be heard;
And pleads the prize is wrongfully conferr'd.
But favor for Euryalus appears;
His blooming beauty, with his tender tears,
Had brib'd the judges for the promis'd prize.
Besides, Diores fills the court with cries,
Who vainly reaches at the last reward,
If the first palm on Salius be conferr'd.
Then thus the prince: "Let no disputes arise:
Where fortune plac'd it, I award the prize.
But fortune's errors give me leave to mend,
At least to pity my deserving friend."
He said, and, from among the spoils, he draws
(Pond'rous with shaggy mane and golden paws)
A lion's hide: to Salius this he gives.
Nisus with envy sees the gift, and grieves.
"If such rewards to vanquish'd men are due."
He said, "and falling is to rise by you,
What prize may Nisus from your bounty claim,
Who merited the first rewards and fame?

In falling, both an equal fortune tried;
Would fortune for my fall so well provide!"
With this he pointed to his face, and show'd
His hand and all his habit smear'd with blood.
Th' indulgent father of the people smil'd,
And caus'd to be produc'd an ample shield,
Of wondrous art, by Didymaon wrought,
Long since from Neptune's bars
in triumph brought.
This giv'n to Nisus, he divides the rest,
And equal justice in his gifts express'd.

The race thus ended, and rewards bestow'd,
Once more the princes bespeaks
th' attentive crowd:
"If there he here whose dauntless courage dare
In gauntlet-fight, with limbs and body bare,
His opposite sustain in open view,
Stand forth the champion, and the games renew.
Two prizes I propose, and thus divide:
A bull with gilded horns, and fillets tied,
Shall be the portion of the conqu'ring chief;
A sword and helm shall cheer the loser's grief."

Then haughty Dares in the lists appears;
Stalking he strides, his head erected bears:
His nervous arms the weighty gauntlet wield,
And loud applauses echo thro' the field.
Dares alone in combat us'd to stand
The match of mighty Paris, hand to hand;
The same, at Hector's fun'rals, undertook
Gigantic Butes, of th' Amycian stock,
And, by the stroke of his resistless hand,
Stretch'd the vast bulk upon the yellow sand.
Such Dares was; and such he strode along,
And drew the wonder of the gazing throng.
His brawny back and ample breast he shows,

His lifted arms around his head he throws,
And deals in whistling air his empty blows.
His match is sought; but, thro' the trembling band,
Not one dares answer to the proud demand.
Presuming of his force, with sparkling eyes
Already he devours the promis'd prize.
He claims the bull with awless insolence,
And having seiz'd his horns, accosts the prince:
"If none my matchless valor dares oppose,
How long shall Dares wait his dastard foes?
Permit me, chief, permit without delay,
To lead this uncontended gift away."
The crowd assents, and with redoubled cries
For the proud challenger demands the prize.

Acestes, fir'd with just disdain, to see
The palm usurp'd without a victory,
Reproach'd Entellus thus, who sate beside,
And heard and saw, unmov'd, the Trojan's pride:
"Once, but in vain, a champion of renown,
So tamely can you bear the ravish'd crown,
A prize in triumph borne before your sight,
And shun, for fear, the danger of the fight?
Where is our Eryx now, the boasted name,
The god who taught your thund'ring arm the game?
Where now your baffled honor? Where the spoil
That fill'd your house, and fame that fill'd our isle?"
Entellus, thus: "My soul is still the same,
Unmov'd with fear, and mov'd with martial fame;
But my chill blood is curdled in my veins,
And scarce the shadow of a man remains.
O could I turn to that fair prime again,
That prime of which this boaster is so vain,

The brave, who this decrepid age defies,
Should feel my force, without the promis'd prize."

He said; and, rising at the word, he threw
Two pond'rous gauntlets down in open view;
Gauntlets which Eryx wont in fight to wield,
And sheathe his hands with in the listed field.
With fear and wonder seiz'd, the crowd beholds
The gloves of death, with sev'n distinguish'd folds
Of tough bull hides; the space within is spread
With iron, or with loads of heavy lead:
Dares himself was daunted at the sight,
Renounc'd his challenge, and refus'd to fight.
Astonish'd at their weight, the hero stands,
And pois'd the pond'rous engines in his hands.
"What had your wonder," said Entellus, "been,
Had you the gauntlets of Alcides seen,
Or view'd the stern debate on this unhappy green!
These which I bear your brother Eryx bore,
Still mark'd with batter'd brains and mingled gore.
With these he long sustain'd th' Herculean arm;
And these I wielded while my blood was warm,
This languish'd frame while better spirits fed,
Ere age unstrung my nerves,
or time o'ersnow'd my head.
But if the challenger these arms refuse,
And cannot wield their weight, or dare not use;
If great Æneas and Acestes join
In his request, these gauntlets I resign;
Let us with equal arms perform the fight,
And let him leave to fear, since I resign my right."

This said, Entellus for the strife prepares;
Stripp'd of his quilted coat, his body bares;
Compos'd of mighty bones and brawn he stands,
A goodly tow'ring object on the sands.
Then just Æneas equal arms supplied,

Which round their shoulders to their
wrists they tied.
Both on the tiptoe stand, at full extent,
Their arms aloft, their bodies inly bent;
Their heads from aiming blows they bear afar;
With clashing gauntlets then provoke the war.
One on his youth and pliant limbs relies;
One on his sinews and his giant size.
The last is stiff with age, his motion slow;
He heaves for breath, he staggers to and fro,
And clouds of issuing smoke his nostrils
loudly blow.
Yet equal in success, they ward, they strike;
Their ways are diff'rent, but their art alike.
Before, behind, the blows are dealt; around
Their hollow sides the rattling thumps resound.
A storm of strokes, well meant, with fury flies,
And errs about their temples, ears, and eyes.
Nor always errs; for oft the gauntlet draws
A sweeping stroke along the crackling jaws.
Heavy with age, Entellus stands his ground,
But with his warping body wards the wound.
His hand and watchful eye keep even pace;
While Dares traverses and shifts his place,
And, like a captain who beleaguers round
Some strong-built castle on a rising ground,
Views all th' approaches with observing eyes:
This and that other part in vain he tries,
And more on industry than force relies.
With hands on high, Entellus threats the foe;
But Dares watch'd the motion from below,
And slipp'd aside, and shunn'd
the long descending blow.
Entellus wastes his forces on the wind,
And, thus deluded of the stroke design'd,
Headlong and heavy fell; his ample breast
And weighty limbs his ancient mother press'd.

So falls a hollow pine, that long had stood
On Ida's height, or Erymanthus' wood,
Torn from the roots. The diff'ring nations rise,
And shouts and mingled murmurs rend the skies,
Acestus runs with eager haste, to raise
The fall'n companion of his youthful days.
Dauntless he rose, and to the fight return'd;
With shame his glowing cheeks,
his eyes with fury burn'd.
Disdain and conscious virtue fir'd his breast,
And with redoubled force his foe he press'd.
He lays on load with either hand, amain,
And headlong drives the Trojan o'er the plain;
Nor stops, nor stays; nor rest nor breath allows;
But storms of strokes descend about his brows,
A rattling tempest, and a hail of blows.
But now the prince, who saw the wild increase
Of wounds, commands the combatants to cease,
And bounds Entellus' wrath, and bids the peace.
First to the Trojan, spent with toil, he came,
And sooth'd his sorrow for the suffer'd shame.
"What fury seiz'd my friend? The gods," said he,
"To him propitious, and averse to thee,
Have giv'n his arm superior force to thine.
'Tis madness to contend with strength divine."
The gauntlet fight thus ended, from the shore
His faithful friends unhappy Dares bore:
His mouth and nostrils pour'd a purple flood,
And pounded teeth came rushing with his blood.
Faintly he stagger'd thro' the hissing throng,
And hung his head, and trail'd his legs along.
The sword and casque are carried by his train;
But with his foe the palm and ox remain.

The champion, then, before Æneas came,
Proud of his prize, but prouder of his fame:
"O goddess-born, and you, Dardanian host,

Mark with attention, and forgive my boast;
Learn what I was, by what remains; and know
From what impending fate you sav'd my foe."
Sternly he spoke, and then confronts the bull;
And, on his ample forehead aiming full,
The deadly stroke, descending, pierc'd the skull.
Down drops the beast,
nor needs a second wound,
But sprawls in pangs of death,
and spurns the ground.
Then, thus: "In Dares' stead I offer this.
Eryx, accept a nobler sacrifice;
Take the last gift my wither'd arms can yield:
Thy gauntlets I resign, and here renounce the field."

This done, Æneas orders, for the close,
The strife of archers with contending bows.
The mast Sergesthus' shatter'd galley bore
With his own hands he raises on the shore.
A flutt'ring dove upon the top they tie,
The living mark at which their arrows fly.
The rival archers in a line advance,
Their turn of shooting to receive from chance.
A helmet holds their names; the lots are drawn:
On the first scroll was read Hippocoon.
The people shout. Upon the next was found
Young Mnestheus, late with naval honors crown'd.
The third contain'd Eurytion's noble name,
Thy brother, Pandarus, and next in fame,
Whom Pallas urg'd the treaty to confound,
And send among the Greeks a feather'd wound.
Acestes in the bottom last remain'd,
Whom not his age from youthful
sports restrain'd.
Soon all with vigor bend their trusty bows,
And from the quiver each his arrow chose.
Hippocoon's was the first: with forceful sway

It flew, and, whizzing, cut the liquid way.
Fix'd in the mast the feather'd weapon stands:
The fearful pigeon flutters in her bands,
And the tree trembled, and the shouting cries
Of the pleas'd people rend the vaulted skies.
Then Mnestheus to the head his arrow drove,
With lifted eyes, and took his aim above,
But made a glancing shot, and missed the dove;
Yet miss'd so narrow, that he cut the cord
Which fasten'd by the foot the flitting bird.
The captive thus releas'd, away she flies,
And beats with clapping wings the yielding skies.
His bow already bent, Eurytion stood;
And, having first invok'd his brother god,
His winged shaft with eager haste he sped.
The fatal message reach'd her as she fled:
She leaves her life aloft; she strikes the ground,
And renders back the weapon in the wound.
Acestes, grudging at his lot, remains,
Without a prize to gratify his pains.
Yet, shooting upward, sends his shaft, to show
An archer's art, and boast his twanging bow.
The feather'd arrow gave a dire portent,
And latter augurs judge from this event.
Chaf'd by the speed, it fir'd; and, as it flew,
A trail of following flames ascending drew:
Kindling they mount, and mark the shiny way;
Across the skies as falling meteors play,
And vanish into wind, or in a blaze decay.
The Trojans and Sicilians wildly stare,
And, trembling, turn their wonder into pray'r.
The Dardan prince put on a smiling face,
And strain'd Acestes with a close embrace;
Then, hon'ring him with gifts above the rest,
Turn'd the bad omen, nor his fears confess'd.
"The gods," said he, "this miracle have wrought,
And order'd you the prize without the lot.

Accept this goblet, rough with figur'd gold,
Which Thracian Cisseus gave my sire of old:
This pledge of ancient amity receive,
Which to my second sire I justly give."
He said, and, with the trumpets' cheerful sound,
Proclaim'd him victor, and with laurel-crown'd.
Nor good Eurytion envied him the prize,
Tho' he transfix'd the pigeon in the skies.
Who cut the line, with second gifts was grac'd;
The third was his whose arrow pierc'd the mast.

The chief, before the games were wholly done,
Call'd Periphantes, tutor to his son,
And whisper'd thus: "With speed Ascanius find;
And, if his childish troop be ready join'd,
On horseback let him grace his grandsire's day,
And lead his equals arm'd in just array."
He said; and, calling out, the cirque he clears.
The crowd withdrawn, an open plain appears.
And now the noble youths, of form divine,
Advance before their fathers, in a line;
The riders grace the steeds; the steeds
with glory shine.

Thus marching on in military pride,
Shouts of applause resound from side to side.
Their casques adorn'd with laurel wreaths
they wear,
Each brandishing aloft a cornel spear.
Some at their backs their gilded quivers bore;
Their chains of burnish'd gold hung down before.
Three graceful troops they form'd upon the green;
Three graceful leaders at their head were seen;
Twelve follow'd ev'ry chief, and left a
space between.
The first young Priam led; a lovely boy,
Whose grandsire was th' unhappy king of Troy;

His race in after times was known to fame,
New honors adding to the Latian name;
And well the royal boy his Thracian steed became.
White were the fetlocks of his feet before,
And on his front a snowy star he bore.
Then beauteous Atys, with Iulus bred,
Of equal age, the second squadron led.
The last in order, but the first in place,
First in the lovely features of his face,
Rode fair Ascanius on a fiery steed,
Queen Dido's gift, and of the Tyrian breed.
Sure coursers for the rest the king ordains,
With golden bits adorn'd, and purple reins.

The pleas'd spectators peals of shouts renew,
And all the parents in the children view;
Their make, their motions, and their
    sprightly grace,
And hopes and fears alternate in their face.

Th' unfledg'd commanders and their martial train
First make the circuit of the sandy plain
Around their sires, and, at th' appointed sign,
Drawn up in beauteous order, form a line.
The second signal sounds, the troop divides
In three distinguish'd parts,
    with three distinguish'd guides
Again they close, and once again disjoin;
In troop to troop oppos'd, and line to line.
They meet; they wheel; they throw their darts afar
With harmless rage and well-dissembled war.
Then in a round the mingled bodies run:
Flying they follow, and pursuing shun;
Broken, they break; and, rallying, they renew
In other forms the military shew.
At last, in order, undiscern'd they join,
And march together in a friendly line.

And, as the Cretan labyrinth of old,
With wand'ring ways and many a winding fold,
Involv'd the weary feet, without redress,
In a round error, which denied recess;
So fought the Trojan boys in warlike play,
Turn'd and return'd, and still a diff'rent way.
Thus dolphins in the deep each other chase
In circles, when they swim around the wat'ry race.
This game, these carousels, Ascanius taught;
And, building Alba, to the Latins brought;
Shew'd what he learn'd: the Latin sires impart
To their succeeding sons the graceful art;
From these imperial Rome receiv'd the game,
Which Troy, the youths the Trojan troop, they name.

Thus far the sacred sports they celebrate:
But Fortune soon resum'd her ancient hate;
For, while they pay the dead his annual dues,
Those envied rites Saturnian Juno views;
And sends the goddess of the various bow,
To try new methods of revenge below;
Supplies the winds to wing her airy way,
Where in the port secure the navy lay.
Swiftly fair Iris down her arch descends,
And, undiscern'd, her fatal voyage ends.
She saw the gath'ring crowd; and, gliding thence,
The desert shore, and fleet without defense.
The Trojan matrons, on the sands alone,
With sighs and tears Anchises' death bemoan;
Then, turning to the sea their weeping eyes,
Their pity to themselves renews their cries.
"Alas!" said one, "what oceans yet remain
For us to sail! what labors to sustain!"
All take the word, and, with a gen'ral groan,

Implore the gods for peace, and places
of their own.

The goddess, great in mischief, views their pains,
And in a woman's form her heav'nly
limbs restrains.
In face and shape old Berœ she became,
Doryclus' wife, a venerable dame,
Once blest with riches, and a mother's name.
Thus chang'd, amidst the crying crowd she ran,
Mix'd with the matrons, and these words began:
"O wretched we, whom not the Grecian pow'r,
Nor flames, destroy'd, in Troy's unhappy hour!
O wretched we, reserv'd by cruel fate,
Beyond the ruins of the sinking state!
Now sev'n revolving years are wholly run,
Since this improsp'rous voyage we begun;
Since, toss'd from shores to shores,
from lands to lands,
Inhospitable rocks and barren sands,
Wand'ring in exile thro' the stormy sea,
We search in vain for flying Italy.
Now cast by fortune on this kindred land,
What should our rest and rising walls withstand,
Or hinder here to fix our banish'd band?
O country lost, and gods redeem'd in vain,
If still in endless exile we remain!
Shall we no more the Trojan walls renew,
Or streams of some dissembled Simoïs view!
Haste, join with me, th' unhappy fleet consume!
Cassandra bids; and I declare her doom.
In sleep I saw her; she supplied my hands
(For this I more than dreamt) with
flaming brands:
'With these,' said she, 'these wand'ring
ships destroy:
These are your fatal seats, and this your Troy.'

Time calls you now; the precious hour employ:
Slack not the good presage, while Heav'n inspires
Our minds to dare, and gives the ready fires.
See! Neptune's altars minister their brands:
The god is pleas'd; the god supplies our hands."
Then from the pile a flaming fire she drew,
And, toss'd in air, amidst the galleys threw.

Wrapp'd in amaze, the matrons wildly stare:
Then Pyrgo, reverenc'd for her hoary hair,
Pyrgo, the nurse of Priam's num'rous race:
"No Berœ this, tho' she belies her face!
What terrors from her frowning front arise!
Behold a goddess in her ardent eyes!
What rays around her heav'nly face are seen!
Mark her majestic voice, and more than mortal mien!
Berœ but now I left, whom, pin'd with pain,
Her age and anguish from these rites detain,"
She said. The matrons, seiz'd with new amaze,
Roll their malignant eyes, and on the navy gaze.
They fear, and hope, and neither part obey:
They hope the fated land, but fear the fatal way.
The goddess, having done her task below,
Mounts up on equal wings, and bends her painted bow.
Struck with the sight, and seiz'd with rage divine,
The matrons prosecute their mad design:
They shriek aloud; they snatch, with impious hands,
The food of altars; fires and flaming brands.
Green boughs and saplings, mingled in their haste,
And smoking torches, on the ships they cast.
The flame, unstopp'd at first, more fury gains,
And Vulcan rides at large with loosen'd reins:
Triumphant to the painted sterns he soars,
And seizes, in this way, the banks and crackling oars.

Eumelus was the first the news to bear,
While yet they crowd the rural theater.
Then, what they hear, is witness'd by their eyes:
A storm of sparkles and of flames arise.
Ascanius took th' alarm, while yet he led
His early warriors on his prancing steed,
And, spurring on, his equals soon o'erpass'd;
Nor could his frighted friends reclaim his haste.
Soon as the royal youth appear'd in view,
He sent his voice before him as he flew:
"What madness moves you, matrons, to destroy
The last remainders of unhappy Troy!
Not hostile fleets, but your own hopes, you burn,
And on your friends your fatal fury turn.
Behold your own Ascanius!" While he said,
He drew his glitt'ring helmet from his head,
In which the youths to sportful arms he led.
By this, Æneas and his train appear;
And now the women, seiz'd with shame and fear,
Dispers'd, to woods and caverns take their flight,
Abhor their actions, and avoid the light;
Their friends acknowledge, and their error find,
And shake the goddess from their alter'd mind.

Not so the raging fires their fury cease,
But, lurking in the seams, with seeming peace,
Work on their way amid the smold'ring tow,
Sure in destruction, but in motion slow.
The silent plague thro' the green timber eats,
And vomits out a tardy flame by fits.
Down to the keels, and upward to the sails,
The fire descends, or mounts, but still prevails;
Nor buckets pour'd, nor strength of human hand,
Can the victorious element withstand.

The pious hero rends his robe, and throws
To heav'n his hands, and with his hands his vows.

"O Jove," he cried, "if pray'rs can yet have place;
If thou abhorr'st not all the Dardan race;
If any spark of pity still remain;
If gods are gods, and not invok'd in vain;
Yet spare the relics of the Trojan train!
Yet from the flames our burning vessels free,
Or let thy fury fall alone on me!
At this devoted head thy thunder throw,
And send the willing sacrifice below!"

Scarce had he said, when southern storms arise:
From pole to pole the forky lightning flies;
Loud rattling shakes the mountains and the plain;
Heav'n bellies downward, and descends in rain.
Whole sheets of water from the clouds are sent,
Which, hissing thro' the planks, the flames prevent,
And stop the fiery pest. Four ships alone
Burn to the waist, and for the fleet atone.

But doubtful thoughts the hero's heart divide;
If he should still in Sicily reside,
Forgetful of his fates, or tempt the main,
In hope the promis'd Italy to gain.
Then Nautes, old and wise, to whom alone
The will of Heav'n by Pallas was foreshown;
Vers'd in portents, experienc'd, and inspir'd
To tell events, and what the fates requir'd;
Thus while he stood, to neither part inclin'd,
With cheerful words reliev'd his lab'ring mind:
"O goddess-born, resign'd in ev'ry state,
With patience bear, with prudence push your fate.
By suff'ring well, our Fortune we subdue;
Fly when she frowns, and, when she calls, pursue.
Your friend Acestes is of Trojan kind;
To him disclose the secrets of your mind:

Trust in his hands your old and useless train;
Too num'rous for the ships which yet remain:
The feeble, old, indulgent of their ease,
The dames who dread the dangers of the seas,
With all the dastard crew, who dare not stand
The shock of battle with your foes by land.
Here you may build a common town for all,
And, from Acestes' name, Acesta call."
The reasons, with his friend's experience join'd,
Encourag'd much, but more disturb'd his mind.

'Twas dead of night; when to his slumb'ring eyes
His father's shade descended from the skies,
And thus he spoke: "O more than vital breath,
Lov'd while I liv'd, and dear ev'n after death;
O son, in various toils and troubles toss'd,
The King of Heav'n employs my careful ghost
On his commands: the god, who sav'd from fire
Your flaming fleet, and heard your just desire.
The wholesome counsel of your friend receive,
And here the coward train and woman leave:
The chosen youth, and those who nobly dare,
Transport, to tempt the dangers of the war.
The stern Italians will their courage try;
Rough are their manners, and their minds
are high.
But first to Pluto's palace you shall go,
And seek my shade among the blest below:
For not with impious ghosts my soul remains,
Nor suffers with the damn'd perpetual pains,
But breathes the living air of soft Elysian plains.
The chaste Sibylla shall your steps convey,
And blood of offer'd victims free the way.
There shall you know what realms the
gods assign,
And learn the fates and fortunes of your line.

But now, farewell! I vanish with the night,
And feel the blast of heav'n's approaching light."
He said, and mix'd with shades, and took
his airy flight.
"Whither so fast?" the filial duty cried;
"And why, ah why, the wish'd embrace denied?"

He said, and rose; as holy zeal inspires,
He rakes hot embers, and renews the fires;
His country gods and Vesta then adores
With cakes and incense, and their aid implores.
Next, for his friends and royal host he sent,
Reveal'd his vision, and the gods' intent,
With his own purpose. All, without delay,
The will of Jove, and his desires obey.
They list with women each degenerate name,
Who dares not hazard life for future fame.
These they cashier: the brave remaining few,
Oars, banks, and cables, half consum'd, renew.
The prince designs a city with the plow;
The lots their sev'ral tenements allow.
This part is nam'd from Ilium, that from Troy,
And the new king ascends the throne with joy;
A chosen senate from the people draws;
Appoints the judges, and ordains the laws.
Then, on the top of Eryx, they begin
A rising temple to the Paphian queen.
Anchises, last, is honor'd as a god;
A priest is added, annual gifts bestow'd,
And groves are planted round his blest abode.
Nine days they pass in feasts, their
temples crown'd;
And fumes of incense in the fanes abound.
Then from the south arose a gentle breeze
That curl'd the smoothness of the glassy seas;
The rising winds a ruffling gale afford,
And call the merry mariners aboard.

Now loud laments along the shores resound,
Of parting friends in close embraces bound.
The trembling women, the degenerate train,
Who shunn'd the frightful dangers of the main,
Ev'n those desire to sail, and take their share
Of the rough passage and the promis'd war:
Whom good Æneas cheers, and recommends
To their new master's care his fearful friends.
On Eryx's altars three fat calves he lays;
A lamb new-fallen to the stormy seas;
Then slips his haulsers, and his anchors weighs.
High on the deck the godlike hero stands,
With olive crown'd, a charger in his hands;
Then cast the reeking entrails in the brine,
And pour'd the sacrifice of purple wine.
Fresh gales arise; with equal strokes they vie,
And brush the buxom seas, and o'er the
billows fly.

Meantime the mother goddess, full of fears,
To Neptune thus address'd, with tender tears:
"The pride of Jove's imperious queen, the rage,
The malice which no suff'rings can assuage,
Compel me to these pray'rs; since neither fate,
Nor time, nor pity, can remove her hate:
Ev'n Jove is thwarted by his haughty wife;
Still vanquish'd, yet she still renews the strife.
As if 'twere little to consume the town
Which aw'd the world, and wore th'
imperial crown,
She prosecutes the ghost of Troy with pains,
And gnaws, ev'n to the bones, the last remains.
Let her the causes of her hatred tell;
But you can witness its effects too well.
You saw the storm she rais'd on Libyan floods,
That mix'd the mounting billows with the clouds;
When, bribing Æolus, she shook the main,

And mov'd rebellion in your wat'ry reign.
With fury she possess'd the Dardan dames,
To burn their fleet with execrable flames,
And forc'd Æneas, when his ships were lost,
To leave his foll'wers on a foreign coast.
For what remains, your godhead I implore,
And trust my son to your protecting pow'r.
If neither Jove's nor Fate's decree withstand,
Secure his passage to the Latian land."

Then thus the mighty Ruler of the Main:
"What may not Venus hope from Neptune's reign?
My kingdom claims your birth; my late defense
Of your endanger'd fleet may claim your confidence.
Nor less by land than sea my deeds declare
How much your lov'd Æneas is my care.
Thee, Xanthus, and thee, Simoïs, I attest.
Your Trojan troops when proud Achilles press'd,
And drove before him headlong on the plain,
And dash'd against the walls the trembling train;
When floods were fill'd with bodies of the slain;
When crimson Xanthus, doubtful of his way,
Stood up on ridges to behold the sea;
(New heaps came tumbling in, and chok'd his way;)
When your Æneas fought, but fought with odds
Of force unequal, and unequal gods;
I spread a cloud before the victor's sight,
Sustain'd the vanquish'd, and secur'd his flight;
Ev'n then secur'd him, when I sought with joy
The vow'd destruction of ungrateful Troy.
My will's the same: fair goddess, fear no more,
Your fleet shall safely gain the Latian shore;
Their lives are giv'n; one destin'd head alone

Shall perish, and for multitudes atone."
Thus having arm'd with hopes her
anxious mind,
His finny team Saturnian Neptune join'd,
Then adds the foamy bridle to their jaws,
And to the loosen'd reins permits the laws.
High on the waves his azure car he guides;
Its axles thunder, and the sea subsides,
And the smooth ocean rolls her silent tides.
The tempests fly before their father's face,
Trains of inferior gods his triumph grace,
And monster whales before their master play,
And choirs of Tritons crowd the wat'ry way.
The marshal'd pow'rs in equal troops divide
To right and left; the gods his better side
Enclose, and on the worse the Nymphs
and Nereids ride.

Now smiling hope, with sweet vicissitude,
Within the hero's mind his joys renew'd.
He calls to raise the masts, the sheets display;
The cheerful crew with diligence obey;
They scud before the wind, and sail in open sea.
Ahead of all the master pilot steers;
And, as he leads, the following navy veers.
The steeds of Night had travel'd half the sky,
The drowsy rowers on their benches lie,
When the soft God of Sleep, with easy flight,
Descends, and draws behind a trail of light.
Thou, Palinurus, art his destin'd prey;
To thee alone he takes his fatal way.
Dire dreams to thee, and iron sleep, he bears;
And, lighting on thy prow, the form of
Phorbas wears.
Then thus the traitor god began his tale:
"The winds, my friend, inspire a pleasing gale;
The ships, without thy care, securely sail.

Now steal an hour of sweet repose; and I
Will take the rudder and thy room supply."
To whom the yawning pilot, half asleep:
"Me dost thou bid to trust the treach'rous deep,
The harlot smiles of her dissembling face,
And to her faith commit the Trojan race?
Shall I believe the Siren South again,
And, oft betray'd, not know the monster main?"
He said: his fasten'd hands the rudder keep,
And, fix'd on heav'n, his eyes repel invading sleep.
The god was wroth, and at his temples threw
A branch in Lethe dipp'd, and drunk with
Stygian dew:
The pilot, vanquish'd by the pow'r divine,
Soon clos'd his swimming eyes, and lay supine.
Scarce were his limbs extended at their length,
The god, insulting with superior strength,
Fell heavy on him, plung'd him in the sea,
And, with the stern, the rudder tore away.
Headlong he fell, and, struggling in the main,
Cried out for helping hands, but cried in vain.
The victor dæmon mounts obscure in air,
While the ship sails without the pilot's care.
On Neptune's faith the floating fleet relies;
But what the man forsook, the god supplies,
And o'er the dang'rous deep secure the navy flies;
Glides by the Sirens' cliffs, a shelfy coast,
Long infamous for ships and sailors lost,
And white with bones. Th' impetuous ocean roars,
And rocks rebellow from the sounding shores.
The watchful hero felt the knocks, and found
The tossing vessel sail'd on shoaly ground.
Sure of his pilot's loss, he takes himself
The helm, and steers aloof, and shuns the shelf.
Inly he griev'd, and, groaning from the breast,
Deplor'd his death; and thus his pain express'd:
"For faith repos'd on seas, and on the

flatt'ring sky,
Thy naked corpse is doom'd on shores
unknown to lie."

Book VI

The Sibyl foretells Æneas the adventures he should meet with in Italy. She attends him to hell; describing to him the various scenes of that place, and conducting him to his father Anchises, who instructs him in those sublime mysteries of the soul of the world, and the transmigration; and shows him that glorious race of heroes which was to descend from him, and his posterity.

He said, and wept; then spread his sails before
The winds, and reach'd at length the Cumæan shore:
Their anchors dropp'd, his crew the vessels moor.
They turn their heads to sea, their sterns to land,
And greet with greedy joy th' Italian strand.
Some strike from clashing flints their fiery seed;
Some gather sticks, the kindled flames to feed,
Or search for hollow trees, and fell the woods,
Or trace thro' valleys the discover'd floods.
Thus, while their sev'ral charges they fulfill,
The pious prince ascends the sacred hill
Where Phœbus is ador'd; and seeks the shade
Which hides from sight his venerable maid.
Deep in a cave the Sibyl makes abode;
Thence full of fate returns, and of the god.
Thro' Trivia's grove they walk; and now behold,
And enter now, the temple roof'd with gold.
When Dædalus, to fly the Cretan shore,
His heavy limbs on jointed pinions bore,
(The first who sail'd in air,) 'tis sung by Fame,
To the Cumæan coast at length he came,
And here alighting, built this costly frame.

Inscrib'd to Phœbus, here he hung on high
The steerage of his wings, that cut the sky:
Then o'er the lofty gate his art emboss'd
Androgeos' death, and off'rings to his ghost;
Sev'n youths from Athens yearly sent, to meet
The fate appointed by revengeful Crete.
And next to those the dreadful urn was plac'd,
In which the destin'd names by lots were cast:
The mournful parents stand around in tears,
And rising Crete against their shore appears.
There too, in living sculpture, might be seen
The mad affection of the Cretan queen;
Then how she cheats her bellowing lover's eye;
The rushing leap, the doubtful progeny,
The lower part a beast, a man above,
The monument of their polluted love.
Not far from thence he grav'd the wondrous maze,
A thousand doors, a thousand winding ways:
Here dwells the monster, hid from human view,
Not to be found, but by the faithful clew;
Till the kind artist, mov'd with pious grief,
Lent to the loving maid this last relief,
And all those erring paths describ'd so well
That Theseus conquer'd and the monster fell.
Here hapless Icarus had found his part,
Had not the father's grief restrain'd his art.
He twice assay'd to cast his son in gold;
Twice from his hands he dropp'd the
        forming mold.

All this with wond'ring eyes Æneas view'd;
Each varying object his delight renew'd:
Eager to read the rest—Achates came,
And by his side the mad divining dame,
The priestess of the god, Deïphobe her name.
"Time suffers not," she said, "to feed your eyes
With empty pleasures; haste the sacrifice.

Sev'n bullocks, yet unyok'd, for Phœbus choose,
And for Diana sev'n unspotted ewes."
This said, the servants urge the sacred rites,
While to the temple she the prince invites.
A spacious cave, within its farmost part,
Was hew'd and fashion'd by laborious art
Thro' the hill's hollow sides: before the place,
A hundred doors a hundred entries grace;
As many voices issue, and the sound
Of Sybil's words as many times rebound.
Now to the mouth they come. Aloud she cries:
"This is the time; inquire your destinies.
He comes; behold the god!" Thus while she said,
(And shiv'ring at the sacred entry stay'd,)
Her color chang'd; her face was not the same,
And hollow groans from her deep spirit came.
Her hair stood up; convulsive rage possess'd
Her trembling limbs, and heav'd her lab'ring breast.
Greater than humankind she seem'd to look,
And with an accent more than mortal spoke.
Her staring eyes with sparkling fury roll;
When all the god came rushing on her soul.
Swiftly she turn'd, and, foaming as she spoke:
"Why this delay?" she cried—"the pow'rs invoke!
Thy pray'rs alone can open this abode;
Else vain are my demands, and dumb the god."

She said no more. The trembling Trojans hear,
O'erspread with a damp sweat and holy fear.
The prince himself, with awful dread possess'd,
His vows to great Apollo thus address'd:
"Indulgent god, propitious pow'r to Troy,
Swift to relieve, unwilling to destroy,
Directed by whose hand the Dardan dart
Pierc'd the proud Grecian's only mortal part:
Thus far, by fate's decrees and thy commands,
Thro' ambient seas and thro' devouring sands,

Our exil'd crew has sought th' Ausonian ground;
And now, at length, the flying coast is found.
Thus far the fate of Troy, from place to place,
With fury has pursued her wand'ring race.
Here cease, ye pow'rs, and let your vengeance end:
Troy is no more, and can no more offend.
And thou, O sacred maid, inspir'd to see
Th' event of things in dark futurity;
Give me what Heav'n has promis'd to my fate,
To conquer and command the Latian state;
To fix my wand'ring gods, and find a place
For the long exiles of the Trojan race.
Then shall my grateful hands a temple rear
To the twin gods, with vows and solemn pray'r;
And annual rites, and festivals, and games,
Shall be perform'd to their auspicious names.
Nor shalt thou want thy honors in my land;
For there thy faithful oracles shall stand,
Preserv'd in shrines; and ev'ry sacred lay,
Which, by thy mouth, Apollo shall convey:
All shall be treasur'd by a chosen train
Of holy priests, and ever shall remain.
But O! commit not thy prophetic mind
To flitting leaves, the sport of ev'ry wind,
Lest they disperse in air our empty fate;
Write not, but, what the pow'rs ordain, relate."

Struggling in vain, impatient of her load,
And lab'ring underneath the pond'rous god,
The more she strove to shake him from her breast,
With more and far superior force he press'd;
Commands his entrance, and, without control,
Usurps her organs and inspires her soul.
Now, with a furious blast, the hundred doors
Ope of themselves; a rushing whirlwind roars
Within the cave, and Sibyl's voice restores:
"Escap'd the dangers of the wat'ry reign,

Yet more and greater ills by land remain.
The coast, so long desir'd (nor doubt th' event),
Thy troops shall reach, but, having reach'd, repent.
Wars, horrid wars, I view—a field of blood,
And Tiber rolling with a purple flood.
Simoïs nor Xanthus shall be wanting there:
A new Achilles shall in arms appear,
And he, too, goddess-born. Fierce Juno's hate,
Added to hostile force, shall urge thy fate.
To what strange nations shalt not thou resort,
Driv'n to solicit aid at ev'ry court!
The cause the same which Ilium once oppress'd;
A foreign mistress, and a foreign guest.
But thou, secure of soul, unbent with woes,
The more thy fortune frowns, the more oppose.
The dawnings of thy safety shall be shown
From whence thou least shalt hope,
    a Grecian town."

Thus, from the dark recess, the Sibyl spoke,
And the resisting air the thunder broke;
The cave rebellow'd, and the temple shook.
Th' ambiguous god, who rul'd her
    lab'ring breast,
In these mysterious words his mind express'd;
Some truths reveal'd, in terms involv'd the rest.
At length her fury fell, her foaming ceas'd,
And, ebbing in her soul, the god decreas'd.
Then thus the chief: "No terror to my view,
No frightful face of danger can be new.
Inur'd to suffer, and resolv'd to dare,
The Fates, without my pow'r,
    shall be without my care.
This let me crave, since near your grove the road
To hell lies open, and the dark abode
Which Acheron surrounds, th' innavigable flood;
Conduct me thro' the regions void of light,

And lead me longing to my father's sight.
For him, a thousand dangers I have sought,
And, rushing where the thickest Grecians fought,
Safe on my back the sacred burthen brought.
He, for my sake, the raging ocean tried,
And wrath of Heav'n, my still auspicious guide,
And bore beyond the strength decrepit age supplied.
Oft, since he breath'd his last, in dead of night
His reverend image stood before my sight;
Enjoin'd to seek, below, his holy shade;
Conducted there by your unerring aid.
But you, if pious minds by pray'rs are won,
Oblige the father, and protect the son.
Yours is the pow'r; nor Proserpine in vain
Has made you priestess of her nightly reign.
If Orpheus, arm'd with his enchanting lyre,
The ruthless king with pity could inspire,
And from the shades below redeem his wife;
If Pollux, off'ring his alternate life,
Could free his brother, and can daily go
By turns aloft, by turns descend below—
Why name I Theseus, or his greater friend,
Who trod the downward path, and upward could ascend?
Not less than theirs from Jove my lineage came;
My mother greater, my descent the same."
So pray'd the Trojan prince, and, while he pray'd,
His hand upon the holy altar laid.

Then thus replied the prophetess divine:
"O goddess-born of great Anchises' line,
The gates of hell are open night and day;
Smooth the descent, and easy is the way:
But to return, and view the cheerful skies,
In this the task and mighty labor lies.
To few great Jupiter imparts this grace,

And those of shining worth and heav'nly race.
Betwixt those regions and our upper light,
Deep forests and impenetrable night
Possess the middle space: th' infernal bounds
Cocytus, with his sable waves, surrounds.
But if so dire a love your soul invades,
As twice below to view the trembling shades;
If you so hard a toil will undertake,
As twice to pass th' innavigable lake;
Receive my counsel. In the neighb'ring grove
There stands a tree; the queen of Stygian Jove
Claims it her own; thick woods and gloomy night
Conceal the happy plant from human sight.
One bough it bears; but (wondrous to behold!)
The ductile rind and leaves of radiant gold:
This from the vulgar branches must be torn,
And to fair Proserpine the present borne,
Ere leave be giv'n to tempt the nether skies.
The first thus rent a second will arise,
And the same metal the same room supplies.
Look round the wood, with lifted eyes, to see
The lurking gold upon the fatal tree:
Then rend it off, as holy rites command;
The willing metal will obey thy hand,
Following with ease, if favor'd by thy fate,
Thou art foredoom'd to view the Stygian state:
If not, no labor can the tree constrain;
And strength of stubborn arms and steel are vain.
Besides, you know not, while you here attend,
Th' unworthy fate of your unhappy friend:
Breathless he lies; and his unburied ghost,
Depriv'd of fun'ral rites, pollutes your host.
Pay first his pious dues; and, for the dead,
Two sable sheep around his hearse be led;
Then, living turfs upon his body lay:
This done, securely take the destin'd way,
To find the regions destitute of day."

She said, and held her peace. Æneas went
Sad from the cave, and full of discontent,
Unknowing whom the sacred Sibyl meant.
Achates, the companion of his breast,
Goes grieving by his side,
with equal cares oppress'd.
Walking, they talk'd, and fruitlessly divin'd
What friend the priestess by those
words design'd.
But soon they found an object to deplore:
Misenus lay extended the shore;
Son of the God of Winds: none so renown'd
The warrior trumpet in the field to sound;
With breathing brass to kindle fierce alarms,
And rouse to dare their fate in honorable arms.
He serv'd great Hector, and was ever near,
Not with his trumpet only, but his spear.
But by Pelides' arms when Hector fell,
He chose Æneas; and he chose as well.
Swoln with applause, and aiming still at more,
He now provokes the sea gods from the shore;
With envy Triton heard the martial sound,
And the bold champion, for his challenge, drown'd;
Then cast his mangled carcass on the strand:
The gazing crowd around the body stand.
All weep; but most Æneas mourns his fate,
And hastens to perform the funeral state.
In altar-wise, a stately pile they rear;
The basis broad below, and top advanc'd in air.
An ancient wood, fit for the work design'd,
(The shady covert of the salvage kind,)
The Trojans found: the sounding ax is plied;
Firs, pines, and pitch trees, and the tow'ring pride
Of forest ashes, feel the fatal stroke,
And piercing wedges cleave the stubborn oak.
Huge trunks of trees, fell'd from the steepy crown
Of the bare mountains, roll with ruin down.

Arm'd like the rest the Trojan prince appears,
And by his pious labor urges theirs.

Thus while he wrought, revolving in his mind
The ways to compass what his wish design'd,
He cast his eyes upon the gloomy grove,
And then with vows implor'd the Queen of Love:
"O may thy pow'r, propitious still to me,
Conduct my steps to find the fatal tree,
In this deep forest; since the Sibyl's breath
Foretold, alas! too true, Misenus' death."
Scarce had he said, when, full before his sight,
Two doves, descending from their airy flight,
Secure upon the grassy plain alight.
He knew his mother's birds; and thus he pray'd:
"Be you my guides, with your auspicious aid,
And lead my footsteps, till the branch be found,
Whose glitt'ring shadow gilds the sacred ground.
And thou, great parent, with celestial care,
In this distress be present to my pray'r!"
Thus having said, he stopp'd with watchful sight,
Observing still the motions of their flight,
What course they took, what happy signs they shew.
They fed, and, flutt'ring, by degrees withdrew
Still farther from the place, but still in view:
Hopping and flying, thus they led him on
To the slow lake, whose baleful stench to shun
They wing'd their flight aloft; then, stooping low,
Perch'd on the double tree that bears the golden bough.
Thro' the green leafs the glitt'ring shadows glow;
As, on the sacred oak, the wintry mistletoe,
Where the proud mother views her precious brood,
And happier branches, which she never sow'd.
Such was the glitt'ring; such the ruddy rind,

And dancing leaves, that wanton'd in the wind.
He seiz'd the shining bough with griping hold,
And rent away, with ease, the ling'ring gold;
Then to the Sibyl's palace bore the prize.
Meantime the Trojan troops, with weeping eyes,
To dead Misenus pay his obsequies.
First, from the ground a lofty pile they rear,
Of pitch trees, oaks, and pines, and unctuous fir:
The fabric's front with cypress twigs they strew,
And stick the sides with boughs of baleful yew.
The topmost part his glitt'ring arms adorn;
Warm waters, then, in brazen cauldrons borne,
Are pour'd to wash his body, joint by joint,
And fragrant oils the stiffen'd limbs anoint.
With groans and cries Misenus they deplore:
Then on a bier, with purple cover'd o'er,
The breathless body, thus bewail'd, they lay,
And fire the pile, their faces turn'd away—
Such reverend rites their fathers us'd to pay.
Pure oil and incense on the fire they throw,
And fat of victims, which his friends bestow.
These gifts the greedy flames to dust devour;
Then on the living coals red wine they pour;
And, last, the relics by themselves dispose,
Which in a brazen urn the priests enclose.
Old Corynæus compass'd thrice the crew,
And dipp'd an olive branch in holy dew;
Which thrice he sprinkled round, and thrice aloud
Invok'd the dead, and then dismissed the crowd.
But good Æneas order'd on the shore
A stately tomb, whose top a trumpet bore,
A soldier's fauchion, and a seaman's oar.
Thus was his friend interr'd; and deathless fame
Still to the lofty cape consigns his name.
These rites perform'd, the prince, without delay,
Hastes to the nether world his destin'd way.

Deep was the cave; and, downward as it went
From the wide mouth, a rocky rough descent;
And here th' access a gloomy grove defends,
And there th' unnavigable lake extends,
O'er whose unhappy waters, void of light,
No bird presumes to steer his airy flight;
Such deadly stenches from the depths arise,
And steaming sulphur, that infects the skies.
From hence the Grecian bards their legends make,
And give the name Avernus to the lake.
Four sable bullocks, in the yoke untaught,
For sacrifice the pious hero brought.
The priestess pours the wine betwixt their horns;
Then cuts the curling hair; that first oblation burns,
Invoking Hecate hither to repair:
A pow'rful name in hell and upper air.
The sacred priests with ready knives bereave
The beasts of life, and in full bowls receive
The streaming blood: a lamb to Hell and Night
(The sable wool without a streak of white)
Æneas offers; and, by fate's decree,
A barren heifer, Proserpine, to thee,
With holocausts he Pluto's altar fills;
Sev'n brawny bulls with his own hand he kills;
Then on the broiling entrails oil he pours;
Which, anointed thus, the raging flame devours.
Late the nocturnal sacrifice begun,
Nor ended till the next returning sun.
Then earth began to bellow, trees to dance,
And howling dogs in glimm'ring light advance,
Ere Hecate came. "Far hence be souls profane!"
The Sibyl cried, "and from the grove abstain!
Now, Trojan, take the way thy fates afford;
Assume thy courage, and unsheathe thy sword."
She said, and pass'd along the gloomy space;
The prince pursued her steps with equal pace.

Ye realms, yet unreveal'd to human sight,
Ye gods who rule the regions of the night,
Ye gliding ghosts, permit me to relate
The mystic wonders of your silent state!

Obscure they went thro' dreary shades, that led
Along the waste dominions of the dead.
Thus wander travelers in woods by night,
By the moon's doubtful and malignant light,
When Jove in dusky clouds involves the skies,
And the faint crescent shoots
    by fits before their eyes.

Just in the gate and in the jaws of hell,
Revengeful Cares and sullen Sorrows dwell,
And pale Diseases, and repining Age,
Want, Fear, and Famine's unresisted rage;
Here Toils, and Death,
    and Death's half-brother, Sleep,
Forms terrible to view, their sentry keep;
With anxious Pleasures of a guilty mind,
Deep Frauds before, and open Force behind;
The Furies' iron beds; and Strife, that shakes
Her hissing tresses and unfolds her snakes.
Full in the midst of this infernal road,
An elm displays her dusky arms abroad:
The God of Sleep there hides his heavy head,
And empty dreams on ev'ry leaf are spread.
Of various forms unnumber'd specters more,
Centaurs, and double shapes, besiege the door.
Before the passage, horrid Hydra stands,
And Briareus with all his hundred hands;
Gorgons, Geryon with his triple frame;
And vain Chimæra vomits empty flame.
The chief unsheath'd his shining steel, prepar'd,
Tho' seiz'd with sudden fear, to force the guard,
Off'ring his brandish'd weapon at their face;

Had not the Sibyl stopp'd his eager pace,
And told him what those empty phantoms were:
Forms without bodies, and impassive air.
Hence to deep Acheron they take their way,
Whose troubled eddies, thick with ooze and clay,
Are whirl'd aloft, and in Cocytus lost.
There Charon stands, who rules the dreary coast—
A sordid god: down from his hoary chin
A length of beard descends, uncomb'd, unclean;
His eyes, like hollow furnaces on fire;
A girdle, foul with grease, binds his obscene attire.
He spreads his canvas; with his pole he steers;
The freights of flitting ghosts in his thin bottom bears.
He look'd in years; yet in his years were seen
A youthful vigor and autumnal green.
An airy crowd came rushing where he stood,
Which fill'd the margin of the fatal flood:
Husbands and wives, boys and unmarried maids,
And mighty heroes' more majestic shades,
And youths, entomb'd before their fathers' eyes,
With hollow groans, and shrieks, and feeble cries.
Thick as the leaves in autumn strow the woods,
Or fowls, by winter forc'd, forsake the floods,
And wing their hasty flight to happier lands;
Such, and so thick, the shiv'ring army stands,
And press for passage with extended hands.
Now these, now those, the surly boatman bore:
The rest he drove to distance from the shore.
The hero, who beheld with wond'ring eyes
The tumult mix'd with shrieks, laments, and cries,
Ask'd of his guide, what the rude concourse meant;
Why to the shore the thronging people bent;

What forms of law among the ghosts were us'd;
Why some were ferried o'er, and some refus'd.

"Son of Anchises, offspring of the gods,"
The Sibyl said, "you see the Stygian floods,
The sacred stream which heav'n's imperial state
Attests in oaths, and fears to violate.
The ghosts rejected are th' unhappy crew
Depriv'd of sepulchers and fun'ral due:
The boatman, Charon; those, the buried host,
He ferries over to the farther coast;
Nor dares his transport vessel cross the waves
With such whose bones are not compos'd
 in graves.
A hundred years they wander on the shore;
At length, their penance done, are wafted o'er."
The Trojan chief his forward pace repress'd,
Revolving anxious thoughts within his breast,
He saw his friends, who,
 whelm'd beneath the waves,
Their fun'ral honors claim'd,
 and ask'd their quiet graves.
The lost Leucaspis in the crowd he knew,
And the brave leader of the Lycian crew,
Whom, on the Tyrrhene seas, the tempests met;
The sailors master'd, and the ship o'erset.

Amidst the spirits, Palinurus press'd,
Yet fresh from life, a new-admitted guest,
Who, while he steering view'd the stars, and bore
His course from Afric to the Latian shore,
Fell headlong down. The Trojan fix'd his view,
And scarcely thro' the gloom the sullen shadow knew.
Then thus the prince: "What envious pow'r, O friend,
Brought your lov'd life to this disastrous end?
For Phœbus, ever true in all he said,
Has in your fate alone my faith betray'd.

The god foretold you should not die, before
You reach'd, secure from seas, th' Italian shore.
Is this th' unerring pow'r?" The ghost replied;
"Nor Phœbus flatter'd, nor his answers lied;
Nor envious gods have sent me to the deep:
But, while the stars and course of heav'n I keep,
My wearied eyes were seiz'd with fatal sleep.
I fell; and, with my weight, the helm constrain'd
Was drawn along, which yet my gripe retain'd.
Now by the winds and raging waves I swear,
Your safety, more than mine, was then my care;
Lest, of the guide bereft, the rudder lost,
Your ship should run against the rocky coast.
Three blust'ring nights, borne by the southern blast,
I floated, and discover'd land at last:
High on a mounting wave my head I bore,
Forcing my strength, and gath'ring to the shore.
Panting, but past the danger, now I seiz'd
The craggy cliffs, and my tir'd members eas'd.
While, cumber'd with my dropping clothes, I lay,
The cruel nation, covetous of prey,
Stain'd with my blood th' unhospitable coast;
And now, by winds and waves,
my lifeless limbs are toss'd:
Which O avert, by yon ethereal light,
Which I have lost for this eternal night!
Or, if by dearer ties you may be won,
By your dead sire, and by your living son,
Redeem from this reproach my wand'ring ghost;
Or with your navy seek the Velin coast,
And in a peaceful grave my corpse compose;
Or, if a nearer way your mother shows,
Without whose aid you durst not undertake
This frightful passage o'er the Stygian lake,
Lend to this wretch your hand, and waft him o'er
To the sweet banks of yon forbidden shore."
Scarce had he said, the prophetess began:

"What hopes delude thee, miserable man?
Think'st thou, thus unintomb'd, to cross
the floods,
To view the Furies and infernal gods,
And visit, without leave, the dark abodes?
Attend the term of long revolving years;
Fate, and the dooming gods, are deaf to tears.
This comfort of thy dire misfortune take:
The wrath of Heav'n, inflicted for thy sake,
With vengeance shall pursue th' inhuman coast,
Till they propitiate thy offended ghost,
And raise a tomb, with vows and solemn pray'r;
And Palinurus' name the place shall bear."
This calm'd his cares; sooth'd with his
future fame,
And pleas'd to hear his propagated name.

Now nearer to the Stygian lake they draw:
Whom, from the shore, the surly boatman saw;
Observ'd their passage thro' the shady wood,
And mark'd their near approaches to the flood.
Then thus he call'd aloud, inflam'd with wrath:
"Mortal, whate'er, who this forbidden path
In arms presum'st to tread, I charge thee, stand,
And tell thy name, and bus'ness in the land.
Know this, the realm of night—the Stygian shore:
My boat conveys no living bodies o'er;
Nor was I pleas'd great Theseus once to bear,
Who forc'd a passage with his pointed spear,
Nor strong Alcides—men of mighty fame,
And from th' immortal gods their lineage came.
In fetters one the barking porter tied,
And took him trembling from his sov'reign's side:
Two sought by force to seize his beauteous bride."
To whom the Sibyl thus: "Compose thy mind;
Nor frauds are here contriv'd, nor force design'd.
Still may the dog the wand'ring troops constrain

Of airy ghosts, and vex the guilty train,
And with her grisly lord his lovely queen remain.
The Trojan chief, whose lineage is from Jove,
Much fam'd for arms, and more for filial love,
Is sent to seek his sire in your Elysian grove.
If neither piety, nor Heav'n's command,
Can gain his passage to the Stygian strand,
This fatal present shall prevail at least."
Then shew'd the shining bough, conceal'd within her vest.
No more was needful: for the gloomy god
Stood mute with awe, to see the golden rod;
Admir'd the destin'd off'ring to his queen—
A venerable gift, so rarely seen.
His fury thus appeas'd, he puts to land;
The ghosts forsake their seats at his command:
He clears the deck, receives the mighty freight;
The leaky vessel groans beneath the weight.
Slowly she sails, and scarcely stems the tides;
The pressing water pours within her sides.
His passengers at length are wafted o'er,
Expos'd, in muddy weeds, upon the miry shore.

No sooner landed, in his den they found
The triple porter of the Stygian sound,
Grim Cerberus, who soon began to rear
His crested snakes, and arm'd his bristling hair.
The prudent Sibyl had before prepar'd
A sop, in honey steep'd, to charm the guard;
Which, mix'd with pow'rful drugs, she cast before
His greedy grinning jaws, just op'd to roar.
With three enormous mouths he gapes; and straight,
With hunger press'd, devours the pleasing bait.
Long draughts of sleep his monstrous limbs enslave;
He reels, and, falling, fills the spacious cave.
The keeper charm'd, the chief without delay

Pass'd on, and took th' irremeable way.
Before the gates, the cries of babes new born,
Whom fate had from their tender mothers torn,
Assault his ears: then those, whom form of laws
Condemn'd to die, when traitors judg'd their cause.
Nor want they lots, nor judges to review
The wrongful sentence, and award a new.
Minos, the strict inquisitor, appears;
And lives and crimes, with his assessors, hears.
Round in his urn the blended balls he rolls,
Absolves the just, and dooms the guilty souls.
The next, in place and punishment, are they
Who prodigally throw their souls away;
Fools, who, repining at their wretched state,
And loathing anxious life, suborn'd their fate.
With late repentance now they would retrieve
The bodies they forsook, and wish to live;
Their pains and poverty desire to bear,
To view the light of heav'n, and breathe the vital air:
But fate forbids; the Stygian floods oppose,
And with nine circling streams
 the captive souls enclose.

Not far from thence, the Mournful Fields appear
So call'd from lovers that inhabit there.
The souls whom that unhappy flame invades,
In secret solitude and myrtle shades
Make endless moans, and, pining with desire,
Lament too late their unextinguish'd fire.
Here Procris, Eriphyle here he found,
Baring her breast, yet bleeding with the wound
Made by her son. He saw Pasiphæ there,
With Phædra's ghost, a foul incestuous pair.
There Laodamia, with Evadne, moves,
Unhappy both, but loyal in their loves:
Cæneus, a woman once, and once a man,
But ending in the sex she first began.

Not far from these Phœnician Dido stood,
Fresh from her wound, her bosom bath'd
in blood;
Whom when the Trojan hero hardly knew,
Obscure in shades, and with a doubtful view,
(Doubtful as he who sees, thro' dusky night,
Or thinks he sees, the moon's uncertain light,)
With tears he first approach'd the sullen shade;
And, as his love inspir'd him, thus he said:
"Unhappy queen! then is the common breath
Of rumor true, in your reported death,
And I, alas! the cause? By Heav'n, I vow,
And all the pow'rs that rule the realms below,
Unwilling I forsook your friendly state,
Commanded by the gods, and forc'd by fate—
Those gods, that fate, whose unresisted might
Have sent me to these regions void of light,
Thro' the vast empire of eternal night.
Nor dar'd I to presume, that, press'd with grief,
My flight should urge you to this dire relief.
Stay, stay your steps, and listen to my vows:
'Tis the last interview that fate allows!"
In vain he thus attempts her mind to move
With tears, and pray'rs, and late-repenting love.
Disdainfully she look'd; then turning round,
But fix'd her eyes unmov'd upon the ground,
And what he says and swears, regards no more
Than the deaf rocks, when the loud billows roar;
But whirl'd away, to shun his hateful sight,
Hid in the forest and the shades of night;
Then sought Sichæus thro' the shady grove,
Who answer'd all her cares,
and equal'd all her love.

Some pious tears the pitying hero paid,
And follow'd with his eyes the flitting shade,
Then took the forward way, by fate ordain'd,

And, with his guide, the farther fields attain'd,
Where, sever'd from the rest, the warrior souls remain'd.
Tydeus he met, with Meleager's race,
The pride of armies, and the soldiers' grace;
And pale Adrastus with his ghastly face.
Of Trojan chiefs he view'd a num'rous train,
All much lamented, all in battle slain;
Glaucus and Medon, high above the rest,
Antenor's sons, and Ceres' sacred priest.
And proud Idæus, Priam's charioteer,
Who shakes his empty reins, and aims his airy spear.
The gladsome ghosts, in circling troops, attend
And with unwearied eyes behold their friend;
Delight to hover near, and long to know
What bus'ness brought him to the realms below.
But Argive chiefs, and Agamemnon's train,
When his refulgent arms flash'd thro' the shady plain,
Fled from his well-known face, with wonted fear,
As when his thund'ring sword and pointed spear
Drove headlong to their ships, and glean'd the routed rear.
They rais'd a feeble cry, with trembling notes;
But the weak voice deceiv'd their gasping throats.

Here Priam's son, Deïphobus, he found,
Whose face and limbs were one continued wound:
Dishonest, with lopp'd arms, the youth appears,
Spoil'd of his nose, and shorten'd of his ears.
He scarcely knew him, striving to disown
His blotted form, and blushing to be known;
And therefore first began: "O Teucer's race,
Who durst thy faultless figure thus deface?
What heart could wish, what hand inflict this dire disgrace?
'Twas fam'd, that in our last and fatal night

Your single prowess long sustain'd the fight,
Till tir'd, not forc'd, a glorious fate you chose,
And fell upon a heap of slaughter'd foes.
But, in remembrance of so brave a deed,
A tomb and fun'ral honors I decreed;
Thrice call'd your manes on the Trojan plains:
The place your armor and your name retains.
Your body too I sought, and, had I found,
Design'd for burial in your native ground."

The ghost replied: "Your piety has paid
All needful rites, to rest my wand'ring shade;
But cruel fate, and my more cruel wife,
To Grecian swords betray'd my sleeping life.
These are the monuments of Helen's love:
The shame I bear below, the marks I bore above.
You know in what deluding joys we pass'd
The night that was by Heav'n decreed our last:
For, when the fatal horse, descending down,
Pregnant with arms, o'erwhelm'd th' unhappy town
She feign'd nocturnal orgies; left my bed,
And, mix'd with Trojan dames, the dances led
Then, waving high her torch, the signal made,
Which rous'd the Grecians from their ambuscade.
With watching overworn, with cares oppress'd,
Unhappy I had laid me down to rest,
And heavy sleep my weary limbs possess'd.
Meantime my worthy wife our arms mislaid,
And from beneath my head my sword convey'd;
The door unlatch'd, and, with repeated calls,
Invites her former lord within my walls.
Thus in her crime her confidence she plac'd,
And with new treasons would redeem the past.
What need I more? Into the room they ran,
And meanly murther'd a defenseless man.
Ulysses, basely born, first led the way.
Avenging pow'rs! with justice if I pray,

That fortune be their own another day!
But answer you; and in your turn relate,
What brought you, living, to the Stygian state:
Driv'n by the winds and errors of the sea,
Or did you Heav'n's superior doom obey?
Or tell what other chance conducts your way,
To view with mortal eyes our dark retreats,
Tumults and torments of th' infernal seats."

While thus in talk the flying hours they pass,
The sun had finish'd more than half his race:
And they, perhaps, in words and tears had spent
The little time of stay which Heav'n had lent;
But thus the Sibyl chides their long delay:
"Night rushes down, and headlong drives the day:
'Tis here, in different paths, the way divides;
The right to Pluto's golden palace guides;
The left to that unhappy region tends,
Which to the depth of Tartarus descends;
The seat of night profound, and punish'd fiends."
Then thus Deïphobus: "O sacred maid,
Forbear to chide, and be your will obey'd!
Lo! to the secret shadows I retire,
To pay my penance till my years expire.
Proceed, auspicious prince, with glory crown'd,
And born to better fates than I have found."
He said; and, while he said, his steps he turn'd
To secret shadows, and in silence mourn'd.

The hero, looking on the left, espied
A lofty tow'r, and strong on ev'ry side
With treble walls, which Phlegethon surrounds,
Whose fiery flood the burning empire bounds;
And, press'd betwixt the rocks
    the bellowing noise resounds
Wide is the fronting gate, and, rais'd on high

With adamantine columns, threats the sky.
Vain is the force of man, and Heav'n's as vain,
To crush the pillars which the pile sustain.
Sublime on these a tow'r of steel is rear'd;
And dire Tisiphone there keeps the ward,
Girt in her sanguine gown, by night and day,
Observant of the souls that pass the
downward way.
From hence are heard the groans of ghosts,
the pains
Of sounding lashes and of dragging chains.
The Trojan stood astonish'd at their cries,
And ask'd his guide from whence those yells arise;
And what the crimes, and what the tortures were,
And loud laments that rent the liquid air.

She thus replied: "The chaste and holy race
Are all forbidden this polluted place.
But Hecate, when she gave to rule the woods,
Then led me trembling thro' these dire abodes,
And taught the tortures of th' avenging gods.
These are the realms of unrelenting fate;
And awful Rhadamanthus rules the state.
He hears and judges each committed crime;
Inquires into the manner, place, and time.
The conscious wretch must all his acts reveal,
(Loth to confess, unable to conceal),
From the first moment of his vital breath,
To his last hour of unrepenting death.
Straight, o'er the guilty ghost, the Fury shakes
The sounding whip and brandishes her snakes,
And the pale sinner, with her sisters, takes.
Then, of itself, unfolds th' eternal door;
With dreadful sounds the brazen hinges roar.
You see, before the gate, what stalking ghost
Commands the guard, what sentries keep the post.
More formidable Hydra stands within,

Whose jaws with iron teeth severely grin.
The gaping gulf low to the center lies,
And twice as deep as earth is distant from
the skies.
The rivals of the gods, the Titan race,
Here, sing'd with lightning,
roll within th' unfathom'd space.
Here lie th' Alæan twins, (I saw them both,)
Enormous bodies, of gigantic growth,
Who dar'd in fight the Thund'rer to defy,
Affect his heav'n, and force him from the sky.
Salmoneus, suff'ring cruel pains, I found,
For emulating Jove; the rattling sound
Of mimic thunder, and the glitt'ring blaze
Of pointed lightnings, and their forky rays.
Thro' Elis and the Grecian towns he flew;
Th' audacious wretch four fiery coursers drew:
He wav'd a torch aloft, and, madly vain,
Sought godlike worship from a servile train.
Ambitious fool! with horny hoofs to pass
O'er hollow arches of resounding brass,
To rival thunder in its rapid course,
And imitate inimitable force!
But he, the King of Heav'n, obscure on high,
Bar'd his red arm, and, launching from the sky
His writhen bolt, not shaking empty smoke,
Down to the deep abyss the flaming felon strook.
There Tityus was to see, who took his birth
From heav'n, his nursing from the foodful earth.
Here his gigantic limbs, with large embrace,
Enfold nine acres of infernal space.
A rav'nous vulture, in his open'd side,
Her crooked beak and cruel talons tried;
Still for the growing liver digg'd his breast;
The growing liver still supplied the feast;
Still are his entrails fruitful to their pains:

Th' immortal hunger lasts, th' immortal food remains.
Ixion and Perithous I could name,
And more Thessalian chiefs of mighty fame.
High o'er their heads a mold'ring rock is plac'd,
That promises a fall, and shakes at ev'ry blast.
They lie below, on golden beds display'd;
And genial feasts with regal pomp are made.
The Queen of Furies by their sides is set,
And snatches from their mouths th' untasted meat,
Which if they touch, her hissing snakes she rears,
Tossing her torch, and thund'ring in their ears.
Then they, who brothers' better claim disown,
Expel their parents, and usurp the throne;
Defraud their clients, and, to lucre sold,
Sit brooding on unprofitable gold;
Who dare not give, and ev'n refuse to lend
To their poor kindred, or a wanting friend.
Vast is the throng of these; nor less the train
Of lustful youths, for foul adult'ry slain:
Hosts of deserters, who their honor sold,
And basely broke their faith for bribes of gold.
All these within the dungeon's depth remain,
Despairing pardon, and expecting pain.
Ask not what pains; nor farther seek to know
Their process, or the forms of law below.
Some roll a weighty stone; some, laid along,
And bound with burning wires, on spokes of wheels are hung
Unhappy Theseus, doom'd for ever there,
Is fix'd by fate on his eternal chair;
And wretched Phlegyas warns the world with cries
(Could warning make the world more just or wise):

'Learn righteousness, and dread th' avenging deities.'
To tyrants others have their country sold,
Imposing foreign lords, for foreign gold;
Some have old laws repeal'd, new statutes made,
Not as the people pleas'd, but as they paid;
With incest some their daughters' bed profan'd:
All dar'd the worst of ills, and,
what they dar'd, attain'd.
Had I a hundred mouths, a hundred tongues,
And throats of brass, inspir'd with iron lungs,
I could not half those horrid crimes repeat,
Nor half the punishments those crimes have met.
But let us haste our voyage to pursue:
The walls of Pluto's palace are in view;
The gate, and iron arch above it, stands
On anvils labor'd by the Cyclops' hands.
Before our farther way the Fates allow,
Here must we fix on high the golden bough."

She said: and thro' the gloomy shades they pass'd,
And chose the middle path. Arriv'd at last,
The prince with living water sprinkled o'er
His limbs and body; then approach'd the door,
Possess'd the porch, and on the front above
He fix'd the fatal bough requir'd by Pluto's love.
These holy rites perform'd, they took their way
Where long extended plains of pleasure lay:
The verdant fields with those of heav'n may vie,
With ether vested, and a purple sky;
The blissful seats of happy souls below.
Stars of their own, and their own suns, they know;
Their airy limbs in sports they exercise,
And on the green contend the wrestler's prize.
Some in heroic verse divinely sing;
Others in artful measures led the ring.
The Thracian bard, surrounded by the rest,
There stands conspicuous in his flowing vest;

His flying fingers, and harmonious quill,
Strikes sev'n distinguish'd notes,
and sev'n at once they fill.
Here found they Teucer's old heroic race,
Born better times and happier years to grace.
Assaracus and Ilus here enjoy
Perpetual fame, with him who founded Troy.
The chief beheld their chariots from afar,
Their shining arms, and coursers train'd to war:
Their lances fix'd in earth, their steeds around,
Free from their harness, graze the flow'ry ground.
The love of horses which they had, alive,
And care of chariots, after death survive.
Some cheerful souls were feasting on the plain;
Some did the song, and some the choir maintain,
Beneath a laurel shade, where mighty Po
Mounts up to woods above, and hides
his head below.
Here patriots live, who, for their country's good,
In fighting fields, were prodigal of blood:
Priests of unblemish'd lives here make abode,
And poets worthy their inspiring god;
And searching wits, of more mechanic parts,
Who grac'd their age with new-invented arts:
Those who to worth their bounty did extend,
And those who knew that bounty to commend.
The heads of these with holy fillets bound,
And all their temples were with garlands crown'd.

To these the Sibyl thus her speech address'd,
And first to him surrounded by the rest
(Tow'ring his height, and ample was his breast):
"Say, happy souls, divine Musæus, say,
Where lives Anchises, and where lies our way
To find the hero, for whose only sake
We sought the dark abodes,
and cross'd the bitter lake?"

To this the sacred poet thus replied:
"In no fix'd place the happy souls reside.
In groves we live, and lie on mossy beds,
By crystal streams, that murmur thro' the meads:
But pass yon easy hill, and thence descend;
The path conducts you to your journey's end."
This said, he led them up the mountain's brow,
And shews them all the shining fields below.
They wind the hill,
 and thro' the blissful meadows go.

But old Anchises, in a flow'ry vale,
Review'd his muster'd race, and took the tale:
Those happy spirits, which, ordain'd by fate,
For future beings and new bodies wait—
With studious thought observ'd th'
 illustrious throng,
In nature's order as they pass'd along:
Their names, their fates, their conduct,
 and their care,
In peaceful senates and successful war.
He, when Æneas on the plain appears,
Meets him with open arms, and falling tears.
"Welcome," he said, "the gods' undoubted race!
O long expected to my dear embrace!
Once more 'tis giv'n me to behold your face!
The love and pious duty which you pay
Have pass'd the perils of so hard a way.
'Tis true, computing times, I now believ'd
The happy day approach'd; nor are
 my hopes deceiv'd.
What length of lands, what oceans
 have you pass'd;
What storms sustain'd, and on what shores
 been cast?
How have I fear'd your fate! but fear'd it most,
When love assail'd you, on the Libyan coast."

To this, the filial duty thus replies:
"Your sacred ghost before my sleeping eyes
Appear'd, and often urg'd this painful enterprise.
After long tossing on the Tyrrhene sea,
My navy rides at anchor in the bay.
But reach your hand, O parent shade, nor shun
The dear embraces of your longing son!"
He said; and falling tears his face bedew:
Then thrice around his neck his arms he threw;
And thrice the flitting shadow slipp'd away,
Like winds, or empty dreams that fly the day.

Now, in a secret vale, the Trojan sees
A sep'rate grove, thro' which a gentle breeze
Plays with a passing breath, and whispers thro' the trees;
And, just before the confines of the wood,
The gliding Lethe leads her silent flood.
About the boughs an airy nation flew,
Thick as the humming bees, that hunt the golden dew;
In summer's heat on tops of lilies feed,
And creep within their bells, to suck the balmy seed:
The winged army roams the fields around;
The rivers and the rocks remurmur to the sound.
Æneas wond'ring stood, then ask'd the cause
Which to the stream the crowding people draws.
Then thus the sire: "The souls that throng the flood
Are those to whom, by fate, are other bodies ow'd:
In Lethe's lake they long oblivion taste,
Of future life secure, forgetful of the past.
Long has my soul desir'd this time and place,
To set before your sight your glorious race,
That this presaging joy may fire your mind
To seek the shores by destiny design'd."
"O father, can it be, that souls sublime

Return to visit our terrestrial clime,
And that the gen'rous mind, releas'd by death,
Can covet lazy limbs and mortal breath?"

Anchises then, in order, thus begun
To clear those wonders to his godlike son:
"Know, first, that heav'n,
    and earth's compacted frame,
And flowing waters, and the starry flame,
And both the radiant lights, one common soul
Inspires and feeds, and animates the whole.
This active mind, infus'd thro' all the space,
Unites and mingles with the mighty mass.
Hence men and beasts the breath of life obtain,
And birds of air, and monsters of the main.
Th' ethereal vigor is in all the same,
And every soul is fill'd with equal flame;
As much as earthy limbs, and gross allay
Of mortal members, subject to decay,
Blunt not the beams of heav'n and edge of day.
From this coarse mixture of terrestrial parts,
Desire and fear by turns possess their hearts,
And grief, and joy; nor can the groveling mind,
In the dark dungeon of the limbs confin'd,
Assert the native skies, or own its heav'nly kind:
Nor death itself can wholly wash their stains;
But long-contracted filth ev'n in the soul remains.
The relics of inveterate vice they wear,
And spots of sin obscene in ev'ry face appear.
For this are various penances enjoin'd;
And some are hung to bleach upon the wind,
Some plung'd in waters, others purg'd in fires,
Till all the dregs are drain'd, and all the rust expires.
All have their manes, and those manes bear:
The few, so cleans'd, to these abodes repair,
And breathe, in ample fields, the soft Elysian air.
Then are they happy, when by length of time

The scurf is worn away of each committed crime;
No speck is left of their habitual stains,
But the pure ether of the soul remains.
But, when a thousand rolling years are past,
(So long their punishments and penance last,)
Whole droves of minds are, by the driving god,
Compell'd to drink the deep Lethæan flood,
In large forgetful draughts to steep the cares
Of their past labors, and their irksome years,
That, unrememb'ring of its former pain,
The soul may suffer mortal flesh again."

Thus having said, the father spirit leads
The priestess and his son thro' swarms of shades,
And takes a rising ground, from thence to see
The long procession of his progeny.
"Survey," pursued the sire, "this airy throng,
As, offer'd to thy view, they pass along.
These are th' Italian names, which fate will join
With ours, and graff upon the Trojan line.
Observe the youth who first appears in sight,
And holds the nearest station to the light,
Already seems to snuff the vital air,
And leans just forward, on a shining spear:
Silvius is he, thy last-begotten race,
But first in order sent, to fill thy place;
An Alban name, but mix'd with Dardan blood,
Born in the covert of a shady wood:
Him fair Lavinia, thy surviving wife,
Shall breed in groves, to lead a solitary life.
In Alba he shall fix his royal seat,
And, born a king, a race of kings beget.
Then Procas, honor of the Trojan name,
Capys, and Numitor, of endless fame.
A second Silvius after these appears;
Silvius Æneas, for thy name he bears;
For arms and justice equally renown'd,

Who, late restor'd, in Alba shall be crown'd.
How great they look! how vig'rously they wield
Their weighty lances, and sustain the shield!
But they, who crown'd with oaken wreaths appear,
Shall Gabian walls and strong Fidena rear;
Nomentum, Bola, with Pometia, found;
And raise Collatian tow'rs on rocky ground.
All these shall then be towns of mighty fame,
Tho' now they lie obscure, and lands without
a name.
See Romulus the great, born to restore
The crown that once his injur'd grandsire wore.
This prince a priestess of your blood shall bear,
And like his sire in arms he shall appear.
Two rising crests, his royal head adorn;
Born from a god, himself to godhead born:
His sire already signs him for the skies,
And marks the seat amidst the deities.
Auspicious chief! thy race, in times to come,
Shall spread the conquests of imperial Rome—
Rome, whose ascending tow'rs shall
heav'n invade,
Involving earth and ocean in her shade;
High as the Mother of the Gods in place,
And proud, like her, of an immortal race.
Then, when in pomp she makes the
Phrygian round,
With golden turrets on her temples crown'd;
A hundred gods her sweeping train supply;
Her offspring all, and all command the sky.

"Now fix your sight, and stand intent, to see
Your Roman race, and Julian progeny.
The mighty Cæsar waits his vital hour,
Impatient for the world,
and grasps his promis'd pow'r.
But next behold the youth of form divine,

Cæsar himself, exalted in his line;
Augustus, promis'd oft, and long foretold,
Sent to the realm that Saturn rul'd of old;
Born to restore a better age of gold.
Afric and India shall his pow'r obey;
He shall extend his propagated sway
Beyond the solar year, without the starry way,
Where Atlas turns the rolling heav'ns around,
And his broad shoulders
with their lights are crown'd.
At his foreseen approach, already quake
The Caspian kingdoms and Mæotian lake:
Their seers behold the tempest from afar,
And threat'ning oracles denounce the war.
Nile hears him knocking at his sev'nfold gates,
And seeks his hidden spring,
and fears his nephew's fates.
Nor Hercules more lands or labors knew,
Not tho' the brazen-footed hind he slew,
Freed Erymanthus from the foaming boar,
And dipp'd his arrows in Lernæan gore;
Nor Bacchus, turning from his Indian war,
By tigers drawn triumphant in his car,
From Nisus' top descending on the plains,
With curling vines around his purple reins.
And doubt we yet thro' dangers to pursue
The paths of honor, and a crown in view?
But what's the man, who from afar appears?
His head with olive crown'd, his hand a
censer bears,
His hoary beard and holy vestments bring
His lost idea back: I know the Roman king.
He shall to peaceful Rome new laws ordain,
Call'd from his mean abode a scepter to sustain.
Him Tullus next in dignity succeeds,
An active prince, and prone to martial deeds.
He shall his troops for fighting fields prepare,

Disus'd to toils, and triumphs of the war.
By dint of sword his crown he shall increase,
And scour his armor from the rust of peace.
Whom Ancus follows, with a fawning air,
But vain within, and proudly popular.
Next view the Tarquin kings, th' avenging sword
Of Brutus, justly drawn, and Rome restor'd.
He first renews the rods and ax severe,
And gives the consuls royal robes to wear.
His sons, who seek the tyrant to sustain,
And long for arbitrary lords again,
With ignominy scourg'd, in open sight,
He dooms to death deserv'd, asserting public right.
Unhappy man, to break the pious laws
Of nature, pleading in his children's cause!
Howe'er the doubtful fact is understood,
'Tis love of honor, and his country's good:
The consul, not the father, sheds the blood.
Behold Torquatus the same track pursue;
And, next, the two devoted Decii view:
The Drusian line, Camillus loaded home
With standards well redeem'd,
and foreign foes o'ercome
The pair you see in equal armor shine,
Now, friends below, in close embraces join;
But, when they leave the shady realms of night,
And, cloth'd in bodies, breathe your upper light,
With mortal hate each other shall pursue:
What wars, what wounds,
what slaughter shall ensue!
From Alpine heights the father first descends;
His daughter's husband in the plain attends:
His daughter's husband arms his eastern friends.
Embrace again, my sons, be foes no more;
Nor stain your country with her children's gore!
And thou, the first, lay down thy lawless claim,

Thou, of my blood, who bearest the Julian name!
Another comes, who shall in triumph ride,
And to the Capitol his chariot guide,
From conquer'd Corinth, rich with Grecian spoils.
And yet another, fam'd for warlike toils,
On Argos shall impose the Roman laws,
And on the Greeks revenge the Trojan cause;
Shall drag in chains their Achillean race;
Shall vindicate his ancestors' disgrace,
And Pallas, for her violated place.
Great Cato there, for gravity renown'd,
And conqu'ring Cossus goes with laurels crown'd.
Who can omit the Gracchi? who declare
The Scipios' worth, those thunderbolts of war,
The double bane of Carthage? Who can see
Without esteem for virtuous poverty,
Severe Fabricius, or can cease t' admire
The plowman consul in his coarse attire?
Tir'd as I am, my praise the Fabii claim;
And thou, great hero, greatest of thy name,
Ordain'd in war to save the sinking state,
And, by delays, to put a stop to fate!
Let others better mold the running mass
Of metals, and inform the breathing brass,
And soften into flesh a marble face;
Plead better at the bar; describe the skies,
And when the stars descend, and when they rise.
But, Rome, 'tis thine alone, with awful sway,
To rule mankind, and make the world obey,
Disposing peace and war by thy own majestic way;
To tame the proud, the fetter'd slave to free:
These are imperial arts, and worthy thee."

He paus'd; and, while with wond'ring eyes
they view'd
The passing spirits, thus his speech renew'd:
"See great Marcellus! how, untir'd in toils,

He moves with manly grace,
 how rich with regal spoils!
He, when his country, threaten'd with alarms,
Requires his courage and his conqu'ring arms,
Shall more than once the Punic bands affright;
Shall kill the Gaulish king in single fight;
Then to the Capitol in triumph move,
And the third spoils shall grace Feretrian Jove."
Æneas here beheld, of form divine,
A godlike youth in glitt'ring armor shine,
With great Marcellus keeping equal pace;
But gloomy were his eyes, dejected was his face.
He saw, and, wond'ring, ask'd his airy guide,
What and of whence was he,
 who press'd the hero's side:
"His son, or one of his illustrious name?
How like the former, and almost the same!
Observe the crowds that compass him around;
All gaze, and all admire, and raise a shouting sound:
But hov'ring mists around his brows are spread,
And night, with sable shades, involves his head."
"Seek not to know," the ghost replied with tears,
"The sorrows of thy sons in future years.
This youth (the blissful vision of a day)
Shall just be shown on earth, and snatch'd away.
The gods too high had rais'd the Roman state,
Were but their gifts as permanent as great.
What groans of men shall fill the Martian field!
How fierce a blaze his flaming pile shall yield!
What fun'ral pomp shall floating Tiber see,
When, rising from his bed,
 he views the sad solemnity!
No youth shall equal hopes of glory give,
No youth afford so great a cause to grieve;
The Trojan honor, and the Roman boast,
Admir'd when living, and ador'd when lost!
Mirror of ancient faith in early youth!

Undaunted worth, inviolable truth!
No foe, unpunish'd, in the fighting field
Shall dare thee, foot to foot, with sword and shield;
Much less in arms oppose thy matchless force,
When thy sharp spurs shall urge thy foaming horse.
Ah! couldst thou break thro' fate's severe decree,
A new Marcellus shall arise in thee!
Full canisters of fragrant lilies bring,
Mix'd with the purple roses of the spring;
Let me with fun'ral flow'rs his body strow;
This gift which parents to their children owe,
This unavailing gift, at least, I may bestow!"
Thus having said, he led the hero round
The confines of the blest Elysian ground;
Which when Anchises to his son had shown,
And fir'd his mind to mount the promis'd throne,
He tells the future wars, ordain'd by fate;
The strength and customs of the Latian state;
The prince, and people; and forearms his care
With rules, to push his fortune, or to bear.

Two gates the silent house of Sleep adorn;
Of polish'd ivory this, that of transparent horn:
True visions thro' transparent horn arise;
Thro' polish'd ivory pass deluding lies.
Of various things discoursing as he pass'd,
Anchises hither bends his steps at last.
Then, thro' the gate of iv'ry, he dismiss'd
His valiant offspring and divining guest.
Straight to the ships Æneas his way,
Embark'd his men, and skimm'd along the sea,
Still coasting, till he gain'd Cajeta's bay.
At length on oozy ground his galleys moor;
Their heads are turn'd to sea, their sterns to shore.

Book VII

King Latinus entertains Æneas, and promises him his only daughter, Lavinia, the heiress of his crown. Turnus, being in love with her, favored by her mother, and stirred up by Juno and Allecto, breaks the treaty which was made, and engages in his quarrel Mezentius, Camilla, Messapus, and many others of the neighboring princes, whose forces, and the names of their commanders, are here related in a catalogue.

And thou, O matron of immortal fame,
Here dying, to the shore hast left thy name;
Cajeta still the place is call'd from thee,
The nurse of great Æneas' infancy.
Here rest thy bones in rich Hesperia's plains;
Thy name ('t is all a ghost can have) remains.

Now, when the prince her fun'ral rites had paid,
He plow'd the Tyrrhene seas with sails display'd.
From land a gentle breeze arose by night,
Serenely shone the stars, the moon was bright,
And the sea trembled with her silver light.
Now near the shelves of Circe's shores they run,
(Circe the rich, the daughter of the Sun,)
A dang'rous coast: the goddess wastes her days
In joyous songs; the rocks resound her lays:
In spinning, or the loom, she spends the night,
And cedar brands supply her father's light.
From hence were heard, rebellowing to the main,
The roars of lions that refuse the chain,
The grunts of bristled boars, and groans of bears,
And herds of howling wolves that stun
the sailors' ears.

These from their caverns, at the close of night,
Fill the sad isle with horror and affright.
Darkling they mourn their fate, whom Circe's pow'r,
(That watch'd the moon and planetary hour,)
With words and wicked herbs from humankind
Had alter'd, and in brutal shapes confin'd.
Which monsters lest the Trojans' pious host
Should bear, or touch upon th' enchanted coast,
Propitious Neptune steer'd their course by night
With rising gales that sped their happy flight.
Supplied with these, they skim the sounding shore,
And hear the swelling surges vainly roar.
Now, when the rosy morn began to rise,
And wav'd her saffron streamer thro' the skies;
When Thetis blush'd in purple not her own,
And from her face the breathing winds were blown,
A sudden silence sate upon the sea,
And sweeping oars, with struggling, urge their way.

The Trojan, from the main, beheld a wood,
Which thick with shades and a brown horror stood:
Betwixt the trees the Tiber took his course,
With whirlpools dimpled; and with downward force,
That drove the sand along, he took his way,
And roll'd his yellow billows to the sea.
About him, and above, and round the wood,
The birds that haunt the borders of his flood,
That bath'd within, or basked upon his side,
To tuneful songs their narrow throats applied.
The captain gives command; the joyful train
Glide thro' the gloomy shade, and leave the main.

Now, Erato, thy poet's mind inspire,
And fill his soul with thy celestial fire!
Relate what Latium was; her ancient kings;
Declare the past and state of things,
When first the Trojan fleet Ausonia sought,

And how the rivals lov'd, and how they fought.
These are my theme, and how the war began,
And how concluded by the godlike man:
For I shall sing of battles, blood, and rage,
Which princes and their people did engage;
And haughty souls, that, mov'd with mutual hate,
In fighting fields pursued and found their fate;
That rous'd the Tyrrhene realm with loud alarms,
And peaceful Italy involv'd in arms.
A larger scene of action is display'd;
And, rising hence, a greater work is weigh'd.

Latinus, old and mild, had long possess'd
The Latin scepter, and his people blest:
His father Faunus; a Laurentian dame
His mother; fair Marica was her name.
But Faunus came from Picus: Picus drew
His birth from Saturn, if records be true.
Thus King Latinus, in the third degree,
Had Saturn author of his family.
But this old peaceful prince, as Heav'n decreed,
Was blest with no male issue to succeed:
His sons in blooming youth were snatch'd by fate;
One only daughter heir'd the royal state.
Fir'd with her love, and with ambition led,
The neighb'ring princes court her nuptial bed.
Among the crowd, but far above the rest,
Young Turnus to the beauteous maid address'd.
Turnus, for high descent and graceful mien,
Was first, and favor'd by the Latian queen;
With him she strove to join Lavinia's hand,
But dire portents the purpos'd match withstand.

Deep in the palace, of long growth, there stood
A laurel's trunk, a venerable wood;
Where rites divine were paid; whose holy hair
Was kept and cut with superstitious care.

This plant Latinus, when his town he wall'd,
Then found, and from the tree Laurentum call'd;
And last, in honor of his new abode,
He vow'd the laurel to the laurel's god.
It happen'd once (a boding prodigy!)
A swarm of bees, that cut the liquid sky,
(Unknown from whence they took their airy flight,)
Upon the topmost branch in clouds alight;
There with their clasping feet together clung,
And a long cluster from the laurel hung.
An ancient augur prophesied from hence:
"Behold on Latian shores a foreign prince!
From the same parts of heav'n his navy stands,
To the same parts on earth; his army lands;
The town he conquers, and the tow'r commands."

Yet more, when fair Lavinia fed the fire
Before the gods, and stood beside her sire,
(Strange to relate!) the flames, involv'd in smoke
Of incense, from the sacred altar broke,
Caught her dishevel'd hair and rich attire;
Her crown and jewels crackled in the fire:
From thence the fuming trail began to spread
And lambent glories danc'd about her head.
This new portent the seer with wonder views,
Then pausing, thus his prophecy renews:
"The nymph, who scatters flaming fires around,
Shall shine with honor, shall herself be crown'd;
But, caus'd by her irrevocable fate,
War shall the country waste, and change the state."

Latinus, frighted with this dire ostent,
For counsel to his father Faunus went,
And sought the shades renown'd for prophecy
Which near Albunea's sulph'rous fountain lie.
To these the Latian and the Sabine land
Fly, when distress'd, and thence relief demand.

The priest on skins of off'rings takes his ease,
And nightly visions in his slumber sees;
A swarm of thin ærial shapes appears,
And, flutt'ring round his temples, deafs his ears:
These he consults, the future fates to know,
From pow'rs above, and from the fiends below.
Here, for the gods' advice, Latinus flies,
Off'ring a hundred sheep for sacrifice:
Their woolly fleeces, as the rites requir'd,
He laid beneath him, and to rest retir'd.
No sooner were his eyes in slumber bound,
When, from above, a more than mortal sound
Invades his ears; and thus the vision spoke:
"Seek not, my seed, in Latian bands to yoke
Our fair Lavinia, nor the gods provoke.
A foreign son upon thy shore descends,
Whose martial fame from pole to pole extends.
His race, in arms and arts of peace renown'd,
Not Latium shall contain, nor Europe bound:
'Tis theirs whate'er the sun surveys around."
These answers, in the silent night receiv'd,
The king himself divulg'd, the land believ'd:
The fame thro' all the neighb'ring nations flew,
When now the Trojan navy was in view.

Beneath a shady tree, the hero spread
His table on the turf, with cakes of bread;
And, with his chiefs, on forest fruits he fed.
They sate; and, (not without the god's command,)
Their homely fare dispatch'd, the hungry band
Invade their trenchers next, and soon devour,
To mend the scanty meal, their cakes of flour.
Ascanius this observ'd, and smiling said:
"See, we devour the plates on which we fed."
The speech had omen, that the Trojan race
Should find repose, and this the time and place.

Æneas took the word, and thus replies,
Confessing fate with wonder in his eyes:
"All hail, O earth! all hail, my household gods!
Behold the destin'd place of your abodes!
For thus Anchises prophesied of old,
And this our fatal place of rest foretold:
'When, on a foreign shore, instead of meat,
By famine forc'd, your trenchers you shall eat,
Then ease your weary Trojans will attend,
And the long labors of your voyage end.
Remember on that happy coast to build,
And with a trench enclose the fruitful field.'
This was that famine, this the fatal place
Which ends the wand'ring of our exil'd race.
Then, on to-morrow's dawn, your care employ,
To search the land, and where the cities lie,
And what the men; but give this day to joy.
Now pour to Jove; and, after Jove is blest,
Call great Anchises to the genial feast:
Crown high the goblets with a cheerful draught;
Enjoy the present hour; adjourn the
future thought."

Thus having said, the hero bound his brows
With leafy branches, then perform'd his vows;
Adoring first the genius of the place,
Then Earth, the mother of the heav'nly race,
The nymphs, and native godheads yet unknown,
And Night, and all the stars that gild her
sable throne,
And ancient Cybel, and Iæan Jove,
And last his sire below, and mother queen above.
Then heav'n's high monarch thunder'd
thrice aloud,
And thrice he shook aloft a golden cloud.
Soon thro' the joyful camp a rumor flew,
The time was come their city to renew.

Then ev'ry brow with cheerful green is crown'd,
The feasts are doubled, and the bowls go round.

When next the rosy morn disclos'd the day,
The scouts to sev'ral parts divide their way,
To learn the natives' names, their towns explore,
The coasts and trendings of the crooked shore:
Here Tiber flows, and here Numicus stands;
Here warlike Latins hold the happy lands.
The pious chief, who sought by peaceful ways
To found his empire, and his town to raise,
A hundred youths from all his train selects,
And to the Latian court their course directs,
(The spacious palace where their prince resides,)
And all their heads with wreaths of olive hides.
They go commission'd to require a peace,
And carry presents to procure access.
Thus while they speed their pace, the prince designs
His new-elected seat, and draws the lines.
The Trojans round the place a rampire cast,
And palisades about the trenches plac'd.

Meantime the train, proceeding on their way,
From far the town and lofty tow'rs survey;
At length approach the walls. Without the gate,
They see the boys and Latian youth debate
The martial prizes on the dusty plain:
Some drive the cars, and some the coursers rein;
Some bend the stubborn bow for victory,
And some with darts their active sinews try.
A posting messenger, dispatch'd from hence,
Of this fair troop advis'd their aged prince,
That foreign men of mighty stature came;
Uncouth their habit, and unknown their name.
The king ordains their entrance, and ascends
His regal seat, surrounded by his friends.

The palace built by Picus, vast and proud,
Supported by a hundred pillars stood,
And round encompass'd with a rising wood.
The pile o'erlook'd the town, and drew the sight;
Surpris'd at once with reverence and delight.
There kings receiv'd the marks of sov'reign pow'r;
In state the monarchs march'd; the lictors bore
Their awful axes and the rods before.
Here the tribunal stood, the house of pray'r,
And here the sacred senators repair;
All at large tables, in long order set,
A ram their off'ring, and a ram their meat.
Above the portal, carv'd in cedar wood,
Plac'd in their ranks, their godlike grandsires stood;
Old Saturn, with his crooked scythe, on high;
And Italus, that led the colony;
And ancient Janus, with his double face,
And bunch of keys, the porter of the place.
There good Sabinus, planter of the vines,
On a short pruning hook his head reclines,
And studiously surveys his gen'rous wines;
Then warlike kings, who for their country fought,
And honorable wounds from battle brought.
Around the posts hung helmets, darts, and spears,
And captive chariots, axes, shields, and bars,
And broken beaks of ships, the trophies of their wars.
Above the rest, as chief of all the band,
Was Picus plac'd, a buckler in his hand;
His other wav'd a long divining wand.
Girt in his Gabin gown the hero sate,
Yet could not with his art avoid his fate:
For Circe long had lov'd the youth in vain,
Till love, refus'd, converted to disdain:
Then, mixing pow'rful herbs, with magic art,
She chang'd his form, who could not change his heart;

Constrain'd him in a bird, and made him fly,
With party-color'd plumes, a chatt'ring pie.

In this high temple, on a chair of state,
The seat of audience, old Latinus sate;
Then gave admission to the Trojan train;
And thus with pleasing accents he began:
"Tell me, ye Trojans, for that name you own,
Nor is your course upon our coasts unknown—
Say what you seek, and whither were you bound:
Were you by stress of weather cast aground?
(Such dangers as on seas are often seen,
And oft befall to miserable men,)
Or come, your shipping in our ports to lay,
Spent and disabled in so long a way
Say what you want: the Latians you shall find
Not forc'd to goodness, but by will inclin'd;
For, since the time of Saturn's holy reign,
His hospitable customs we retain.
I call to mind (but time the tale has worn)
Th' Arunci told, that Dardanus, tho' born
On Latian plains, yet sought the Phrygian shore,
And Samothracia, Samos call'd before.
From Tuscan Coritum he claim'd his birth;
But after, when exempt from mortal earth,
From thence ascended to his kindred skies,
A god, and, as a god, augments their sacrifice,"

He said. Ilioneus made this reply:
"O king, of Faunus' royal family!
Nor wintry winds to Latium forc'd our way,
Nor did the stars our wand'ring course betray.
Willing we sought your shores; and, hither bound,
The port, so long desir'd, at length we found;
From our sweet homes and ancient realms expell'd;
Great as the greatest that the sun beheld.
The god began our line, who rules above;

And, as our race, our king descends from Jove:
And hither are we come, by his command,
To crave admission in your happy land.
How dire a tempest, from Mycenæ pour'd,
Our plains, our temples, and our town devour'd;
What was the waste of war, what fierce alarms
Shook Asia's crown with European arms;
Ev'n such have heard, if any such there be,
Whose earth is bounded by the frozen sea;
And such as, born beneath the burning sky
And sultry sun, betwixt the tropics lie.
From that dire deluge, thro' the wat'ry waste,
Such length of years, such various perils past,
At last escap'd, to Latium we repair,
To beg what you without your want may spare:
The common water, and the common air;
Sheds which ourselves will build, and mean abodes,
Fit to receive and serve our banish'd gods.
Nor our admission shall your realm disgrace,
Nor length of time our gratitude efface.
Besides, what endless honor you shall gain,
To save and shelter Troy's unhappy train!
Now, by my sov'reign, and his fate, I swear,
Renown'd for faith in peace, for force in war;
Oft our alliance other lands desir'd,
And, what we seek of you, of us requir'd.
Despite not then, that in our hands we bear
These holy boughs, sue with words of pray'r.
Fate and the gods, by their supreme command,
Have doom'd our ships to seek the Latian land.
To these abodes our fleet Apollo sends;
Here Dardanus was born, and hither tends;
Where Tuscan Tiber rolls with rapid force,
And where Numicus opes his holy source.
Besides, our prince presents, with his request,
Some small remains of what his sire possess'd.
This golden charger, snatch'd from burning Troy,

Anchises did in sacrifice employ;
This royal robe and this tiara wore
Old Priam, and this golden scepter bore
In full assemblies, and in solemn games;
These purple vests were weav'd by
Dardan dames."

Thus while he spoke, Latinus roll'd around
His eyes, and fix'd a while upon the ground.
Intent he seem'd, and anxious in his breast;
Not by the scepter mov'd, or kingly vest,
But pond'ring future things of wondrous weight;
Succession, empire, and his daughter's fate.
On these he mus'd within his thoughtful mind,
And then revolv'd what Faunus had divin'd.
This was the foreign prince, by fate decreed
To share his scepter, and Lavinia's bed;
This was the race that sure portents foreshew
To sway the world, and land and sea subdue.
At length he rais'd his cheerful head, and spoke:
"The pow'rs," said he, "the pow'rs we both invoke,
To you, and yours, and mine, propitious be,
And firm our purpose with their augury!
Have what you ask; your presents I receive;
Land, where and when you please,
with ample leave;
Partake and use my kingdom as your own;
All shall be yours, while I command the crown:
And, if my wish'd alliance please your king,
Tell him he should not send the peace, but bring.
Then let him not a friend's embraces fear;
The peace is made when I behold him here.
Besides this answer, tell my royal guest,
I add to his commands my own request:
One only daughter heirs my crown and state,
Whom not our oracles, nor Heav'n, nor fate,
Nor frequent prodigies, permit to join

With any native of th' Ausonian line.
A foreign son-in-law shall come from far
(Such is our doom), a chief renown'd in war,
Whose race shall bear aloft the Latian name,
And thro' the conquer'd world diffuse our fame.
Himself to be the man the fates require,
I firmly judge, and, what I judge, desire."

He said, and then on each bestow'd a steed.
Three hundred horses, in high stables fed,
Stood ready, shining all, and smoothly dress'd:
Of these he chose the fairest and the best,
To mount the Trojan troop. At his command
The steeds caparison'd with purple stand,
With golden trappings, glorious to behold,
And champ betwixt their teeth the foaming gold.
Then to his absent guest the king decreed
A pair of coursers born of heav'nly breed,
Who from their nostrils breath'd ethereal fire;
Whom Circe stole from her celestial sire,
By substituting mares produc'd on earth,
Whose wombs conceiv'd a more than mortal birth.
These draw the chariot which Latinus sends,
And the rich present to the prince commends.
Sublime on stately steeds the Trojans borne,
To their expecting lord with peace return.

But jealous Juno, from Pachynus' height,
As she from Argos took her airy flight,
Beheld with envious eyes this hateful sight.
She saw the Trojan and his joyful train
Descend upon the shore, desert the main,
Design a town, and, with unhop'd success,
Th' ambassadors return with promis'd peace.
Then, pierc'd with pain, she shook her haughty head,
Sigh'd from her inward soul, and thus she said:
"O hated offspring of my Phrygian foes!

O fates of Troy, which Juno's fates oppose!
Could they not fall unpitied on the plain,
But slain revive, and, taken, scape again?
When execrable Troy in ashes lay,
Thro' fires and swords and seas they forc'd their way.
Then vanquish'd Juno must in vain contend,
Her rage disarm'd, her empire at an end.
Breathless and tir'd, is all my fury spent?
Or does my glutted spleen at length relent?
As if 'twere little from their town to chase,
I thro' the seas pursued their exil'd race;
Engag'd the heav'ns, oppos'd the stormy main;
But billows roar'd, and tempests rag'd in vain.
What have my Scyllas and my Syrtes done,
When these they overpass, and those they shun?
On Tiber's shores they land, secure of fate,
Triumphant o'er the storms and Juno's hate.
Mars could in mutual blood the Centaurs bathe,
And Jove himself gave way to Cynthia's wrath,
Who sent the tusky boar to Calydon;
(What great offense had either people done?)
But I, the consort of the Thunderer,
Have wag'd a long and unsuccessful war,
With various arts and arms in vain have toil'd,
And by a mortal man at length am foil'd.
If native pow'r prevail not, shall I doubt
To seek for needful succor from without?
If Jove and Heav'n my just desires deny,
Hell shall the pow'r of Heav'n and Jove supply.
Grant that the Fates have firm'd, by their decree,
The Trojan race to reign in Italy;
At least I can defer the nuptial day,
And with protracted wars the peace delay:
With blood the dear alliance shall be bought,
And both the people near destruction brought;
So shall the son-in-law and father join,

With ruin, war, and waste of either line.
O fatal maid, thy marriage is endow'd
With Phrygian, Latian, and Rutulian blood!
Bellona leads thee to thy lover's hand;
Another queen brings forth another brand,
To burn with foreign fires another land!
A second Paris, diff'ring but in name,
Shall fire his country with a second flame."

Thus having said, she sinks beneath the ground,
With furious haste, and shoots the Stygian sound,
To rouse Alecto from th' infernal seat
Of her dire sisters, and their dark retreat.
This Fury, fit for her intent, she chose;
One who delights in wars and human woes.
Ev'n Pluto hates his own misshapen race;
Her sister Furies fly her hideous face;
So frightful are the forms the monster takes,
So fierce the hissings of her speckled snakes.
Her Juno finds, and thus inflames her spite:
"O virgin daughter of eternal Night,
Give me this once thy labor, to sustain
My right, and execute my just disdain.
Let not the Trojans, with a feign'd pretense
Of proffer'd peace, delude the Latian prince.
Expel from Italy that odious name,
And let not Juno suffer in her fame.
'Tis thine to ruin realms, o'erturn a state,
Betwixt the dearest friends to raise debate,
And kindle kindred blood to mutual hate.
Thy hand o'er towns the fun'ral torch displays,
And forms a thousand ills ten thousand ways.
Now shake, out thy fruitful breast, the seeds
Of envy, discord, and of cruel deeds:
Confound the peace establish'd, and prepare
Their souls to hatred, and their hands to war."

Smear'd as she was with black Gorgonian blood,
The Fury sprang above the Stygian flood;
And on her wicker wings, sublime thro' night,
She to the Latian palace took her flight:
There sought the queen's apartment,
stood before
The peaceful threshold, and besieg'd the door.
Restless Amata lay, her swelling breast
Fir'd with disdain for Turnus dispossess'd,
And the new nuptials of the Trojan guest.
From her black bloody locks the Fury shakes
Her darling plague, the fav'rite of her snakes;
With her full force she threw the poisonous dart,
And fix'd it deep within Amata's heart,
That, thus envenom'd, she might kindle rage,
And sacrifice to strife her house husband's age.
Unseen, unfelt, the fiery serpent skims
Betwixt her linen and her naked limbs;
His baleful breath inspiring, as he glides,
Now like a chain around her neck he rides,
Now like a fillet to her head repairs,
And with his circling volumes folds her hairs.
At first the silent venom slid with ease,
And seiz'd her cooler senses by degrees;
Then, ere th' infected mass was fir'd too far,
In plaintive accents she began the war,
And thus bespoke her husband: "Shall," she said,
"A wand'ring prince enjoy Lavinia's bed?
If nature plead not in a parent's heart,
Pity my tears, and pity her desert.
I know, my dearest lord, the time will come,
You in vain, reverse your cruel doom;
The faithless pirate soon will set to sea,
And bear the royal virgin far away!
A guest like him, a Trojan guest before,
In shew of friendship sought the Spartan shore,
And ravish'd Helen from her husband bore.

Think on a king's inviolable word;
And think on Turnus, her once plighted lord:
To this false foreigner you give your throne,
And wrong a friend, a kinsman, and a son.
Resume your ancient care; and, if the god
Your sire, and you, resolve on foreign blood,
Know all are foreign, in a larger sense,
Not born your subjects, or deriv'd from hence.
Then, if the line of Turnus you retrace,
He springs from Inachus of Argive race."

But when she saw her reasons idly spent,
And could not move him from his fix'd intent,
She flew to rage; for now the snake possess'd
Her vital parts, and poison'd all her breast;
She raves, she runs with a distracted pace,
And fills with horrid howls the public place.
And, as young striplings whip the top for sport,
On the smooth pavement of an empty court;
The wooden engine flies and whirls about,
Admir'd, with clamors, of the beardless rout;
They lash aloud; each other they provoke,
And lend their little souls at ev'ry stroke:
Thus fares the queen; and thus her fury blows
Amidst the crowd, and kindles as she goes.
Nor yet content, she strains her malice more,
And adds new ills to those contriv'd before:
She flies the town, and, mixing with a throng
Of madding matrons, bears the bride along,
Wand'ring thro' woods and wilds, and devious ways,
And with these arts the Trojan match delays.
She feign'd the rites of Bacchus; cried aloud,
And to the buxom god the virgin vow'd.
"Evoe! O Bacchus!" thus began the song;
And "Evoe!" answer'd all the female throng.
"O virgin! worthy thee alone!" she cried;

"O worthy thee alone!" the crew replied.
"For thee she feeds her hair, she leads thy dance,
And with thy winding ivy wreathes her lance."
Like fury seiz'd the rest; the progress known,
All seek the mountains, and forsake the town:
All, clad in skins of beasts, the jav'lin bear,
Give to the wanton winds their flowing hair,
And shrieks and shoutings rend the suff'ring air.
The queen herself, inspir'd with rage divine,
Shook high above her head a flaming pine;
Then roll'd her haggard eyes around the throng,
And sung, in Turnus' name, the nuptial song:
"Io, ye Latian dames! if any here
Hold your unhappy queen, Amata, dear;
If there be here," she said, "who dare maintain
My right, nor think the name of mother vain;
Unbind your fillets, loose your flowing hair,
And orgies and nocturnal rites prepare."

Amata's breast the Fury thus invades,
And fires with rage, amid the sylvan shades;
Then, when she found her venom spread so far,
The royal house embroil'd in civil war,
Rais'd on her dusky wings, she cleaves the skies,
And seeks the palace where young Turnus lies.
His town, as fame reports, was built of old
By Danæ, pregnant with almighty gold,
Who fled her father's rage, and, with a train
Of following Argives, thro' the stormy main,
Driv'n by the southern blasts, was fated here to reign.
'Twas Ardua once; now Ardea's name it bears;
Once a fair city, now consum'd with years.
Here, in his lofty palace, Turnus lay,
Betwixt the confines of the night and day,
Secure in sleep. The Fury laid aside
Her looks and limbs, and with new methods tried

The foulness of th' infernal form to hide.
Propp'd on a staff, she takes a trembling mien:
Her face is furrow'd, and her front obscene;
Deep-dinted wrinkles on her cheek she draws;
Sunk are her eyes, and toothless are her jaws;
Her hoary hair with holy fillets bound,
Her temples with an olive wreath are crown'd.
Old Chalybe, who kept the sacred fane
Of Juno, now she seem'd, and thus began,
Appearing in a dream, to rouse the careless man:
"Shall Turnus then such endless toil sustain
In fighting fields, and conquer towns in vain?
Win, for a Trojan head to wear the prize,
Usurp thy crown, enjoy thy victories?
The bride and scepter which thy blood has bought,
The king transfers; and foreign heirs are sought.
Go now, deluded man, and seek again
New toils, new dangers, on the dusty plain.
Repel the Tuscan foes; their city seize;
Protect the Latians in luxurious ease.
This dream all-pow'rful Juno sends; I bear
Her mighty mandates, and her words you hear.
Haste; arm your Ardeans; issue to the plain;
With fate to friend, assault the Trojan train:
Their thoughtless chiefs, their painted ships, that lie
In Tiber's mouth, with fire and sword destroy.
The Latian king, unless he shall submit,
Own his old promise, and his new forget—
Let him, in arms, the pow'r of Turnus prove,
And learn to fear whom he disdains to love.
For such is Heav'n's command."
The youthful prince
With scorn replied, and made this bold defense:
"You tell me, mother, what I knew before:
The Phrygian fleet is landed on the shore.
I neither fear nor will provoke the war;

My fate is Juno's most peculiar care.
But time has made you dote, and vainly tell
Of arms imagin'd in your lonely cell.
Go; be the temple and the gods your care;
Permit to men the thought of peace and war."

These haughty words Alecto's rage provoke,
And frighted Turnus trembled as she spoke.
Her eyes grow stiffen'd, and with sulphur burn;
Her hideous looks and hellish form return;
Her curling snakes with hissings fill the place,
And open all the furies of her face:
Then, darting fire from her malignant eyes,
She cast him backward as he strove to rise,
And, ling'ring, sought to frame some new replies.
High on her head she rears two twisted snakes,
Her chains she rattles, and her whip she shakes;
And, churning bloody foam, thus loudly speaks:
"Behold whom time has made to dote, and tell
Of arms imagin'd in her lonely cell!
Behold the Fates' infernal minister!
War, death, destruction, in my hand I bear."

Thus having said, her smold'ring torch, impress'd
With her full force, she plung'd into his breast.
Aghast he wak'd; and, starting from his bed,
Cold sweat, in clammy drops, his limbs o'erspread.
"Arms! arms!" he cries: "my sword and
shield prepare!"
He breathes defiance, blood, and mortal war.
So, when with crackling flames a cauldron fries,
The bubbling waters from the bottom rise:
Above the brims they force their fiery way;
Black vapors climb aloft, and cloud the day.

The peace polluted thus, a chosen band
He first commissions to the Latian land,

In threat'ning embassy; then rais'd the rest,
To meet in arms th' intruding Trojan guest,
To force the foes from the Lavinian shore,
And Italy's endanger'd peace restore.
Himself alone an equal match he boasts,
To fight the Phrygian and Ausonian hosts.
The gods invok'd, the Rutuli prepare
Their arms, and warn each other to the war.
His beauty these, and those his blooming age,
The rest his house and his own fame engage.

While Turnus urges thus his enterprise,
The Stygian Fury to the Trojans flies;
New frauds invents, and takes a steepy stand,
Which overlooks the vale with wide command;
Where fair Ascanius and his youthful train,
With horns and hounds, a hunting match ordain,
And pitch their toils around the shady plain.
The Fury fires the pack; they snuff, they vent,
And feed their hungry nostrils with the scent.
'Twas of a well-grown stag, whose antlers rise
High o'er his front; his beams invade the skies.
From this light cause th' infernal maid prepares
The country churls to mischief, hate, and wars.

The stately beast the two Tyrrhidæ bred,
Snatch'd from his dams, and the tame
 youngling fed.
Their father Tyrrheus did his fodder bring,
Tyrrheus, chief ranger to the Latian king:
Their sister Silvia cherish'd with her care
The little wanton, and did wreaths prepare
To hang his budding horns, with ribbons tied
His tender neck, and comb'd his silken hide,
And bathed his body. Patient of command
In time he grew, and, growing us'd to hand,
He waited at his master's board for food;

Then sought his salvage kindred in the wood,
Where grazing all the day, at night he came
To his known lodgings, and his country dame.

This household beast, that us'd the woodland grounds,
Was view'd at first by the young hero's hounds,
As down the stream he swam, to seek retreat
In the cool waters, and to quench his heat.
Ascanius young, and eager of his game,
Soon bent his bow, uncertain in his aim;
But the dire fiend the fatal arrow guides,
Which pierc'd his bowels thro' his panting sides.
The bleeding creature issues from the floods,
Possess'd with fear, and seeks his known abodes,
His old familiar hearth and household gods.
He falls; he fills the house with heavy groans,
Implores their pity, and his pain bemoans.
Young Silvia beats her breast, and cries aloud
For succor from the clownish neighborhood:
The churls assemble; for the fiend, who lay
In the close woody covert, urg'd their way.
One with a brand yet burning from the flame,
Arm'd with a knotty club another came:
Whate'er they catch or find, without their care,
Their fury makes an instrument of war.
Tyrrheus, the foster father of the beast,
Then clench'd a hatchet in his horny fist,
But held his hand from the descending stroke,
And left his wedge within the cloven oak,
To whet their courage and their rage provoke.
And now the goddess, exercis'd in ill,
Who watch'd an hour to work her impious will,
Ascends the roof, and to her crooked horn,
Such as was then by Latian shepherds borne,
Adds all her breath: the rocks and woods around,

And mountains, tremble at th' infernal sound.
The sacred lake of Trivia from afar,
The Veline fountains, and sulphureous Nar,
Shake at the baleful blast, the signal of the war.
Young mothers wildly stare, with fear possess'd,
And strain their helpless infants to their breast.

The clowns, a boist'rous, rude, ungovern'd crew,
With furious haste to the loud summons flew.
The pow'rs of Troy, then issuing on the plain,
With fresh recruits their youthful chief sustain:
Not theirs a raw and unexperienc'd train,
But a firm body of embattled men.
At first, while fortune favor'd neither side,
The fight with clubs and burning brands was tried;
But now, both parties reinforc'd, the fields
Are bright with flaming swords and brazen shields.
A shining harvest either host displays,
And shoots against the sun with equal rays.
Thus, when a black-brow'd gust begins to rise,
White foam at first on the curl'd ocean fries;
Then roars the main, the billows mount the skies;
Till, by the fury of the storm full blown,
The muddy bottom o'er the clouds is thrown.
First Almon falls, old Tyrrheus' eldest care,
Pierc'd with an arrow from the distant war:
Fix'd in his throat the flying weapon stood,
And stopp'd his breath, and drank his vital blood
Huge heaps of slain around the body rise:
Among the rest, the rich Galesus lies;
A good old man, while peace he preach'd in vain,
Amidst the madness of th' unruly train:
Five herds, five bleating flocks, his pastures fill'd;
His lands a hundred yoke of oxen till'd.

Thus, while in equal scales their fortune stood
The Fury bath'd them in each other's blood;

Then, having fix'd the fight, exulting flies,
And bears fulfill'd her promise to the skies.
To Juno thus she speaks: "Behold! It is done,
The blood already drawn, the war begun;
The discord is complete; nor can they cease
The dire debate, nor you command the peace.
Now, since the Latian and the Trojan brood
Have tasted vengeance and the sweets of blood;
Speak, and my pow'r shall add this office more:
The neighb'ing nations of th' Ausonian shore
Shall hear the dreadful rumor, from afar,
Of arm'd invasion, and embrace the war."
Then Juno thus: "The grateful work is done,
The seeds of discord sow'd, the war begun;
Frauds, fears, and fury have possess'd the state,
And fix'd the causes of a lasting hate.
A bloody Hymen shall th' alliance join
Betwixt the Trojan and Ausonian line:
But thou with speed to night and hell repair;
For not the gods, nor angry Jove, will bear
Thy lawless wand'ring walks in upper air.
Leave what remains to me." Saturnia said:
The sullen fiend her sounding wings display'd,
Unwilling left the light, and sought the
nether shade.

In midst of Italy, well known to fame,
There lies a lake (Amsanctus is the name)
Below the lofty mounts: on either side
Thick forests the forbidden entrance hide.
Full in the center of the sacred wood
An arm arises of the Stygian flood,
Which, breaking from beneath with
bellowing sound,
Whirls the black waves and rattling
stones around.
Here Pluto pants for breath from out his cell,

And opens wide the grinning jaws of hell.
To this infernal lake the Fury flies;
Here hides her hated head, and frees
the lab'ring skies.

Saturnian Juno now, with double care,
Attends the fatal process of the war.
The clowns, return'd, from battle bear the slain,
Implore the gods, and to their king complain.
The corps of Almon and the rest are shown;
Shrieks, clamors, murmurs, fill the frighted town.
Ambitious Turnus in the press appears,
And, aggravating crimes, augments their fears;
Proclaims his private injuries aloud,
A solemn promise made, and disavow'd;
A foreign son is sought, and a mix'd
mungril brood.
Then they, whose mothers, frantic with their fear,
In woods and wilds the flags of Bacchus bear,
And lead his dances with dishevel'd hair,
Increase the clamor, and the war demand,
(Such was Amata's interest in the land,)
Against the public sanctions of the peace,
Against all omens of their ill success.
With fates averse, the rout in arms resort,
To force their monarch, and insult the court.
But, like a rock unmov'd, a rock that braves
The raging tempest and the rising waves—
Propp'd on himself he stands; his solid sides
Wash off the seaweeds, and the sounding tides—
So stood the pious prince, unmov'd, and long
Sustain'd the madness of the noisy throng.
But, when he found that Juno's pow'r prevail'd,
And all the methods of cool counsel fail'd,
He calls the gods to witness their offense,
Disclaims the war, asserts his innocence.
"Hurried by fate," he cries, "and borne before

A furious wind, we have the faithful shore.
O more than madmen! you yourselves shall bear
The guilt of blood and sacrilegious war:
Thou, Turnus, shalt atone it by thy fate,
And pray to Heav'n for peace, but pray too late.
For me, my stormy voyage at an end,
I to the port of death securely tend.
The fun'ral pomp which to your kings you pay,
Is all I want, and all you take away."
He said no more, but, in his walls confin'd,
Shut out the woes which he too well divin'd
Nor with the rising storm would vainly strive,
But left the helm, and let the vessel drive.

A solemn custom was observ'd of old,
Which Latium held, and now the Romans hold,
Their standard when in fighting fields they rear
Against the fierce Hyrcanians, or declare
The Scythian, Indian, or Arabian war;
Or from the boasting Parthians would regain
Their eagles, lost in Carrhæ's bloody plain.
Two gates of steel (the name of Mars they bear,
And still are worship'd with religious fear)
Before his temple stand: the dire abode,
And the fear'd issues of the furious god,
Are fenc'd with brazen bolts; without the gates,
The wary guardian Janus doubly waits.
Then, when the sacred senate votes the wars,
The Roman consul their decree declares,
And in his robes the sounding gates unbars.
The youth in military shouts arise,
And the loud trumpets break the yielding skies.
These rites, of old by sov'reign princes us'd,
Were the king's office; but the king refus'd,
Deaf to their cries, nor would the gates unbar
Of sacred peace, or loose th' imprison'd war;
But hid his head, and, safe from loud alarms,

Abhorr'd the wicked ministry of arms.
Then heav'n's imperious queen shot down
from high:
At her approach the brazen hinges fly;
The gates are forc'd, and ev'ry falling bar;
And, like a tempest, issues out the war.

The peaceful cities of th' Ausonian shore,
Lull'd in their ease, and undisturb'd before,
Are all on fire; and some, with studious care,
Their restiff steeds in sandy plains prepare;
Some their soft limbs in painful marches try,
And war is all their wish, and arms the gen'ral cry.
Part scour the rusty shields with seam; and part
New grind the blunted ax, and point the dart:
With joy they view the waving ensigns fly,
And hear the trumpet's clangor pierce the sky.
Five cities forge their arms: th' Atinian pow'rs,
Antemnæ, Tibur with her lofty tow'rs,
Ardea the proud, the Crustumerian town:
All these of old were places of renown.
Some hammer helmets for the fighting field;
Some twine young sallows to support the shield;
The croslet some, and some the cuishes mold,
With silver plated, and with ductile gold.
The rustic honors of the scythe and share
Give place to swords and plumes, the pride of war.
Old fauchions are new temper'd in the fires;
The sounding trumpet ev'ry soul inspires.
The word is giv'n; with eager speed they lace
The shining headpiece, and the shield embrace.
The neighing steeds are to the chariot tied;
The trusty weapon sits on ev'ry side

And now the mighty labor is begun
Ye Muses, open all your Helicon.
Sing you the chiefs that sway'd th' Ausonian land,

Their arms, and armies under their command;
What warriors in our ancient clime were bred;
What soldiers follow'd, and what heroes led.
For well you know, and can record alone,
What fame to future times conveys but darkly down.

Mezentius first appear'd upon the plain:
Scorn sate upon his brows, and sour disdain,
Defying earth and heav'n. Etruria lost,
He brings to Turnus' aid his baffled host.
The charming Lausus, full of youthful fire,
Rode in the rank, and next his sullen sire;
To Turnus only second in the grace
Of manly mien, and features of the face.
A skillful horseman, and a huntsman bred,
With fates averse a thousand men he led:
His sire unworthy of so brave a son;
Himself well worthy of a happier throne.

Next Aventinus drives his chariot round
The Latian plains, with palms and laurels crown'd.
Proud of his steeds, he smokes along the field;
His father's hydra fills his ample shield:
A hundred serpents hiss about the brims;
The son of Hercules he justly seems
By his broad shoulders and gigantic limbs;
Of heav'nly part, and part of earthly blood,
A mortal woman mixing with a god.
For strong Alcides, after he had slain
The triple Geryon, drove from conquer'd Spain
His captive herds; and, thence in triumph led,
On Tuscan Tiber's flow'ry banks they fed.
Then on Mount Aventine the son of Jove
The priestess Rhea found, and forc'd to love.
For arms, his men long piles and jav'lins bore;
And poles with pointed steel their foes in battle gore.
Like Hercules himself his son appears,

In salvage pomp; a lion's hide he wears;
About his shoulders hangs the shaggy skin;
The teeth and gaping jaws severely grin.
Thus, like the god his father, homely dress'd,
He strides into the hall, a horrid guest.

Then two twin brothers from fair Tibur came,
(Which from their brother Tiburs took the name,)
Fierce Coras and Catillus, void of fear:
Arm'd Argive horse they led, and in the front appear.
Like cloud-born Centaurs, from the mountain's height
With rapid course descending to the fight;
They rush along; the rattling woods give way;
The branches bend before their sweepy sway.

Nor was Præneste's founder wanting there,
Whom fame reports the son of Mulciber:
Found in the fire, and foster'd in the plains,
A shepherd and a king at once he reigns,
And leads to Turnus' aid his country swains.
His own Præneste sends a chosen band,
With those who plow Saturnia's Gabine land;
Besides the succor which cold Anien yields,
The rocks of Hernicus, and dewy fields,
Anagnia fat, and Father Amasene,
A num'rous rout, but all of naked men:
Nor arms they wear, nor swords and bucklers wield,
Nor drive the chariot thro' the dusty field,
But whirl from leathern slings huge balls of lead,
And spoils of yellow wolves adorn their head;
The left foot naked, when they march to fight,
But in a bull's raw hide they sheathe the right.

Messapus next, (great Neptune was his sire,)
Secure of steel, and fated from the fire,

In pomp appears, and with his ardor warms
A heartless train, unexercis'd in arms:
The just Faliscans he to battle brings,
And those who live where Lake Ciminia springs;
And where Feronia's grove and temple stands,
Who till Fescennian or Flavinian lands.
All these in order march, and marching sing
The warlike actions of their sea-born king;
Like a long team of snowy swans on high,
Which clap their wings, and cleave the liquid sky,
When, homeward from their wat'ry pastures borne,
They sing, and Asia's lakes their notes return.
Not one who heard their music from afar,
Would think these troops an army train'd to war,
But flocks of fowl, that, when the tempests roar,
With their hoarse gabbling seek the silent shore.

Then Clausus came, who led a num'rous band
Of troops embodied from the Sabine land,
And, in himself alone, an army brought.
'Twas he, the noble Claudian race begot,
The Claudian race, ordain'd, in times to come,
To share the greatness of imperial Rome.
He led the Cures forth, of old renown,
Mutuscans from their olive-bearing town,
And all th' Eretian pow'rs; besides a band
That follow'd from Velinum's dewy land,
And Amiternian troops, of mighty fame,
And mountaineers, that from Severus came,
And from the craggy cliffs of Tetrica,
And those where yellow Tiber takes his way,
And where Himella's wanton waters play.
Casperia sends her arms, with those that lie
By Fabaris, and fruitful Foruli:
The warlike aids of Horta next appear,

And the cold Nursians come to close the rear,
Mix'd with the natives born of Latine blood,
Whom Allia washes with her fatal flood.
Not thicker billows beat the Libyan main,
When pale Orion sets in wintry rain;
Nor thicker harvests on rich Hermus rise,
Or Lycian fields, when Phœbus burns the skies,
Than stand these troops: their bucklers ring around;
Their trampling turns the turf,
and shakes the solid ground.

High in his chariot then Halesus came,
A foe by birth to Troy's unhappy name:
From Agamemnon born to Turnus' aid
A thousand men the youthful hero led,
Who till the Massic soil, for wine renown'd,
And fierce Auruncans from their hilly ground,
And those who live by Sidicinian shores,
And where with shoaly fords Vulturnus roars,
Cales' and Osca's old inhabitants,
And rough Saticulans, inur'd to wants:
Light demi-lances from afar they throw,
Fasten'd with leathern thongs, to gall the foe.
Short crooked swords in closer fight they wear;
And on their warding arm light bucklers bear.

Nor Œbalus, shalt thou be left unsung,
From nymph Semethis and old Telon sprung,
Who then in Teleboan Capri reign'd;
But that short isle th' ambitious youth disdain'd,
And o'er Campania stretch'd his ample sway,
Where swelling Sarnus seeks the Tyrrhene sea;
O'er Batulum, and where Abella sees,
From her high tow'rs, the harvest of her trees.
And these (as was the Teuton use of old)
Wield brazen swords, and brazen bucklers hold;
Sling weighty stones, when from afar they fight;
Their casques are cork, a covering thick and light.

Next these in rank, the warlike Ufens went,
And led the mountain troops that Nursia sent.
The rude Equicolæ his rule obey'd;
Hunting their sport, and plund'ring was
their trade.
In arms they plow'd, to battle still prepar'd:
Their soil was barren, and their hearts were hard.

Umbro the priest the proud Marrubians led,
By King Archippus sent to Turnus' aid,
And peaceful olives crown'd his hoary head.
His wand and holy words, the viper's rage,
And venom'd wounds of serpents could assuage.
He, when he pleas'd with powerful juice to steep
Their temples, shut their eyes in pleasing sleep.
But vain were Marsian herbs, and magic art,
To cure the wound giv'n by the Dardan dart:
Yet his untimely fate th' Angitian woods
In sighs remurmur'd to the Fucine floods.

The son of fam'd Hippolytus was there,
Fam'd as his sire, and, as his mother, fair;
Whom in Egerian groves Aricia bore,
And nurs'd his youth along the marshy shore,
Where great Diana's peaceful altars flame,
In fruitful fields; and Virbius was his name.
Hippolytus, as old records have said,
Was by his stepdam sought to share her bed;
But, when no female arts his mind could move,
She turn'd to furious hate her impious love.
Torn by wild horses on the sandy shore,
Another's crimes th' unhappy hunter bore,
Glutting his father's eyes with guiltless gore.
But chaste Diana, who his death deplor'd,
With Æsculapian herbs his life restor'd.
Then Jove, who saw from high, with just disdain,
The dead inspir'd with vital breath again,

Struck to the center, with his flaming dart,
Th' unhappy founder of the godlike art.
But Trivia kept in secret shades alone
Her care, Hippolytus, to fate unknown;
And call'd him Virbius in th' Egerian grove,
Where then he liv'd obscure, but safe from Jove.
For this, from Trivia's temple and her wood
Are coursers driv'n, who shed their master's blood,
Affrighted by the monsters of the flood.
His son, the second Virbius, yet retain'd
His father's art, and warrior steeds he rein'd.

Amid the troops, and like the leading god,
High o'er the rest in arms the graceful Turnus rode:
A triple of plumes his crest adorn'd,
On which with belching flames Chimæra burn'd:
The more the kindled combat rises high'r,
The more with fury burns the blazing fire.
Fair Io grac'd his shield; but Io now
With horns exalted stands, and seems to low—
A noble charge! Her keeper by her side,
To watch her walks, his hundred eyes applied;
And on the brims her sire, the wat'ry god,
Roll'd from a silver urn his crystal flood.
A cloud of foot succeeds, and fills the fields
With swords, and pointed spears, and clatt'ring shields;
Of Argives, and of old Sicanian bands,
And those who plow the rich Rutulian lands;
Auruncan youth, and those Sacrana yields,
And the proud Labicans, with painted shields,
And those who near Numician streams reside,
And those whom Tiber's holy forests hide,
Or Circe's hills from the main land divide;

Where Ufens glides along the lowly lands,
Or the black water of Pomptina stands.

Last, from the Volscians fair Camilla came,
And led her warlike troops, a warrior dame;
Unbred to spinning, in the loom unskill'd,
She chose the nobler Pallas of the field.
Mix'd with the first, the fierce virago fought,
Sustain'd the toils of arms, the danger sought,
Outstripp'd the winds in speed upon the plain,
Flew o'er the fields, nor hurt the bearded grain:
She swept the seas, and, as she skimm'd along,
Her flying feet unbath'd on billows hung.
Men, boys, and women, stupid with surprise,
Where'er she passes, fix their wond'ring eyes:
Longing they look, and, gaping at the sight,
Devour her o'er and o'er with vast delight;
Her purple habit sits with such a grace
On her smooth shoulders, and so suits her face;
Her head with ringlets of her hair is crown'd,
And in a golden caul the curls are bound.
She shakes her myrtle jav'lin; and, behind,
Her Lycian quiver dances in the wind.

Book VIII

The war being now begun, both the generals make all possible preparations. Turnus sends to Diomedes. Æneas goes in person to beg aid from Evander and the Tuscans (the Etruscans). Evander receives him kindly, furnishes him with men, and sends his son Pallas with him. Vulcan, at the request of Venus, makes arms for her son Æneas, and draws on his shield the most memorable actions of his posterity.

When Turnus had assembled all his pow'rs,
His standard planted on Laurentum's tow'rs;
When now the sprightly trumpet, from afar,
Had giv'n the signal of approaching war,
Had rous'd the neighing steeds to scour the fields,
While the fierce riders clatter'd on their shields;
Trembling with rage, the Latian youth prepare
To join th' allies, and headlong rush to war.
Fierce Ufens, and Messapus, led the crowd,
With bold Mezentius, who blasphem'd aloud.
These thro' the country took their
wasteful course,
The fields to forage, and to gather force.
Then Venulus to Diomedes they send,
To beg his aid Ausonia to defend,
Declare the common danger, and inform
The Grecian leader of the growing storm:
Æneas, landed on the Latian coast,
With banish'd gods, and with a baffled host,
Yet now aspir'd to conquest of the state,
And claim'd a title from the gods and fate;
What num'rous nations in his quarrel came,

And how they spread his formidable name.
What he design'd, what mischief might arise,
If fortune favor'd his first enterprise,
Was left for him to weigh, whose equal fears,
And common interest, was involv'd in theirs.

While Turnus and th' allies thus urge the war,
The Trojan, floating in a flood of care,
Beholds the tempest which his foes prepare.
This way and that he turns his anxious mind;
Thinks, and rejects the counsels he design'd;
Explores himself in vain, in ev'ry part,
And gives no rest to his distracted heart.
So, when the sun by day, or moon by night,
Strike on the polish'd brass their trembling light,
The glitt'ring species here and there divide,
And cast their dubious beams from side to side;
Now on the walls, now on the pavement play,
And to the ceiling flash the glaring day.

'Twas night; and weary nature lull'd asleep
The birds of air, and fishes of the deep,
And beasts, and mortal men. The Trojan chief
Was laid on Tiber's banks, oppress'd with grief,
And found in silent slumber late relief.
Then, thro' the shadows of the poplar wood,
Arose the father of the Roman flood;
An azure robe was o'er his body spread,
A wreath of shady reeds adorn'd his head:
Thus, manifest to sight, the god appear'd,
And with these pleasing words his sorrow cheer'd:
"Undoubted offspring of ethereal race,
O long expected in this promis'd place!
Who thro' the foes hast borne thy banish'd gods,
Restor'd them to their hearths, and old abodes;
This is thy happy home, the clime where fate
Ordains thee to restore the Trojan state.

Fear not! The war shall end in lasting peace,
And all the rage of haughty Juno cease.
And that this nightly vision may not seem
Th' effect of fancy, or an idle dream,
A sow beneath an oak shall lie along,
All white herself, and white her thirty young.
When thirty rolling years have run their race,
Thy son Ascanius, on this empty space,
Shall build a royal town, of lasting fame,
Which from this omen shall receive the name.
Time shall approve the truth. For what remains,
And how with sure success to crown thy pains,
With patience next attend. A banish'd band,
Driv'n with Evander from th' Arcadian land,
Have planted here, and plac'd on high their walls;
Their town the founder Pallanteum calls,
Deriv'd from Pallas, his great-grandsire's name:
But the fierce Latians old possession claim,
With war infesting the new colony.
These make thy friends, and on their aid rely.
To thy free passage I submit my streams.
Wake, son of Venus, from thy pleasing dreams;
And, when the setting stars are lost in day,
To Juno's pow'r thy just devotion pay;
With sacrifice the wrathful queen appease:
Her pride at length shall fall, her fury cease.
When thou return'st victorious from the war,
Perform thy vows to me with grateful care.
The god am I, whose yellow water flows
Around these fields, and fattens as it goes:
Tiber my name; among the rolling floods
Renown'd on earth, esteem'd among the gods.
This is my certain seat. In times to come,
My waves shall wash the walls of mighty Rome."

He said, and plung'd below. While yet he spoke,
His dream Æneas and his sleep forsook.

He rose, and looking up, beheld the skies
With purple blushing, and the day arise.
Then water in his hollow palm he took
From Tiber's flood, and thus the pow'rs bespoke:
"Laurentian nymphs, by whom the streams are fed,
And Father Tiber, in thy sacred bed
Receive Æneas, and from danger keep.
Whatever fount, whatever holy deep,
Conceals thy wat'ry stores; where'er they rise,
And, bubbling from below, salute the skies;
Thou, king of horned floods, whose plenteous urn
Suffices fatness to the fruitful corn,
For this thy kind compassion of our woes,
Shalt share my morning song and ev'ning vows.
But, O be present to thy people's aid,
And firm the gracious promise thou hast made!"
Thus having said, two galleys from his stores,
With care he chooses, mans, and fits with oars.
Now on the shore the fatal swine is found.
Wondrous to tell!—She lay along the ground:
Her well-fed offspring at her udders hung;
She white herself, and white her thirty young.
Æneas takes the mother and her brood,
And all on Juno's altar are bestow'd.

The foll'wing night, and the succeeding day,
Propitious Tiber smooth'd his wat'ry way:
He roll'd his river back, and pois'd he stood,
A gentle swelling, and a peaceful flood.
The Trojans mount their ships; they put
    from shore,
Borne on the waves, and scarcely dip an oar.
Shouts from the land give omen to their course,
And the pitch'd vessels glide with easy force.
The woods and waters wonder at the gleam
Of shields, and painted ships that stem the stream.
One summer's night and one whole day they pass

Betwixt the greenwood shades, and cut the liquid glass.
The fiery sun had finish'd half his race,
Look'd back, and doubted in the middle space,
When they from far beheld the rising tow'rs,
The tops of sheds, and shepherds' lowly bow'rs,
Thin as they stood, which, then of homely clay,
Now rise in marble, from the Roman sway.
These cots (Evander's kingdom, mean and poor)
The Trojan saw, and turn'd his ships to shore.
'Twas on a solemn day: th' Arcadian states,
The king and prince, without the city gates,
Then paid their off'rings in a sacred grove
To Hercules, the warrior son of Jove.
Thick clouds of rolling smoke involve the skies,
And fat of entrails on his altar fries.

But, when they saw the ships that stemm'd the flood,
And glitter'd thro' the covert of the wood,
They rose with fear, and left th' unfinish'd feast,
Till dauntless Pallas reassur'd the rest
To pay the rites. Himself without delay
A jav'lin seiz'd, and singly took his way;
Then gain'd a rising ground, and call'd from far:
"Resolve me, strangers, whence, and what you are;
Your bus'ness here; and bring you peace or war?"
High on the stern Æneas his stand,
And held a branch of olive in his hand,
While thus he spoke: "The Phrygians' arms you see,
Expell'd from Troy, provok'd in Italy
By Latian foes, with war unjustly made;
At first affianc'd, and at last betray'd.

This message bear: 'The Trojans and their chief
Bring holy peace, and beg the king's relief.'
Struck with so great a name, and all on fire,
The youth replies: "Whatever you require,
Your fame exacts. Upon our shores descend.
A welcome guest, and, what you wish, a friend."
He said, and, downward hasting to the strand,
Embrac'd the stranger prince, and join'd his hand.

Conducted to the grove, Æneas broke
The silence first, and thus the king bespoke:
"Best of the Greeks, to whom, by fate's command,
I bear these peaceful branches in my hand,
Undaunted I approach you, tho' I know
Your birth is Grecian, and your land my foe;
From Atreus tho' your ancient lineage came,
And both the brother kings your kindred claim;
Yet, my self-conscious worth, your high renown,
Your virtue, thro' the neighb'ring nations blown,
Our fathers' mingled blood, Apollo's voice,
Have led me hither, less by need than choice.
Our founder Dardanus, as fame has sung,
And Greeks acknowledge, from Electra sprung:
Electra from the loins of Atlas came;
Atlas, whose head sustains the starry frame.
Your sire is Mercury, whom long before
On cold Cyllene's top fair Maia bore.
Maia the fair, on fame if we rely,
Was Atlas' daughter, who sustains the sky.
Thus from one common source our streams divide;
Ours is the Trojan, yours th' Arcadian side.
Rais'd by these hopes, I sent no news before,
Nor ask'd your leave, nor did your faith implore;
But come, without a pledge, my own ambassador.
The same Rutulians, who with arms pursue
The Trojan race, are equal foes to you.
Our host expell'd, what farther force can stay

The victor troops from universal sway?
Then will they stretch their pow'r athwart the land,
And either sea from side to side command.
Receive our offer'd faith, and give us thine;
Ours is a gen'rous and experienc'd line:
We want not hearts nor bodies for the war;
In council cautious, and in fields we dare."

He said; and while spoke, with piercing eyes
Evander view'd the man with vast surprise,
Pleas'd with his action, ravish'd with his face:
Then answer'd briefly, with a royal grace:
"O valiant leader of the Trojan line,
In whom the features of thy father shine,
How I recall Anchises! how I see
His motions, mien, and all my friend, in thee!
Long tho' it be, 'tis fresh within my mind,
When Priam to his sister's court design'd
A welcome visit, with a friendly stay,
And thro' th' Arcadian kingdom took his way.
Then, past a boy, the callow down began
To shade my chin, and call me first a man.
I saw the shining train with vast delight,
And Priam's goodly person pleas'd my sight:
But great Anchises, far above the rest,
With awful wonder fir'd my youthful breast.
I long'd to join in friendship's holy bands
Our mutual hearts, and plight our mutual hands.
I first accosted him: I sued, I sought,
And, with a loving force, to Pheneus brought.
He gave me, when at length constrain'd to go,
A Lycian quiver and a Gnossian bow,
A vest embroider'd, glorious to behold,
And two rich bridles, with their bits of gold,
Which my son's coursers in obedience hold.
The league you ask, I offer, as your right;
And, when to-morrow's sun reveals the light,

With swift supplies you shall be sent away.
Now celebrate with us this solemn day,
Whose holy rites admit no long delay.
Honor our annual feast; and take your seat,
With friendly welcome, at a homely treat."
Thus having said, the bowls (remov'd for fear)
The youths replac'd, and soon restor'd the cheer.
On sods of turf he set the soldiers round:
A maple throne, rais'd higher from the ground,
Receiv'd the Trojan chief; and, o'er the bed,
A lion's shaggy hide for ornament they spread.
The loaves were serv'd in canisters; the wine
In bowls; the priest renew'd the rites divine:
Broil'd entrails are their food, and beef's
continued chine.

But when the rage of hunger was repress'd,
Thus spoke Evander to his royal guest:
"These rites, these altars, and this feast, O king,
From no vain fears or superstition spring,
Or blind devotion, or from blinder chance,
Or heady zeal, or brutal ignorance;
But, sav'd from danger, with a grateful sense,
The labors of a god we recompense.
See, from afar, yon rock that mates the sky,
About whose feet such heaps of rubbish lie;
Such indigested ruin; bleak and bare,
How desert now it stands, expos'd in air!
'Twas once a robber's den, enclos'd around
With living stone, and deep beneath the ground.
The monster Cacus, more than half a beast,
This hold, impervious to the sun, possess'd.
The pavement ever foul with human gore;
Heads, and their mangled members, hung the door.
Vulcan this plague begot; and, like his sire,
Black clouds he belch'd, and flakes of livid fire.
Time, long expected, eas'd us of our load,

And brought the needful presence of a god.
Th' avenging force of Hercules, from Spain,
Arriv'd in triumph, from Geryon slain:
Thrice liv'd the giant, and thrice liv'd in vain.
His prize, the lowing herds, Alcides drove
Near Tiber's bank, to graze the shady grove.
Allur'd with hope of plunder, and intent
By force to rob, by fraud to circumvent,
The brutal Cacus, as by chance they stray'd,
Four oxen thence, and four fair kine convey'd;
And, lest the printed footsteps might be seen,
He dragg'd 'em backwards to his rocky den.
The tracks averse a lying notice gave,
And led the searcher backward from the cave.

"Meantime the herdsman hero shifts his place,
To find fresh pasture and untrodden grass.
The beasts, who miss'd their mates, fill'd all around
With bellowings, and the rocks restor'd the sound.
One heifer, who had heard her love complain,
Roar'd from the cave, and made the project vain.
Alcides found the fraud; with rage he shook,
And toss'd about his head his knotted oak.
Swift as the winds, or Scythian arrows' flight,
He clomb, with eager haste, th' ærial height.
Then first we saw the monster mend his pace;
Fear his eyes, and paleness in his face,
Confess'd the god's approach. Trembling he springs,
As terror had increas'd his feet with wings;
Nor stay'd for stairs; but down the depth he threw
His body, on his back the door he drew
(The door, a rib of living rock; with pains
His father hew'd it out, and bound with iron chains):

He broke the heavy links, the mountain clos'd,
And bars and levers to his foe oppos'd.
The wretch had hardly made his dungeon fast;
The fierce avenger came with bounding haste;
Survey'd the mouth of the forbidden hold,
And here and there his raging eyes he roll'd.
He gnash'd his teeth; and thrice he compass'd round
With winged speed the circuit of the ground.
Thrice at the cavern's mouth he pull'd in vain,
And, panting, thrice desisted from his pain.
A pointed flinty rock, all bare and black,
Grew gibbous from behind the mountain's back;
Owls, ravens, all ill omens of the night,
Here built their nests, and hither wing'd their flight.
The leaning head hung threat'ning o'er the flood,
And nodded to the left. The hero stood
Adverse, with planted feet, and, from the right,
Tugg'd at the solid stone with all his might.
Thus heav'd, the fix'd foundations of the rock
Gave way; heav'n echo'd at the rattling shock.
Tumbling, it chok'd the flood: on either side
The banks leap backward, and the streams divide;
The sky shrunk upward with unusual dread,
And trembling Tiber div'd beneath his bed.
The court of Cacus stands reveal'd to sight;
The cavern glares with new-admitted light.
So the pent vapors, with a rumbling sound,
Heave from below, and rend the hollow ground;
A sounding flaw succeeds; and, from on high,
The gods with hate beheld the nether sky:
The ghosts repine at violated night,
And curse th' invading sun, and sicken at the sight.
The graceless monster, caught in open day,
Enclos'd, and in despair to fly away,

Howls horrible from underneath, and fills
His hollow palace with unmanly yells.
The hero stands above, and from afar
Plies him with darts, and stones, and distant war.
He, from his nostrils huge mouth, expires
Black clouds of smoke, amidst his father's fires,
Gath'ring, with each repeated blast, the night,
To make uncertain aim, and erring sight.
The wrathful god then plunges from above,
And, where in thickest waves the sparkles drove,
There lights; and wades thro' fumes, and gropes his way,
Half sing'd, half stifled, till he grasps his prey.
The monster, spewing fruitless flames, he found;
He squeez'd his throat; he writh'd his neck around,
And in a knot his crippled members bound;
Then from their sockets tore his burning eyes:
Roll'd on a heap, the breathless robber lies.
The doors, unbarr'd, receive the rushing day,
And thoro' lights disclose the ravish'd prey.
The bulls, redeem'd, breathe open air again.
Next, by the feet, they drag him from his den.
The wond'ring neighborhood, with glad surprise,
Behold his shagged breast, his giant size,
His mouth that flames no more, and his extinguish'd eyes.
From that auspicious day, with rites divine,
We worship at the hero's holy shrine.
Potitius first ordain'd these annual vows:
As priests, were added the Pinarian house,
Who rais'd this altar in the sacred shade,
Where honors, ever due, for ever shall be paid.
For these deserts, and this high virtue shown,
Ye warlike youths, your heads with garlands crown:
Fill high the goblets with a sparkling flood,
And with deep draughts invoke our common god."

This said, a double wreath Evander twin'd,
And poplars black and white his temples bind.
Then brims his ample bowl. With like design
The rest invoke the gods, with sprinkled wine.
Meantime the sun descended from the skies,
And the bright evening star began to rise.
And now the priests, Potitius at their head,
In skins of beasts involv'd, the long procession led;
Held high the flaming tapers in their hands,
As custom had prescrib'd their holy bands;
Then with a second course the tables load,
And with full chargers offer to the god.
The Salii sing, and cense his altars round
With Saban smoke, their heads with poplar bound—
One choir of old, another of the young,
To dance, and bear the burthen of the song.
The lay records the labors, and the praise,
And all th' immortal acts of Hercules:
First, how the mighty babe, when swath'd in bands,
The serpents strangled with his infant hands;
Then, as in years and matchless force he grew,
Th' Œchalian walls, and Trojan, overthrew.
Besides, a thousand hazards they relate,
Procur'd by Juno's and Eurystheus' hate:
"Thy hands, unconquer'd hero, could subdue
The cloud-born Centaurs, and the monster crew:
Nor thy resistless arm the bull withstood,
Nor he, the roaring terror of the wood.
The triple porter of the Stygian seat,
With lolling tongue, lay fawning at thy feet,
And, seiz'd with fear, forgot his mangled meat.
Th' infernal waters trembled at thy sight;
Thee, god, no face of danger could affright;
Not huge Typhœus, nor th' unnumber'd snake,
Increas'd with hissing heads, in Lerna's lake.

Hail, Jove's undoubted son! an added grace
To heav'n and the great author of thy race!
Receive the grateful off'rings which we pay,
And smile propitious on thy solemn day!"
In numbers thus they sung; above the rest,
The den and death of Cacus crown the feast.
The woods to hollow vales convey the sound,
The vales to hills, and hills the notes rebound.
The rites perform'd, the cheerful train retire.

Betwixt young Pallas and his aged sire,
The Trojan pass'd, the city to survey,
And pleasing talk beguil'd the tedious way.
The stranger cast around his curious eyes,
New objects viewing still, with new surprise;
With greedy joy inquires of various things,
And acts and monuments of ancient kings.
Then thus the founder of the Roman tow'rs:
"These woods were first the seat of sylvan pow'rs,
Of Nymphs and Fauns, and salvage men, who took
Their birth from trunks of trees and stubborn oak.
Nor laws they knew, nor manners, nor the care
Of lab'ring oxen, or the shining share,
Nor arts of gain, nor what they gain'd to spare.
Their exercise the chase; the running flood
Supplied their thirst, the trees supplied their food.
Then Saturn came, who fled the pow'r of Jove,
Robb'd of his realms, and banish'd from above.
The men, dispers'd on hills, to towns he brought,
And laws ordain'd, and civil customs taught,
And Latium call'd the land where safe he lay
From his unduteous son, and his usurping sway.
With his mild empire, peace and plenty came;
And hence the golden times deriv'd their name.
A more degenerate and discolor'd age
Succeeded this, with avarice and rage.
Th' Ausonians then, and bold Sicanians came;

And Saturn's empire often chang'd the name.
Then kings, gigantic Tybris, and the rest,
With arbitrary sway the land oppress'd:
For Tiber's flood was Albula before,
Till, from the tyrant's fate, his name it bore.
I last arriv'd, driv'n from my native home
By fortune's pow'r, and fate's resistless doom.
Long toss'd on seas, I sought this happy land,
Warn'd by my mother nymph, and call'd by
 Heav'n's command."

Thus, walking on, he spoke, and shew'd the gate,
Since call'd Carmental by the Roman state;
Where stood an altar, sacred to the name
Of old Carmenta, the prophetic dame,
Who to her son foretold th' Ænean race,
Sublime in fame, and Rome's imperial place:
Then shews the forest, which, in after times,
Fierce Romulus for perpetrated crimes
A sacred refuge made; with this, the shrine
Where Pan below the rock had rites divine:
Then tells of Argus' death, his murder'd guest,
Whose grave and tomb his innocence attest.
Thence, to the steep Tarpeian rock he leads;
Now roof'd with gold, then thatch'd with
 homely reeds.
A reverent fear (such superstition reigns
Among the rude) ev'n then possess'd the swains.
Some god, they knew—what god, they could
 not tell—
Did there amidst the sacred horror dwell.
Th' Arcadians thought him Jove; and said they saw
The mighty Thund'rer with majestic awe,
Who took his shield, and dealt his bolts around,
And scatter'd tempests on the teeming ground.
Then saw two heaps of ruins, (once they stood
Two stately towns, on either side the flood,)

Saturnia's and Janicula's remains;
And either place the founder's name retains.
Discoursing thus together, they resort
Where poor Evander kept his country court.
They view'd the ground of Rome's litigious hall;
(Once oxen low'd, where now the lawyers bawl;)
Then, stooping, thro' the narrow gate they press'd,
When thus the king bespoke his Trojan guest:
"Mean as it is, this palace, and this door,
Receiv'd Alcides, then a conqueror.
Dare to be poor; accept our homely food,
Which feasted him, and emulate a god."
Then underneath a lowly roof he led
The weary prince, and laid him on a bed;
The stuffing leaves, with hides of bears o'erspread.
Now Night had shed her silver dews around,
And with her sable wings embrac'd the ground,
When love's fair goddess, anxious for her son,
(New tumults rising, and new wars begun,)
Couch'd with her husband in his golden bed,
With these alluring words invokes his aid;
And, that her pleasing speech his mind may move,
Inspires each accent with the charms of love:
"While cruel fate conspir'd with Grecian pow'rs,
To level with the ground the Trojan tow'rs,
I ask'd not aid th' unhappy to restore,
Nor did the succor of thy skill implore;
Nor urg'd the labors of my lord in vain,
A sinking empire longer to sustain,
Tho' much I ow'd to Priam's house, and more
The dangers of Æneas did deplore.
But now, by Jove's command, and fate's decree,
His race is doom'd to reign in Italy:
With humble suit I beg thy needful art,
O still propitious pow'r, that rules my heart!
A mother kneels a suppliant for her son.
By Thetis and Aurora thou wert won

To forge impenetrable shields, and grace
With fated arms a less illustrious race.
Behold, what haughty nations are combin'd
Against the relics of the Phrygian kind,
With fire and sword my people to destroy,
And conquer Venus twice, in conqu'ring Troy."
She said; and straight her arms, of snowy hue,
About her unresolving husband threw.
Her soft embraces soon infuse desire;
His bones and marrow sudden warmth inspire;
And all the godhead feels the wonted fire.
Not half so swift the rattling thunder flies,
Or forky lightnings flash along the skies.
The goddess, proud of her successful wiles,
And conscious of her form, in secret smiles.

Then thus the pow'r, obnoxious to her charms,
Panting, and half dissolving in her arms:
"Why seek you reasons for a cause so just,
Or your own beauties or my love distrust?
Long since, had you requir'd my helpful hand,
Th' artificer and art you might command,
To labor arms for Troy: nor Jove, nor fate,
Confin'd their empire to so short a date.
And, if you now desire new wars to wage,
My skill I promise, and my pains engage.
Whatever melting metals can conspire,
Or breathing bellows, or the forming fire,
Is freely yours: your anxious fears remove,
And think no task is difficult to love."
Trembling he spoke; and, eager of her charms,
He snatch'd the willing goddess to his arms;
Till in her lap infus'd, he lay possess'd
Of full desire, and sunk to pleasing rest.
Now when the Night her middle race had rode,
And his first slumber had refresh'd the god—

The time when early housewives leave the bed;
When living embers on the hearth they spread,
Supply the lamp, and call the maids to rise—
With yawning mouths, and with half-open'd eyes,
They ply the distaff by the winking light,
And to their daily labor add the night:
Thus frugally they earn their children's bread,
And uncorrupted keep the nuptial bed—
Not less concern'd, nor at a later hour,
Rose from his downy couch the forging pow'r.

Sacred to Vulcan's name, an isle there lay,
Betwixt Sicilia's coasts and Lipare,
Rais'd high on smoking rocks; and, deep below,
In hollow caves the fires of Ætna glow.
The Cyclops here their heavy hammers deal;
Loud strokes, and hissings of tormented steel,
Are heard around; the boiling waters roar,
And smoky flames thro' fuming tunnels soar.
Hither the Father of the Fire, by night,
Thro' the brown air precipitates his flight.
On their eternal anvils here he found
The brethren beating, and the blows go round.
A load of pointless thunder now there lies
Before their hands, to ripen for the skies:
These darts, for angry Jove, they daily cast;
Consum'd on mortals with prodigious waste.
Three rays of writhen rain, of fire three more,
Of winged southern winds and cloudy store
As many parts, the dreadful mixture frame;
And fears are added, and avenging flame.
Inferior ministers, for Mars, repair
His broken axletrees and blunted war,
And send him forth again with furbish'd arms,
To wake the lazy war with trumpets' loud alarms.
The rest refresh the scaly snakes that fold
The shield of Pallas, and renew their gold.

Full on the crest the Gorgon's head they place,
With eyes that roll in death, and with distorted face.

"My sons," said Vulcan, "set your tasks aside;
Your strength and master-skill must now be tried.
Arms for a hero forge; arms that require
Your force, your speed, and all your forming fire."
He said. They set their former work aside,
And their new toils with eager haste divide.
A flood of molten silver, brass, and gold,
And deadly steel, in the large furnace roll'd;
Of this, their artful hands a shield prepare,
Alone sufficient to sustain the war.
Sev'n orbs within a spacious round they close:
One stirs the fire, and one the bellows blows.
The hissing steel is in the smithy drown'd;
The grot with beaten anvils groans around.
By turns their arms advance, in equal time;
By turns their hands descend, and hammers chime.
They turn the glowing mass with crooked tongs;
The fiery work proceeds, with rustic songs.

While, at the Lemnian god's command, they urge
Their labors thus, and ply th' Æolian forge,
The cheerful morn salutes Evander's eyes,
And songs of chirping birds invite to rise.
He leaves his lowly bed: his buskins meet
Above his ankles; sandals sheathe his feet:
He sets his trusty sword upon his side,
And o'er his shoulder throws a panther's hide.
Two menial dogs before their master press'd.
Thus clad, and guarded thus, he seeks his
kingly guest.
Mindful of promis'd aid, he mends his pace,
But meets Æneas in the middle space.
Young Pallas did his father's steps attend,
And true Achates waited on his friend.

They join their hands; a secret seat they choose;
Th' Arcadian first their former talk renews:
"Undaunted prince, I never can believe
The Trojan empire lost, while you survive.
Command th' assistance of a faithful friend;
But feeble are the succors I can send.
Our narrow kingdom here the Tiber bounds;
That other side the Latian state surrounds,
Insults our walls, and wastes our fruitful grounds.
But mighty nations I prepare, to join
Their arms with yours, and aid your just design.
You come, as by your better genius sent,
And fortune seems to favor your intent.
Not far from hence there stands a hilly town,
Of ancient building, and of high renown,
Torn from the Tuscans by the Lydian race,
Who gave the name of Cære to the place,
Once Agyllina call'd. It flourish'd long,
In pride of wealth and warlike people strong,
Till curs'd Mezentius, in a fatal hour,
Assum'd the crown, with arbitrary pow'r.
What words can paint those execrable times,
The subjects' suff'rings, and the tyrant's crimes!
That blood, those murthers, O ye gods, replace
On his own head, and on his impious race!
The living and the dead at his command
Were coupled, face to face, and hand to hand,
Till, chok'd with stench, in loath'd embraces tied,
The ling'ring wretches pin'd away and died.
Thus plung'd in ills, and meditating more,
The people's patience, tir'd, no longer bore
The raging monster; but with arms beset
His house, and vengeance and destruction threat.
They fire his palace: while the flame ascends,
They force his guards, and execute his friends.
He cleaves the crowd, and, favor'd by the night,
To Turnus' friendly court directs his flight.

By just revenge the Tuscans set on fire,
With arms, their king to punishment require:
Their num'rous troops, now muster'd on the strand,
My counsel shall submit to your command.
Their navy swarms upon the coasts; they cry
To hoist their anchors, but the gods deny.
An ancient augur, skill'd in future fate,
With these foreboding words restrains their hate:
'Ye brave in arms, ye Lydian blood, the flow'r
Of Tuscan youth, and choice of all their pow'r,
Whom just revenge against Mezentius arms,
To seek your tyrant's death by lawful arms;
Know this: no native of our land may lead
This pow'rful people; seek a foreign head.'
Aw'd with these words, in camps they still abide,
And wait with longing looks their promis'd guide.
Tarchon, the Tuscan chief, to me has sent
Their crown, and ev'ry regal ornament:
The people join their own with his desire;
And all my conduct, as their king, require.
But the chill blood that creeps within my veins,
And age, and listless limbs unfit for pains,
And a soul conscious of its own decay,
Have forc'd me to refuse imperial sway.
My Pallas were more fit to mount the throne,
And should, but he's a Sabine mother's son,
And half a native; but, in you, combine
A manly vigor, and a foreign line.
Where Fate and smiling Fortune shew the way,
Pursue the ready path to sov'reign sway.
The staff of my declining days, my son,
Shall make your good or ill success his own;
In fighting fields from you shall learn to dare,
And serve the hard apprenticeship of war;
Your matchless courage and your conduct view,
And early shall begin t' admire and copy you.
Besides, two hundred horse he shall command;

Tho' few, a warlike and well-chosen band.
These in my name are listed; and my son
As many more has added in his own."

Scarce had he said; Achates and his guest,
With downcast eyes, their silent grief express'd;
Who, short of succors, and in deep despair,
Shook at the dismal prospect of the war.
But his bright mother, from a breaking cloud,
To cheer her issue, thunder'd thrice aloud;
Thrice forky lightning flash'd along the sky,
And Tyrrhene trumpets thrice were heard on high.
Then, gazing up, repeated peals they hear;
And, in a heav'n serene, refulgent arms appear:
Redd'ning the skies, and glitt'ring all around,
The temper'd metals clash, and yield a silver sound.
The rest stood trembling, struck with awe divine;
Æneas only, conscious to the sign,
Presag'd th' event, and joyful view'd, above,
Th' accomplish'd promise of the Queen of Love.
Then, to th' Arcadian king: "This prodigy
(Dismiss your fear) belongs alone to me.
Heav'n calls me to the war: th' expected sign
Is giv'n of promis'd aid, and arms divine.
My goddess mother, whose indulgent care
Foresaw the dangers of the growing war,
This omen gave, when bright Vulcanian arms,
Fated from force of steel by Stygian charms,
Suspended, shone on high: she then foreshow'd
Approaching fights, and fields to float in blood.
Turnus shall dearly pay for faith forsworn;
And corps, and swords, and shields, on Tiber borne,
Shall choke his flood: now sound the loud alarms;
And, Latian troops, prepare your perjur'd arms."

He said, and, rising from his homely throne,
The solemn rites of Hercules begun,

And on his altars wak'd the sleeping fires;
Then cheerful to his household gods retires;
There offers chosen sheep. Th' Arcadian king
And Trojan youth the same oblations bring.
Next, of his men and ships he makes review;
Draws out the best and ablest of the crew.
Down with the falling stream the refuse run,
To raise with joyful news his drooping son.
Steeds are prepar'd to mount the Trojan band,
Who wait their leader to the Tyrrhene land.
A sprightly courser, fairer than the rest,
The king himself presents his royal guest:
A lion's hide his back and limbs enfold,
Precious with studded work, and paws of gold.
Fame thro' the little city spreads aloud
Th' intended march, amid the fearful crowd:
The matrons beat their breasts, dissolve in tears,
And double their devotion in their fears.
The war at hand appears with more affright,
And rises ev'ry moment to the sight.

Then old Evander, with a close embrace,
Strain'd his departing friend;
    and tears o'erflow his face.
"Would Heav'n," said he, "my strength
    and youth recall,
Such as I was beneath Præneste's wall;
Then when I made the foremost foes retire,
And set whole heaps of conquer'd shields on fire;
When Herilus in single fight I slew,
Whom with three lives Feronia did endue;
And thrice I sent him to the Stygian shore,
Till the last ebbing soul return'd no more—
Such if I stood renew'd, not these alarms,
Nor death, should rend me from my Pallas' arms;
Nor proud Mezentius, thus unpunish'd, boast
His rapes and murthers on the Tuscan coast.

Ye gods, and mighty Jove, in pity bring
Relief, and hear a father and a king!
If fate and you reserve these eyes, to see
My son return with peace and victory;
If the lov'd boy shall bless his father's sight;
If we shall meet again with more delight;
Then draw my life in length; let me sustain,
In hopes of his embrace, the worst of pain.
But if your hard decrees—which, O! I dread—
Have doom'd to death his undeserving head;
This, O this very moment, let me die!
While hopes and fears in equal balance lie;
While, yet possess'd of all his youthful charms,
I strain him close within these aged arms;
Before that fatal news my soul shall wound!"
He said, and, swooning, sunk upon the ground.
His servants bore him off, and softly laid
His languish'd limbs upon his homely bed.

The horsemen march; the gates are open'd wide;
Æneas at their head, Achates by his side.
Next these, the Trojan leaders rode along;
Last follows in the rear th' Arcadian throng.
Young Pallas shone conspicuous o'er the rest;
Gilded his arms, embroider'd was his vest.
So, from the seas, exerts his radiant head
The star by whom the lights of heav'n are led;
Shakes from his rosy locks the pearly dews,
Dispels the darkness, and the day renews.
The trembling wives the walls and turrets crowd,
And follow, with their eyes, the dusty cloud,
Which winds disperse by fits, and shew from far
The blaze of arms, and shields, and shining war.
The troops, drawn up in beautiful array,
O'er heathy plains pursue the ready way.
Repeated peals of shouts are heard around;

The neighing coursers answer to the sound,
And shake with horny hoofs the solid ground.

A greenwood shade, for long religion known,
Stands by the streams that wash the Tuscan town,
Encompass'd round with gloomy hills above,
Which add a holy horror to the grove.
The first inhabitants of Grecian blood,
That sacred forest to Silvanus vow'd,
The guardian of their flocks and fields; and pay
Their due devotions on his annual day.
Not far from hence, along the river's side,
In tents secure, the Tuscan troops abide,
By Tarchon led. Now, from a rising ground,
Æneas cast his wond'ring eyes around,
And all the Tyrrhene army had in sight,
Stretch'd on the spacious plain from left to right.
Thither his warlike train the Trojan led,
Refresh'd his men, and wearied horses fed.

Meantime the mother goddess, crown'd with charms,
Breaks thro' the clouds, and brings the fated arms.
Within a winding vale she finds her son,
On the cool river's banks, retir'd alone.
She shews her heav'nly form without disguise,
And gives herself to his desiring eyes.
"Behold," she said, "perform'd in ev'ry part,
My promise made, and Vulcan's labor'd art.
Now seek, secure, the Latian enemy,
And haughty Turnus to the field defy."
She said; and, having first her son embrac'd,
The radiant arms beneath an oak she plac'd,
Proud of the gift, he roll'd his greedy sight

Around the work, and gaz'd with vast delight.
He lifts, he turns, he poises, and admires
The crested helm, that vomits radiant fires:
His hands the fatal sword and corslet hold,
One keen with temper'd steel, one stiff with gold:
Both ample, flaming both, and beamy bright;
So shines a cloud, when edg'd with adverse light.
He shakes the pointed spear, and longs to try
The plated cuishes on his manly thigh;
But most admires the shield's mysterious mold,
And Roman triumphs rising on the gold:
For these, emboss'd, the heav'nly smith had wrought
(Not in the rolls of future fate untaught)
The wars in order, and the race divine
Of warriors issuing from the Julian line.
The cave of Mars was dress'd with mossy greens:
There, by the wolf, were laid the martial twins.
Intrepid on her swelling dugs they hung;
The foster dam loll'd out her fawning tongue:
They suck'd secure, while, bending back her head,
She lick'd their tender limbs, and form'd them as they fed.
Not far from thence new Rome appears, with games
Projected for the rape of Sabine dames.
The pit resounds with shrieks; a war succeeds,
For breach of public faith, and unexampled deeds.
Here for revenge the Sabine troops contend;
The Romans there with arms the prey defend.
Wearied with tedious war, at length they cease;
And both the kings and kingdoms plight the peace.
The friendly chiefs before Jove's altar stand,
Both arm'd, with each a charger in his hand:
A fatted sow for sacrifice is led,
With imprecations on the perjur'd head.
Near this, the traitor Metius, stretch'd between

Four fiery steeds, is dragg'd along the green,
By Tullus' doom: the brambles drink his blood,
And his torn limbs are left the vulture's food.
There, Porsena to Rome proud Tarquin brings,
And would by force restore the banish'd kings.
One tyrant for his fellow-tyrant fights;
The Roman youth assert their native rights.
Before the town the Tuscan army lies,
To win by famine, or by fraud surprise.
Their king, half-threat'ning,
half-disdaining stood,
While Cocles broke the bridge, and stemm'd
the flood.
The captive maids there tempt the raging tide,
Scap'd from their chains, with Clœlia
for their guide.
High on a rock heroic Manlius stood,
To guard the temple, and the temple's god.
Then Rome was poor; and there you
might behold
The palace thatch'd with straw,
now roof'd with gold.
The silver goose before the shining gate
There flew, and, by her cackle, sav'd the state.
She told the Gauls' approach;
th' approaching Gauls,
Obscure in night, ascend, and seize the walls.
The gold dissembled well their yellow hair,
And golden chains on their white necks
they wear.
Gold are their vests; long Alpine spears
they wield,
And their left arm sustains a length of shield.
Hard by, the leaping Salian priests advance;
And naked thro' the streets the mad
Luperci dance,

In caps of wool; the targets dropp'd
from heav'n.
Here modest matrons, in soft litters driv'n,
To pay their vows in solemn pomp appear,
And odorous gums in their chaste hands
they bear.
Far hence remov'd, the Stygian seats are seen;
Pains of the damn'd, and punish'd Catiline
Hung on a rock—the traitor; and, around,
The Furies hissing from the nether ground.
Apart from these, the happy souls he draws,
And Cato's holy ghost dispensing laws.

Betwixt the quarters flows a golden sea;
But foaming surges there in silver play.
The dancing dolphins with their tails divide
The glitt'ring waves, and cut the precious tide.
Amid the main, two mighty fleets engage
Their brazen beaks, oppos'd with equal rage.
Actium surveys the well-disputed prize;
Leucate's wat'ry plain with foamy billows fries.
Young Cæsar, on the stern, in armor bright,
Here leads the Romans and their gods to fight:
His beamy temples shoot their flames afar,
And o'er his head is hung the Julian star.
Agrippa seconds him, with prosp'rous gales,
And, with propitious gods, his foes assails:
A naval crown, that binds his manly brows,
The happy fortune of the fight foreshows.
Rang'd on the line oppos'd, Antonius brings
Barbarian aids, and troops of Eastern kings;
Th' Arabians near, and Bactrians from afar,
Of tongues discordant, and a mingled war:
And, rich in gaudy robes, amidst the strife,
His ill fate follows him—th' Egyptian wife.
Moving they fight; with oars and forky prows
The froth is gather'd, and the water glows.

It seems, as if the Cyclades again
Were rooted up, and justled in the main;
Or floating mountains floating mountains meet;
Such is the fierce encounter of the fleet.
Fireballs are thrown, and pointed jav'lins fly;
The fields of Neptune take a purple dye.
The queen herself, amidst the loud alarms,
With cymbals toss'd her fainting soldiers warms—
Fool as she was! who had not yet divin'd
Her cruel fate, nor saw the snakes behind.
Her country gods, the monsters of the sky,
Great Neptune, Pallas, and Love's Queen defy:
The dog Anubis barks, but barks in vain,
Nor longer dares oppose th' ethereal train.
Mars in the middle of the shining shield
Is grav'd, and strides along the liquid field.
The Diræ souse from heav'n with swift descent;
And Discord, dyed in blood, with garments rent,
Divides the prease: her steps Bellona treads,
And shakes her iron rod above their heads.
This seen, Apollo, from his Actian height,
Pours down his arrows; at whose winged flight
The trembling Indians and Egyptians yield,
And soft Sabæans quit the wat'ry field.
The fatal mistress hoists her silken sails,
And, shrinking from the fight, invokes the gales.
Aghast she looks, and heaves her breast for breath,
Panting, and pale with fear of future death.
The god had figur'd her as driv'n along
By winds and waves, and scudding thro' the throng.
Just opposite, sad Nilus opens wide
His arms and ample bosom to the tide,
And spreads his mantle o'er the winding coast,
In which he wraps his queen, and hides the flying host.

The victor to the gods his thanks express'd,
And Rome, triumphant, with his presence bless'd.
Three hundred temples in the town he plac'd;
With spoils and altars ev'ry temple grac'd.
Three shining nights, and three succeeding days,
The fields resound with shouts,
the streets with praise,
The domes with songs, the theaters with plays.
All altars flame: before each altar lies,
Drench'd in his gore, the destin'd sacrifice.
Great Cæsar sits sublime upon his throne,
Before Apollo's porch of Parian stone;
Accepts the presents vow'd for victory,
And hangs the monumental crowns on high.
Vast crowds of vanquish'd nations march along,
Various in arms, in habit, and in tongue.
Here, Mulciber assigns the proper place
For Carians, and th' ungirt Numidian race;
Then ranks the Thracians in the second row,
With Scythians, expert in the dart and bow.
And here the tam'd Euphrates humbly glides,
And there the Rhine submits her swelling tides,
And proud Araxes, whom no bridge could bind;
The Danes' unconquer'd offspring march behind,
And Morini, the last of humankind.

These figures, on the shield divinely wrought,
By Vulcan labor'd, and by Venus brought,
With joy and wonder fill the hero's thought.
Unknown the names, he yet admires the grace,
And bears aloft the fame and fortune of his race.

Book IX

Turnus takes advantage of Æneas's absence, fires some of his ships (which are transformed into sea nymphs), and assaults his camp. The Trojans, reduced to the last extremities, send Nisus and Euryalus to recall Æneas; which furnishes the poet with that admirable episode of their friendship, generosity, and the conclusion of their adventures.

While these affairs in distant places pass'd,
The various Iris Juno sends with haste,
To find bold Turnus, who, with anxious thought,
The secret shade of his great grandsire sought.
Retir'd alone she found the daring man,
And op'd her rosy lips, and thus began:
"What none of all the gods could grant thy vows,
That, Turnus, this auspicious day bestows.
Æneas, gone to seek th' Arcadian prince,
Has left the Trojan camp without defense;
And, short of succors there, employs his pains
In parts remote to raise the Tuscan swains.
Now snatch an hour that favors thy designs;
Unite thy forces, and attack their lines."
This said, on equal wings she pois'd her weight,
And form'd a radiant rainbow in her flight.

The Daunian hero lifts his hands eyes,
And thus invokes the goddess as she flies:
"Iris, the grace of heav'n, what pow'r divine
Has sent thee down, thro' dusky clouds to shine?
See, they divide; immortal day appears,
And glitt'ring planets dancing in their spheres!

With joy, these happy omens I obey,
And follow to the war the god that leads the way."
Thus having said, as by the brook he stood,
He scoop'd the water from the crystal flood;
Then with his hands the drops to heav'n he throws,
And loads the pow'rs above with offer'd vows.

Now march the bold confed'rates thro' the plain,
Well hors'd, well clad; a rich and shining train.
Messapus leads the van; and, in the rear,
The sons of Tyrrheus in bright arms appear.
In the main battle, with his flaming crest,
The mighty Turnus tow'rs above the rest.
Silent they move, majestically slow,
Like ebbing Nile, or Ganges in his flow.
The Trojans view the dusty cloud from far,
And the dark menace of the distant war.
Caicus from the rampire saw it rise,
Black'ning the fields, and thick'ning
thro' the skies.
Then to his fellows thus aloud he calls:
"What rolling clouds, my friends,
approach the walls?
Arm! arm! and man the works!
prepare your spears
And pointed darts! the Latian host appears."

Thus warn'd, they shut their gates;
with shouts ascend
The bulwarks, and, secure, their foes attend:
For their wise gen'ral, with foreseeing care,
Had charg'd them not to tempt the doubtful war,
Nor, tho' provok'd, in open fields advance,
But close within their lines attend their chance.
Unwilling, yet they keep the strict command,
And sourly wait in arms the hostile band.
The fiery Turnus flew before the rest:

A piebald steed of Thracian strain he press'd;
His helm of massy gold, and crimson was his crest.
With twenty horse to second his designs,
An unexpected foe, he fac'd the lines.
"Is there," he said, "in arms, who bravely dare
His leader's honor and his danger share?"
Then spurring on, his brandish'd dart he threw,
In sign of war: applauding shouts ensue.

Amaz'd to find a dastard race, that run
Behind the rampires and the battle shun,
He rides around the camp, with rolling eyes,
And stops at ev'ry post, and ev'ry passage tries.
So roams the nightly wolf about the fold:
Wet with descending show'rs, and stiff with cold,
He howls for hunger, and he grins for pain,
(His gnashing teeth are exercis'd in vain,)
And, impotent of anger, finds no way
In his distended paws to grasp the prey.
The mothers listen; but the bleating lambs
Securely swig the dug, beneath the dams.
Thus ranges eager Turnus o'er the plain.
Sharp with desire, and furious with disdain;
Surveys each passage with a piercing sight,
To force his foes in equal field to fight.
Thus while he gazes round, at length he spies,
Where, fenc'd with strong redoubts, their navy lies,
Close underneath the walls; the washing tide
Secures from all approach this weaker side.
He takes the wish'd occasion, fills his hand
With ready fires, and shakes a flaming brand.
Urg'd by his presence, ev'ry soul is warm'd,
And ev'ry hand with kindled firs is arm'd.
From the fir'd pines the scatt'ring sparkles fly;
Fat vapors, mix'd with flames, involve the sky.
What pow'r, O Muses, could avert the flame
Which threaten'd, in the fleet, the Trojan name?

Tell: for the fact, thro' length of time obscure,
Is hard to faith; yet shall the fame endure.

'Tis said that, when the chief prepar'd his flight,
And fell'd his timber from Mount Ida's height,
The grandam goddess then approach'd her son,
And with a mother's majesty begun:
"Grant me," she said, "the sole request I bring,
Since conquer'd heav'n has own'd you for its king.
On Ida's brows, for ages past, there stood,
With firs and maples fill'd, a shady wood;
And on the summit rose a sacred grove,
Where I was worship'd with religious love.
Those woods, that holy grove, my long delight,
I gave the Trojan prince, to speed his flight.
Now, fill'd with fear, on their behalf I come;
Let neither winds o'erset, nor waves entomb
The floating forests of the sacred pine;
But let it be their safety to be mine."
Then thus replied her awful son, who rolls
The radiant stars, and heav'n and earth controls:
"How dare you, mother, endless date demand
For vessels molded by a mortal hand?
What then is fate? Shall bold Æneas ride,
Of safety certain, on th' uncertain tide?
Yet, what I can, I grant; when, wafted o'er,
The chief is landed on the Latian shore,
Whatever ships escape the raging storms,
At my command shall change their fading forms
To nymphs divine, and plow the wat'ry way,
Like Dotis and the daughters of the sea."
To seal his sacred vow, by Styx he swore,
The lake of liquid pitch, the dreary shore,
And Phlegethon's innavigable flood,
And the black regions of his brother god.
He said; and shook the skies with his
imperial nod.

And now at length the number'd hours were come,
Prefix'd by fate's irrevocable doom,
When the great Mother of the Gods was free
To save her ships, and finish Jove's decree.
First, from the quarter of the morn, there sprung
A light that sign'd the heav'ns, and shot along;
Then from a cloud, fring'd round with golden fires,
Were timbrels heard, and Berecynthian choirs;
And, last, a voice, with more than mortal sounds,
Both hosts, in arms oppos'd, with equal
horror wounds:
"O Trojan race, your needless aid forbear,
And know, my ships are my peculiar care.
With greater ease the bold Rutulian may,
With hissing brands, attempt to burn the sea,
Than singe my sacred pines. But you,
my charge,
Loos'd from your crooked anchors,
launch at large,
Exalted each a nymph: forsake the sand,
And swim the seas, at Cybele's command."
No sooner had the goddess ceas'd to speak,
When, lo! th' obedient ships their haulsers break;
And, strange to tell, like dolphins, in the main
They plunge their prows, and dive, and spring again:
As many beauteous maids the billows sweep,
As rode before tall vessels on the deep

The foes, surpris'd with wonder, stood aghast;
Messapus curb'd his fiery courser's haste;
Old Tiber roar'd, and, raising up his head,
Call'd back his waters to their oozy bed.
Turnus alone, undaunted, bore the shock,
And with these words his trembling troops bespoke:
"These monsters for the Trojans' fate are meant,
And are by Jove for black presages sent.
He takes the cowards' last relief away;

For fly they cannot, and, constrain'd to stay,
Must yield unfought, a base inglorious prey.
The liquid half of all the globe is lost;
Heav'n shuts the seas, and we secure the coast.
Theirs is no more than that small spot of ground
Which myriads of our martial men surround.
Their fates I fear not, or vain oracles.
'Twas giv'n to Venus they should cross the seas,
And land secure upon the Latian plains:
Their promis'd hour is pass'd, and mine remains.
'Tis in the fate of Turnus to destroy,
With sword and fire, the faithless race of Troy.
Shall such affronts as these alone inflame
The Grecian brothers, and the Grecian name?
My cause and theirs is one; a fatal strife,
And final ruin, for a ravish'd wife.
Was't not enough, that, punish'd for the crime,
They fell; but will they fall a second time?
One would have thought they paid enough before,
To curse the costly sex, and durst offend no more.
Can they securely trust their feeble wall,
A slight partition, a thin interval,
Betwixt their fate and them; when Troy, tho' built
By hands divine, yet perish'd by their guilt?
Lend me, for once, my friends, your valiant hands,
To force from out their lines these dastard bands.
Less than a thousand ships will end this war,
Nor Vulcan needs his fated arms prepare.
Let all the Tuscans, all th' Arcadians, join!
Nor these, nor those, shall frustrate my design.
Let them not fear the treasons of the night,
The robb'd Palladium, the pretended flight:
Our onset shall be made in open light.
No wooden engine shall their town betray;
Fires they shall have around, but fires by day.
No Grecian babes before their camp appear,
Whom Hector's arms detain'd to the tenth tardy year.

Now, since the sun is rolling to the west,
Give we the silent night to needful rest:
Refresh your bodies, and your arms prepare;
The morn shall end the small remains of war."

The post of honor to Messapus falls,
To keep the nightly guard, to watch the walls,
To pitch the fires at distances around,
And close the Trojans in their scanty ground.
Twice seven Rutulian captains ready stand,
And twice seven hundred horse these
    chiefs command;
All clad in shining arms the works invest,
Each with a radiant helm and waving crest.
Stretch'd at their length, they press the
    grassy ground;
They laugh, they sing, (the jolly bowls go round,)
With lights and cheerful fires renew the day,
And pass the wakeful night in feasts and play.

The Trojans, from above, their foes beheld,
And with arm'd legions all the rampires fill'd.
Seiz'd with affright, their gates they first explore;
Join works to works with bridges, tow'r to tow'r:
Thus all things needful for defense abound.
Mnestheus and brave Seresthus walk the round,
Commission'd by their absent prince to share
The common danger, and divide the care.
The soldiers draw their lots, and, as they fall,
By turns relieve each other on the wall.

Nigh where the foes their utmost guards advance,
To watch the gate was warlike Nisus' chance.
His father Hyrtacus of noble blood;
His mother was a huntress of the wood,
And sent him to the wars. Well could he bear
His lance in fight, and dart the flying spear,

But better skill'd unerring shafts to send.
Beside him stood Euryalus, his friend:
Euryalus, than whom the Trojan host
No fairer face, or sweeter air, could boast,
Scarce had the down to shade his cheeks begun.
One was their care, and their delight was one:
One common hazard in the war they shar'd,
And now were both by choice upon the guard.

Then Nisus thus: "Or do the gods inspire
This warmth, or make we gods of our desire?
A gen'rous ardor boils within my breast,
Eager of action, enemy to rest:
This urges me to fight, and fires my mind
To leave a memorable name behind.
Thou see'st the foe secure; how faintly shine
Their scatter'd fires! the most, in sleep supine
Along the ground, an easy conquest lie:
The wakeful few the fuming flagon ply;
All hush'd around. Now hear what I revolve—
A thought unripe—and scarcely yet resolve.
Our absent prince both camp and council mourn;
By message both would hasten his return:
If they confer what I demand on thee,
(For fame is recompense enough for me,)
Methinks, beneath yon hill, I have espied
A way that safely will my passage guide."

Euryalus stood list'ning while he spoke,
With love of praise and noble envy struck;
Then to his ardent friend expos'd his mind:
"All this, alone, and leaving me behind!
Am I unworthy, Nisus, to be join'd?
Thinkist thou I can my share of glory yield,
Or send thee unassisted to the field?
Not so my father taught my childhood arms;
Born in a siege, and bred among alarms!

Nor is my youth unworthy of my friend,
Nor of the heav'n-born hero I attend.
The thing call'd life, with ease I can disclaim,
And think it over-sold to purchase fame."

Then Nisus thus: "Alas! thy tender years
Would minister new matter to my fears.
So may the gods, who view this friendly strife,
Restore me to thy lov'd embrace with life,
Condemn'd to pay my vows, (as sure I trust,)
This thy request is cruel and unjust.
But if some chance—as many chances are,
And doubtful hazards, in the deeds of war—
If one should reach my head, there let it fall,
And spare thy life; I would not perish all.
Thy bloomy youth deserves a longer date:
Live thou to mourn thy love's unhappy fate;
To bear my mangled body from the foe,
Or buy it back, and fun'ral rites bestow.
Or, if hard fortune shall those dues deny,
Thou canst at least an empty tomb supply.
O let not me the widow's tears renew!
Nor let a mother's curse my name pursue:
Thy pious parent, who, for love of thee,
Forsook the coasts of friendly Sicily,
Her age committing to the seas and wind,
When ev'ry weary matron stay'd behind."
To this, Euryalus: "You plead in vain,
And but protract the cause you cannot gain.
No more delays, but haste!" With that, he wakes
The nodding watch; each to his office takes.
The guard reliev'd, the gen'rous couple went
To find the council at the royal tent.

All creatures else forgot their daily care,
And sleep, the common gift of nature, share;
Except the Trojan peers, who wakeful sate

In nightly council for th' endanger'd state.
They vote a message to their absent chief,
Shew their distress, and beg a swift relief.
Amid the camp a silent seat they chose,
Remote from clamor, and secure from foes.
On their left arms their ample shields they bear,
The right reclin'd upon the bending spear.
Now Nisus and his friend approach the guard,
And beg admission, eager to be heard:
Th' affair important, not to be deferr'd.
Ascanius bids 'em be conducted in,
Ord'ring the more experienc'd to begin.
Then Nisus thus: "Ye fathers, lend your ears;
Nor judge our bold attempt beyond our years.
The foe, securely drench'd in sleep and wine,
Neglect their watch; the fires but thinly shine;
And where the smoke in cloudy vapors flies,
Cov'ring the plain, and curling to the skies,
Betwixt two paths, which at the gate divide,
Close by the sea, a passage we have spied,
Which will our way to great Æneas guide.
Expect each hour to see him safe again,
Loaded with spoils of foes in battle slain.
Snatch we the lucky minute while we may;
Nor can we be mistaken in the way;
For, hunting in the vale, we both have seen
The rising turrets, and the stream between,
And know the winding course, with ev'ry ford."

He ceas'd; and old Alethes took the word:
"Our country gods, in whom our trust we place,
Will yet from ruin save the Trojan race,
While we behold such dauntless worth appear
In dawning youth, and souls so void of fear."
Then into tears of joy the father broke;
Each in his longing arms by turns he took;
Panted and paus'd; and thus again he spoke:

"Ye brave young men, what equal gifts can we,
In recompense of such desert, decree?
The greatest, sure, and best you can receive,
The gods and your own conscious worth will give.
The rest our grateful gen'ral will bestow,
And young Ascanius till his manhood owe."

"And I, whose welfare in my father lies,"
Ascanius adds, "by the great deities,
By my dear country, by my household gods,
By hoary Vesta's rites and dark abodes,
Adjure you both, (on you my fortune stands;
That and my faith I plight into your hands,)
Make me but happy in his safe return,
Whose wanted presence I can only mourn;
Your common gift shall two large goblets be
Of silver, wrought with curious imagery,
And high emboss'd, which, when
old Priam reign'd,
My conqu'ring sire at sack'd Arisba gain'd;
And more, two tripods cast in antic mold,
With two great talents of the finest gold;
Beside a costly bowl, engrav'd with art,
Which Dido gave, when first she gave her heart.
But, if in conquer'd Italy we reign,
When spoils by lot the victor shall obtain,
Thou saw'st the courser by proud Turnus press'd:
That, Nisus, and his arms, and nodding crest,
And shield, from chance exempt,
shall be thy share:
Twelve lab'ring slaves, twelve handmaids
young and fair
All clad in rich attire, and train'd with care;
And, last, a Latian field with fruitful plains,
And a large portion of the king's domains.
But thou, whose years are more to mine allied,
No fate my vow'd affection shall divide

From thee, heroic youth! Be wholly mine;
Take full possession; all my soul is thine.
One faith, one fame, one fate, shall both attend;
My life's companion, and my bosom friend:
My peace shall be committed to thy care,
And to thy conduct my concerns in war."

Then thus the young Euryalus replied:
"Whatever fortune, good or bad, betide,
The same shall be my age, as now my youth;
No time shall find me wanting to my truth.
This only from your goodness let me gain
(And, this ungranted, all rewards are vain)
Of Priam's royal race my mother came—
And sure the best that ever bore the name—
Whom neither Troy nor Sicily could hold
From me departing, but, o'erspent and old,
My fate she follow'd. Ignorant of this
(Whatever) danger, neither parting kiss,
Nor pious blessing taken, her I leave,
And in this only act of all my life deceive.
By this right hand and conscious Night I swear,
My soul so sad a farewell could not bear.
Be you her comfort; fill my vacant place
(Permit me to presume so great a grace)
Support her age, forsaken and distress'd.
That hope alone will fortify my breast
Against the worst of fortunes, and of fears."
He said. The mov'd assistants melt in tears.

Then thus Ascanius, wonderstruck to see
That image of his filial piety:
"So great beginnings, in so green an age,
Exact the faith which I again engage.
Thy mother all the dues shall justly claim,
Creüsa had, and only want the name.
Whate'er event thy bold attempt shall have,

'Tis merit to have borne a son so brave.
Now by my head, a sacred oath, I swear,
(My father us'd it,) what, returning here
Crown'd with success, I for thyself prepare,
That, if thou fail, shall thy lov'd mother share."

He said, and weeping, while he spoke the word,
From his broad belt he drew a shining sword,
Magnificent with gold. Lycaon made,
And in an ivory scabbard sheath'd the blade.
This was his gift. Great Mnestheus gave
his friend
A lion's hide, his body to defend;
And good Alethes furnish'd him, beside,
With his own trusty helm, of temper tried.

Thus arm'd they went. The noble Trojans wait
Their issuing forth, and follow to the gate
With prayers and vows. Above the rest appears
Ascanius, manly far beyond his years,
And messages committed to their care,
Which all in winds were lost, and flitting air.

The trenches first they pass'd; then took their way
Where their proud foes in pitch'd pavilions lay;
To many fatal, ere themselves were slain.
They found the careless host dispers'd
upon the plain,
Who, gorg'd, and drunk with wine,
supinely snore.
Unharness'd chariots stand along the shore:
Amidst the wheels and reins, the goblet by,
A medley of debauch and war, they lie.
Observing Nisus shew'd his friend the sight:
"Behold a conquest gain'd without a fight.
Occasion offers, and I stand prepar'd;
There lies our way; be thou upon the guard,
And look around, while I securely go,

And hew a passage thro' the sleeping foe."
Softly he spoke; then striding took his way,
With his drawn sword, where haughty Rhamnes lay;
His head rais'd high on tapestry beneath,
And heaving from his breast, he drew his breath;
A king and prophet, by King Turnus lov'd:
But fate by prescience cannot be remov'd.
Him and his sleeping slaves he slew; then spies
Where Remus, with his rich retinue, lies.
His armor-bearer first, and next he kills
His charioteer, entrench'd betwixt the wheels
And his lov'd horses; last invades their lord;
Full on his neck he drives the fatal sword:
The gasping head flies off; a purple flood
Flows from the trunk, that welters in the blood,
Which, by the spurning heels dispers'd around,
The bed besprinkles and bedews the ground.
Lamus the bold, and Lamyrus the strong,
He slew, and then Serranus fair and young.
From dice and wine the youth retir'd to rest,
And puff'd the fumy god from out his breast:
Ev'n then he dreamt of drink and lucky play—
More lucky, had it lasted till the day.
The famish'd lion thus, with hunger bold,
O'erleaps the fences of the nightly fold,
And tears the peaceful flocks: with silent awe
Trembling they lie, and pant beneath his paw.

Nor with less rage Euryalus employs
The wrathful sword, or fewer foes destroys;
But on th' ignoble crowd his fury flew;
He Fadus, Hebesus, and Rhœtus slew.
Oppress'd with heavy sleep the former fell,
But Rhœtus wakeful, and observing all:
Behind a spacious jar he slink'd for fear;
The fatal iron found and reach'd him there;
For, as he rose, it pierc'd his naked side,

And, reeking, thence return'd in crimson dyed.
The wound pours out a stream of wine and blood;
The purple soul comes floating in the flood.

Now, where Messapus quarter'd, they arrive.
The fires were fainting there, and just alive;
The warrior-horses, tied in order, fed.
Nisus observ'd the discipline, and said:
"Our eager thirst of blood may both betray;
And see the scatter'd streaks of dawning day,
Foe to nocturnal thefts. No more, my friend;
Here let our glutted execution end.
A lane thro' slaughter'd bodies we have made."
The bold Euryalus, tho' loth, obey'd.
Of arms, and arras, and of plate, they find
A precious load; but these they leave behind.
Yet, fond of gaudy spoils, the boy would stay
To make the rich caparison his prey,
Which on the steed of conquer'd Rhamnes lay.
Nor did his eyes less longingly behold
The girdle-belt, with nails of burnish'd gold.
This present Cædicus the rich bestow'd
On Remulus, when friendship first they vow'd,
And, absent, join'd in hospitable ties:
He, dying, to his heir bequeath'd the prize;
Till, by the conqu'ring Ardean troops oppress'd,
He fell; and they the glorious gift possess'd.
These glitt'ring spoils (now made the victor's gain)
He to his body suits, but suits in vain:
Messapus' helm he finds among the rest,
And laces on, and wears the waving crest.
Proud of their conquest, prouder of their prey,
They leave the camp, and take the ready way.

But far they had not pass'd, before they spied
Three hundred horse, with Volscens for
their guide.
The queen a legion to King Turnus sent;

But the swift horse the slower foot prevent,
And now, advancing, sought the leader's tent.
They saw the pair; for, thro' the doubtful shade,
His shining helm Euryalus betray'd,
On which the moon with full reflection play'd.
"'Tis not for naught," cried Volscens from the crowd,
"These men go there;" then rais'd his voice aloud:
"Stand! stand! why thus in arms? And whither bent?
From whence, to whom, and on what errand sent?"
Silent they scud away, and haste their flight
To neighb'ring woods, and trust themselves to night.
The speedy horse all passages belay,
And spur their smoking steeds to cross their way,
And watch each entrance of the winding wood.
Black was the forest: thick with beech it stood,
Horrid with fern, and intricate with thorn;
Few paths of human feet, or tracks of beasts, were worn.
The darkness of the shades, his heavy prey,
And fear, misled the younger from his way.
But Nisus hit the turns with happier haste,
And, thoughtless of his friend, the forest pass'd,
And Alban plains, from Alba's name so call'd,
Where King Latinus then his oxen stall'd;
Till, turning at the length, he stood his ground,
And miss'd his friend, and cast his eyes around:
"Ah wretch!" he cried, "where have I left behind
Th' unhappy youth? where shall I hope to find?
Or what way take?" Again he ventures back,
And treads the mazes of his former track.
He winds the wood, and, list'ning, hears the noise
Of tramping coursers, and the riders' voice.
The sound approach'd; and suddenly he view'd
The foes enclosing, and his friend pursued,

Forelaid and taken, while he strove in vain
The shelter of the friendly shades to gain.
What should he next attempt? what arms employ,
What fruitless force, to free the captive boy?
Or desperate should he rush and lose his life,
With odds oppress'd, in such unequal strife?

Resolv'd at length, his pointed spear he shook;
And, casting on the moon a mournful look:
"Guardian of groves, and goddess of the night,
Fair queen," he said, "direct my dart aright.
If e'er my pious father, for my sake,
Did grateful off'rings on thy altars make,
Or I increas'd them with my sylvan toils,
And hung thy holy roofs with savage spoils,
Give me to scatter these." Then from his ear
He pois'd, and aim'd, and launch'd the trembling spear.
The deadly weapon, hissing from the grove,
Impetuous on the back of Sulmo drove;
Pierc'd his thin armor, drank his vital blood,
And in his body left the broken
He staggers round; his eyeballs roll in death,
And with short sobs he gasps away his breath.
All stand amaz'd; a second jav'lin flies
With equal strength, and quivers thro' the skies.
This thro' thy temples, Tagus, forc'd the way,
And in the brainpan warmly buried lay.
Fierce Volscens foams with rage, and, gazing round,
Descried not him who gave the fatal wound,
Nor knew to fix revenge: "But thou," he cries,
"Shalt pay for both," and at the pris'ner flies
With his drawn sword. Then, struck with deep despair,
That cruel sight the lover could not bear;
But from his covert rush'd in open view,

And sent his voice before him as he flew:
"Me! me!" he cried, "turn all your swords alone
On me; the fact confess'd, the fault my own.
He neither could nor durst, the guiltless youth:
Ye moon and stars, bear witness to the truth!
His only crime (if friendship can offend)
Is too much love to his unhappy friend."
Too late he speaks: the sword, which fury guides,
Driv'n with full force, had pierc'd his tender sides.
Down fell the beauteous youth: the yawning wound
Gush'd out a purple stream, and stain'd the ground.
His snowy neck reclines upon his breast,
Like a fair flow'r by the keen share oppress'd;
Like a white poppy sinking on the plain,
Whose heavy head is overcharg'd with rain.
Despair, and rage, and vengeance justly vow'd,
Drove Nisus headlong on the hostile crowd.
Volscens he seeks; on him alone he bends:
Borne back and bor'd by his surrounding friends,
Onward he press'd, and kept him still in sight;
Then whirl'd aloft his sword with all his might:
Th' unerring steel descended while he spoke,
Pierced his wide mouth, and thro' his weazon broke.
Dying, he slew; and, stagg'ring on the plain,
With swimming eyes he sought his lover slain;
Then quiet on his bleeding bosom fell,
Content, in death, to be reveng'd so well.

O happy friends! for, if my verse can give
Immortal life, your fame shall ever live,
Fix'd as the Capitol's foundation lies,
And spread, where'er the Roman eagle flies!

The conqu'ring party first divide the prey,
Then their slain leader to the camp convey.
With wonder, as they went, the troops were fill'd,
To see such numbers whom so few had kill'd.
Serranus, Rhamnes, and the rest, they found:

Vast crowds the dying and the dead surround;
And the yet reeking blood o'erflows the ground.
All knew the helmet which Messapus lost,
But mourn'd a purchase that so dear had cost.
Now rose the ruddy morn from Tithon's bed,
And with the dawn of day the skies o'erspread;
Nor long the sun his daily course withheld,
But added colors to the world reveal'd:
When early Turnus, wak'ning with the light,
All clad in armor, calls his troops to fight.
His martial men with fierce harangue he fir'd,
And his own ardor in their souls inspir'd.
This done- to give new terror to his foes,
The heads of Nisus and his friend he shows,
Rais'd high on pointed spears—a ghastly sight:
Loud peals of shouts ensue,
and barbarous delight.

Meantime the Trojans run, where danger calls;
They line their trenches, and they man their walls.
In front extended to the left they stood;
Safe was the right, surrounded by the flood.
But, casting from their tow'rs a frightful view,
They saw the faces, which too well they knew,
Tho' then disguis'd in death, and smear'd all o'er
With filth obscene, and dropping putrid gore.
Soon hasty fame thro' the sad city bears
The mournful message to the mother's ears.
An icy cold benumbs her limbs; she shakes;
Her cheeks the blood, her hand the web forsakes.
She runs the rampires round amidst the war,
Nor fears the flying darts; she rends her hair,
And fills with loud laments the liquid air.
"Thus, then, my lov'd Euryalus appears!
Thus looks the prop my declining years!
Was't on this face my famish'd eyes I fed?
Ah! how unlike the living is the dead!

And could'st thou leave me, cruel, thus alone?
Not one kind kiss from a departing son!
No look, no last adieu before he went,
In an ill-boding hour to slaughter sent!
Cold on the ground, and pressing foreign clay,
To Latian dogs and fowls he lies a prey!
Nor was I near to close his dying eyes,
To wash his wounds, to weep his obsequies,
To call about his corpse his crying friends,
Or spread the mantle (made for other ends)
On his dear body, which I wove with care,
Nor did my daily pains or nightly labor spare.
Where shall I find his corpse? what earth sustains
His trunk dismember'd, and his cold remains?
For this, alas! I left my needful ease,
Expos'd my life to winds and winter seas!
If any pity touch Rutulian hearts,
Here empty all your quivers, all your darts;
Or, if they fail, thou, Jove, conclude my woe,
And send me thunderstruck to shades below!"
Her shrieks and clamors pierce the Trojans' ears,
Unman their courage, and augment their fears;
Nor young Ascanius could the sight sustain,
Nor old Ilioneus his tears restrain,
But Actor and Idæus jointly sent,
To bear the madding mother to her tent.

And now the trumpets terribly, from far,
With rattling clangor, rouse the sleepy war.
The soldiers' shouts succeed the brazen sounds;
And heav'n, from pole to pole, the noise rebounds.
The Volscians bear their shields upon their head,
And, rushing forward, form a moving shed.
These fill the ditch; those pull the bulwarks down:
Some raise the ladders; others scale the town.
But, where void spaces on the walls appear,

Or thin defense, they pour their forces there.
With poles and missive weapons, from afar,
The Trojans keep aloof the rising war.
Taught, by their ten years' siege,
defensive fight,
They roll down ribs of rocks,
an unresisted weight,
To break the penthouse with the pond'rous blow,
Which yet the patient Volscians undergo:
But could not bear th' unequal combat long;
For, where the Trojans find the thickest throng,
The ruin falls: their shatter'd shields give way,
And their crush'd heads become an easy prey.
They shrink for fear, abated of their rage,
Nor longer dare in a blind fight engage;
Contented now to gall them from below
With darts and slings, and with the distant bow.

Elsewhere Mezentius, terrible to view,
A blazing pine within the trenches threw.
But brave Messapus, Neptune's warlike son,
Broke down the palisades, the trenches won,
And loud for ladders calls, to scale the town.

Calliope, begin! Ye sacred Nine,
Inspire your poet in his high design,
To sing what slaughter manly Turnus made,
What souls he sent below the Stygian shade,
What fame the soldiers with their captain share,
And the vast circuit of the fatal war;
For you in singing martial facts excel;
You best remember, and alone can tell.

There stood a tow'r, amazing to the sight,
Built up of beams, and of stupendous height:
Art, and the nature of the place, conspir'd
To furnish all the strength that war requir'd.
To level this, the bold Italians join;

The wary Trojans obviate their design;
With weighty stones o'erwhelm their troops below,
Shoot thro' the loopholes, and sharp jav'lins throw.
Turnus, the chief, toss'd from his thund'ring hand
Against the wooden walls, a flaming brand:
It stuck, the fiery plague; the winds were high;
The planks were season'd, and the timber dry.
Contagion caught the posts; it spread along,
Scorch'd, and to distance drove the scatter'd throng.
The Trojans fled; the fire pursued amain,
Still gath'ring fast upon the trembling train;
Till, crowding to the corners of the wall,
Down the defense and the defenders fall.
The mighty flaw makes heav'n itself resound:
The dead and dying Trojans strew the ground.
The tow'r, that follow'd on the fallen crew,
Whelm'd o'er their heads, and buried whom it slew:
Some stuck upon the darts themselves had sent;
All the same equal ruin underwent.

Young Lycus and Helenor only scape;
Sav'd—how, they know not—from the steepy leap.
Helenor, elder of the two: by birth,
On one side royal, one a son of earth,
Whom to the Lydian king Licymnia bare,
And sent her boasted bastard to the war
(A privilege which none but freemen share).
Slight were his arms, a sword and silver shield:
No marks of honor charg'd its empty field.
Light as he fell, so light the youth arose,
And rising, found himself amidst his foes;
Nor flight was left, nor hopes to force his way.

Embolden'd by despair, he stood at bay;
And—like a stag, whom all the troop surrounds
Of eager huntsmen and invading hounds—
Resolv'd on death, he dissipates his fears,
And bounds aloft against the pointed spears:
So dares the youth, secure of death; and throws
His dying body on his thickest foes.

But Lycus, swifter of his feet by far,
Runs, doubles, winds and turns, amidst the war;
Springs to the walls, and leaves his foes behind,
And snatches at the beam he first can find;
Looks up, and leaps aloft at all the stretch,
In hopes the helping hand of some kind
    friend to reach.
But Turnus follow'd hard his hunted prey
(His spear had almost reach'd him in the way,
Short of his reins, and scarce a span behind)
"Fool!" said the chief, "tho' fleeter than the wind,
Couldst thou presume to scape, when I pursue?"
He said, and downward by the feet he drew
The trembling dastard; at the tug he falls;
Vast ruins come along, rent from the
    smoking walls.
Thus on some silver swan, or tim'rous hare,
Jove's bird comes sousing down from upper air;
Her crooked talons truss the fearful prey:
Then out of sight she soars, and wings her way.
So seizes the grim wolf the tender lamb,
In vain lamented by the bleating dam.

Then rushing onward with a barb'rous cry,
The troops of Turnus to the combat fly.
The ditch with fagots fill'd, the daring foe
Toss'd firebrands to the steepy turrets throw.

Ilioneus, as bold Lucetius came
To force the gate, and feed the kindling flame,

Roll'd down the fragment of a rock so right,
It crush'd him double underneath the weight.
Two more young Liger and Asylas slew:
To bend the bow young Liger better knew;
Asylas best the pointed jav'lin threw.
Brave Cæneus laid Ortygius on the plain;
The victor Cæneus was by Turnus slain.
By the same hand, Clonius and Itys fall,
Sagar, and Ida, standing on the wall.
From Capys' arms his fate Privernus found:
Hurt by Themilla first—but slight the wound—
His shield thrown by, to mitigate the smart,
He clapp'd his hand upon the wounded part:
The second shaft came swift and unespied,
And pierc'd his hand, and nail'd it to his side,
Transfix'd his breathing lungs and beating heart:
The soul came issuing out,
    and hiss'd against the dart.

The son of Arcens shone amid the rest,
In glitt'ring armor and a purple vest,
(Fair was his face, his eyes inspiring love,)
Bred by his father in the Martian grove,
Where the fat altars of Palicus flame,
And send in arms to purchase early fame.
Him when he spied from far, the Tuscan king
Laid by the lance, and took him to the sling,
Thrice whirl'd the thong around his head,
    and threw:
The heated lead half melted as it flew;
It pierc'd his hollow temples and his brain;
The youth came tumbling down,
    and spurn'd the plain.

Then young Ascanius, who, before this day,
Was wont in woods to shoot the savage prey,
First bent in martial strife the twanging bow,
And exercis'd against a human foe,

With this bereft Numanus of his life,
Who Turnus' younger sister took to wife.
Proud of his realm, and of his royal bride,
Vaunting before his troops, and lengthen'd with a stride,
In these insulting terms the Trojans he defied:
"Twice-conquer'd cowards, now your shame is shown,
Coop'd up a second time within your town!
Who dare not issue forth in open field,
But hold your walls before you for a shield.
Thus threat you war? thus our alliance force?
What gods, what madness, hither steer'd your course?
You shall not find the sons of Atreus here,
Nor need the frauds of sly Ulysses fear.
Strong from the cradle, of a sturdy brood,
We bear our newborn infants to the flood;
There bath'd amid the stream, our boys we hold,
With winter harden'd, and inur'd to cold.
They wake before the day to range the wood,
Kill ere they eat, nor taste unconquer'd food.
No sports, but what belong to war, they know:
To break the stubborn colt, to bend the bow.
Our youth, of labor patient, earn their bread;
Hardly they work, with frugal diet fed.
From plows and harrows sent to seek renown,
They fight in fields, and storm the shaken town.
No part of life from toils of war is free,
No change in age, or diff'rence in degree.
We plow and till in arms; our oxen feel,
Instead of goads, the spur and pointed steel;
Th' inverted lance makes furrows in the plain.
Ev'n time, that changes all, yet changes us in vain:
The body, not the mind; nor can control
Th' immortal vigor, or abate the soul.
Our helms defend the young, disguise the gray:

We live by plunder, and delight in prey.
Your vests embroider'd with rich purple shine;
In sloth you glory, and in dances join.
Your vests have sweeping sleeves; with female pride
Your turbants underneath your chins are tied.
Go, Phrygians, to your Dindymus again!
Go, less than women, in the shapes of men!
Go, mix'd with eunuchs, in the Mother's rites,
Where with unequal sound the flute invites;
Sing, dance, and howl, by turns, in Ida's shade:
Resign the war to men, who know the martial trade!"

This foul reproach Ascanius could not hear
With patience, or a vow'd revenge forbear.
At the full stretch of both his hands he drew,
And almost join'd the horns of the tough yew.
But, first, before the throne of Jove he stood,
And thus with lifted hands invok'd the god:
"My first attempt, great Jupiter, succeed!
An annual off'ring in thy grove shall bleed;
A snow-white steer, before thy altar led,
Who, like his mother, bears aloft his head,
Butts with his threat'ning brows, and bellowing stands,
And dares the fight, and spurns the yellow sands."

Jove bow'd the heav'ns, and lent a gracious ear,
And thunder'd on the left, amidst the clear.
Sounded at once the bow; and swiftly flies
The feather'd death, and hisses thro' the skies.
The steel thro' both his temples forc'd the way:
Extended on the ground, Numanus lay.
"Go now, vain boaster, and true valor scorn!
The Phrygians, twice subdued, yet make this third return."

Ascanius said no more. The Trojans shake
The heav'ns with shouting, and new vigor take.

Apollo then bestrode a golden cloud,
To view the feats of arms, and fighting crowd;
And thus the beardless victor he bespoke aloud:
"Advance, illustrious youth, increase in fame,
And wide from east to west extend thy name;
Offspring of gods thyself; and Rome shall owe
To thee a race of demigods below.
This is the way to heav'n: the pow'rs divine
From this beginning date the Julian line.
To thee, to them, and their victorious heirs,
The conquer'd war is due, and the vast
world is theirs.
Troy is too narrow for thy name." He said,
And plunging downward shot his radiant head;
Dispell'd the breathing air, that broke his flight:
Shorn of his beams, a man to mortal sight.
Old Butes' form he took, Anchises' squire,
Now left, to rule Ascanius, by his sire:
His wrinkled visage, and his hoary hairs,
His mien, his habit, and his arms, he wears,
And thus salutes the boy, too forward for his years:
"Suffice it thee, thy father's worthy son,
The warlike prize thou hast already won.
The god of archers gives thy youth a part
Of his own praise, nor envies equal art.
Now tempt the war no more." He said, and flew
Obscure in air, and vanish'd from their view.
The Trojans, by his arms, their patron know,
And hear the twanging of his heav'nly bow.
Then duteous force they use, and Phœbus' name,
To keep from fight the youth too fond of fame.
Undaunted, they themselves no danger shun;
From wall to wall the shouts and clamors run.
They bend their bows; they whirl their slings around;

Heaps of spent arrows fall, and strew the ground;
And helms, and shields, and rattling arms resound.
The combat thickens, like the storm that flies
From westward, when the show'ry Kids arise;
Or patt'ring hail comes pouring on the main,
When Jupiter descends in harden'd rain,
Or bellowing clouds burst with a stormy sound,
And with an armed winter strew the ground.

Pand'rus and Bitias, thunderbolts of war,
Whom Hiera to bold Alcanor bare
On Ida's top, two youths of height and size
Like firs that on their mother mountain rise,
Presuming on their force, the gates unbar,
And of their own accord invite the war.
With fates averse, against their king's command,
Arm'd, on the right and on the left they stand,
And flank the passage: shining steel they wear,
And waving crests above their heads appear.
Thus two tall oaks, that Padus' banks adorn,
Lift up to heav'n their leafy heads unshorn,
And, overpress'd with nature's heavy load,
Dance to the whistling winds, and
at each other nod.
In flows a tide of Latians, when they see
The gate set open, and the passage free;
Bold Quercens, with rash Tmarus, rushing on,
Equicolus, that in bright armor shone,
And Hæmon first; but soon repuls'd they fly,
Or in the well-defended pass they die.
These with success are fir'd, and those with rage,
And each on equal terms at length engage.
Drawn from their lines, and issuing on the plain,
The Trojans hand to hand the fight maintain.

Fierce Turnus in another quarter fought,
When suddenly th' unhop'd-for news
was brought,

The foes had left the fastness of their place,
Prevail'd in fight, and had his men in chase.
He quits th' attack, and, to prevent their fate,
Runs where the giant brothers guard the gate.
The first he met, Antiphates the brave,
But base-begotten on a Theban slave,
Sarpedon's son, he slew: the deadly dart
Found passage thro' his breast, and pierc'd his heart.
Fix'd in the wound th' Italian cornel stood,
Warm'd in his lungs, and in his vital blood.
Aphidnus next, and Erymanthus dies,
And Meropes, and the gigantic size
Of Bitias, threat'ning with his ardent eyes.
Not by the feeble dart he fell oppress'd
(A dart were lost within that roomy breast),
But from a knotted lance, large, heavy, strong,
Which roar'd like thunder as it whirl'd along:
Not two bull hides th' impetuous force withhold,
Nor coat of double mail, with scales of gold.
Down sunk the monster bulk and press'd the ground;
His arms and clatt'ring shield on the vast body sound,
Not with less ruin than the Bajan mole,
Rais'd on the seas, the surges to control,
At once comes tumbling down the rocky wall;
Prone to the deep, the stones disjointed fall
Of the vast pile; the scatter'd ocean flies;
Black sands, discolor'd froth, and mingled mud arise:
The frighted billows roll, and seek the shores;
Then trembles Prochyta, then Ischia roars:
Typhœus, thrown beneath, by Jove's command,
Astonish'd at the flaw that shakes the land,
Soon shifts his weary side, and, scarce awake,
With wonder feels the weight press lighter on his back.

The warrior god the Latian troops inspir'd,
New strung their sinews, and their courage fir'd,
But chills the Trojan hearts with cold affright:
Then black despair precipitates their flight

When Pandarus beheld his brother kill'd,
The town with fear and wild confusion fill'd,
He turns the hinges of the heavy gate
With both his hands, and adds his
  shoulders to the weight
Some happier friends within the walls enclos'd;
The rest shut out, to certain death expos'd:
Fool as he was, and frantic in his care,
T' admit young Turnus, and include the war!
He thrust amid the crowd, securely bold,
Like a fierce tiger pent amid the fold.
Too late his blazing buckler they descry,
And sparkling fires that shot from either eye,
His mighty members, and his ample breast,
His rattling armor, and his crimson crest.

Far from that hated face the Trojans fly,
All but the fool who sought his destiny.
Mad Pandarus steps forth, with vengeance vow'd
For Bitias' death, and threatens thus aloud:
"These are not Ardea's walls, nor this the town
Amata proffers with Lavinia's crown:
'Tis hostile earth you tread. Of hope bereft,
No means of safe return by flight are left."
To whom, with count'nance calm, and soul sedate,
Thus Turnus: "Then begin, and try thy fate:
My message to the ghost of Priam bear;
Tell him a new Achilles sent thee there."

A lance of tough ground ash the Trojan threw,
Rough in the rind, and knotted as it grew:
With his full force he whirl'd it first around;
But the soft yielding air receiv'd the wound:

Imperial Juno turn'd the course before,
And fix'd the wand'ring weapon in the door.

"But hope not thou," said Turnus, "when I strike,
To shun thy fate: our force is not alike,
Nor thy steel temper'd by the Lemnian god."
Then rising, on his utmost stretch he stood,
And aim'd from high: the full descending blow
Cleaves the broad front and beardless cheeks
in two.
Down sinks the giant with a thund'ring sound:
His pond'rous limbs oppress the
trembling ground;
Blood, brains, and foam gush from the
gaping wound:
Scalp, face, and shoulders the keen steel divides,
And the shar'd visage hangs on equal sides.
The Trojans fly from their approaching fate;
And, had the victor then secur'd the gate,
And to his troops without unclos'd the bars,
One lucky day had ended all his wars.
But boiling youth, and blind desire of blood,
Push'd on his fury, to pursue the crowd.
Hamstring'd behind, unhappy Gyges died;
Then Phalaris is added to his side.
The pointed jav'lins from the dead he drew,
And their friends' arms against their fellows threw.
Strong Halys stands in vain; weak Phlegys flies;
Saturnia, still at hand, new force and fire supplies.
Then Halius, Prytanis, Alcander fall,
Engag'd against the foes who scal'd the wall:
But, whom they fear'd without, they found within.
At last, tho' late, by Lynceus he was seen.
He calls new succors, and assaults the prince:
But weak his force, and vain is their defense.
Turn'd to the right, his sword the hero drew,
And at one blow the bold aggressor slew.
He joints the neck; and, with a stroke so strong,

The helm flies off, and bears the head along.
Next him, the huntsman Amycus he kill'd,
In darts invenom'd and in poison skill'd.
Then Clytius fell beneath his fatal spear,
And Creteus, whom the Muses held so dear:
He fought with courage, and he sung the fight;
Arms were his bus'ness, verses his delight.

The Trojan chiefs behold, with rage and grief,
Their slaughter'd friends, and hasten their relief.
Bold Mnestheus rallies first the broken train,
Whom brave Seresthus and his troop sustain.
To save the living, and revenge the dead,
Against one warrior's arms all Troy they led.
"O, void of sense and courage!" Mnestheus cried,
"Where can you hope your coward heads to hide?
Ah! where beyond these rampires can you run?
One man, and in your camp enclos'd, you shun!
Shall then a single sword such slaughter boast,
And pass unpunish'd from a num'rous host?
Forsaking honor, and renouncing fame,
Your gods, your country, and your king
    you shame!"
This just reproach their virtue does excite:
They stand, they join, they thicken to the fight.

Now Turnus doubts, and yet disdains to yield,
But with slow paces measures back the field,
And inches to the walls, where Tiber's tide,
Washing the camp, defends the weaker side.
The more he loses, they advance the more,
And tread in ev'ry step he trod before.
They shout: they bear him back;
    and, whom by might
They cannot conquer, they oppress with weight.

As, compass'd with a wood of spears around,
The lordly lion still maintains his ground;

Grins horrible, retires, and turns again;
Threats his distended paws, and shakes his mane;
He loses while in vain he presses on,
Nor will his courage let him dare to run:
So Turnus fares, and, unresolved of flight,
Moves tardy back, and just recedes from fight.
Yet twice, enrag'd, the combat he renews,
Twice breaks, and twice his broken foes pursues.
But now they swarm, and, with fresh troops supplied,
Come rolling on, and rush from ev'ry side:
Nor Juno, who sustain'd his arms before,
Dares with new strength suffice th' exhausted store;
For Jove, with sour commands, sent Iris down,
To force th' invader from the frighted town.

With labor spent, no longer can he wield
The heavy fanchion, or sustain the shield,
O'erwhelm'd with darts, which from afar they fling:
The weapons round his hollow temples ring;
His golden helm gives way, with stony blows
Batter'd, and flat, and beaten to his brows.
His crest is rash'd away; his ample shield
Is falsified, and round with jav'lins fill'd.

The foe, now faint, the Trojans overwhelm;
And Mnestheus lays hard load upon his helm.
Sick sweat succeeds; he drops at ev'ry pore;
With driving dust his cheeks are pasted o'er;
Shorter and shorter ev'ry gasp he takes;
And vain efforts and hurtless blows he makes.
Plung'd in the flood, and made the waters fly.
The yellow god the welcome burthen bore,
And wip'd the sweat, and wash'd away the gore;
Then gently wafts him to the farther coast,
And sends him safe to cheer his anxious host.

Nullius
Interventu
Divina

Book X

Jupiter calls a council of the gods, and forbids them to intervene on either side. At Æneas's return there is a bloody battle with Turnus killing Pallas and Æneas, Lausus and Mezentius. Mezentius is described as an atheist; Lausas as a pious and virtuous youth. The different actions and death of these two are the subject of a noble episode.

The gates of heav'n unfold: Jove summons all
The gods to council in the common hall.
Sublimely seated, he surveys from far
The fields, the camp, the fortune of the war,
And all th' inferior world. From first to last,
The sov'reign senate in degrees are plac'd.

Then thus th' almighty sire began: "Ye gods,
Natives or denizens of blest abodes,
From whence these murmurs,
and this change of mind,
This backward fate from what was first design'd?
Why this protracted war, when my commands
Pronounc'd a peace, and gave the Latian lands?
What fear or hope on either part divides
Our heav'ns, and arms our powers
on diff'rent sides?
A lawful time of war at length will come,
(Nor need your haste anticipate the doom),
When Carthage shall contend the world with Rome,
Shall force the rigid rocks and Alpine chains,
And, like a flood, come pouring on the plains.
Then is your time for faction and debate,

For partial favor, and permitted hate.
Let now your immature dissension cease;
Sit quiet, and compose your souls to peace."

Thus Jupiter in few unfolds the charge;
But lovely Venus thus replies at large:
"O pow'r immense, eternal energy,
(For to what else protection can we fly?)
Seest thou the proud Rutulians, how they dare
In fields, unpunish'd, and insult my care?
How lofty Turnus vaunts amidst his train,
In shining arms, triumphant on the plain?
Ev'n in their lines and trenches they contend,
And scarce their walls the Trojan troops defend:
The town is fill'd with slaughter, and o'erfloats,
With a red deluge, their increasing moats.
Æneas, ignorant, and far from thence,
Has left a camp expos'd, without defense.
This endless outrage shall they still sustain?
Shall Troy renew'd be forc'd and fir'd again?
A second siege my banish'd issue fears,
And a new Diomede in arms appears.
One more audacious mortal will be found;
And I, thy daughter, wait another wound.
Yet, if with fates averse, without thy leave,
The Latian lands my progeny receive,
Bear they the pains of violated law,
And thy protection from their aid withdraw.
But, if the gods their sure success foretell;
If those of heav'n consent with those of hell,
To promise Italy; who dare debate
The pow'r of Jove, or fix another fate?
What should I tell of tempests on the main,
Of Æolus usurping Neptune's reign?
Of Iris sent, with Bacchanalian heat
T' inspire the matrons, and destroy the fleet?
Now Juno to the Stygian sky descends,

Solicits hell for aid, and arms the fiends.
That new example wanted yet above:
An act that well became the wife of Jove!
Alecto, rais'd by her, with rage inflames
The peaceful bosoms of the Latian dames.
Imperial sway no more exalts my mind;
(Such hopes I had indeed, while Heav'n was kind;)
Now let my happier foes possess my place,
Whom Jove prefers before the Trojan race;
And conquer they, whom you with conquest grace.
Since you can spare, from all your wide command,
No spot of earth, no hospitable land,
Which may my wand'ring fugitives receive;
(Since haughty Juno will not give you leave;)
Then, father, (if I still may use that name,)
By ruin'd Troy, yet smoking from the flame,
I beg you, let Ascanius, by my care,
Be freed from danger, and dismiss'd the war:
Inglorious let him live, without a crown.
The father may be cast on coasts unknown,
Struggling with fate; but let me save the son.
Mine is Cythera, mine the Cyprian tow'rs:
In those recesses, and those sacred bow'rs,
Obscurely let him rest; his right resign
To promis'd empire, and his Julian line.
Then Carthage may th' Ausonian towns destroy,
Nor fear the race of a rejected boy.
What profits it my son to scape the fire,
Arm'd with his gods, and loaded with his sire;
To pass the perils of the seas and wind;
Evade the Greeks, and leave the war behind;
To reach th' Italian shores; if, after all,
Our second Pergamus is doom'd to fall?
Much better had he curb'd his high desires,
And hover'd o'er his ill-extinguish'd fires.
To Simoïs' banks the fugitives restore,
And give them back to war, and all the woes before."

Deep indignation swell'd Saturnia's heart:
"And must I own," she said, "my secret smart,
What with more decence were in silence kept,
And, but for this unjust reproach, had slept?
Did god or man your fav'rite son advise,
With war unhop'd the Latians to surprise?
By fate, you boast, and by the gods' decree,
He left his native land for Italy!
Confess the truth; by mad Cassandra, more
Than Heav'n inspir'd, he sought a foreign shore!
Did I persuade to trust his second Troy
To the raw conduct of a beardless boy,
With walls unfinish'd, which himself forsakes,
And thro' the waves a wand'ring voyage takes?
When have I urg'd him meanly to demand
The Tuscan aid, and arm a quiet land?
Did I or Iris give this mad advice,
Or made the fool himself the fatal choice?
You think it hard, the Latians should destroy
With swords your Trojans, and with fires your Troy!
Hard and unjust indeed, for men to draw
Their native air, nor take a foreign law!
That Turnus is permitted still to live,
To whom his birth a god and goddess give!
But yet is just and lawful for your line
To drive their fields, and force with fraud to join;
Realms, not your own, among your clans divide,
And from the bridegroom tear the promis'd bride;
Petition, while you public arms prepare;
Pretend a peace, and yet provoke a war!
'Twas giv'n to you, your darling son to shroud,
To draw the dastard from the fighting crowd,
And, for a man, obtend an empty cloud.
From flaming fleets you turn'd the fire away,
And chang'd the ships to daughters of the sea.
But is my crime the Queen of Heav'n offends,
If she presume to save her suff'ring friends!

Your son, not knowing what his foes decree,
You say, is absent: absent let him be.
Yours is Cythera, yours the Cyprian tow'rs,
The soft recesses, and the sacred bow'rs.
Why do you then these needless arms prepare,
And thus provoke a people prone to war?
Did I with fire the Trojan town deface,
Or hinder from return your exil'd race?
Was I the cause of mischief, or the man
Whose lawless lust the fatal war began?
Think on whose faith th' adult'rous youth relied;
Who promis'd, who procur'd, the Spartan bride?
When all th' united states of Greece combin'd,
To purge the world of the perfidious kind,
Then was your time to fear the Trojan fate:
Your quarrels and complaints are now too late."

Thus Juno. Murmurs rise, with mix'd applause,
Just as they favor or dislike the cause.
So winds, when yet unfledg'd in woods they lie,
In whispers first their tender voices try,
Then issue on the main with bellowing rage,
And storms to trembling mariners presage.

Then thus to both replied th' imperial god,
Who shakes heav'n's axles with his awful nod.
(When he begins, the silent senate stand
With rev'rence, list'ning to the dread command:
The clouds dispel; the winds their breath restrain;
And the hush'd waves lie flatted on the main.)
"Celestials, your attentive ears incline!
Since," said the god, "the Trojans must not join
In wish'd alliance with the Latian line;
Since endless jarrings and immortal hate
Tend but to discompose our happy state;
The war henceforward be resign'd to fate:
Each to his proper fortune stand or fall;

Equal and unconcern'd I look on all.
Rutulians, Trojans, are the same to me;
And both shall draw the lots their fates decree.
Let these assault, if Fortune be their friend;
And, if she favors those, let those defend:
The Fates will find their way." The Thund'rer said,
And shook the sacred honors of his head,
Attesting Styx, th' inviolable flood,
And the black regions of his brother god.
Trembled the poles of heav'n, and earth
confess'd the nod.
This end the sessions had: the senate rise,
And to his palace wait their sov'reign
thro' the skies.

Meantime, intent upon their siege, the foes
Within their walls the Trojan host enclose:
They wound, they kill, they watch at ev'ry gate;
Renew the fires, and urge their happy fate.

Th' Æneans wish in vain their wanted chief,
Hopeless of flight, more hopeless of relief.
Thin on the tow'rs they stand; and ev'n those few
A feeble, fainting, and dejected crew.
Yet in the face of danger some there stood:
The two bold brothers of Sarpedon's blood,
Asius and Acmon; both th' Assaraci;
Young Hæmon, and tho' young, resolv'd to die.
With these were Clarus and Thymœtes join'd;
Tibris and Castor, both of Lycian kind.
From Acmon's hands a rolling stone there came,
So large, it half deserv'd a mountain's name:
Strong-sinew'd was the youth, and big of bone;
His brother Mnestheus could not more have done,
Or the great father of th' intrepid son.
Some firebrands throw, some flights of arrows send;
And some with darts, and some with stones defend.

Amid the press appears the beauteous boy,
The care of Venus, and the hope of Troy.
His lovely face unarm'd, his head was bare;
In ringlets o'er his shoulders hung his hair.
His forehead circled with a diadem;
Distinguish'd from the crowd,
he shines a gem,
Enchas'd in gold, or polish'd iv'ry set,
Amidst the meaner foil of sable jet.

Nor Ismarus was wanting to the war,
Directing pointed arrows from afar,
And death with poison arm'd—in Lydia born,
Where plenteous harvests the fat fields adorn;
Where proud Pactolus floats the fruitful lands,
And leaves a rich manure of golden sands.
There Capys, author of the Capuan name,
And there was Mnestheus too, increas'd in fame,
Since Turnus from the camp he cast with shame.

Thus mortal war was wag'd on either side.
Meantime the hero cuts the nightly tide:
For, anxious, from Evander when he went,
He sought the Tyrrhene camp,
and Tarchon's tent;
Expos'd the cause of coming to the chief;
His name and country told, and ask'd relief;
Propos'd the terms; his own small
strength declar'd;
What vengeance proud Mezentius had prepar'd:
What Turnus, bold and violent, design'd;
Then shew'd the slipp'ry state of humankind,
And fickle fortune; warn'd him to beware,
And to his wholesome counsel added pray'r.
Tarchon, without delay, the treaty signs,
And to the Trojan troops the Tuscan joins.

They soon set sail; nor now the fates withstand;
Their forces trusted with a foreign hand.
Æneas leads; upon his stern appear
Two lions carv'd, which rising Ida bear—
Ida, to wand'ring Trojans ever dear.
Under their grateful shade Æneas sate,
Revolving war's events, and various fate.
His left young Pallas kept, fix'd to his side,
And oft of winds enquir'd, and of the tide;
Oft of the stars, and of their wat'ry way;
And what he suffer'd both by land and sea.

Now, sacred sisters, open all your spring!
The Tuscan leaders, and their army sing,
Which follow'd great Æneas to the war:
Their arms, their numbers, and their
names declare.

A thousand youths brave Massicus obey,
Borne in the Tiger thro' the foaming sea;
From Asium brought, and Cosa, by his care:
For arms, light quivers, bows and shafts,
they bear.
Fierce Abas next: his men bright armor wore;
His stern Apollo's golden statue bore.
Six hundred Populonia sent along,
All skill'd in martial exercise, and strong.
Three hundred more for battle Ilva joins,
An isle renown'd for steel,
and unexhausted mines.
Asylas on his prow the third appears,
Who heav'n interprets, and the wand'ring stars;
From offer'd entrails prodigies expounds,
And peals of thunder, with presaging sounds.
A thousand spears in warlike order stand,
Sent by the Pisans under his command.

Fair Astur follows in the wat'ry field,
Proud of his manag'd horse and painted shield.
Gravisca, noisome from the neighb'ring fen,
And his own Cære, sent three hundred men;
With those which Minio's fields and Pyrgi gave,
All bred in arms, unanimous, and brave.

Thou, Muse, the name of Cinyras renew,
And brave Cupavo follow'd but by few;
Whose helm confess'd the lineage of the man,
And bore, with wings display'd, a silver swan.
Love was the fault of his fam'd ancestry,
Whose forms and fortunes in his ensigns fly.
For Cycnus lov'd unhappy Phæton,
And sung his loss in poplar groves, alone,
Beneath the sister shades, to soothe his grief.
Heav'n heard his song, and hasten'd his relief,
And chang'd to snowy plumes his hoary hair,
And wing'd his flight, to chant aloft in air.
His son Cupavo brush'd the briny flood:
Upon his stern a brawny Centaur stood,
Who heav'd a rock, and, threat'ning still to throw,
With lifted hands alarm'd the seas below:
They seem'd to fear the formidable sight,
And roll'd their billows on, to speed his flight.

Ocnus was next, who led his native train
Of hardy warriors thro' the wat'ry plain:
The son of Manto by the Tuscan stream,
From whence the Mantuan town
    derives the name—
An ancient city, but of mix'd descent:
Three sev'ral tribes compose the government;
Four towns are under each; but all obey
The Mantuan laws, and own the Tuscan sway.

Hate to Mezentius arm'd five hundred more,

Whom Mincius from his sire Benacus bore:
Mincius, with wreaths of reeds his forehead
 cover'd o'er.
These grave Auletes leads: a hundred sweep
With stretching oars at once the glassy deep.
Him and his martial train the Triton bears;
High on his poop the sea-green god appears:
Frowning he seems his crooked shell to sound,
And at the blast the billows dance around.
A hairy man above the waist he shows;
A porpoise tail beneath his belly grows;
And ends a fish: his breast the waves divides,
And froth and foam augment the murm'ring tides.

Full thirty ships transport the chosen train
For Troy's relief, and scour the briny main.

Now was the world forsaken by the sun,
And Phœbe half her nightly race had run.
The careful chief, who never clos'd his eyes,
Himself the rudder holds, the sails supplies.
A choir of Nereids meet him on the flood,
Once his own galleys, hewn from Ida's wood;
But now, as many nymphs, the sea they sweep,
As rode, before, tall vessels on the deep.
They know him from afar; and in a ring
Enclose the ship that bore the Trojan king.
Cymodoce, whose voice excell'd the rest,
Above the waves advanc'd her snowy breast;
Her right hand stops the stern; her left divides
The curling ocean, and corrects the tides.
She spoke for all the choir, and thus began
With pleasing words to warn th' unknowing man:
"Sleeps our lov'd lord? O goddess-born, awake!
Spread ev'ry sail, pursue your wat'ry track,
And haste your course. Your navy once were we,
From Ida's height descending to the sea;

Till Turnus, as at anchor fix'd we stood,
Presum'd to violate our holy wood.
Then, loos'd from shore, we fled his fires profane
(Unwillingly we broke our master's chain),
And since have sought you thro' the Tuscan main.
The mighty Mother chang'd our forms to these,
And gave us life immortal in the seas.
But young Ascanius, in his camp distress'd,
By your insulting foes is hardly press'd.
Th' Arcadian horsemen, and Etrurian host,
Advance in order on the Latian coast:
To cut their way the Daunian chief designs,
Before their troops can reach the Trojan lines.
Thou, when the rosy morn restores the light,
First arm thy soldiers for th' ensuing fight:
Thyself the fated sword of Vulcan wield,
And bear aloft th' impenetrable shield.
To-morrow's sun, unless my skill be vain,
Shall see huge heaps of foes in battle slain."
Parting, she spoke; and with immortal force
Push'd on the vessel in her wat'ry course;
For well she knew the way. Impell'd behind,
The ship flew forward, and outstripp'd the wind.
The rest make up. Unknowing of the cause,
The chief admires their speed, and happy
omens draws.

Then thus he pray'd, and fix'd on heav'n his eyes:
"Hear thou, great Mother of the deities.
With turrets crown'd! (on Ida's holy hill
Fierce tigers, rein'd and curb'd, obey thy will.)
Firm thy own omens; lead us on to fight;
And let thy Phrygians conquer in thy right."

He said no more. And now renewing day
Had chas'd the shadows of the night away.
He charg'd the soldiers, with preventing care,

Their flags to follow, and their arms prepare;
Warn'd of th' ensuing fight, and bade 'em hope the war.
Now, his lofty poop, he view'd below
His camp encompass'd, and th' enclosing foe.
His blazing shield, embrac'd, he held on high;
The camp receive the sign, and with loud shouts reply.
Hope arms their courage: from their tow'rs they throw
Their darts with double force, and drive the foe.
Thus, at the signal giv'n, the cranes arise
Before the stormy south, and blacken all the skies.

King Turnus wonder'd at the fight renew'd,
Till, looking back, the Trojan fleet he view'd,
The seas with swelling canvas cover'd o'er,
And the swift ships descending on the shore.
The Latians saw from far, with dazzled eyes,
The radiant crest that seem'd in flames to rise,
And dart diffusive fires around the field,
And the keen glitt'ring the golden shield.
Thus threat'ning comets, when by night they rise,
Shoot sanguine streams, and sadden all the skies:
So Sirius, flashing forth sinister lights,
Pale humankind with plagues and with dry famine frights:

Yet Turnus with undaunted mind is bent
To man the shores, and hinder their descent,
And thus awakes the courage of his friends:
"What you so long have wish'd, kind Fortune sends;
In ardent arms to meet th' invading foe:
You find, and find him at advantage now.
Yours is the day: you need but only dare;
Your swords will make you masters of the war.

Your sires, your sons, your houses, and your lands,
And dearest wifes, are all within your hands.
Be mindful of the race from whence you came,
And emulate in arms your fathers' fame.
Now take the time, while stagg'ring yet they stand
With feet unfirm, and prepossess the strand:
Fortune befriends the bold." Nor more he said,
But balanc'd whom to leave, and whom to lead;
Then these elects, the landing to prevent;
And those he leaves, to keep the city pent.

Meantime the Trojan sends his troops ashore:
Some are by boats expos'd, by bridges more.
With lab'ring oars they bear along the strand,
Where the tide languishes, and leap aland.
Tarchon observes the coast with careful eyes,
And, where no ford he finds, no water fries,
Nor billows with unequal murmurs roar,
But smoothly slide along, and swell the shore,
That course he steer'd, and thus he gave command:
"Here ply your oars, and at all hazard land:
Force on the vessel, that her keel may wound
This hated soil, and furrow hostile ground.
Let me securely land—I ask no more;
Then sink my ships, or shatter on the shore."

This fiery speech inflames his fearful friends:
They tug at ev'ry oar, and ev'ry stretcher bends;
They run their ships aground; the vessels knock,
(Thus forc'd ashore,) and tremble with the shock.
Tarchon's alone was lost, that stranded stood,
Stuck on a bank, and beaten by the flood:
She breaks her back; the loosen'd sides give way,
And plunge the Tuscan soldiers in the sea.
Their broken oars and floating planks withstand
Their passage, while they labor to the land,
And ebbing tides bear back upon th' uncertain sand.

Now Turnus leads his troops without delay,
Advancing to the margin of the sea.
The trumpets sound: Æneas first assail'd
The clowns new-rais'd and raw, and soon prevail'd.
Great Theron fell, an omen of the fight;
Great Theron, large of limbs, of giant height.
He first in open field defied the prince:
But armor scal'd with gold was no defense
Against the fated sword, which open'd wide
His plated shield, and pierc'd his naked side.
Next, Lichas fell, who, not like others born,
Was from his wretched mother ripp'd and torn;
Sacred, O Phœbus, from his birth to thee;
For his beginning life from biting steel was free.
Not far from him was Gyas laid along,
Of monstrous bulk; with Cisseus fierce and strong:
Vain bulk and strength! for, when the chief assail'd,
Nor valor nor Herculean arms avail'd,
Nor their fam'd father, wont in war to go
With great Alcides, while he toil'd below.
The noisy Pharos next receiv'd his death:
Æneas writh'd his dart, and stopp'd his bawling breath.
Then wretched Cydon had receiv'd his doom,
Who courted Clytius in his beardless bloom,
And sought with lust obscene polluted joys:
The Trojan sword had curd his love of boys,
Had not his sev'n bold brethren stopp'd the course
Of the fierce champions, with united force.
Sev'n darts were thrown at once; and some rebound
From his bright shield, some on his helmet sound:
The rest had reach'd him; but his mother's care
Prevented those, and turn'd aside in air.

The prince then call'd Achates, to supply
The spears that knew the way to victory:
"Those fatal weapons, which, inur'd to blood,
In Grecian bodies under Ilium stood:
Not one of those my hand shall toss in vain
Against our foes, on this contended plain."
He said; then seiz'd a mighty spear, and threw;
Which, wing'd with fate, thro' Mæon's buckler flew,
Pierc'd all the brazen plates, and reach'd his heart:
He stagger'd with intolerable smart.
Alcanor saw; and reach'd, but reach'd in vain,
His helping hand, his brother to sustain.
A second spear, which kept the former course,
From the same hand, and sent with equal force,
His right arm pierc'd, and holding on, bereft
His use of both, and pinion'd down his left.
Then Numitor from his dead brother drew
Th' ill-omen'd spear, and at the Trojan threw:
Preventing fate directs the lance awry,
Which, glancing, only mark'd Achates' thigh.

In pride of youth the Sabine Clausus came,
And, from afar, at Dryops took his aim.
The spear flew hissing thro' the middle space,
And pierc'd his throat, directed at his face;
It stopp'd at once the passage of his wind,
And the free soul to flitting air resign'd:
His forehead was the first that struck the ground;
Lifeblood and life rush'd mingled thro' the wound.
He slew three brothers of the Borean race,
And three, whom Ismarus, their native place,
Had sent to war, but all the sons of Thrace.
Halesus, next, the bold Aurunci leads:
The son of Neptune to his aid succeeds,
Conspicuous on his horse. On either hand,

These fight to keep, and those to win, the land.
With mutual blood th' Ausonian soil is dyed,
While on its borders each their claim decide.
As wintry winds, contending in the sky,
With equal force of lungs their titles try:
They rage, they roar; the doubtful rack of heav'n
Stands without motion, and the tide undriv'n:
Each bent to conquer, neither side to yield,
They long suspend the fortune of the field.
Both armies thus perform what courage can;
Foot set to foot, and mingled man to man.

But, in another part, th' Arcadian horse
With ill success engage the Latin force:
For, where th' impetuous torrent, rushing down,
Huge craggy stones and rooted trees had thrown,
They left their coursers, and, unus'd to fight
On foot, were scatter'd in a shameful flight.
Pallas, who with disdain and grief had view'd
His foes pursuing, and his friends pursued,
Us'd threat'nings mix'd with pray'rs,
his last resource,
With these to move their minds, with those
to fire their force:
"Which way, companions? whither would you run?
By you yourselves, and mighty battles won,
By my great sire, by his establish'd name,
And early promise of my future fame;
By my youth, emulous of equal right
To share his honors—shun ignoble flight!
Trust not your feet: your hands must hew way
Thro' yon black body, and that thick array:
'Tis thro' that forward path that we must come;
There lies our way, and that our passage home.
Nor pow'rs above, nor destinies below
Oppress our arms: with equal strength we go,
With mortal hands to meet a mortal foe.

See on what foot we stand: a scanty shore,
The sea behind, our enemies before;
No passage left, unless we swim the main;
Or, forcing these, the Trojan trenches gain."
This said, he strode with eager haste along,
And bore amidst the thickest of the throng.
Lagus, the first he met, with fate to foe,
Had heav'd a stone of mighty weight, to throw:
Stooping, the spear descended on his chine,
Just where the bone distinguished either loin:
It stuck so fast, so deeply buried lay,
That scarce the victor forc'd the steel away.
Hisbon came on: but, while he mov'd too slow
To wish'd revenge, the prince prevents his blow;
For, warding his at once, at once he press'd,
And plung'd the fatal weapon in his breast.
Then lewd Anchemolus he laid in dust,
Who stain'd his stepdam's bed with impious lust.
And, after him, the Daucian twins were slain,
Laris and Thymbrus, on the Latian plain;
So wondrous like in feature, shape, and size,
As caus'd an error in their parents' eyes—
Grateful mistake!—but soon the sword decides
The nice distinction, and their fate divides:
For Thymbrus' head was lopp'd; and Laris' hand,
Dismember'd, sought its owner on the strand:
The trembling fingers yet the fauchion strain,
And threaten still th' intended stroke in vain.

Now, to renew the charge, th' Arcadians came:
Sight of such acts, and sense of honest shame,
And grief, with anger mix'd, their minds inflame.
Then, with a casual blow was Rhœteus slain,
Who chanc'd, as Pallas threw, to cross the plain:
The flying spear was after Ilus sent;
But Rhœteus happen'd on a death unmeant:
From Teuthras and from Tyres while he fled,

The lance, athwart his body, laid him dead:
Roll'd from his chariot with a mortal wound,
And intercepted fate, he spurn'd the ground.
As when, in summer, welcome winds arise,
The watchful shepherd to the forest flies,
And fires the midmost plants; contagion spreads,
And catching flames infect the neighb'ring heads;
Around the forest flies the furious blast,
And all the leafy nation sinks at last,
And Vulcan rides in triumph o'er the waste;
The pastor, pleas'd with his dire victory,
Beholds the satiate flames in sheets ascend the sky:
So Pallas' troops their scatter'd strength unite,
And, pouring on their foes, their prince delight.

Halesus came, fierce with desire of blood;
But first collected in his arms he stood:
Advancing then, he plied the spear so well,
Ladon, Demodocus, and Pheres fell.
Around his head he toss'd his glitt'ring brand,
And from Strymonius hew'd his better hand,
Held up to guard his throat; then hurl'd a stone
At Thoas' ample front, and pierc'd the bone:
It struck beneath the space of either eye;
And blood, and mingled brains, together fly.
Deep skill'd in future fates, Halesus' sire
Did with the youth to lonely groves retire:
But, when the father's mortal race was run,
Dire destiny laid hold upon the son,
And haul'd him to the war, to find, beneath
Th' Evandrian spear, a memorable death.
Pallas th' encounter seeks, but, ere he throws,
To Tuscan Tiber thus address'd his vows:
"O sacred stream, direct my flying dart,
And give to pass the proud Halesus' heart!
His arms and spoils thy holy oak shall bear."
Pleas'd with the bribe, the god receiv'd his pray'r:

For, while his shield protects a friend distress'd,
The dart came driving on, and pierc'd his breast.

But Lausus, no small portion of the war,
Permits not panic fear to reign too far,
Caus'd by the death of so renown'd a knight;
But by his own example cheers the fight.
Fierce Abas first he slew; Abas, the stay
Of Trojan hopes, and hindrance of the day.
The Phrygian troops escap'd the Greeks in vain:
They, and their mix'd allies, now load the plain.
To the rude shock of war both armies came;
Their leaders equal, and their strength the same.
The rear so press'd the front, they could not wield
Their angry weapons, to dispute the field.
Here Pallas urges on, and Lausus there:
Of equal youth and beauty both appear,
But both by fate forbid to breathe their native air.
Their congress in the field great Jove withstands:
Both doom'd to fall, but fall by greater hands.

Meantime Juturna warns the Daunian chief
Of Lausus' danger, urging swift relief.
With his driv'n chariot he divides the crowd,
And, making to his friends, thus calls aloud:
"Let none presume his needless aid to join;
Retire, and clear the field; the fight is mine:
To this right hand is Pallas only due;
O were his father here, my just revenge to view!"
From the forbidden space his men retir'd.
Pallas their awe, and his stern words, admir'd;
Survey'd him o'er and o'er with wond'ring sight,
Struck with his haughty mien, and tow'ring height.
Then to the king: "Your empty vaunts forbear;
Success I hope, and fate I cannot fear;
Alive or dead, I shall deserve a name;
Jove is impartial, and to both the same."

He said, and to the void advanc'd his pace:
Pale horror sate on each Arcadian face.
Then Turnus, from his chariot leaping light,
Address'd himself on foot to single fight.
And, as a lion—when he spies from far
A bull that seems to meditate the war,
Bending his neck, and spurning back the sand—
Runs roaring downward from his hilly stand:
Imagine eager Turnus not more slow,
To rush from high on his unequal foe.

Young Pallas, when he saw the chief advance
Within due distance of his flying lance,
Prepares to charge him first, resolv'd to try
If fortune would his want of force supply;
And thus to Heav'n and Hercules address'd:
"Alcides, once on earth Evander's guest,
His son adjures you by those holy rites,
That hospitable board, those genial nights;
Assist my great attempt to gain this prize,
And let proud Turnus view, with dying eyes,
His ravish'd spoils." 'Twas heard,
the vain request;
Alcides mourn'd, and stifled sighs within
his breast.
Then Jove, to soothe his sorrow, thus began:
"Short bounds of life are set to mortal man.
'Tis virtue's work alone to stretch the narrow span.
So many sons of gods, in bloody fight,
Around the walls of Troy, have lost the light:
My own Sarpedon fell beneath his foe;
Nor I, his mighty sire, could ward the blow.
Ev'n Turnus shortly shall resign his breath,
And stands already on the verge of death."
This said, the god permits the fatal fight,
But from the Latian fields averts his sight.

Now with full force his spear young Pallas threw,
And, having thrown, his shining fauchion drew
The steel just graz'd along the shoulder joint,
And mark'd it slightly with the glancing point,
Fierce Turnus first to nearer distance drew,
And pois'd his pointed spear, before he threw:
Then, as the winged weapon whizz'd along,
"See now," said he, "whose arm is better strung."
The spear kept on the fatal course, unstay'd
By plates of ir'n, which o'er the shield were laid:
Thro' folded brass and tough bull hides it pass'd,
His corslet pierc'd, and reach'd his heart at last.
In vain the youth tugs at the broken wood;
The soul comes issuing with the vital blood:
He falls; his arms upon his body sound;
And with his bloody teeth he bites the ground.

Turnus bestrode the corpse: "Arcadians, hear,"
Said he; "my message to your master bear:
Such as the sire deserv'd, the son I send;
It costs him dear to be the Phrygians' friend.
The lifeless body, tell him, I bestow,
Unask'd, to rest his wand'ring ghost below."
He said, and trampled down with all the force
Of his left foot, and spurn'd the wretched corpse;
Then snatch'd the shining belt, with gold inlaid;
The belt Eurytion's artful hands had made,
Where fifty fatal brides, express'd to sight,
All in the compass of one mournful night,
Depriv'd their bridegrooms of returning light.

In an ill hour insulting Turnus tore
Those golden spoils, and in a worse he wore.
O mortals, blind in fate, who never know
To bear high fortune, or endure the low!
The time shall come, when Turnus, but in vain,
Shall wish untouch'd the trophies of the slain;

Shall wish the fatal belt were far away,
And curse the dire remembrance of the day.

The sad Arcadians, from th' unhappy field,
Bear back the breathless body on a shield.
O grace and grief of war! at once restor'd,
With praises, to thy sire, at once deplor'd!
One day first sent thee to the fighting field,
Beheld whole heaps of foes in battle kill'd;
One day beheld thee dead, and borne
upon thy shield.
This dismal news, not from uncertain fame,
But sad spectators, to the hero came:
His friends upon the brink of ruin stand,
Unless reliev'd by his victorious hand.
He whirls his sword around, without delay,
And hews thro' adverse foes an ample way,
To find fierce Turnus, of his conquest proud:
Evander, Pallas, all that friendship ow'd
To large deserts, are present to his eyes;
His plighted hand, and hospitable ties.

Four sons of Sulmo, four whom Ufens bred,
He took in fight, and living victims led,
To please the ghost of Pallas, and expire,
In sacrifice, before his fun'ral fire.
At Magus next he threw: he stoop'd below
The flying spear, and shunn'd the promis'd blow;
Then, creeping, clasp'd the hero's knees, and pray'd:
"By young Iülus, by thy father's shade,
O spare my life, and send me back to see
My longing sire, and tender progeny!
A lofty house I have, and wealth untold,
In silver ingots, and in bars of gold:
All these, and sums besides, which see no day,
The ransom of this one poor life shall pay.
If I survive, will Troy the less prevail?

A single soul's too light to turn the scale."
He said. The hero sternly thus replied:
"Thy bars and ingots, and the sums beside,
Leave for thy children's lot. Thy Turnus broke
All rules of war by one relentless stroke,
When Pallas fell: so deems, nor deems alone
My father's shadow, but my living son."
Thus having said, of kind remorse bereft,
He seiz'd his helm, and dragg'd him with his left;
Then with his right hand, while his neck
he wreath'd,
Up to the hilts his shining fauchion sheath'd.

Apollo's priest, Emonides, was near;
His holy fillets on his front appear;
Glitt'ring in arms, he shone amidst the crowd;
Much of his god, more of his purple, proud.
Him the fierce Trojan follow'd thro' the field:
The holy coward fell; and, forc'd to yield,
The prince stood o'er the priest, and, at one blow,
Sent him an off'ring to the shades below.
His arms Seresthus on his shoulders bears,
Design'd a trophy to the God of Wars.

Vulcanian Cæculus renews the fight,
And Umbro, born upon the mountains' height.
The champion cheers his troops t' encounter those,
And seeks revenge himself on other foes.
At Anxur's shield he drove; and, at the blow,
Both shield and arm to ground together go.
Anxur had boasted much of magic charms,
And thought he wore impenetrable arms,
So made by mutter'd spells; and, from the spheres,
Had life secur'd, in vain, for length of years.
Then Tarquitus the field triumph trod;
A nymph his mother, his sire a god.
Exulting in bright arms, he braves the prince:

With his protended lance he makes defense;
Bears back his feeble foe; then, pressing on,
Arrests his better hand, and drags him down;
Stands o'er the prostrate wretch, and, as he lay,
Vain tales inventing, and prepar'd to pray,
Mows off his head: the trunk a moment stood,
Then sunk, and roll'd along the sand in blood.
The vengeful victor thus upbraids the slain:
"Lie there, proud man, unpitied, on the plain;
Lie there, inglorious, and without a tomb,
Far from thy mother and thy native home,
Exposed to savage beasts, and birds of prey,
Or thrown for food to monsters of the sea."

On Lycas and Antæus next he ran,
Two chiefs of Turnus, and who led his van.
They fled for fear; with these, he chas'd along
Camers the yellow-lock'd, and Numa strong;
Both great in arms, and both were fair and young.
Camers was son to Volscens lately slain,
In wealth surpassing all the Latian train,
And in Amycla fix'd his silent easy reign.
And, as Ægæon, when with heav'n he strove,
Stood opposite in arms to mighty Jove;
Mov'd all his hundred hands, provok'd the war,
Defied the forky lightning from afar;
At fifty mouths his flaming breath expires,
And flash for flash returns, and fires for fires;
In his right hand as many swords he wields,
And takes the thunder on as many shields:
With strength like his, the Trojan hero stood;
And soon the fields with falling corps were strow'd,
When once his fauchion found the taste of blood.
With fury scarce to be conceiv'd, he flew
Against Niphæus, whom four coursers drew.
They, when they see the fiery chief advance,
And pushing at their chests his pointed lance,

Wheel'd with so swift a motion, mad with fear,
They threw their master headlong from the chair.
They stare, they start, nor stop their course, before
They bear the bounding chariot to the shore.

Now Lucagus and Liger scour the plains,
With two white steeds; but Liger holds the reins,
And Lucagus the lofty seat maintains:
Bold brethren both. The former wav'd in air
His flaming sword: Æneas couch'd his spear,
Unus'd to threats, and more unus'd to fear.
Then Liger thus: "Thy confidence is vain
To scape from hence, as from the Trojan plain:
Nor these the steeds which Diomede bestrode,
Nor this the chariot where Achilles rode;
Nor Venus' veil is here, near Neptune's shield;
Thy fatal hour is come, and this the field."
Thus Liger vainly vaunts: the Trojan
Return'd his answer with his flying spear.
As Lucagus, to lash his horses, bends,
Prone to the wheels, and his left foot protends,
Prepar'd for fight; the fatal dart arrives,
And thro' the borders of his buckler drives;
Pass'd thro' and pierc'd his groin: the deadly wound,
Cast from his chariot, roll'd him on the ground.
Whom thus the chief upbraids with scornful spite:
"Blame not the slowness of your steeds in flight;
Vain shadows did not force their swift retreat;
But you yourself forsake your empty seat."
He said, and seiz'd at once the loosen'd rein;
For Liger lay already on the plain,
By the same shock: then, stretching out his hands,
The recreant thus his wretched life demands:
"Now, by thyself, O more than mortal man!

By her and him from whom thy breath began,
Who form'd thee thus divine, I beg thee, spare
This forfeit life, and hear thy suppliant's pray'r."
Thus much he spoke, and more he would have said;
But the stern hero turn'd aside his head,
And cut him short: "I hear another man;
You talk'd not thus before the fight began.
Now take your turn; and, as a brother should,
Attend your brother to the Stygian flood."
Then thro' his breast his fatal sword he sent,
And the soul issued at the gaping vent.

As storms the skies, and torrents tear the ground,
Thus rag'd the prince, and scatter'd deaths around.
At length Ascanius and the Trojan train
Broke from the camp, so long besieg'd in vain.

Meantime the King of Gods and Mortal Man
Held conference with his queen, and thus began:
"My sister goddess, and well-pleasing wife,
Still think you Venus' aid supports the strife—
Sustains her Trojans—or themselves, alone,
With inborn valor force their fortune on?
How fierce in fight, with courage undecay'd!
Judge if such warriors want immortal aid."
To whom the goddess with the charming eyes,
Soft in her tone, submissively replies:
"Why, O my sov'reign lord, whose frown I fear,
And cannot, unconcern'd, your anger bear;
Why urge you thus my grief? when, if I still
(As once I was) were mistress of your will,
From your almighty pow'r your pleasing wife
Might gain the grace of length'ning Turnus' life,
Securely snatch him from the fatal fight,
And give him to his aged father's sight.
Now let him perish, since you hold it good,
And glut the Trojans with his pious blood.

Yet from our lineage he derives his name,
And, in the fourth degree, from god
Pilumnus came;
Yet he devoutly pays you rites divine,
And offers daily incense at your shrine."

Then shortly thus the sov'reign god replied:
"Since in my pow'r and goodness you confide,
If for a little space, a lengthen'd span,
You beg reprieve for this expiring man,
I grant you leave to take your Turnus hence
From instant fate, and can so far dispense.
But, if some secret meaning lies beneath,
To save the short-liv'd youth from destin'd death,
Or if a farther thought you entertain,
To change the fates; you feed your hopes in vain."
To whom the goddess thus, with weeping eyes:
"And what if that request, your tongue denies,
Your heart should grant; and not a short reprieve,
But length of certain life, to Turnus give?
Now speedy death attends the guiltless youth,
If my presaging soul divines with truth;
Which, O! I wish, might err thro' causeless fears,
And you (for you have pow'r) prolong his years!"

Thus having said, involv'd in clouds, she flies,
And drives a storm before her thro' the skies.
Swift she descends, alighting on the plain,
Where the fierce foes a dubious fight maintain.
Of air condens'd a specter soon she made;
And, what Æneas was, such seem'd the shade.
Adorn'd with Dardan arms, the phantom bore
His head aloft; a plumy crest he wore;
This hand appear'd a shining sword to wield,
And that sustain'd an imitated shield.
With manly mien he stalk'd along the ground,
Nor wanted voice belied, nor vaunting sound.

(Thus haunting ghosts appear to waking sight,
Or dreadful visions in our dreams by night.)
The specter seems the Daunian chief to dare,
And flourishes his empty sword in air.
At this, advancing, Turnus hurl'd his spear:
The phantom wheel'd, and seem'd to fly for fear.
Deluded Turnus thought the Trojan fled,
And with vain hopes his haughty fancy fed.
"Whether, O coward?" (thus he calls aloud,
Nor found he spoke to wind, and chas'd a cloud,)
"Why thus forsake your bride! Receive from me
The fated land you sought so long by sea."
He said, and, brandishing at once his blade,
With eager pace pursued the flying shade.
By chance a ship was fasten'd to the shore,
Which from old Clusium King Osinius bore:
The plank was ready laid for safe ascent;
For shelter there the trembling shadow bent,
And skipp't and skulk'd, and under hatches went.
Exulting Turnus, with regardless haste,
Ascends the plank, and to the galley pass'd.
Scarce had he reach'd the prow: Saturnia's hand
The haulsers cuts, and shoots the ship from land.
With wind in poop, the vessel plows the sea,
And measures back with speed her former way.
Meantime Æneas seeks his absent foe,
And sends his slaughter'd troops to shades below.

The guileful phantom now forsook the shroud,
And flew sublime, and vanish'd in a cloud.
Too late young Turnus the delusion found,
Far on the sea, still making from the ground.
Then, thankless for a life redeem'd by shame,
With sense of honor stung, and forfeit fame,
Fearful besides of what in fight had pass'd,
His hands and haggard eyes to heav'n he cast;
"O Jove!" he cried, "for what offense have

Deserv'd to bear this endless infamy?
Whence am I forc'd, and whether am I borne?
How, and with what reproach, shall I return?
Shall ever I behold the Latian plain,
Or see Laurentum's lofty tow'rs again?
What will they say of their deserting chief
The war was mine: I fly from their relief;
I led to slaughter, and in slaughter leave;
And ev'n from hence their dying groans receive.
Here, overmatch'd in fight, in heaps they lie;
There, scatter'd o'er the fields, ignobly fly.
Gape wide, O earth, and draw me down alive!
Or, O ye pitying winds, a wretch relieve!
On sands or shelves the splitting vessel drive;
Or set me shipwreck'd on some desert shore,
Where no Rutulian eyes may see me more,
Unknown to friends, or foes, or conscious Fame,
Lest she should follow, and my flight proclaim."

Thus Turnus rav'd, and various fates revolv'd:
The choice was doubtful, but the death resolv'd.
And now the sword, and now the sea took place,
That to revenge, and this to purge disgrace.
Sometimes he thought to swim the stormy main,
By stretch of arms the distant shore to gain.
Thrice he the sword assay'd, and thrice the flood;
But Juno, mov'd with pity, both withstood.
And thrice repress'd his rage; strong gales supplied,
And push'd the vessel o'er the swelling tide.
At length she lands him on his native shores,
And to his father's longing arms restores.

Meantime, by Jove's impulse, Mezentius arm'd,
Succeeding Turnus, with his ardor warm'd
His fainting friends, reproach'd their shameful flight,
Repell'd the victors, and renew'd the fight.
Against their king the Tuscan troops conspire;

Such is their hate, and such their fierce desire
Of wish'd revenge: on him, and him alone,
All hands employ'd, and all their darts are thrown.
He, like a solid rock by seas enclos'd,
To raging winds and roaring waves oppos'd,
From his proud summit looking down, disdains
Their empty menace, and unmov'd remains.

Beneath his feet fell haughty Hebrus dead,
Then Latagus, and Palmus as he fled.
At Latagus a weighty stone he flung:
His face was flatted, and his helmet rung.
But Palmus from behind receives his wound;
Hamstring'd he falls, and grovels on the ground:
His crest and armor, from his body torn,
Thy shoulders, Lausus, and thy head adorn.
Evas and Mimas, both of Troy, he slew.
Mimas his birth from fair Theano drew,
Born on that fatal night, when, big with fire,
The queen produc'd young Paris to his sire:
But Paris in the Phrygian fields was slain,
Unthinking Mimas on the Latian plain.

And, as a savage boar, on mountains bred,
With forest mast and fatt'ning marshes fed,
When once he sees himself in toils enclos'd,
By huntsmen and their eager hounds oppos'd,
He whets his tusks, and turns, and dares the war;
Th' invaders dart their jav'lins from afar:
All keep aloof, and safely shout around;
But none presumes to give a nearer wound:
He frets and froths, erects his bristled hide,
And shakes a grove of lances from his side:
Not otherwise the troops, with hate inspir'd,
And just revenge against the tyrant fir'd,
Their darts with clamor at a distance drive,
And only keep the languish'd war alive.

From Coritus came Acron to the fight,
Who left his spouse betroth'd,
and unconsummate night.
Mezentius sees him thro' the squadrons ride,
Proud of the purple favors of his bride.
Then, as a hungry lion, who beholds
A gamesome goat, who frisks about the folds,
Or beamy stag, that grazes on the plain,
He runs, he roars, he shakes his rising mane,
He grins, and opens wide his greedy jaws;
The prey lies panting underneath his paws:
He fills his famish'd maw; his mouth runs o'er
With unchew'd morsels, while he churns the gore:
So proud Mezentius rushes on his foes,
And first unhappy Acron overthrows:
Stretch'd at his length, he spurns the
swarthy ground;
The lance, besmear'd with blood, lies broken
in the wound.
Then with disdain the haughty victor view'd
Orodes flying, nor the wretch pursued,
Nor thought the dastard's back deserv'd a wound,
But, running, gain'd th' advantage of the ground:
Then turning short, he met him face to face,
To give his victor the better grace.
Orodes falls, equal fight oppress'd:
Mezentius fix'd his foot upon his breast,
And rested lance; and thus aloud he cries:
"Lo! here the champion of my rebels lies!"
The fields around with Io Pæan! ring;
And peals of shouts applaud the conqu'ring king.
At this the vanquish'd, with his dying breath,
Thus faintly spoke, and prophesied in death:
"Nor thou, proud man, unpunish'd shalt remain:
Like death attends thee on this fatal plain."
Then, sourly smiling, thus the king replied:
"For what belongs to me, let Jove provide;

But die thou first, whatever chance ensue."
He said, and from the wound the weapon drew.
A hov'ring mist came swimming o'er his sight,
And seal'd his eyes in everlasting night.

By Cædicus, Alcathous was slain;
Sacrator laid Hydaspes on the plain;
Orses the strong to greater strength must yield;
He, with Parthenius, were by Rapo kill'd.
Then brave Messapus Ericetes slew,
Who from Lycaon's blood his lineage drew.
But from his headstrong horse his fate he found,
Who threw his master, as he made a bound:
The chief, alighting, stuck him to the ground;
Then Clonius, hand to hand, on foot assails:
The Trojan sinks, and Neptune's son prevails.
Agis the Lycian, stepping forth with pride,
To single fight the boldest foe defied;
Whom Tuscan Valerus by force o'ercame,
And not belied his mighty father's fame.
Salius to death the great Antronius sent:
But the same fate the victor underwent,
Slain by Nealces' hand, well-skill'd to throw
The flying dart, and draw the far-deceiving bow.

Thus equal deaths are dealt with equal chance;
By turns they quit their ground, by turns advance:
Victors and vanquish'd, in the various field,
Nor wholly overcome, nor wholly yield.
The gods from heav'n survey the fatal strife,
And mourn the miseries of human life.
Above the rest, two goddesses appear
Concern'd for each: here Venus, Juno there.
Amidst the crowd, infernal Ate shakes
Her scourge aloft, and crest of hissing snakes.

Once more the proud Mezentius, with disdain,
Brandish'd his spear, and rush'd into the plain,

Where tow'ring in the midmost rank she stood,
Like tall Orion stalking o'er the flood.
(When with his brawny breast he cuts the waves,
His shoulders scarce the topmost billow laves),
Or like a mountain ash, whose roots are spread,
Deep fix'd in earth; in clouds he hides his head.

The Trojan prince beheld him from afar,
And dauntless undertook the doubtful war.
Collected in his strength, and like a rock,
Pois'd on his base, Mezentius stood the shock.
He stood, and, measuring first with careful eyes
The space his spear could reach, aloud he cries:
"My strong right hand, and sword, assist my stroke!
(Those only gods Mezentius will invoke.)
His armor, from the Trojan pirate torn,
By my triumphant Lausus shall be worn."
He said; and with his utmost force he threw
The massy spear, which, hissing as it flew,
Reach'd the celestial shield, that stopp'd
the course;
But, glancing thence, the yet unbroken force
Took a new bent obliquely, and betwixt
The side and bowels fam'd Anthores fix'd.
Anthores had from Argos travel'd far,
Alcides' friend, and brother of the war;
Till, tir'd with toils, fair Italy he chose,
And in Evander's palace sought repose.
Now, falling by another's wound, his eyes
He cast to heav'n, on Argos thinks, and dies.

The pious Trojan then his jav'lin sent;
The shield gave way; thro' treble plates it went
Of solid brass, of linen trebly roll'd,
And three bull hides which round the buckler fold.
All these it pass'd, resistless in the course,
Transpierc'd his thigh, and spent its dying force.

The gaping wound gush'd out a crimson flood.
The Trojan, glad with sight of hostile blood,
His faunchion drew, to closer fight address'd,
And with new force his fainting foe oppress'd.

His father's peril Lausus view'd with grief;
He sigh'd, he wept, he ran to his relief.
And here, heroic youth, 'tis here I must
To thy immortal memory be just,
And sing an act so noble and so new,
Posterity will scarce believe 'tis true.
Pain'd with his wound, and useless for the fight,
The father sought to save himself by flight:
Encumber'd, slow he dragg'd the spear along,
Which pierc'd his thigh, and in his buckler hung.
The pious youth, resolv'd on death, below
The lifted sword springs forth to face the foe;
Protects his parent, and prevents the blow.
Shouts of applause ran ringing thro' the field,
To see the son the vanquish'd father shield.
All, fir'd with gen'rous indignation, strive,
And with a storm of darts to distance drive
The Trojan chief, who, held at bay from far,
On his Vulcanian orb sustain'd the war.

As, when thick hail comes rattling in the wind,
The plowman, passenger, and lab'ring hind
For shelter to the neighb'ring covert fly,
Or hous'd, or safe in hollow caverns lie;
But, that o'erblown, when heav'n above 'em smiles,
Return to travel, and renew their toils:
Æneas thus, o'erwhelmed on ev'ry side,
The storm of darts, undaunted, did abide;
And thus to Lausus loud with friendly
threat'ning cried:
"Why wilt thou rush to certain death, and rage
In rash attempts, beyond thy tender age,

Betray'd by pious love?" Nor, thus forborne,
The youth desists, but with insulting scorn
Provokes the ling'ring prince, whose patience, tir'd,
Gave place; and all his breast with fury fir'd.
For now the Fates prepar'd their sharpen'd shears;
And lifted high the flaming sword appears,
Which, full descending with a frightful sway,
Thro' shield and corslet forc'd th' impetuous way,
And buried deep in his fair bosom lay.
The purple streams thro' the thin armor strove,
And drench'd th' embroider'd coat his mother wove;
And life at length forsook his heaving heart,
Loth from so sweet a mansion to depart.

But when, with blood and paleness all o'erspread,
The pious prince beheld young Lausus dead,
He griev'd; he wept; the sight an image brought
Of his own filial love, a sadly pleasing thought:
Then stretch'd his hand to hold him up, and said:
"Poor hapless youth! what praises can be paid
To love so great, to such transcendent store
Of early worth, and sure presage of more?
Accept whate'er Æneas can afford;
Untouch'd thy arms, untaken be thy sword;
And all that pleas'd thee living, still remain
Inviolate, and sacred to the slain.
Thy body on thy parents I bestow,
To rest thy soul, at least, if shadows know,
Or have a sense of human things below.
There to thy fellow ghosts with glory tell:
"Twas by the great Æneas hand I fell.'"

With this, his distant friends he beckons near,
Provokes their duty, and prevents their fear:
Himself assists to lift him from the ground,
With clotted locks, and blood that
well'd from out the wound.

Meantime, his father, now no father, stood,
And wash'd his wounds by Tiber's yellow flood:
Oppress'd with anguish, panting, and o'erspent,
His fainting limbs against an oak he leant.
A bough his brazen helmet did sustain;
His heavier arms lay scatter'd on the plain:
A chosen train of youth around him stand;
His drooping head was rested on his hand:
His grisly beard his pensive bosom sought;
And all on Lausus ran his restless thought.
Careful, concern'd his danger to prevent,
He much inquir'd, and many a message sent
To warn him from the field—alas! in vain!
Behold, his mournful followers bear him slain!
O'er his broad shield still gush'd the
yawning wound,
And drew a bloody trail along the ground.
Far off he heard their cries, far off divin'd
The dire event, with a foreboding mind.
With dust he sprinkled first his hoary head;
Then both his lifted hands to heav'n he spread;
Last, the dear corpse embracing, thus he said:
"What joys, alas! could this frail being give,
That I have been so covetous to live?
To see my son, and such a son, resign
His life, a ransom for preserving mine!
And am I then preserv'd, and art thou lost?
How much too dear has that redemption cost!
'Tis now my bitter banishment I feel:
This is a wound too deep for time to heal.
My guilt thy growing virtues did defame;

My blackness blotted thy unblemish'd name.
Chas'd from a throne, abandon'd, and exil'd
For foul misdeeds, were punishments too mild:
I ow'd my people these, and, from their hate,
With less resentment could have borne my fate.
And yet I live, and yet sustain the sight
Of hated men, and of more hated light:
But will not long." With that he rais'd from ground
His fainting limbs, that stagger'd with his wound;
Yet, with a mind resolv'd, and unappall'd
With pains or perils, for his courser call'd
Well-mouth'd, well-manag'd, whom himself
did dress
With daily care, and mounted with success;
His aid in arms, his ornament in peace

Soothing his courage with a gentle stroke,
The steed seem'd sensible, while thus he spoke:
"O Rhœbus, we have liv'd too long for me—
If life and long were terms that could agree!
This day thou either shalt bring back the head
And bloody trophies of the Trojan dead;
This day thou either shalt revenge my woe,
For murther'd Lausus, on his cruel foe;
Or, if inexorable fate deny
Our conquest, with thy conquer'd master die:
For, after such a lord, rest secure,
Thou wilt no foreign reins, or Trojan
load endure."
He said; and straight th' officious courser kneels,
To take his wonted weight. His hands he fills
With pointed jav'lins; on his head he lac'd
His glitt'ring helm, which terribly was grac'd
With waving horsehair, nodding from afar;
Then spurr'd his thund'ring steed amidst the war.
Love, anguish, wrath, and grief, to madness wrought,
Despair, and secret shame, and conscious thought

Of inborn worth, his lab'ring soul oppress'd,
Roll'd in his eyes, and rag'd within his breast.
Then loud he call'd Æneas thrice by name:
The loud repeated voice to glad Æneas came.
"Great Jove," he said, "and the far-shooting god,
Inspire thy mind to make thy challenge good!"
He spoke no more; but hasten'd, void of fear,
And threaten'd with his long protended spear.

To whom Mezentius thus: "Thy vaunts are vain.
My Lausus lies extended on the plain:
He's lost! thy conquest is already won;
The wretched sire is murther'd in the son.
Nor fate I fear, but all the gods defy.
Forbear thy threats: my bus'ness is to die;
But first receive this parting legacy."
He said; and straight a whirling dart he sent;
Another after, and another went.
Round in a spacious ring he rides the field,
And vainly plies th' impenetrable shield.
Thrice rode he round; and thrice Æneas wheel'd,
Turn'd as he turn'd: the golden orb withstood
The strokes, and bore about an iron wood.
Impatient of delay, and weary grown,
Still to defend, and to defend alone,
To wrench the darts which in his buckler light,
Urg'd and o'er-labor'd in unequal fight;
At length resolv'd, he throws with all his force
Full at the temples of the warrior horse.
Just where the stroke was aim'd, th' unerring spear
Made way, and stood transfix'd thro' either ear.
Seiz'd with unwonted pain, surpris'd with fright,
The wounded steed curvets, and, rais'd upright,
Lights on his feet before; his hoofs behind
Spring up in air aloft, and lash the wind.
Down comes the rider headlong from his height:
His horse came after with unwieldy weight,

And, flound'ring forward, pitching on his head,
His lord's encumber'd shoulder overlaid.

From either host, the mingled shouts and cries
Of Trojans and Rutulians rend the skies.
Æneas, hast'ning, wav'd his fatal sword
High o'er his head, with this reproachful word:
"Now; where are now thy vaunts,
the fierce disdain
Of proud Mezentius, and the lofty strain?"

Struggling, and wildly staring on the skies,
With scarce recover'd sight he thus replies:
"Why these insulting words,
this waste of breath,
To souls undaunted, and secure of death?
'Tis no dishonor for the brave to die,
Nor came I here with hope victory;
Nor ask I life, nor fought with that design:
As I had us'd my fortune, use thou thine.
My dying son contracted no such band;
The gift is hateful from his murd'rer's hand.
For this, this only favor let me sue,
If pity can to conquer'd foes be due:
Refuse it not; but let my body have
The last retreat of humankind, a grave.
Too well I know th' insulting people's hate;
Protect me from their vengeance after fate:
This refuge for my poor remains provide,
And lay my much-lov'd Lausus by my side."
He said, and to the sword his throat applied.
The crimson stream distain'd his arms around,
And the disdainful soul came rushing
thro' the wound.

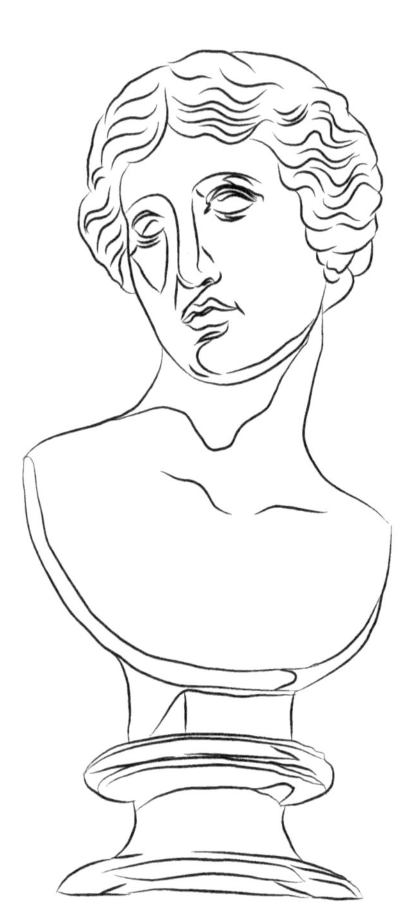

Book XI

Æneas erects a trophy of the spoils of Mezentius, grants a truce for burying the dead, and sends home the body of Pallas with great solemnity. Latinus calls a council, to propose offers of peace to Æneas; which occasions great animosity betwixt Turnus and Drances. In the meantime there is a sharp engagement of the horse; wherein Camilla shows herself remarkable; is killed; and the Latin troops are entirely defeated.

Scarce had the rosy Morning rais'd her head
Above the waves, and left her wat'ry bed;
The pious chief, whom double cares attend
For his unburied soldiers and his friend,
Yet first to Heav'n perform'd a victor's vows:
He bar'd an ancient oak of all her boughs;
Then on a rising ground the trunk he plac'd,
Which with the spoils of his dead foe he grac'd.
The coat of arms by proud Mezentius worn,
Now on a naked snag in triumph borne,
Was hung on high, and glitter'd from afar,
A trophy sacred to the God of War.
Above his arms, fix'd on the leafless wood,
Appear'd his plumy crest, besmear'd with blood:
His brazen buckler on the left was seen;
Truncheons of shiver'd lances hung between;
And on the right was placed his corslet, bor'd;
And to the neck was tied his unavailing sword.

A crowd of chiefs enclose the godlike man,
Who thus, conspicuous in the midst, began:
"Our toils, my friends, are crown'd with
sure success;

The greater part perform'd, achieve the less.
Now follow cheerful to the trembling town;
Press but an entrance, and presume it won.
Fear is no more, for fierce Mezentius lies,
As the first fruits of war, a sacrifice.
Turnus shall fall extended on the plain,
And, in this omen, is already slain.
Prepar'd in arms, pursue your happy chance;
That none unwarn'd may plead his ignorance,
And I, at Heav'n's appointed hour, may find
Your warlike ensigns waving in the wind.
Meantime the rites and fun'ral pomps prepare,
Due to your dead companions of the war:
The last respect the living can bestow,
To shield their shadows from contempt below.
That conquer'd earth be theirs, for which they fought,
And which for us with their own blood they bought;
But first the corpse of our unhappy friend
To the sad city of Evander send,
Who, not inglorious, in his age's bloom,
Was hurried hence by too severe a doom."

Thus, weeping while he spoke, he took his way,
Where, new in death, lamented Pallas lay.
Acœtes watch'd the corpse; whose youth deserv'd
The father's trust; and now the son he serv'd
With equal faith, but less auspicious care.
Th' attendants of the slain his sorrow share.
A troop of Trojans mix'd with these appear,
And mourning matrons with dishevel'd hair.
Soon as the prince appears, they raise a cry;
All beat their breasts, and echoes rend the sky.
They rear his drooping forehead from the ground;
But, when Æneas view'd the grisly wound
Which Pallas in his manly bosom bore,

And the fair flesh distain'd with purple gore;
First, melting into tears, the pious man
Deplor'd so sad a sight, then thus began:
"Unhappy youth! when Fortune gave the rest
Of my full wishes, she refus'd the best!
She came; but brought not thee along, to bless
My longing eyes, and share in my success:
She grudg'd thy safe return, the triumphs due
To prosp'rous valor, in the public view.
Not thus I promis'd, when thy father lent
Thy needless succor with a sad consent;
Embrac'd me, parting for th' Etrurian land,
And sent me to possess a large command.
He warn'd, and from his own experience told,
Our foes were warlike, disciplin'd, and bold.
And now perhaps, in hopes of thy return,
Rich odors on his loaded altars burn,
While we, with vain officious pomp, prepare
To send him back his portion of the war,
A bloody breathless body, which can owe
No farther debt, but to the pow'rs below.
The wretched father, ere his race is run,
Shall view the fun'ral honors of his son.
These are my triumphs of the Latian war,
Fruits of my plighted faith and boasted care!
And yet, unhappy sire, thou shalt not see
A son whose death disgrac'd his ancestry;
Thou shalt not blush, old man, however griev'd:
Thy Pallas no dishonest wound receiv'd.
He died no death to make thee wish, too late,
Thou hadst not liv'd to see his shameful fate:
But what a champion has th' Ausonian coast,
And what a friend hast thou, Ascanius, lost!"

Thus having mourn'd, he gave the word around,
To raise the breathless body from the ground;
And chose a thousand horse, the flow'r of all

His warlike troops, to wait the funeral,
To bear him back and share Evander's grief:
A well-becoming, but a weak relief.
Of oaken twigs they twist an easy bier,
Then on their shoulders the sad burden rear.
The body on this rural hearse is borne:
Strew'd leaves and funeral greens the bier adorn.
All pale he lies, and looks a lovely flow'r,
New cropp'd by virgin hands, to dress the bow'r:
Unfaded yet, but yet unfed below,
No more to mother earth or the green stern
shall owe.
Then two fair vests, of wondrous work and cost,
Of purple woven, and with gold emboss'd,
For ornament the Trojan hero brought,
Which with her hands Sidonian Dido wrought.
One vest array'd the corpse; and one they spread
O'er his clos'd eyes, and wrapp'd around his head,
That, when the yellow hair in flame should fall,
The catching fire might burn the golden caul.
Besides, the spoils of foes in battle slain,
When he descended on the Latian plain;
Arms, trappings, horses, by the hearse are led
In long array- th' achievements of the dead.
Then, pinion'd with their hands behind, appear
Th' unhappy captives, marching in the rear,
Appointed off'rings in the victor's name,
To sprinkle with their blood the fun'ral flame.
Inferior trophies by the chiefs are borne;
Gauntlets and helms their loaded hands adorn;
And fair inscriptions fix'd, and titles read
Of Latian leaders conquer'd by the dead.

Acœtes on his pupil's corpse attends,
With feeble steps, supported by his friends.
Pausing at ev'ry pace, in sorrow drown'd,
Betwixt their arms he sinks upon the ground;

Where grov'ling while he lies in deep despair,
He beats his breast, and rends his hoary hair.
The champion's chariot next is seen to roll,
Besmear'd with hostile blood, and honorably foul.
To close the pomp, Æthon, the steed of state,
Is led, the fun'rals of his lord to wait.
Stripp'd of his trappings, with a sullen pace
He walks; and the big tears run rolling down his face.
The lance of Pallas, and the crimson crest,
Are borne behind: the victor seiz'd the rest.
The march begins: the trumpets hoarsely sound;
The pikes and lances trail along the ground.
Thus while the Trojan and Arcadian horse
To Pallantean tow'rs direct their course,
In long procession rank'd, the pious chief
Stopp'd in the rear, and gave a vent to grief:
"The public care," he said, "which war attends,
Diverts our present woes, at least suspends.
Peace with the manes of great Pallas dwell!
Hail, holy relics! and a last farewell!"
He said no more, but, inly thro' he mourn'd,
Restrained his tears, and to the camp return'd.

Now suppliants, from Laurentum sent, demand
A truce, with olive branches in their hand;
Obtest his clemency, and from the plain
Beg leave to draw the bodies of their slain.
They plead, that none those common rites deny
To conquer'd foes that in fair battle die.
All cause of hate was ended in their death;
Nor could he war with bodies void of breath.
A king, they hop'd, would hear a king's request,
Whose son he once was call'd, and once his guest.

Their suit, which was too just to be denied,
The hero grants, and farther thus replied:
"O Latian princes, how severe a fate

In causeless quarrels has involv'd your state,
And arm'd against an unoffending man,
Who sought your friendship ere the war began!
You beg a truce, which I would gladly give,
Not only for the slain, but those who live.
I came not hither but by Heav'n's command,
And sent by fate to share the Latian land.
Nor wage I wars unjust: your king denied
My proffer'd friendship, and my promis'd bride;
Left me for Turnus. Turnus then should try
His cause in arms, to conquer or to die.
My right and his are in dispute: the slain
Fell without fault, our quarrel to maintain.
In equal arms let us alone contend;
And let him vanquish, whom his fates befriend.
This is the way (so tell him) to possess
The royal virgin, and restore the peace.
Bear this message back, with ample leave,
That your slain friends may fun'ral rites receive."

Thus having said—th' ambassadors, amaz'd,
Stood mute a while, and on each other gaz'd.
Drances, their chief, who harbor'd in his breast
Long hate to Turnus, as his foe profess'd,
Broke silence first, and to the godlike man,
With graceful action bowing, thus began:
"Auspicious prince, in arms a mighty name,
But yet whose actions far transcend your fame;
Would I your justice or your force express,
Thought can but equal; and all words are less.
Your answer we shall thankfully relate,
And favors granted to the Latian state.
If wish'd success our labor shall attend,
Think peace concluded, and the king your friend:
Let Turnus leave the realm to your command,
And seek alliance in some other land:

Build you the city which your fates assign;
We shall be proud in the great work to join."

Thus Drances; and his words so well persuade
The rest empower'd, that soon a truce is made.
Twelve days the term allow'd: and, during those,
Latians and Trojans, now no longer foes,
Mix'd in the woods, for fun'ral piles prepare
To fell the timber, and forget the war.
Loud axes thro' the groaning groves resound;
Oak, mountain ash, and poplar spread the ground;
First fall from high; and some the trunks receive
In loaden wains; with wedges some they cleave.

And now the fatal news by Fame is blown
Thro' the short circuit of th' Arcadian town,
Of Pallas slain—by Fame, which just before
His triumphs on distended pinions bore.
Rushing from out the gate, the people stand,
Each with a fun'ral flambeau in his hand.
Wildly they stare, distracted with amaze:
The fields are lighten'd with a fiery blaze,
That cast a sullen splendor on their friends,
The marching troop which their dead
prince attends.
Both parties meet: they raise a doleful cry;
The matrons from the walls with shrieks reply,
And their mix'd mourning rends the vaulted sky.
The town is fill'd with tumult and with tears,
Till the loud clamors reach Evander's ears:
Forgetful of his state, he runs along,
With a disorder'd pace, and cleaves the throng;
Falls on the corpse; and groaning there he lies,
With silent grief, that speaks but at his eyes.
Short sighs and sobs succeed; till sorrow breaks
A passage, and at once he weeps and speaks:

"O Pallas! thou hast fail'd thy plighted word,
To fight with caution, not to tempt the sword!
I warn'd thee, but in vain; for well I knew
What perils youthful ardor would pursue,
That boiling blood would carry thee too far,
Young as thou wert in dangers, raw to war!
O curst essay of arms, disastrous doom,
Prelude of bloody fields, and fights to come!
Hard elements of unauspicious war,
Vain vows to Heav'n, and unavailing care!
Thrice happy thou, dear partner of my bed,
Whose holy soul the stroke of Fortune fled,
Præscious of ills, and leaving me behind,
To drink the dregs of life by fate assign'd!
Beyond the goal of nature I have gone:
My Pallas late set out, but reach'd too soon.
If, for my league against th' Ausonian state,
Amidst their weapons I had found my fate,
(Deserv'd from them,) then I had been return'd
A breathless victor, and my son had mourn'd.
Yet will I not my Trojan friend upbraid,
Nor grudge th' alliance I so gladly made.
'T was not his fault, my Pallas fell so young,
But my own crime, for having liv'd too long.
Yet, since the gods had destin'd him to die,
At least he led the way to victory:
First for his friends he won the fatal shore,
And sent whole herds of slaughter'd foes before;
A death too great, too glorious to deplore.
Nor will I add new honors to thy grave,
Content with those the Trojan hero gave:
That funeral pomp thy Phrygian friends design'd,
In which the Tuscan chiefs and army join'd.
Great spoils and trophies, gain'd by thee, they bear:
Then let thy own achievements be thy share.
Even thou, O Turnus, hadst a trophy stood,
Whose mighty trunk had better grac'd the wood,

If Pallas had arriv'd, with equal length
Of years, to match thy bulk with equal strength.
But why, unhappy man, dost thou detain
These troops, to view the tears thou shedd'st in vain?
Go, friends, this message to your lord relate:
Tell him, that, if I bear my bitter fate,
And, after Pallas' death, live ling'ring on,
'Tis to behold his vengeance for my son.
I stay for Turnus, whose devoted head
Is owing to the living and the dead.
My son and I expect it from his hand;
'Tis all that he can give, or we demand.
Joy is no more; but I would gladly go,
To greet my Pallas with such news below."

The morn had now dispell'd the shades of night,
Restoring toils, when she restor'd the light.
The Trojan king and Tuscan chief command
To raise the piles along the winding strand.
Their friends convey the dead fun'ral fires;
Black smold'ring smoke from the green wood expires;
The light of heav'n is chok'd, and the new day retires.
Then thrice around the kindled piles they go
(For ancient custom had ordain'd it so)
Thrice horse and foot about the fires are led;
And thrice, with loud laments, they hail the dead.
Tears, trickling down their breasts, bedew the ground,
And drums and trumpets mix their mournful sound.
Amid the blaze, their pious brethren throw
The spoils, in battle taken from the foe:
Helms, bits emboss'd, and swords of shining steel;
One casts a target, one a chariot wheel;

Some to their fellows their own arms restore:
The fauchions which in luckless fight they bore,
Their bucklers pierc'd, their darts bestow'd in vain,
And shiver'd lances gather'd from the plain.
Whole herds of offer'd bulls, about the fire,
And bristled boars, and woolly sheep expire.
Around the piles a careful troop attends,
To watch the wasting flames, and weep their burning friends;
Ling'ring along the shore, till dewy night
New decks the face of heav'n with starry light.

The conquer'd Latians, with like pious care,
Piles without number for their dead prepare.
Part in the places where they fell are laid;
And part are to the neighb'ring fields convey'd.
The corps of kings, and captains of renown,
Borne off in state, are buried in the town;
The rest, unhonor'd, and without a name,
Are cast a common heap to feed the flame.
Trojans and Latians vie with like desires
To make the field of battle shine with fires,
And the promiscuous blaze to heav'n aspires.

Now had the morning thrice renew'd the light,
And thrice dispell'd the shadows of the night,
When those who round the wasted fires remain,
Perform the last sad office to the slain.
They rake the yet warm ashes from below;
These, and the bones unburn'd, in earth bestow;
These relics with their country rites they grace,
And raise a mount of turf to mark the place.

But, in the palace of the king, appears
A scene more solemn, and a pomp of tears.
Maids, matrons, widows, mix their common moans;
Orphans their sires, and sires lament their sons.

All in that universal sorrow share,
And curse the cause of this unhappy war:
A broken league, a bride unjustly sought,
A crown usurp'd, which with their blood
is bought!
These are the crimes with which they load
the name
Of Turnus, and on him alone exclaim:
"Let him who lords it o'er th' Ausonian land
Engage the Trojan hero hand to hand:
His is the gain; our lot is but to serve;
'Tis just, the sway he seeks, he should deserve."
This Drances aggravates; and adds, with spite:
"His foe expects, and dares him to the fight."
Nor Turnus wants a party, to support
His cause and credit in the Latian court.
His former acts secure his present fame,
And the queen shades him with her mighty name.

While thus their factious minds with fury burn,
The legates from th' Ætolian prince return:
Sad news they bring, that, after all the cost
And care employ'd, their embassy is lost;
That Diomedes refus'd his aid in war,
Unmov'd with presents, and as deaf to pray'r.
Some new alliance must elsewhere be sought,
Or peace with Troy on hard conditions bought.

Latinus, sunk in sorrow, finds too late,
A foreign son is pointed out by fate;
And, till Æneas shall Lavinia wed,
The wrath of Heav'n is hov'ring o'er his head.
The gods, he saw, espous'd the juster side,
When late their titles in the field were tried:
Witness the fresh laments, and fun'ral
tears undried.
Thus, full of anxious thought, he summons all

The Latian senate to the council hall.
The princes come, commanded by their head,
And crowd the paths that to the palace lead.
Supreme in pow'r, and reverenc'd for his years,
He takes the throne, and in the midst appears.
Majestically sad, he sits in state,
And bids his envoys their success relate.

When Venulus began, the murmuring sound
Was hush'd, and sacred silence reign'd around.
"We have," said he, "perform'd your high command,
And pass'd with peril a long tract of land:
We reach'd the place desir'd; with wonder fill'd,
The Grecian tents and rising tow'rs beheld.
Great Diomede has compass'd round with walls
The city, which Argyripa he calls,
From his own Argos nam'd. We touch'd, with joy,
The royal hand that raz'd unhappy Troy.
When introduc'd, our presents first we bring,
Then crave an instant audience from the king.
His leave obtain'd, our native soil we name,
And tell th' important cause for which we came.
Attentively he heard us, while we spoke;
Then, with soft accents, and a pleasing look,
Made this return: 'Ausonian race, of old
Renown'd for peace, and for an age of gold,
What madness has your alter'd minds possess'd,
To change for war hereditary rest,
Solicit arms unknown, and tempt the sword,
A needless ill your ancestors abhorr'd?
We—for myself I speak, and all the name
Of Grecians, who to Troy's destruction came,
Omitting those who were in battle slain,
Or borne by rolling Simoïs to the main—
Not one but suffer'd, and too dearly bought
The prize of honor which in arms he sought;
Some doom'd to death, and some in exile driv'n.

Outcasts, abandon'd by the care of Heav'n;
So worn, so wretched, so despis'd a crew,
As ev'n old Priam might with pity view.
Witness the vessels by Minerva toss'd
In storms; the vengeful Capharean coast;
Th' Eubœan rocks! the prince, whose brother led
Our armies to revenge his injur'd bed,
In Egypt lost! Ulysses with his men
Have seen Charybdis and the Cyclops' den.
Why should I name Idomeneus, in vain
Restor'd to scepters, and expell'd again?
Or young Achilles, by his rival slain?
Ev'n he, the King of Men, the foremost name
Of all the Greeks, and most renown'd by fame,
The proud revenger of another's wife,
Yet by his own adult'ress lost his life;
Fell at his threshold; and the spoils of Troy
The foul polluters of his bed enjoy.
The gods have envied me the sweets of life,
My much lov'd country, and my more lov'd wife:
Banish'd from both, I mourn; while in the sky,
Transform'd to birds, my lost companions fly:
Hov'ring about the coasts, they make their moan,
And cuff the cliffs with pinions not their own.
What squalid specters, in the dead of night,
Break my short sleep, and skim before my sight!
I might have promis'd to myself those harms,
Mad as I was, when I, with mortal arms,
Presum'd against immortal pow'rs to move,
And violate with wounds the Queen of Love.
Such arms this hand shall never more employ;
No hate remains with me to ruin'd Troy.
I war not with its dust; nor am I glad
To think of past events, or good or bad.
Your presents I return: whate'er you bring
To buy my friendship, send the Trojan king.
We met in fight; I know him, to my cost:

With what a whirling force his lance he toss'd!
Heav'ns! what a spring was in his arm, to throw!
How high he held his shield, and rose at ev'ry blow!
Had Troy produc'd two more his match in might,
They would have chang'd the fortune of the fight:
Th' invasion of the Greeks had been return'd,
Our empire wasted, and our cities burn'd.
The long defense the Trojan people made,
The war protracted, and the siege delay'd,
Were due to Hector's and this hero's hand:
Both brave alike, and equal in command;
Æneas, not inferior in the field,
In pious reverence to the gods excell'd.
Make peace, ye Latians, and avoid with care
Th' impending dangers of a fatal war.'
He said no more; but, with this cold excuse,
Refus'd th' alliance, and advis'd a truce."

Thus Venulus concluded his report.
A jarring murmur fill'd the factious court:
As, when a torrent rolls with rapid force,
And dashes o'er the stones that stop the course,
The flood, constrain'd within a scanty space,
Roars horrible along th' uneasy race;
White foam in gath'ring eddies floats around;
The rocky shores rebellow to the sound.

The murmur ceas'd: then from his lofty throne
The king invok'd the gods, and thus begun:
"I wish, ye Latins, what we now debate
Had been resolv'd before it was too late.
Much better had it been for you and me,
Unforc'd by this our last necessity,
To have been earlier wise, than now to call
A council, when the foe surrounds the wall.
O citizens, we wage unequal war,
With men not only Heav'n's peculiar care,
But Heav'n's own race; unconquer'd in the field,

Or, conquer'd, yet unknowing how to yield.
What hopes you had in Diomedes, lay down:
Our hopes must center on ourselves alone.
Yet those how feeble, and, indeed, how vain,
You see too well; nor need my words explain.
Vanquish'd without resource; laid flat by fate;
Factions within, a foe without the gate!
Not but I grant that all perform'd their parts
With manly force, and with undaunted hearts:
With our united strength the war we wag'd;
With equal numbers, equal arms, engag'd.
You see th' event.—Now hear what I propose,
To save our friends, and satisfy our foes.
A tract of land the Latins have possess'd
Along the Tiber, stretching to the west,
Which now Rutulians and Auruncans till,
And their mix'd cattle graze the fruitful hill.
Those mountains fill'd with firs, that lower land,
If you consent, the Trojan shall command,
Call'd into part of what is ours; and there,
On terms agreed, the common country share.
There let 'em build and settle, if they please;
Unless they choose once more to cross the seas,
In search of seats remote from Italy,
And from unwelcome inmates set us free.
Then twice ten galleys let us build with speed,
Or twice as many more, if more they need.
Materials are at hand; a well-grown wood
Runs equal with the margin of the flood:
Let them the number and the form assign;
The care and cost of all the stores be mine.
To treat the peace, a hundred senators
Shall be commission'd hence with ample pow'rs,
With olive the presents they shall bear,
A purple robe, a royal iv'ry chair,
And all the marks of sway that Latian
monarchs wear,

And sums of gold. Among yourselves debate
This great affair, and save the sinking state."

Then Drances took the word, who grudg'd, long since,
The rising glories of the Daunian prince
Factious and rich, bold at the council board,
But cautious in the field, he shunn'd the sword;
A close caballer, and tongue-valiant lord.
Noble his mother was, and near the throne;
But, what his father's parentage, unknown.
He rose, and took th' advantage of the times,
To load young Turnus with invidious crimes.
"Such truths, O king," said he, "your words contain,
As strike the sense, and all replies are vain;
Nor are your loyal subjects now to seek
What common needs require, but fear to speak.
Let him give leave of speech, that haughty man,
Whose pride this unauspicious war began;
For whose ambition (let me dare to say,
Fear set apart, tho' death is in my way)
The plains of Latium run with blood around.
So many valiant heroes bite the ground;
Dejected grief in ev'ry face appears;
A town in mourning, and a land in tears;
While he, th' undoubted author of our harms,
The man who menaces the gods with arms,
Yet, after all his boasts, forsook the fight,
And sought his safety in ignoble flight.
Now, best of kings, since you propose to send
Such bounteous presents to your Trojan friend;
Add yet a greater at our joint request,
One which he values more than all the rest:
Give him the fair Lavinia for his bride;
With that alliance let the league be tied,
And for the bleeding land a lasting peace provide.

Let insolence no longer awe the throne;
But, with a father's right, bestow your own.
For this maligner of the general good,
If still we fear his force, he must be woo'd;
His haughty godhead we with pray'rs implore,
Your scepter to release, and our just rights restore.
O cursed cause of all our ills, must we
Wage wars unjust, and fall in fight, for thee!
What right hast thou to rule the Latian state,
And send us out to meet our certain fate?
'Tis a destructive war: from Turnus' hand
Our peace and public safety we demand.
Let the fair bride to the brave chief remain;
If not, the peace, without the pledge, is vain.
Turnus, I know you think me not your friend,
Nor will I much with your belief contend:
I beg your greatness not to give the law
In others' realms, but, beaten, to withdraw.
Pity your own, or pity our estate;
Nor twist our fortunes with your sinking fate.
Your interest is, the war should never cease;
But we have felt enough to wish the peace:
A land exhausted to the last remains,
Depopulated towns, and driven plains.
Yet, if desire of fame, and thirst of pow'r,
A beauteous princess, with a crown in dow'r,
So fire your mind, in arms assert your right,
And meet your foe, who dares you to the fight.
Mankind, it seems, is made for you alone;
We, but the slaves who mount you to the throne:
A base ignoble crowd, without a name,
Unwept, unworthy, of the fun'ral flame,
By duty bound to forfeit each his life,
That Turnus may possess a royal wife.
Permit not, mighty man, so mean a crew
Should share such triumphs, and detain from you
The post of honor, your undoubted due.

Rather alone your matchless force employ,
To merit what alone you must enjoy."

These words, so full of malice mix'd with art,
Inflam'd with rage the youthful hero's heart.
Then, groaning from the bottom of his breast,
He heav'd for wind, and thus his wrath express'd:
"You, Drances, never want a stream of words,
Then, when the public need requires our swords.
First in the council hall to steer the state,
And ever foremost in a tongue-debate,
While our strong walls secure us from the foe,
Ere yet with blood our ditches overflow:
But let the potent orator declaim,
And with the brand of coward blot my name;
Free leave is giv'n him, when his fatal hand
Has cover'd with more corps the sanguine strand,
And high as mine his tow'ring trophies stand.
If any doubt remains, who dares the most,
Let us decide it at the Trojan's cost,
And issue both abreast, where honor calls—
Foes are not far to seek without the walls—
Unless his noisy tongue can only fight,
And feet were giv'n him but to speed his flight.
I beaten from the field? I forc'd away?
Who, but so known a dastard, dares to say?
Had he but ev'n beheld the fight, his eyes
Had witness'd for me what his tongue denies:
What heaps of Trojans by this hand were slain,
And how the bloody Tiber swell'd the main.
All saw, but he, th' Arcadian troops retire
In scatter'd squadrons, and their prince expire.
The giant brothers, in their camp, have found,
I was not forc'd with ease to quit my ground.
Not such the Trojans tried me, when, enclos'd,
I singly their united arms oppos'd:
First forc'd an entrance thro' their thick array;

Then, glutted with their slaughter, freed my way.
'Tis a destructive war? So let it be,
But to the Phrygian pirate, and to thee!
Meantime proceed to fill the people's ears
With false reports, their minds with panic fears:
Extol the strength of a twice-conquer'd race;
Our foes encourage, and our friends debase.
Believe thy fables, and the Trojan town
Triumphant stands; the Grecians are o'erthrown;
Suppliant at Hector's feet Achilles lies,
And Diomede from fierce Æneas flies.
Say rapid Aufidus with awful dread
Runs backward from the sea, and hides his head,
When the great Trojan on his bank appears;
For that's as true as thy dissembled fears
Of my revenge. Dismiss that vanity:
Thou, Drances, art below a death from me.
Let that vile soul in that vile body rest;
The lodging is well worthy of the guest.

"Now, royal father, to the present state
Of our affairs, and of this high debate:
If in your arms thus early you diffide,
And think your fortune is already tried;
If one defeat has brought us down so low,
As never more in fields to meet the foe;
Then I conclude for peace: 'tis time to treat,
And lie like vassals at the victor's feet.
But, O! if any ancient blood remains,
One drop of all our fathers', in our veins,
That man would I prefer before the rest,
Who dar'd his death with an undaunted breast;
Who comely fell, by no dishonest wound,
To shun that sight, and, dying, gnaw'd the ground.
But, if we still have fresh recruits in store,
If our confederates can afford us more;
If the contended field we bravely fought,

And not a bloodless victory was bought;
Their losses equal'd ours; and, for their slain,
With equal fires they fill'd the shining plain;
Why thus, unforc'd, should we so tamely yield,
And, ere the trumpet sounds, resign the field?
Good unexpected, evils unforeseen,
Appear by turns, as fortune shifts the scene:
Some, rais'd aloft, come tumbling down amain;
Then fall so hard, they bound and rise again.
If Diomede refuse his aid to lend,
The great Messapus yet remains our friend:
Tolumnius, who foretells events, is ours;
Th' Italian chiefs and princes join their pow'rs:
Nor least in number, nor in name the last,
Your own brave subjects have your cause embrac'd
Above the rest, the Volscian Amazon
Contains an army in herself alone,
And heads a squadron, terrible to sight,
With glitt'ring shields, in brazen armor bright.
Yet, if the foe a single fight demand,
And I alone the public peace withstand;
If you consent, he shall not be refus'd,
Nor find a hand to victory unus'd.
This new Achilles, let him take the field,
With fated armor, and Vulcanian shield!
For you, my royal father, and my fame,
I, Turnus, not the least of all my name,
Devote my soul. He calls me hand to hand,
And I alone will answer his demand.
Drances shall rest secure, and neither share
The danger, nor divide the prize of war."

While they debate, nor these nor those will yield,
Æneas draws his forces to the field,
And moves his camp. The scouts with flying speed
Return, and thro' the frighted city spread
Th' unpleasing news, the Trojans are descried,

In battle marching by the river side,
And bending to the town. They take th' alarm:
Some tremble, some are bold; all in confusion arm.
Th' impetuous youth press forward to the field;
They clash the sword, and clatter on the shield:
The fearful matrons raise a screaming cry;
Old feeble men with fainter groans reply;
A jarring sound results, and mingles in the sky,
Like that of swans remurm'ring to the floods,
Or birds of diff'ring kinds in hollow woods

Turnus th' occasion takes, and cries aloud:
"Talk on, ye quaint haranguers of the crowd:
Declaim in praise of peace, when danger calls,
And the fierce foes in arms approach the walls."
He said, and, turning short, with speedy pace,
Casts back a scornful glance, and quits the place:
"Thou, Volusus, the Volscian troops command
To mount; and lead thyself our Ardean band.
Messapus and Catillus, post your force
Along the fields, to charge the Trojan horse.
Some guard the passes, others man the wall;
Drawn up in arms, the rest attend my call."

They swarm from ev'ry quarter of the town,
And with disorder'd haste the rampires crown.
Good old Latinus, when he saw, too late,
The gath'ring storm just breaking on the state,
Dismiss'd the council till a fitter time,
And own'd his easy temper as his crime,
Who, forc'd against his reason, had complied
To break the treaty for the promis'd bride.

Some help to sink new trenches; others aid
To ram the stones, or raise the palisade.
Hoarse trumpets sound th' alarm; around the walls
Runs a distracted crew, whom their last labor calls.

A sad procession in the streets is seen,
Of matrons, that attend the mother queen:
High in her chair she sits, and, at her side,
With downcast eyes, appears the fatal bride.
They mount the cliff, where Pallas' temple stands;
Pray'rs in their mouths, and presents in their hands,
With censers first they fume the sacred shrine,
Then in this common supplication join:
"O patroness of arms, unspotted maid,
Propitious hear, and lend thy Latins aid!
Break short the pirate's lance; pronounce his fate,
And lay the Phrygian low before the gate."

Now Turnus arms for fight. His back and breast
Well-temper'd steel and scaly brass invest:
The cuishes which his brawny thighs enfold
Are mingled metal damask'd o'er with gold.
His faithful fauchion sits upon his side;
Nor casque, nor crest, his manly features hide:
But, bare to view, amid surrounding friends,
With godlike grace, he from the tow'r descends.
Exulting in his strength, he seems to dare
His absent rival, and to promise war.
Freed from his keepers, thus, with broken reins,
The wanton courser prances o'er the plains,
Or in the pride of youth o'erleaps the mounds,
And snuffs the females in forbidden grounds.
Or seeks his wat'ring in the well-known flood,
To quench his thirst, and cool his fiery blood:
He swims luxuriant in the liquid plain,
And o'er his shoulder flows his waving mane:
He neighs, he snorts, he bears his head on high;
Before his ample chest the frothy waters fly.

Soon as the prince appears without the gate,
The Volscians, with their virgin leader, wait
His last commands. Then, with a graceful mien,

Lights from her lofty steed the warrior queen:
Her squadron imitates, and each descends; *500*
Whose common suit Camilla thus commends:
“If sense of honor, if a soul secure
Of inborn worth, that can all tests endure,
Can promise aught, or on itself rely
Greatly to dare, to conquer or to die;
Then, I alone, sustain’d by these, will meet
The Tyrrhene troops, and promise their defeat.
Ours be the danger, ours the sole renown:
You, gen’ral, stay behind, and guard the town:”

Turnus a while stood mute, with glad surprise,
And on the fierce virago fix’d his eyes;
Then thus return’d: “O grace of Italy,
With what becoming thanks can I reply?
Not only words lie lab’ring in my breast,
But thought itself is by thy praise oppress’d.
Yet rob me not of all; but let me join
My toils, my hazard, and my fame, with thine.
The Trojan, not in stratagem unskill’d,
Sends his light horse before to scour the field:
Himself, thro’ steep ascents and thorny brakes,
A larger compass to the city takes.
This news my scouts confirm, and I prepare
To foil his cunning, and his force to dare;
With chosen foot his passage to forelay,
And place an ambush in the winding way.
Thou, with thy Volscians, face the Tuscan horse;
The brave Messapus shall thy troops enforce
With those of Tibur, and the Latian band,
Subjected all to thy supreme command.”
This said, he warns Messapus to the war,
Then ev’ry chief exhorts with equal care.
All thus encourag’d, his own troops he joins,
And hastes to prosecute his deep designs.

Enclos'd with hills, a winding valley lies,
By nature form'd for fraud, and fitted
for surprise.
A narrow track, by human steps untrode,
Leads, thro' perplexing thorns, to this
obscure abode.
High o'er the vale a steepy mountain stands,
Whence the surveying sight the nether
ground commands.
The top is level, an offensive seat
Of war; and from the war a safe retreat:
For, on the right and left, is room to press
The foes at hand, or from afar distress;
To drive 'em headlong downward, and to pour
On their descending backs a stony show'r.
Thither young Turnus took the well-known way,
Possess'd the pass, and in blind ambush lay.

Meantime Latonian Phœbe, from the skies,
Beheld th' approaching war with hateful eyes,
And call'd the light-foot Opis to her aid,
Her most belov'd and ever-trusty maid;
Then with a sigh began: "Camilla goes
To meet her death amidst her fatal foes:
The nymphs I lov'd of all my mortal train,
Invested with Diana's arms, in vain.
Nor is my kindness for the virgin new:
'T was born with her; and with her years it grew.
Her father Metabus, when forc'd away
From old Privernum, for tyrannic sway,
Snatch'd up, and sav'd from his prevailing foes,
This tender babe, companion of his woes.
Casmilla was her mother; but he drown'd
One hissing letter in a softer sound,
And call'd Camilla. Thro' the woods he flies;
Wrapp'd in his robe the royal infant lies.
His foes in sight, he mends his weary pace;

With shout and clamors they pursue the chase.
The banks of Amasene at length he gains:

The raging flood his farther flight restrains,
Rais'd o'er the borders with unusual rains.
Prepar'd to plunge into the stream, he fears,
Not for himself, but for the charge he bears.
Anxious, he stops a while, and thinks in haste;
Then, desp'rate in distress, resolves at last.
A knotty lance of well-boil'd oak he bore;
The middle part with cork he cover'd o'er:
He clos'd the child within the hollow space;
With twigs of bending osier bound the case;
Then pois'd the spear, heavy with human weight,
And thus invok'd my favor for the freight:
'Accept, great goddess of the woods,' he said,
'Sent by her sire, this dedicated maid!
Thro' air she flies a suppliant to thy shrine;
And the first weapons that she knows, are thine.'
He said; and with full force the spear he threw:
Above the sounding waves Camilla flew.
Then, press'd by foes, he stemm'd the stormy tide,
And gain'd, by stress of arms, the farther side.
His fasten'd spear he pull'd from out the ground,
And, victor of his vows, his infant nymph unbound;
Nor, after that, in towns which walls enclose,
Would trust his hunted life amidst his foes;
But, rough, in open air he chose to lie;
Earth was his couch, his cov'ring was the sky.
On hills unshorn, or in a desert den,
He shunn'd the dire society of men.
A shepherd's solitary life he led;
His daughter with the milk of mares he fed.
The dugs of bears, and ev'ry salvage beast,
He drew, and thro' her lips the liquor press'd.
The little Amazon could scarcely go:
He loads her with a quiver and a bow;

And, that she might her stagg'ring
steps command,
He with a slender jav'lin fills her hand.
Her flowing hair no golden fillet bound;
Nor swept her trailing robe the dusty ground.
Instead of these, a tiger's hide o'erspread
Her back and shoulders, fasten'd to her head.
The flying dart she first attempts to fling,
And round her tender temples toss'd the sling;
Then, as her strength with years increas'd, began
To pierce aloft in air the soaring swan,
And from the clouds to fetch the heron
and the crane.
The Tuscan matrons with each other vied,
To bless their rival sons with such a bride;
But she disdains their love, to share with me
The sylvan shades and vow'd virginity.
And, O! I wish, contented with my cares
Of salvage spoils, she had not sought the wars!
Then had she been of my celestial train,
And shunn'd the fate that dooms her to be slain.
But since, opposing Heav'n's decree, she goes
To find her death among forbidden foes,
Haste with these arms, and take thy steepy flight.
Where, with the gods, averse, the Latins fight.
This bow to thee, this quiver I bequeath,
This chosen arrow, to revenge her death:
By whate'er hand Camilla shall be slain,
Or of the Trojan or Italian train,
Let him not pass unpunish'd from the plain.
Then, in a hollow cloud, myself will aid
To bear the breathless body of my maid:
Unspoil'd shall be her arms, and unprofan'd
Her holy limbs with any human hand,
And in a marble tomb laid in her native land."

She said. The faithful nymph descends from high

With rapid flight, and cuts the sounding sky:
Black clouds and stormy winds around her body fly.

By this, the Trojan and the Tuscan horse,
Drawn up in squadrons, with united force,
Approach the walls: the sprightly coursers bound,
Press forward on their bits, and shift their ground.
Shields, arms, and spears flash horribly from far;
And the fields glitter with a waving war.
Oppos'd to these, come on with furious force
Messapus, Coras, and the Latian horse;
These in the body plac'd, on either hand
Sustain'd and clos'd by fair Camilla's band.
Advancing in a line, they couch their spears;
And less and less the middle space appears.
Thick smoke obscures the field; and scarce are seen
The neighing coursers, and the shouting men.
In distance of their darts they stop their course;
Then man to man they rush, and horse to horse.
The face of heav'n their flying jav'lins hide,
And deaths unseen are dealt on either side.
Tyrrhenus, and Aconteus, void of fear,
By mettled coursers borne in full career,
Meet first oppos'd; and, with a mighty shock,
Their horses' heads against each other knock.
Far from his steed is fierce Aconteus cast,
As with an engine's force, or lightning's blast:
He rolls along in blood, and breathes his last.
The Latin squadrons take a sudden fright,
And sling their shields behind, to save their backs in flight
Spurring at speed to their own walls they drew;
Close in the rear the Tuscan troops pursue,
And urge their flight: Asylas leads the chase;
Till, seiz'd, with shame, they wheel about and face,
Receive their foes, and raise a threat'ning cry.
The Tuscans take their turn to fear and fly.

So swelling surges, with a thund'ring roar,
Driv'n on each other's backs, insult the shore,
Bound o'er the rocks, encroach upon the land,
And far upon the beach eject the sand;
Then backward, with a swing, they take their way,
Repuls'd from upper ground, and seek their
 mother sea;
With equal hurry quit th' invaded shore,
And swallow back the sand and stones
 they spew'd before.

Twice were the Tuscans masters of the field,
Twice by the Latins, in their turn, repell'd.
Asham'd at length, to the third charge they ran;
Both hosts resolv'd, and mingled man to man.
Now dying groans are heard; the fields are strow'd
With falling bodies, and are drunk with blood.
Arms, horses, men, on heaps together lie:
Confus'd the fight, and more confus'd the cry.
Orsilochus, who durst not press too near
Strong Remulus, at distance drove his spear,
And stuck the steel beneath his horse's ear.
The fiery steed, impatient of the wound,
Curvets, and, springing upward with a bound,
His helpless lord cast backward on the ground.
Catillus pierc'd Iolas first; then drew
His reeking lance, and at Herminius threw,
The mighty champion of the Tuscan crew.
His neck and throat unarm'd, his head was bare,
But shaded with a length of yellow hair:
Secure, he fought, expos'd on ev'ry part,
A spacious mark for swords, and for the flying dart.
Across the shoulders came the feather'd wound;
Transfix'd he fell, and doubled to the ground.
The sands with streaming blood are sanguine dyed,
And death with honor sought on either side.

Resistless thro' the war Camilla rode,
In danger unappall'd, and pleas'd with blood.
One side was bare for her exerted breast;
One shoulder with her painted quiver press'd.
Now from afar her fatal jav'lins play;
Now with her ax's edge she hews her way:
Diana's arms upon her shoulder sound;
And when, too closely press'd, she quits
the ground,
From her bent bow she sends a
backward wound.
Her maids, in martial pomp, on either side,
Larina, Tulla, fierce Tarpeia, ride:
Italians all; in peace, their queen's delight;
In war, the bold companions of the fight.
So march'd the Tracian Amazons of old,
When Thermodon with bloody billows roll'd:
Such troops as these in shining arms were seen,
When Theseus met in fight their maiden queen:
Such to the field Penthisilea led,
From the fierce virgin when the Grecians fled;
With such, return'd triumphant from the war,
Her maids with cries attend the lofty car;
They clash with manly force their moony shields;
With female shouts resound the Phrygian fields.

Who foremost, and who last, heroic maid,
On the cold earth were by thy courage laid?
Thy spear, of mountain ash, Eumenius first,
With fury driv'n, from side to side transpierc'd:
A purple stream came spouting from the wound;
Bath'd in his blood he lies, and bites the ground.
Liris and Pegasus at once she slew:
The former, as the slacken'd reins he drew
Of his faint steed; the latter, as he stretch'd
His arm to prop his friend, the jav'lin reach'd.
By the same weapon, sent from the same hand,

Both fall together, and both spurn the sand.
Amastrus next is added to the slain:
The rest in rout she follows o'er the plain:
Tereus, Harpalycus, Demophoon,
And Chromis, at full speed her fury shun.
Of all her deadly darts, not one she lost;
Each was attended with a Trojan ghost.
Young Ornithus bestrode a hunter steed,
Swift for the chase, and of Apulian breed.
Him from afar she spied, in arms unknown:
O'er his broad back an ox's hide was thrown;
His helm a wolf, whose gaping jaws were spread
A cov'ring for his cheeks, and grinn'd around his head,
He clench'd within his hand an iron prong,
And tower'd above the rest, conspicuous in the throng.
Him soon she singled from the flying train,
And slew with ease; then thus insults the slain:
"Vain hunter, didst thou think thro' woods to chase
The savage herd, a vile and trembling race?
Here cease thy vaunts, and own my victory:
A woman warrior was too strong for thee.
Yet, if the ghosts demand the conqu'ror's name,
Confessing great Camilla, save thy shame."
Then Butes and Orsilochus she slew,
The bulkiest bodies of the Trojan crew;
But Butes breast to breast: the spear descends
Above the gorget, where his helmet ends,
And o'er the shield which his left side defends.
Orsilochus and she their courses ply:
He seems to follow, and she seems to fly;
But in a narrower ring she makes the race;
And then he flies, and she pursues the chase.
Gath'ring at length on her deluded foe,
She swings her ax, and rises to the blow
Full on the helm behind, with such a sway

The weapon falls, the riven steel gives way:
He groans, he roars, he sues in vain for grace;
Brains, mingled with his blood, besmear his face.

Astonish'd Aunus just arrives by chance,
To see his fall; nor farther dares advance;
But, fixing on the horrid maid his eye,
He stares, and shakes, and finds it vain to fly;
Yet, like a true Ligurian, born to cheat,
(At least while fortune favor'd his deceit,)
Cries out aloud: "What courage have you shown,
Who trust your courser's strength, and not your own?
Forego the vantage of your horse, alight,
And then on equal terms begin the fight:
It shall be seen, weak woman, what you can,
When, foot to foot, you combat with a man,"
He said. She glows with anger and disdain,
Dismounts with speed to dare him on the plain,
And leaves her horse at large among her train;
With her drawn sword defies him to the field,
And, marching, lifts aloft her maiden shield.
The youth, who thought his cunning did succeed,
Reins round his horse, and urges all his speed;
Adds the remembrance of the spur, and hides
The goring rowels in his bleeding sides.
"Vain fool, and coward!" cries the lofty maid,
"Caught in the train which thou thyself hast laid!
On others practice thy Ligurian arts;
Thin stratagems and tricks of little hearts
Are lost on me: nor shalt thou safe retire,
With vaunting lies, to thy fallacious sire."
At this, so fast her flying feet she sped,
That soon she strain'd beyond his horse's head:
Then turning short, at once she seiz'd the rein,
And laid the boaster grov'ling on the plain.

Not with more ease the falcon, from above,
Trusses in middle air the trembling dove,
Then plumes the prey, in her strong
pounces bound:
The feathers, foul with blood, come tumbling
to the ground.

Now mighty Jove, from his superior height,
With his broad eye surveys th' unequal fight.
He fires the breast of Tarchon with disdain,
And sends him to redeem th' abandon'd plain.
Betwixt the broken ranks the Tuscan rides,
And these encourages, and those he chides;
Recalls each leader, by his name, from flight;
Renews their ardor, and restores the fight.
"What panic fear has seiz'd your souls? O shame,
O brand perpetual of th' Etrurian name!
Cowards incurable, a woman's hand
Drives, breaks, and scatters your ignoble band!
Now cast away the sword, and quit the shield!
What use of weapons which you dare not wield?
Not thus you fly your female foes by night,
Nor shun the feast, when the full bowls invite;
When to fat off'rings the glad augur calls,
And the shrill hornpipe sounds to bacchanals.
These are your studied cares, your lewd delight:
Swift to debauch, but slow to manly fight."
Thus having said, he spurs amid the foes,
Not managing the life he meant to lose.
The first he found he seiz'd with headlong haste,
In his strong gripe, and clasp'd around the waist;
'Twas Venulus, whom from his horse he tore,
And, laid athwart his own, in triumph bore.
Loud shouts ensue; the Latins turn their eyes,
And view th' unusual sight with vast surprise.
The fiery Tarchon, flying o'er the plains,
Press'd in his arms the pond'rous prey sustains;

Then, with his shorten'd spear, explores around
His jointed arms, to fix a deadly wound.
Nor less the captive struggles for his life:
He writhes his body to prolong the strife,
And, fencing for his naked throat, exerts
His utmost vigor, and the point averts.
So stoops the yellow eagle from on high,
And bears a speckled serpent thro' the sky,
Fast'ning his crooked talons on the prey:
The pris'ner hisses thro' the liquid way;
Resists the royal hawk; and, tho' oppress'd,
She fights in volumes, and erects her crest:
Turn'd to her foe, she stiffens ev'ry scale,
And shoots her forky tongue, and whisks her
threat'ning tail.
Against the victor, all defense is weak:
Th' imperial bird still plies her with his beak;
He tears her bowels, and her breast he gores;
Then claps his pinions, and securely soars.
Thus, thro' the midst of circling enemies,
Strong Tarchon snatch'd and bore away his prize.
The Tyrrhene troops, that shrunk before,
now press
The Latins, and presume the like success.

Then Aruns, doom'd to death, his arts assay'd,
To murther, unespied, the Volscian maid:
This way and that his winding course he bends,
And, whereso'er she turns, her steps attends.
When she retires victorious from the chase,
He wheels about with care, and shifts his place;
When, rushing on, she seeks her foes flight,
He keeps aloof, but keeps her still in sight:
He threats, and trembles, trying ev'ry way,
Unseen to kill, and safely to betray.
Chloreus, the priest of Cybele, from far,
Glitt'ring in Phrygian arms amidst the war,

Was by the virgin view'd. The steed he press'd
Was proud with trappings, and his brawny chest
With scales of gilded brass was cover'd o'er;
A robe of Tyrian dye the rider wore.
With deadly wounds he gall'd the distant foe;
Gnossian his shafts, and Lycian was his bow:
A golden helm his front and head surrounds
A gilded quiver from his shoulder sounds.
Gold, weav'd with linen, on his thighs he wore,
With flowers of needlework distinguish'd o'er,
With golden buckles bound, and gather'd up before.
Him the fierce maid beheld with ardent eyes,
Fond and ambitious of so rich a prize,
Or that the temple might his trophies hold,
Or else to shine herself in Trojan gold.
Blind in her haste, she chases him alone.
And seeks his life, regardless of her own.

This lucky moment the sly traitor chose:
Then, starting from his ambush, up he rose,
And threw, but first to Heav'n address'd his vows:
"O patron of Socrates' high abodes,
Phœbus, the ruling pow'r among the gods,
Whom first we serve, whole woods of
unctuous pine
Are fell'd for thee, and to thy glory shine;
By thee protected with our naked soles,
Thro' flames unsing'd we march, and tread
the kindled coals
Give me, propitious pow'r, to wash away
The stains of this dishonorable day:
Nor spoils, nor triumph, from the fact I claim,
But with my future actions trust my fame.
Let me, by stealth, this female plague o'ercome,
And from the field return inglorious home."
Apollo heard, and, granting half his pray'r,
Shuffled in winds the rest, and toss'd in empty air.

He gives the death desir'd; his safe return
By southern tempests to the seas is borne.

Now, when the jav'lin whizz'd along the skies,
Both armies on Camilla turn'd their eyes,
Directed by the sound. Of either host,
Th' unhappy virgin, tho' concern'd the most,
Was only deaf; so greedy was she bent
On golden spoils, and on her prey intent;
Till in her pap the winged weapon stood
Infix'd, and deeply drunk the purple blood.
Her sad attendants hasten to sustain
Their dying lady, drooping on the plain.
Far from their sight the trembling Aruns flies,
With beating heart, and fear confus'd with joys;
Nor dares he farther to pursue his blow,
Or ev'n to bear the sight of his expiring foe.
As, when the wolf has torn a bullock's hide
At unawares, or ranch'd a shepherd's side,
Conscious of his audacious deed, he flies,
And claps his quiv'ring tail between his thighs:
So, speeding once, the wretch no more attends,
But, spurring forward, herds among his friends.

She wrench'd the jav'lin with her dying hands,
But wedg'd within her breast the weapon stands;
The wood she draws, the steely point remains;
She staggers in her seat with agonizing pains:
(A gath'ring mist o'erclouds her cheerful eyes,
And from her cheeks the rosy color flies:)
Then turns to her, whom of her female train
She trusted most, and thus she speaks with pain:
"Acca, 'tis past! he swims before my sight,
Inexorable Death; and claims his right.
Bear my last words to Turnus; fly with speed,
And bid him timely to my charge succeed,
Repel the Trojans, and the town relieve:

Farewell! and in this kiss my parting breath receive."
She said, and, sliding, sunk upon the plain:
Dying, her open'd hand forsakes the rein;
Short, and more short, she pants; by slow degrees
Her mind the passage from her body frees.
She drops her sword; she nods her plumy crest,
Her drooping head declining on her breast:
In the last sigh her struggling soul expires,
And, murm'ring with disdain, to Stygian
sounds retires.

A shout, that struck the golden stars, ensued;
Despair and rage the languish'd fight renew'd.
The Trojan troops and Tuscans, in a line,
Advance to charge; the mix'd Arcadians join.

But Cynthia's maid, high seated, from afar
Surveys the field, and fortune of the war,
Unmov'd a while, till, prostrate on the plain,
Welt'ring in blood, she sees Camilla slain,
And, round her corpse, of friends and foes
a fighting train.
Then, from the bottom of her breast, she drew
A mournful sigh, and these sad words ensue:
"Too dear a fine, ah much lamented maid,
For warring with the Trojans, thou hast paid!
Nor aught avail'd, in this unhappy strife,
Diana's sacred arms, to save thy life.
Yet unreveng'd thy goddess will not leave
Her vot'ry's death, nor; with vain sorrow grieve.
Branded the wretch, and be his name abhorr'd;
But after ages shall thy praise record.
Th' inglorious coward soon shall press the plain:
Thus vows thy queen, and thus the Fates ordain."

High o'er the field there stood a hilly mound,
Sacred the place, and spread with oaks around,

Where, in a marble tomb, Dercennus lay,
A king that once in Latium bore the sway.
The beauteous Opis thither bent her flight,
To mark the traitor Aruns from the height.
Him in refulgent arms she soon espied,
Swoln with success; and loudly thus she cried:
"Thy backward steps, vain boaster, are too late;
Turn like a man, at length, and meet thy fate.
Charg'd with my message, to Camilla go,
And say I sent thee to the shades below,
An honor undeserv'd from Cynthia's bow."

She said, and from her quiver chose with speed
The winged shaft, predestin'd for the deed;
Then to the stubborn yew her strength applied,
Till the far distant horns approach'd on either side.
The bowstring touch'd her breast, so strong she drew;
Whizzing in air the fatal arrow flew.
At once the twanging bow and sounding dart
The traitor heard, and felt the point within his heart.
Him, beating with his heels in pangs of death,
His flying friends to foreign fields bequeath.
The conqu'ring damsel, with expanded wings,
The welcome message to her mistress brings.

Their leader lost, the Volscians quit the field,
And, unsustain'd, the chiefs of Turnus yield.
The frighted soldiers, when their captains fly,
More on their speed than on their strength rely.
Confus'd in flight, they bear each other down,
And spur their horses headlong to the town.
Driv'n by their foes, and to their fears resign'd,
Not once they turn, but take their wounds behind.
These drop the shield, and those the lance forego,
Or on their shoulders bear the slacken'd bow.

The hoofs of horses, with a rattling sound,
Beat short and thick, and shake the rotten ground.
Black clouds of dust come rolling in the sky,
And o'er the darken'd walls and rampires fly.
The trembling matrons, from their lofty stands,
Rend heav'n with female shrieks, and wring
their hands.
All pressing on, pursuers and pursued,
Are crush'd in crowds, a mingled multitude.
Some happy few escape: the throng too late
Rush on for entrance, till they choke the gate.
Ev'n in the sight of home, the wretched sire
Looks on, and sees his helpless son expire.
Then, in a fright, the folding gates they close,
But leave their friends excluded with their foes.
The vanquish'd cry; the victors loudly shout;
'Tis terror all within, and slaughter all without.
Blind in their fear, they bounce against the wall,
Or, to the moats pursued, precipitate their fall.

The Latian virgins, valiant with despair,
Arm'd on the tow'rs, the common danger share:
So much of zeal their country's cause inspir'd;
So much Camilla's great example fir'd.
Poles, sharpen'd in the flames, from high they throw,
With imitated darts, to gall the foe.
Their lives for godlike freedom they bequeath,
And crowd each other to be first in death.
Meantime to Turnus, ambush'd in the shade,
With heavy tidings came th' unhappy maid:
"The Volscians overthrown, Camilla kill'd;
The foes, entirely masters of the field,
Like a resistless flood, come rolling on:
The cry goes off the plain, and thickens to the town."

Inflam'd with rage, (for so the Furies fire
The Daunian's breast, and so the Fates require,)

He leaves the hilly pass, the woods in vain
Possess'd, and downward issues on the plain.
Scarce was he gone, when to the straits, now freed
From secret foes, the Trojan troops succeed.
Thro' the black forest and the ferny brake,
Unknowingly secure, their way they take;
From the rough mountains to the plain descend,
And there, in order drawn, their line extend.
Both armies now in open fields are seen;
Nor far the distance of the space between.
Both to the city bend. Æneas sees,
Thro' smoking fields, his hast'ning enemies;
And Turnus views the Trojans in array,
And hears th' approaching horses proudly neigh.
Soon had their hosts in bloody battle join'd;
But westward to the sea the sun declin'd.
Entrench'd before the town both armies lie,
While Night with sable wings involves the sky.

Book XII

Turnus challenges Æneas to a single combat: articles are agreed on, but broken by the Rutuli, who wound Æneas. He is miraculously cured by Venus, forces Turnus to a duel, and concludes the poem with his death.

When Turnus saw the Latins leave the field,
Their armies broken, and their courage quell'd,
Himself become the mark of public spite,
His honor question'd for the promis'd fight;
The more he was with vulgar hate oppress'd,
The more his fury boil'd within his breast:
He rous'd his vigor for the last debate,
And rais'd his haughty soul to meet his fate.

As, when the swains the Libyan lion chase,
He makes a sour retreat, nor mends his pace;
But, if the pointed jav'lin pierce his side,
The lordly beast returns with double pride:
He wrenches out the steel, he roars for pain;
His sides he lashes, and erects his mane:
So Turnus fares; his eyeballs flash with fire,
Thro' his wide nostrils clouds of smoke expire.

Trembling with rage, around the court he ran,
At length approach'd the king, and thus began:
"No more excuses or delays: I stand
In arms prepar'd to combat, hand to hand,
This base deserter of his native land.
The Trojan, by his word, is bound to take
The same conditions which himself did make.
Renew the truce; the solemn rites prepare,

And to my single virtue trust the war.
The Latians unconcern'd shall see the fight;
This arm unaided shall assert your right:
Then, if my prostrate body press the plain,
To him the crown and beauteous bride remain."

To whom the king sedately thus replied:
"Brave youth, the more your valor has been tried,
The more becomes it us, with due respect,
To weigh the chance of war, which you neglect.
You want not wealth, or a successive throne,
Or cities which your arms have made your own:
My towns and treasures are at your command,
And stor'd with blooming beauties is my land;
Laurentum more than one Lavinia sees,
Unmarried, fair, of noble families.
Now let me speak, and you with patience hear,
Things which perhaps may grate a lover's ear,
But sound advice, proceeding from a heart
Sincerely yours, and free from fraudful art.
The gods, by signs, have manifestly shown,
No prince Italian born should heir my throne:
Oft have our augurs, in prediction skill'd,
And oft our priests, foreign son reveal'd.
Yet, won by worth that cannot be withstood,
Brib'd by my kindness to my kindred blood,
Urg'd by my wife, who would not be denied,
I promis'd my Lavinia for your bride:
Her from her plighted lord by force I took;
All ties of treaties, and of honor, broke:
On your account I wag'd an impious war—
With what success, 'tis needless to declare—
I and my subjects feel, and you have had your share.
Twice vanquish'd while in bloody fields we strive,
Scarce in our walls we keep our hopes alive:
The rolling flood runs warm with human gore;
The bones of Latians blanch the neighb'ring shore.

Why put I not an end to this debate,
Still unresolv'd, and still a slave to fate?
If Turnus' death a lasting peace can give,
Why should I not procure it whilst you live?
Should I to doubtful arms your youth betray,
What would my kinsmen the Rutulians say?
And, should you fall in fight, (which Heav'n defend!)
How curse the cause which hasten'd to his end
The daughter's lover and the father's friend?
Weigh in your mind the various chance of war;
Pity your parent's age, and ease his care."

Such balmy words he pour'd, but all in vain:
The proffer'd med'cine but provok'd the pain.
The wrathful youth, disdaining the relief,
With intermitting sobs thus vents his grief:
"The care, O best of fathers, which you take
For my concerns, at my desire forsake.
Permit me not to languish out my days,
But make the best exchange of life for praise.
This arm, this lance, can well dispute the prize;
And the blood follows, where the weapon flies.
His goddess mother is not near, to shroud
The flying coward with an empty cloud."

But now the queen, who fear'd for Turnus' life,
And loath'd the hard conditions of the strife,
Held him by force; and, dying in his death,
In these sad accents gave her sorrow breath:
"O Turnus, I adjure thee by these tears,
And whate'er price Amata's honor bears
Within thy breast, since thou art all my hope,
My sickly mind's repose, my sinking age's prop;
Since on the safety of thy life alone
Depends Latinus, and the Latian throne:
Refuse me not this one, this only pray'r,
To waive the combat, and pursue the war.

Whatever chance attends this fatal strife,
Think it includes, in thine, Amata's life.
I cannot live a slave, or see my throne
Usurp'd by strangers or a Trojan son."

At this, a flood of tears Lavinia shed;
A crimson blush her beauteous face o'erspread,
Varying her cheeks by turns with white and red.
The driving colors, never at a stay,
Run here and there, and flush, and fade away.
Delightful change! Thus Indian iv'ry shows,
Which with the bord'ring paint of purple glows;
Or lilies damask'd by the neighb'ring rose.

The lover gaz'd, and, burning with desire,
The more he look'd, the more he fed the fire:
Revenge, and jealous rage, and secret spite,
Roll in his breast, and rouse him to the fight.
Then fixing on the queen his ardent eyes,
Firm to his first intent, he thus replies:
"O mother, do not by your tears prepare
Such boding omens, and prejudge the war.
Resolv'd on fight, I am no longer free
To shun my death, if Heav'n my death decree."
Then turning to the herald, thus pursues:
"Go, greet the Trojan with ungrateful news;
Denounce from me, that, when to-morrow's light
Shall gild the heav'ns, he need not urge the fight;
The Trojan and Rutulian troops no more
Shall dye, with mutual blood, the Latian shore:
Our single swords the quarrel shall decide,
And to the victor be the beauteous bride."

He said, and striding on, with speedy pace,
He sought his coursers of the Thracian race.
At his approach they toss their heads on high,
And, proudly neighing, promise victory.

The sires of these Orythia sent from far,
To grace Pilumnus, when he went to war.
The drifts of Thracian snows were scarce
so white,
Nor northern winds in fleetness match'd
their flight.
Officious grooms stand ready by his side;
And some with combs their flowing manes divide,
And others stroke their chests and gently
soothe their pride.

He sheath'd his limbs in arms; a temper'd mass
Of golden metal those, and mountain brass.
Then to his head his glitt'ring helm he tied,
And girt his faithful fauchion to his side.
In his Ætnæan forge, the God of Fire
That fauchion labor'd for the hero's sire;
Immortal keenness on the blade bestow'd,
And plung'd it hissing in the Stygian flood.
Propp'd on a pillar, which the ceiling bore,
Was plac'd the lance Auruncan Actor wore;
Which with such force he brandish'd in his hand,
The tough ash trembled like an osier wand:
Then cried: "O pond'rous spoil of Actor slain,
And never yet by Turnus toss'd in vain,
Fail not this day thy wonted force; but go,
Sent by this hand, to pierce the Trojan foe!
Give me to tear his corslet from his breast,
And from that eunuch head to rend the crest;
Dragg'd in the dust, his frizzled hair to soil,
Hot from the vexing ir'n, and smear'd
with fragrant oil!"

Thus while he raves, from his wide nostrils flies
A fiery steam, and sparkles from his eyes.
So fares the bull in his lov'd female's sight:
Proudly he bellows, and preludes the fight;

He tries his goring horns against a tree,
And meditates his absent enemy;
He pushes at the winds; he digs the strand
With his black hoofs, and spurns the yellow sand.

Nor less the Trojan, in his Lemnian arms,
To future fight his manly courage warms:
He whets his fury, and with joy prepares
To terminate at once the ling'ring wars;
To cheer his chiefs and tender son, relates
What Heav'n had promis'd,
and expounds the fates.
Then to the Latian king he sends, to cease
The rage of arms, and ratify the peace.

The morn ensuing, from the mountain's height,
Had scarcely spread the skies with rosy light;
Th' ethereal coursers, bounding from the sea,
From out their flaming nostrils breath'd the day;
When now the Trojan and Rutulian guard,
In friendly labor join'd, the list prepar'd.
Beneath the walls they measure out the space;
Then sacred altars rear, on sods of grass,
Where, with religious their common gods
they place.
In purest white the priests their heads attire;
And living waters bear, and holy fire;
And, o'er their linen hoods and shaded hair,
Long twisted wreaths of sacred veryain wear.

In order issuing from the town appears
The Latin legion, arm'd with pointed spears;
And from the fields, advancing on a line,
The Trojan and the Tuscan forces join:
Their various arms afford a pleasing sight;
A peaceful train they seem, in peace
prepar'd for fight.

Betwixt the ranks the proud commanders ride,
Glitt'ring with gold, and vests in purple dyed;
Here Mnestheus, author of the Memmian line,
And there Messapus, born of seed divine.
The sign is giv'n; and, round the listed space,
Each man in order fills his proper place.
Reclining on their ample shields, they stand,
And fix their pointed lances in the sand.
Now, studious of the sight, a num'rous throng
Of either sex promiscuous, old and young,
Swarm the town: by those who rest behind,
The gates and walls and houses' tops are lin'd.
Meantime the Queen of Heav'n beheld the sight,
With eyes unpleas'd, from Mount Albano's height
(Since call'd Albano by succeeding fame,
But then an empty hill, without a name).
She thence survey'd the field, the Trojan pow'rs,
The Latian squadrons, and Laurentine tow'rs.
Then thus the goddess of the skies bespoke,
With sighs and tears, the goddess of the lake,
King Turnus' sister, once a lovely maid,
Ere to the lust of lawless Jove betray'd:
Compress'd by force, but, by the grateful god,
Now made the Nais of the neighb'ring flood.
"O nymph, the pride of living lakes," said she,
"O most renown'd, and most belov'd by me,
Long hast thou known, nor need I to record,
The wanton sallies of my wand'ring lord.
Of ev'ry Latian fair whom Jove misled
To mount by stealth my violated bed,
To thee alone I grudg'd not his embrace,
But gave a part of heav'n, and an unenvied place.
Now learn from me thy near approaching grief,
Nor think my wishes want to thy relief.
While fortune favor'd, nor Heav'n's King denied
To lend my succor to the Latian side,
I sav'd thy brother, and the sinking state:

But now he struggles with unequal fate,
And goes, with gods averse, o'ermatch'd in might,
To meet inevitable death in fight;
Nor must I break the truce, nor can sustain
the sight.
Thou, if thou dar'st thy present aid supply;
It well becomes a sister's care to try."

At this the lovely nymph, with grief oppress'd,
Thrice tore her hair, and beat her comely breast.
To whom Saturnia thus: "Thy tears are late:
Haste, snatch him, if he can be snatch'd from fate:
New tumults kindle; violate the truce:
Who knows what changeful fortune may produce?
'Tis not a crime t' attempt what I decree;
Or, if it were, discharge the crime on me."
She said, and, sailing on the winged wind,
Left the sad nymph suspended in her mind.

And now pomp the peaceful kings appear:
Four steeds the chariot of Latinus bear;
Twelve golden beams around his temples play,
To mark his lineage from the God of Day.
Two snowy coursers Turnus' chariot yoke,
And in his hand two massy spears he shook:
Then issued from the camp, in arms divine,
Æneas, author of the Roman line;
And by his side Ascanius took his place,
The second hope of Rome's immortal race.
Adorn'd in white, a rev'rend priest appears,
And off'rings to the flaming altars bears;
A porket, and a lamb that never suffer'd shears.
Then to the rising sun he turns his eyes,
And strews the beasts, design'd for sacrifice,
With salt and meal: with like officious care
He marks their foreheads, and he clips their hair.
Betwixt their horns the purple wine he sheds;
With the same gen'rous juice the flame he feeds.

Æneas then unsheath'd his shining sword,
And thus with pious pray'rs the gods ador'd:
"All-seeing sun, and thou, Ausonian soil,
For which I have sustain'd so long a toil,
Thou, King of Heav'n, and thou,
the Queen of Air,
Propitious now, and reconcil'd by pray'r;
Thou, God of War, whose unresisted sway
The labors and events of arms obey;
Ye living fountains, and ye running floods,
All pow'rs of ocean, all ethereal gods,
Hear, and bear record: if I fall in field,
Or, recreant in the fight, to Turnus yield,
My Trojans shall Increase Evander's town;
Ascanius shall renounce th' Ausonian crown:
All claims, all questions of debate, shall cease;
Nor he, nor they, with force infringe the peace.
But, if my juster arms prevail in fight,
(As sure they shall, if I divine aright,)
My Trojans shall not o'er th' Italians reign:
Both equal, both unconquer'd shall remain,
Join'd in their laws, their lands, and their abodes;
I ask but altars for my weary gods.
The care of those religious rites be mine;
The crown to King Latinus I resign:
His be the sov'reign sway. Nor will I share
His pow'r in peace, or his command in war.
For me, my friends another town shall frame,
And bless the rising tow'rs with fair
Lavinia's name."

Thus he. Then, with erected eyes and hands,
The Latian king before his altar stands.
"By the same heav'n," said he, "and earth,
and main,
And all the pow'rs that all the three contain;
By hell below, and by that upper god

Whose thunder signs the peace, who seals it with his nod;
So let Latona's double offspring hear,
And double-fronted Janus, what I swear:
I touch the sacred altars, touch the flames,
And all those pow'rs attest, and all their names;
Whatever chance befall on either side,
No term of time this union shall divide:
No force, no fortune, shall my vows unbind,
Or shake the steadfast tenor of my mind;
Not tho' the circling seas should break their bound,
O'erflow the shores, or sap the solid ground;
Not tho' the lamps of heav'n their spheres forsake,
Hurl'd down, and hissing in the nether lake:
Ev'n as this royal scepter" (for he bore
A scepter in his hand) "shall never more
Shoot out in branches, or renew the birth:
An orphan now, cut from the mother earth
By the keen ax, dishonor'd of its hair,
And cas'd in brass, for Latian kings to bear."

When thus in public view the peace was tied
With solemn vows, and sworn on either side,
All dues perform'd which holy rites require;
The victim beasts are slain before the fire,
The trembling entrails from their bodies torn,
And to the fatten'd flames in chargers borne.

Already the Rutulians deem their man
O'ermatch'd in arms, before the fight began.
First rising fears are whisper'd thro' the crowd;
Then, gath'ring sound, they murmur more aloud.
Now, side to side, they measure with their eyes
The champions' bulk, their sinews, and their size:
The nearer they approach, the more is known
Th' apparent disadvantage of their own.
Turnus himself appears in public sight

Conscious of fate, desponding of the fight.
Slowly he moves, and at his altar stands
With eyes dejected, and with trembling hands;
And, while he mutters undistinguish'd pray'rs,
A livid deadness in his cheeks appears.

With anxious pleasure when Juturna view'd
Th' increasing fright of the mad multitude,
When their short sighs and thick'ning sobs she heard,
And found their ready minds for change prepar'd;
Dissembling her immortal form, she took
Camertus' mien, his habit, and his look;
A chief of ancient blood; in arms well known
Was his great sire, and he his greater son.
His shape assum'd, amid the ranks she ran,
And humoring their first motions, thus began:
"For shame, Rutulians, can you bear the sight
Of one expos'd for all, in single fight?
Can we, before the face of heav'n, confess
Our courage colder, or our numbers less?
View all the Trojan host, th' Arcadian band,
And Tuscan army; count 'em as they stand:
Undaunted to the battle if we go,
Scarce ev'ry second man will share a foe.
Turnus, 'tis true, in this unequal strife,
Shall lose, with honor, his devoted life,
Or change it rather for immortal fame,
Succeeding to the gods, from whence he came:
But you, a servile and inglorious band,
For foreign lords shall sow your native land,
Those fruitful fields your fighting fathers gain'd,
Which have so long their lazy sons sustain'd."
With words like these, she carried her design:
A rising murmur runs along the line.
Then ev'n the city troops, and Latians, tir'd

With tedious war, seem with new souls inspir'd:
Their champion's fate with pity they lament,
And of the league, so lately sworn, repent.

Nor fails the goddess to foment the rage
With lying wonders, and a false presage;
But adds a sign, which, present to their eyes,
Inspires new courage, and a glad surprise.
For, sudden, in the fiery tracts above,
Appears in pomp th' imperial bird of Jove:
A plump of fowl he spies, that swim the lakes,
And o'er their heads his sounding pinions shakes;
Then, stooping on the fairest of the train,
In his strong talons truss'd a silver swan.
Th' Italians wonder at th' unusual sight;
But, while he lags, and labors in his flight,
Behold, the dastard fowl return anew,
And with united force the foe pursue:
Clam'rous around the royal hawk they fly,
And, thick'ning in a cloud, o'ershade the sky.
They cuff, they scratch, they cross his airy course;
Nor can th' incumber'd bird sustain their force;
But vex'd, not vanquish'd, drops the pond'rous prey,
And, lighten'd of his burthen, wings his way.

Th' Ausonian bands with shouts salute the sight,
Eager of action, and demand the fight.
Then King Tolumnius, vers'd in augurs' arts,
Cries out, and thus his boasted skill imparts:
"At length 'tis granted, what I long desir'd!
This, this is what my frequent vows requir'd.
Ye gods, I take your omen, and obey.
Advance, my friends, and charge! I lead the way.
These are the foreign foes, whose impious band,
Like that rapacious bird, infest our land:
But soon, like him, they shall be forc'd to sea
By strength united, and forego the prey.

Your timely succor to your country bring,
Haste to the rescue, and redeem your king."

He said; and, pressing onward thro' the crew,
Pois'd in his lifted arm, his lance he threw.
The winged weapon, whistling in the wind,
Came driving on, nor miss'd the mark design'd.
At once the cornel rattled in the skies;
At once tumultuous shouts and clamors rise.
Nine brothers in a goodly band there stood,
Born of Arcadian mix'd with Tuscan blood,
Gylippus' sons: the fatal jav'lin flew,
Aim'd at the midmost of the friendly crew.
A passage thro' the jointed arms it found,
Just where the belt was to the body bound,
And struck the gentle youth extended on the ground.
Then, fir'd with pious rage, the gen'rous train
Run madly forward to revenge the slain.
And some with eager haste their jav'lins throw;
And some with sword in hand assault the foe.

The wish'd insult the Latine troops embrace,
And meet their ardor in the middle space.
The Trojans, Tuscans, and Arcadian line,
With equal courage obviate their design.
Peace leaves the violated fields, and hate
Both armies urges to their mutual fate.
With impious haste their altars are o'erturn'd,
The sacrifice half-broil'd, and half-unburn'd.
Thick storms of steel from either army fly,
And clouds of clashing darts obscure the sky;
Brands from the fire are missive weapons made,
With chargers, bowls, and all the priestly trade.
Latinus, frighted, hastens from the fray,
And bears his unregarded gods away.
These on their horses vault; those yoke the car;
The rest, with swords on high, run headlong to the war.

Messapus, eager to confound the peace,
Spurr'd his hot courser thro' the fighting prease,
At King Aulestes, by his purple known
A Tuscan prince, and by his regal crown;
And, with a shock encount'ring, bore him down.
Backward he fell; and, as his fate design'd,
The ruins of an altar were behind:
There, pitching on his shoulders and his head,
Amid the scatt'ring fires he lay supinely spread.
The beamy spear, descending from above,
His cuirass pierc'd, and thro' his body drove.
Then, with a scornful smile, the victor cries:
"The gods have found a fitter sacrifice."
Greedy of spoils, th' Italians strip the dead
Of his rich armor, and uncrown his head.

Priest Corynæus, arm'd his better hand,
From his own altar, with a blazing brand;
And, as Ebusus with a thund'ring pace
Advanc'd to battle, dash'd it on his face:
His bristly beard shines out with sudden fires;
The crackling crop a noisome scent expires.
Following the blow, he seiz'd his curling crown
With his left hand; his other cast him down.
The prostrate body with his knees he press'd,
And plung'd his holy poniard in his breast.

While Podalirius, with his sword, pursued
The shepherd Alsus thro' the flying crowd,
Swiftly he turns, and aims a deadly blow
Full on the front of his unwary foe.
The broad ax enters with a crashing sound,
And cleaves the chin with one continued wound;
Warm blood, and mingled brains, besmear
his arms around
An iron sleep his stupid eyes oppress'd,
And seal'd their heavy lids in endless rest.

But good Æneas rush'd amid the bands;
Bare was his head, and naked were his hands,
In sign of truce: then thus he cries aloud:
"What sudden rage, what new desire of blood,
Enflames your alter'd minds? O Trojans, cease
From impious arms, nor violate the peace!
By human sanctions, and by laws divine,
The terms are all agreed; the war is mine.
Dismiss your fears, and let the fight ensue;
This hand alone shall right the gods and you:
Our injur'd altars, and their broken vow,
To this avenging sword the faithless Turnus owe."

Thus while he spoke, unmindful of defense,
A winged arrow struck the pious prince.
But, whether from some human hand it came,
Or hostile god, is left unknown by fame:
No human hand or hostile god was found,
To boast the triumph of so base a wound.

When Turnus saw the Trojan quit the plain,
His chiefs dismay'd, his troops a fainting train,
Th' unhop'd event his heighten'd soul inspires:
At once his arms and coursers he requires;
Then, with a leap, his lofty chariot gains,
And with a ready hand assumes the reins.
He drives impetuous, and, where'er he goes,
He leaves behind a lane of slaughter'd foes.
These his lance reaches; over those he rolls
His rapid car, and crushes out their souls:
In vain the vanquish'd fly; the victor sends
The dead men's weapons at their living friends.
Thus, on the banks of Hebrus' freezing flood,
The God of Battles, in his angry mood,
Clashing his sword against his brazen shield,
Let loose the reins, and scours along the field:
Before the wind his fiery coursers fly;

Groans the sad earth, resounds the rattling sky.
Wrath, Terror, Treason, Tumult, and Despair
(Dire faces, and deform'd) surround the car;
Friends of the god, and followers of the war.
With fury not unlike, nor less disdain,
Exulting Turnus flies along the plain:
His smoking horses, at their utmost speed,
He lashes on, and urges o'er the dead.
Their fetlocks run with blood; and, when they bound,
The gore and gath'ring dust are dash'd around.
Thamyris and Pholus, masters of the war,
He kill'd at hand, but Sthenelus afar:
From far the sons of Imbracus he slew,
Glaucus and Lades, of the Lycian crew;
Both taught to fight on foot, in battle join'd,
Or mount the courser that outstrips the wind.

Meantime Eumedes, vaunting in the field,
New fir'd the Trojans, and their foes repell'd.
This son of Dolon bore his grandsire's name,
But emulated more his father's fame;
His guileful father, sent a nightly spy,
The Grecian camp and order to descry:
Hard enterprise! and well he might require
Achilles' car and horses, for his hire:
But, met upon the scout, th' Ætolian prince
In death bestow'd a juster recompense.
Fierce Turnus view'd the Trojan from afar,
And launch'd his jav'lin from his lofty car;
Then lightly leaping down, pursued the blow,
And, pressing with his foot his prostrate foe,
Wrench'd from his feeble hold the shining sword,
And plung'd it in the bosom of its lord.
"Possess," said he, "the fruit of all thy pains,
And measure, at thy length, our Latian plains.
Thus are my foes rewarded by my hand;
Thus may they build their town, and thus
enjoy the land!"

Then Dares, Butes, Sybaris he slew,
Whom o'er his neck his flound'ring courser threw.
As when loud Boreas, with his blust'ring train,
Stoops from above, incumbent on the main;
Where'er he flies, he drives the rack before,
And rolls the billows on th' Ægæan shore:
So, where resistless Turnus takes his course,
The scatter'd squadrons bend before his force;
His crest of horses' hair is blown behind
By adverse air, and rustles in the wind.

This haughty Phegeus saw with high disdain,
And, as the chariot roll'd along the plain,
Light from the ground he leapt, and seiz'd the rein.
Thus hung in air, he still retain'd his hold,
The coursers frighted, and their course controll'd.
The lance of Turnus reach'd him as he hung,
And pierc'd his plated arms, but pass'd along,
And only raz'd the skin. He turn'd, and held
Against his threat'ning foe his ample shield;
Then call'd for aid: but, while he cried in vain,
The chariot bore him backward on the plain.
He lies revers'd; the victor king descends,
And strikes so justly where his helmet ends,
He lops the head. The Latian fields are drunk
With streams that issue from the bleeding trunk.

While he triumphs, and while the Trojans yield,
The wounded prince is forc'd to leave the field:
Strong Mnestheus, and Achates often tried,
And young Ascanius, weeping by his side,
Conduct him to his tent. Scarce can he rear
His limbs from earth, supported on his spear.
Resolv'd in mind, regardless of the smart,
He tugs with both his hands, and breaks the dart.
The steel remains. No readier way he found
To draw the weapon, than t' enlarge the wound.

Eager of fight, impatient of delay,
He begs; and his unwilling friends obey.

Iapis was at hand to prove his art,
Whose blooming youth so fir'd Apollo's heart,
That, for his love, he proffer'd to bestow
His tuneful harp and his unerring bow.
The pious youth, more studious how to save
His aged sire, now sinking to the grave,
Preferr'd the pow'r of plants, and silent praise
Of healing arts, before Phœbean bays.

Propp'd on his lance the pensive hero stood,
And heard and saw, unmov'd, the mourning crowd.
The fam'd physician tucks his robes around
With ready hands, and hastens to the wound.
With gentle touches he performs his part,
This way and that, soliciting the dart,
And exercises all his heav'nly art.
All soft'ning simples, known of sov'reign use,
He presses out, and pours their noble juice.
These first infus'd, to lenify the pain,
He tugs with pincers, but he tugs in vain.
Then to the patron of his art he pray'd:
The patron of his art refus'd his aid.

Meantime the war approaches to the tents;
Th' alarm grows hotter, and the noise augments:
The driving dust proclaims the danger near;
And first their friends, and then their foes appear:
Their friends retreat; their foes pursue the rear.
The camp is fill'd with terror and affright:
The hissing shafts within the trench alight;
An undistinguish'd noise ascends the sky,
The shouts those who kill, and groans of those who die.

But now the goddess mother, mov'd with grief,
And pierc'd with pity, hastens her relief.
A branch of healing dittany she brought,
Which in the Cretan fields with care she sought:
Rough is the stern, which woolly leafs surround;
The leafs with flow'rs, the flow'rs with purple crown'd,
Well known to wounded goats; a sure relief
To draw the pointed steel, and ease the grief.
This Venus brings, in clouds involv'd, and brews
Th' extracted liquor with ambrosian dews,
And odorous panacee. Unseen she stands,
Temp'ring the mixture with her heav'nly hands,
And pours it in a bowl, already crown'd
With juice of med'c'nal herbs prepar'd to bathe the wound.
The leech, unknowing of superior art
Which aids the cure, with this foments the part;
And in a moment ceas'd the raging smart.
Stanch'd is the blood, and in the bottom stands:
The steel, but scarcely touch'd with tender hands,
Moves up, and follows of its own accord,
And health and vigor are at once restor'd.
Iapis first perceiv'd the closing wound,
And first the footsteps of a god he found.
"Arms! arms!" he cries; "the sword and shield prepare,
And send the willing chief, renew'd, to war.
This is no mortal work, no cure of mine,
Nor art's effect, but done by hands divine.
Some god our general to the battle sends;
Some god preserves his life for greater ends."

The hero arms in haste; his hands enfold
His thighs with cuishes of refulgent gold:
Inflam'd to fight, and rushing to the field,
That hand sustaining the celestial shield,

This gripes the lance, and with such vigor shakes,
That to the rest the beamy weapon quakes.
Then with a close embrace he strain'd his son,
And, kissing thro' his helmet, thus begun:
"My son, from my example learn the war,
In camps to suffer, and in fields to dare;
But happier chance than mine attend thy care!
This day my hand thy tender age shall shield,
And crown with honors of the conquer'd field:
Thou, when thy riper years shall send thee forth
To toils of war, be mindful of my worth;
Assert thy birthright, and in arms be known,
For Hector's nephew, and Æneas' son."
He said; and, striding, issued on the plain.
Anteus and Mnestheus, and a num'rous train,
Attend his steps; the rest their weapons take,
And, crowding to the field, the camp forsake.
A cloud of blinding dust is rais'd around,
Labors beneath their feet the trembling ground.
Now Turnus, posted on a hill, from far
Beheld the progress of the moving war:
With him the Latins view'd the cover'd plains,
And the chill blood ran backward in their veins.
Juturna saw th' advancing troops appear,
And heard the hostile sound, and fled for fear.
Æneas leads; and draws a sweeping train,
Clos'd in their ranks, and pouring on the plain.
As when a whirlwind, rushing to the shore
From the mid ocean, drives the waves before;
The painful hind with heavy heart foresees
The flatted fields, and slaughter of the trees;
With like impetuous rage the prince appears
Before his doubled front, nor less destruction bears.
And now both armies shock in open field;
Osiris is by strong Thymbræus kill'd.
Archetius, Ufens, Epulon, are slain
(All fam'd in arms, and of the Latian train)

By Gyas', Mnestheus', and Achates' hand.
The fatal augur falls, by whose command
The truce was broken, and whose lance, embrued
With Trojan blood, th' unhappy fight renew'd.
Loud shouts and clamors rend the liquid sky,
And o'er the field the frighted Latins fly.
The prince disdains the dastards to pursue,
Nor moves to meet in arms the fighting few;
Turnus alone, amid the dusky plain,
He seeks, and to the combat calls in vain.
Juturna heard, and, seiz'd with mortal fear,
Forc'd from the beam her brother's charioteer;
Assumes his shape, his armor, and his mien,
And, like Metiscus, in his seat is seen.

As the black swallow near the palace plies;
O'er empty courts, and under arches, flies;
Now hawks aloft, now skims along the flood,
To furnish her loquacious nest with food:
So drives the rapid goddess o'er the plains;
The smoking horses run with loosen'd reins.
She steers a various course among the foes;
Now here, now there, her conqu'ring brother shows;
Now with a straight, now with a wheeling flight,
She turns, and bends, but shuns the single fight.
Æneas, fir'd with fury, breaks the crowd,
And seeks his foe, and calls by name aloud:
He runs within a narrower ring, and tries
To stop the chariot; but the chariot flies.
If he but gain a glimpse, Juturna fears,
And far away the Daunian hero bears.

What should he do! Nor arts nor arms avail;
And various cares in vain his mind assail.
The great Messapus, thund'ring thro' the field,
In his left hand two pointed jav'lins held:
Encount'ring on the prince, one dart he drew,

And with unerring aim and utmost vigor threw.
Æneas saw it come, and, stooping low
Beneath his buckler, shunn'd the threat'ning blow.
The weapon hiss'd above his head, and tore
The waving plume which on his helm he wore.
Forced by this hostile act, and fir'd with spite,
That flying Turnus still declin'd the fight,
The Prince, whose piety had long repell'd
His inborn ardor, now invades the field;
Invokes the pow'rs of violated peace,
Their rites and injur'd altars to redress;
Then, to his rage abandoning the rein,
With blood and slaughter'd bodies fills the plain.

What god can tell, what numbers can display, *500*
The various labors of that fatal day;
What chiefs and champions fell on either side,
In combat slain, or by what deaths they died;
Whom Turnus, whom the Trojan hero kill'd;
Who shar'd the fame and fortune of the field!
Jove, could'st thou view, and not avert thy sight,
Two jarring nations join'd in cruel fight,
Whom leagues of lasting love so shortly shall unite!

Æneas first Rutulian Sucro found,
Whose valor made the Trojans quit their ground;
Betwixt his ribs the jav'lin drove so just,
It reach'd his heart, nor needs a second thrust.
Now Turnus, at two blows, two brethren slew;
First from his horse fierce Amycus he threw:
Then, leaping on the ground, on foot assail'd
Diores, and in equal fight prevail'd.
Their lifeless trunks he leaves upon the place;
Their heads, distilling gore, his chariot grace.

Three cold on earth the Trojan hero threw,
Whom without respite at one charge he slew:

Cethegus, Tanais, Tagus, fell oppress'd,
And sad Onythes, added to the rest,
Of Theban blood, whom Peridia bore.

Turnus two brothers from the Lycian shore,
And from Apollo's fane to battle sent,
O'erthrew; nor Phœbus could their fate prevent.
Peaceful Menœtes after these he kill'd,
Who long had shunn'd the dangers of the field:
On Lerna's lake a silent life he led,
And with his nets and angle earn'd his bread;
Nor pompous cares, nor palaces, he knew,
But wisely from th' infectious world withdrew:
Poor was his house; his father's painful hand
Discharg'd his rent, and plow'd another's land.

As flames among the lofty woods are thrown
On diff'rent sides, and both by winds are blown;
The laurels crackle in the sputt'ring fire;
The frighted sylvans from their shades retire:
Or as two neighb'ring torrents fall from high;
Rapid they run; the foamy waters fry;
They roll to sea with unresisted force,
And down the rocks precipitate their course:
Not with less rage the rival heroes take
Their diff'rent ways, nor less destruction make.
With spears afar, with swords at hand, they strike;
And zeal of slaughter fires their souls alike.
Like them, their dauntless men maintain the field;
And hearts are pierc'd, unknowing how to yield:
They blow for blow return, and wound for wound;
And heaps of bodies raise the level ground.

Murranus, boasting of his blood, that springs
From a long royal race of Latian kings,
Is by the Trojan from his chariot thrown,
Crush'd with the weight of an unwieldy stone:

Betwixt the wheels he fell; the wheels, that bore
His living load, his dying body tore.
His starting steeds, to shun the glitt'ring sword,
Paw down his trampled limbs, forgetful of their lord.

Fierce Hyllus threaten'd high, and, face to face,
Affronted Turnus in the middle space:
The prince encounter'd him in full career,
And at his temples aim'd the deadly spear;
So fatally the flying weapon sped,
That thro' his helm it pierc'd his head.
Nor, Cisseus, couldst thou scape from
Turnus' hand,
In vain the strongest of th' Arcadian band:
Nor to Cupentus could his gods afford
Availing aid against th' Ænean sword,
Which to his naked heart pursued the course;
Nor could his plated shield sustain the force.

Iolas fell, whom not the Grecian pow'rs,
Nor great subverter of the Trojan tow'rs,
Were doom'd to kill, while Heav'n
prolong'd his date;
But who can pass the bounds, prefix'd by fate?
In high Lyrnessus, and in Troy, he held
Two palaces, and was from each expell'd:
Of all the mighty man, the last remains
A little spot of foreign earth contains.

And now both hosts their broken troops unite
In equal ranks, and mix in mortal fight.
Seresthus and undaunted Mnestheus join
The Trojan, Tuscan, and Arcadian line:
Sea-born Messapus, with Atinas, heads
The Latin squadrons, and to battle leads.
They strike, they push, they throng
the scanty space,

Resolv'd on death, impatient of disgrace;
And, where one falls, another fills his place.

The Cyprian goddess now inspires her son
To leave th' unfinish'd fight, and storm the town:
For, while he rolls his eyes around the plain
In quest of Turnus, whom he seeks in vain,
He views th' unguarded city from afar,
In careless quiet, and secure of war.
Occasion offers, and excites his mind
To dare beyond the task he first design'd.
Resolv'd, he calls his chiefs; they leave the fight:
Attended thus, he takes a neighb'ring height;
The crowding troops about their gen'ral stand,
All under arms, and wait his high command.
Then thus the lofty prince: "Hear and obey,
Ye Trojan bands, without the least delay
Jove is with us; and what I have decreed
Requires our utmost vigor, and our speed.
Your instant arms against the town prepare,
The source of mischief, and the seat of war.
This day the Latian tow'rs, that mate the sky,
Shall level with the plain in ashes lie:
The people shall be slaves, unless in time
They kneel for pardon, and repent their crime.
Twice have our foes been vanquish'd on the plain:
Then shall I wait till Turnus will be slain?
Your force against the perjur'd city bend.
There it began, and there the war shall end.
The peace profan'd our rightful arms requires;
Cleanse the polluted place with purging fires."

He finish'd; and, one soul inspiring all,
Form'd in a wedge, the foot approach the wall.
Without the town, an unprovided train
Of gaping, gazing citizens are slain.
Some firebrands, others scaling ladders bear,

And those they toss aloft, and these they rear:
The flames now launch'd, the feather'd arrows fly,
And clouds of missive arms obscure the sky.
Advancing to the front, the hero stands,
And, stretching out to heav'n his pious hands,
Attests the gods, asserts his innocence,
Upbraids with breach of faith th' Ausonian prince;
Declares the royal honor doubly stain'd,
And twice the rites of holy peace profan'd.

Dissenting clamors in the town arise;
Each will be heard, and all at once advise.
One part for peace, and one for war contends;
Some would exclude their foes, and some
admit their friends.
The helpless king is hurried in the throng,
And, whate'er tide prevails, is borne along.
Thus, when the swain, within a hollow rock,
Invades the bees with suffocating smoke,
They run around, or labor on their wings,
Disus'd to flight, and shoot their sleepy stings;
To shun the bitter fumes in vain they try;
Black vapors, issuing from the vent,
involve the sky.

But fate and envious fortune now prepare
To plunge the Latins in the last despair.
The queen, who saw the foes invade the town,
And brands on tops of burning houses thrown,
Cast round her eyes, distracted with her fear—
No troops of Turnus in the field appear.
Once more she stares abroad, but still in vain,
And then concludes the royal youth is slain.
Mad with her anguish, impotent to bear
The mighty grief, she loathes the vital air.
She calls herself the cause of all this ill,
And owns the dire effects of her ungovern'd will;

She raves against the gods; she beats her breast;
She tears with both her hands her purple vest:
Then round a beam a running noose she tied,
And, fasten'd by the neck, obscenely died.

Soon as the fatal news by Fame was blown,
And to her dames and to her daughter known,
The sad Lavinia rends her yellow hair
And rosy cheeks; the rest her sorrow share:
With shrieks the palace rings, and madness of despair.
The spreading rumor fills the public place:
Confusion, fear, distraction, and disgrace,
And silent shame, are seen in ev'ry face.
Latinus tears his garments as he goes,
Both for his public and his private woes;
With filth his venerable beard besmears,
And sordid dust deforms his silver hairs.
And much he blames the softness of his mind,
Obnoxious to the charms of womankind,
And soon seduc'd to change what he so well design'd;
To break the solemn league so long desir'd,
Nor finish what his fates, and those of Troy, requir'd.

Now Turnus rolls aloof o'er empty plains,
And here and there some straggling foes he gleans.
His flying coursers please him less and less,
Asham'd of easy fight and cheap success.
Thus half-contented, anxious in his mind,
The distant cries come driving in the wind,
Shouts from the walls, but shouts in murmurs drown'd;

A jarring mixture, and a boding sound.
"Alas!" said he, "what mean these dismal cries?
What doleful clamors from the town arise?"
Confus'd, he stops, and backward pulls the reins.
She who the driver's office now sustains,
Replies: "Neglect, my lord, these new alarms;
Here fight, and urge the fortune of your arms:
There want not others to defend the wall.
If by your rival's hand th' Italians fall,
So shall your fatal sword his friends oppress,
In honor equal, equal in success."

To this, the prince: "O sister—for I knew
The peace infring'd proceeded first from you;
I knew you, when you mingled first in fight;
And now in vain you would deceive my sight—
Why, goddess, this unprofitable care?
Who sent you down from heav'n, involv'd in air,
Your share of mortal sorrows to sustain,
And see your brother bleeding on the plain?
For to what pow'r can Turnus have recourse,
Or how resist his fate's prevailing force?
These eyes beheld Murranus bite the ground:
Mighty the man, and mighty was the wound.
I heard my dearest friend, with dying breath,
My name invoking to revenge his death.
Brave Ufens fell with honor on the place,
To shun the shameful sight of my disgrace.
On earth supine, a manly corpse he lies;
His vest and armor are the victor's prize.
Then, shall I see Laurentum in a flame,
Which only wanted, to complete my shame?
How will the Latins hoot their champion's flight!
How Drances will insult and point them
to the sight!
Is death so hard to bear? Ye gods below,
(Since those above so small compassion show,)

Receive a soul unsullied yet with shame,
Which not belies my great forefather's name!"

He said; and while he spoke, with flying speed
Came Sages urging on his foamy steed:
Fix'd on his wounded face a shaft he bore,
And, seeking Turnus, sent his voice before:
"Turnus, on you, on you alone, depends
Our last relief: compassionate your friends!
Like lightning, fierce Æneas, rolling on,
With arms invests, with flames invades the town:
The brands are toss'd on high; the winds conspire
To drive along the deluge of the fire.
All eyes are fix'd on you: your foes rejoice;
Ev'n the king staggers, and suspends his choice;
Doubts to deliver or defend the town,
Whom to reject, or whom to call his son.
The queen, on whom your utmost hopes
were plac'd,
Herself suborning death, has breath'd her last.
'Tis true, Messapus, fearless of his fate,
With fierce Atinas' aid, defends the gate:
On ev'ry side surrounded by the foe,
The more they kill, the greater numbers grow;
An iron harvest mounts, and still remains to mow.
You, far aloof from your forsaken bands,
Your rolling chariot drive o'er empty sands."

Stupid he sate, his eyes on earth declin'd,
And various cares revolving in his mind:
Rage, boiling from the bottom of his breast,
And sorrow mix'd with shame, his soul oppress'd;
And conscious worth lay lab'ring in his thought,
And love by jealousy to madness wrought.
By slow degrees his reason drove away
The mists of passion, and resum'd her sway.
Then, rising on his car, he turn'd his look,

And saw the town involv'd in fire and smoke.
A wooden tow'r with flames already blaz'd,
Which his own hands on beams and rafters rais'd;
And bridges laid above to join the space,
And wheels below to roll from place to place.
"Sister, the Fates have vanquish'd: let us go
The way which Heav'n and my hard fortune show.
The fight is fix'd; nor shall the branded name
Of a base coward blot your brother's fame.
Death is my choice; but suffer me to try
My force, and vent my rage before I die."
He said; and, leaping down without delay,
Thro' crowds of scatter'd foes he freed his way.
Striding he pass'd, impetuous as the wind,
And left the grieving goddess far behind.
As when a fragment, from a mountain torn
By raging tempests, or by torrents borne,
Or sapp'd by time, or loosen'd from the roots,
Prone thro' the void the rocky ruin shoots,
Rolling from crag to crag, from steep to steep;
Down sink, at once, the shepherds and their sheep:
Involv'd alike, they rush to nether ground;
Stunn'd with the shock they fall, and stunn'd from earth rebound:
So Turnus, hasting headlong to the town,
Should'ring and shoving, bore the squadrons down.
Still pressing onward, to the walls he drew,
Where shafts, and spears, and darts promiscuous flew,
And sanguine streams the slipp'ry ground embrue.
First stretching out his arm, in sign of peace,
He cries aloud, to make the combat cease:
"Rutulians, hold; and Latin troops, retire!
The fight is mine; and me the gods require.
'Tis just that I should vindicate alone
The broken truce, or for the breach atone.

This day shall free from wars th' Ausonian state,
Or finish my misfortunes in my fate."

Both armies from their bloody work desist,
And, bearing backward, form a spacious list.
The Trojan hero, who receiv'd from fame
The welcome sound, and heard the champion's name,
Soon leaves the taken works and mounted walls,
Greedy of war where greater glory calls.
He springs to fight, exulting in his force
His jointed armor rattles in the course.
Like Eryx, or like Athos, great he shows,
Or Father Apennine, when, white with snows,
His head divine obscure in clouds he hides,
And shakes the sounding forest on his sides.
The nations, overaw'd, surcease the fight;
Immovable their bodies, fix'd their sight.
Ev'n death stands still; nor from above they throw
Their darts, nor drive their batt'ring-rams below.
In silent order either army stands,
And drop their swords, unknowing, from their hands.
Th' Ausonian king beholds, with wond'ring sight,
Two mighty champions match'd in single fight,
Born under climes remote, and brought by fate,
With swords to try their titles to the state.

Now, in clos'd field, each other from afar
They view; and, rushing on, begin the war.
They launch their spears; then hand to hand
they meet;
The trembling soil resounds beneath their feet:
Their bucklers clash; thick blows descend from high,
And flakes of fire from their hard helmets fly.
Courage conspires with chance, and both engage
With equal fortune yet, and mutual rage.
As when two bulls for their fair female fight
In Sila's shades, or on Taburnus' height;

With horns adverse they meet; the keeper flies;
Mute stands the herd; the heifers roll their eyes,
And wait th' event; which victor they shall bear,
And who shall be the lord, to rule the lusty year:
With rage of love the jealous rivals burn,
And push for push, and wound for wound return;
Their dewlaps gor'd, their sides are lav'd in blood;
Loud cries and roaring sounds rebellow
thro' the wood:
Such was the combat in the listed ground;
So clash their swords,
and so their shields resound.

Jove sets the beam; in either scale he lays
The champions' fate, and each exactly weighs.
On this side, life and lucky chance ascends;
Loaded with death, that other scale descends.
Rais'd on the stretch, young Turnus aims a blow
Full on the helm of his unguarded foe:
Shrill shouts and clamors ring on either side,
As hopes and fears their panting hearts divide.
But all in pieces flies the traitor sword,
And, in the middle stroke, deserts his lord.
Now is but death, or flight; disarm'd he flies,
When in his hand an unknown hilt he spies.
Fame says that Turnus, when his steeds he join'd,
Hurrying to war, disorder'd in his mind,
Snatch'd the first weapon which his haste could find.
'Twas not the fated sword his father bore,
But that his charioteer Metiscus wore.
This, while the Trojans fled, the toughness held;
But, vain against the great Vulcanian shield,
The mortal-temper'd steel deceiv'd his hand:
The shiver'd fragments shone amid the sand.

Surpris'd with fear, he fled along the field,
And now forthright, and now in orbits wheel'd;

For here the Trojan troops the list surround,
And there the pass is clos'd with pools and marshy ground.
Æneas hastens, tho' with heavier pace—
His wound, so newly knit, retards the chase,
And oft his trembling knees their aid refuse—
Yet, pressing foot by foot, his foe pursues.

Thus, when a fearful stag is clos'd around
With crimson toils, or in a river found,
High on the bank the deep-mouth'd hound appears,
Still opening, following still, where'er he steers;
The persecuted creature, to and fro,
Turns here and there, to 'scape his Umbrian foe:
Steep is th' ascent, and, if he gains the land,
The purple death is pitch'd along the strand.
His eager foe, determin'd to the chase,
Stretch'd at his length, gains ground at ev'ry pace;
Now to his beamy head he makes his way,
And now he holds, or thinks he holds, his prey:
Just at the pinch, the stag springs out with fear;
He bites the wind, and fills his sounding jaws with air:
The rocks, the lakes, the meadows ring with cries;
The mortal tumult mounts, and thunders in the skies.
Thus flies the Daunian prince, and, flying, blames
His tardy troops, and, calling by their names,
Demands his trusty sword. The Trojan threats
The realm with ruin, and their ancient seats
To lay in ashes, if they dare supply
With arms or aid his vanquish'd enemy:
Thus menacing, he still pursues the course,

With vigor, tho' diminish'd of his force.
Ten times already round the listed place
One chief had fled, and t' other giv'n the chase:
No trivial prize is play'd; for on the life
Or death of Turnus now depends the strife.

Within the space, an olive tree had stood,
A sacred shade, a venerable wood,
For vows to Faunus paid, the Latins' guardian god.
Here hung the vests, and tablets were engrav'd,
Of sinking mariners from shipweck sav'd.
With heedless hands the Trojans fell'd the tree,
To make the ground enclos'd for combat free.
Deep in the root, whether by fate, or chance,
Or erring haste, the Trojan drove his lance;
Then stoop'd, and tugg'd with force immense,
to free
Th' encumber'd spear from the tenacious tree;
That, whom his fainting limbs pursued in vain,
His flying weapon might from far attain.

Confus'd with fear, bereft of human aid,
Then Turnus to the gods, and first to
Faunus pray'd:
"O Faunus, pity! and thou Mother Earth,
Where I thy foster son receiv'd my birth,
Hold fast the steel! If my religious hand
Your plant has honor'd, which your foes
profan'd,
Propitious hear my pious pray'r!" He said,
Nor with successless vows invok'd their aid.
Th' incumbent hero wrench'd, and pull'd,
and strain'd;
But still the stubborn earth the steel detain'd.
Juturna took her time; and, while in vain
He strove, assum'd Meticus' form again,
And, in that imitated shape, restor'd

To the despairing prince his Daunian sword.
The Queen of Love, who, with disdain and grief,
Saw the bold nymph afford this prompt relief,
T' assert her offspring with a greater deed,
From the tough root the ling'ring weapon freed.

Once more erect, the rival chiefs advance:
One trusts the sword, and one the pointed lance;
And both resolv'd alike to try their fatal chance.

Meantime imperial Jove to Juno spoke,
Who from a shining cloud beheld the shock:
"What new arrest, O Queen of Heav'n, is sent
To stop the Fates now lab'ring in th' event?
What farther hopes are left thee to pursue?
Divine Æneas, (and thou know'st it too,)
Foredoom'd, to these celestial seats are due.
What more attempts for Turnus can be made,
That thus thou ling'rest in this lonely shade?
Is it becoming of the due respect
And awful honor of a god elect,
A wound unworthy of our state to feel,
Patient of human hands and earthly steel?
Or seems it just, the sister should restore
A second sword, when one was lost before,
And arm a conquer'd wretch
against his conqueror?
For what, without thy knowledge and avow,
Nay more, thy dictate, durst Juturna do?
At last, in deference to my love, forbear
To lodge within thy soul this anxious care;
Reclin'd upon my breast, thy grief unload:
Who should relieve the goddess, but the god?
Now all things to their utmost issue tend,
Push'd by the Fates to their appointed
While leave was giv'n thee, and a lawful hour
For vengeance, wrath, and unresisted pow'r,

Toss'd on the seas, thou couldst thy foes distress,
And, driv'n ashore, with hostile arms oppress;
Deform the royal house; and, from the side
Of the just bridegroom, tear the plighted bride:
Now cease at my command." The Thund'rer said;
And, with dejected eyes, this answer Juno made:
"Because your dread decree too well I knew,
From Turnus and from earth unwilling I withdrew.
Else should you not behold me here, alone,
Involv'd in empty clouds, my friends bemoan,
But, girt with vengeful flames, in open sight
Engag'd against my foes in mortal fight.
'Tis true, Juturna mingled in the strife
By my command, to save her brother's life—
At least to try—but, by the Stygian lake,
(The most religious oath the gods can take,)
With this restriction, not to bend the bow,
Or toss the spear, or trembling dart to throw.
And now, resign'd to your superior might,
And tir'd with fruitless toils, I loathe the fight.
This let me beg (and this no fates withstand)
Both for myself and for your father's land,
That, when the nuptial bed shall bind the peace,
(Which I, since you ordain, consent to bless,)
The laws of either nation be the same;
But let the Latins still retain their name,
Speak the same language which they spoke before,
Wear the same habits which their grandsires wore.
Call them not Trojans: perish the renown
And name of Troy, with that detested town.
Latium be Latium still; let Alba reign
And Rome's immortal majesty remain."

Then thus the founder of mankind replies
(Unruffled was his front, serene his eyes)
"Can Saturn's issue, and heav'n's other heir,
Such endless anger in her bosom bear?

Be mistress, and your full desires obtain;
But quench the choler you foment in vain.
From ancient blood th' Ausonian
people sprung,
Shall keep their name, their habit,
and their tongue.
The Trojans to their customs shall be tied:
I will, myself, their common rites provide;
The natives shall command,
the foreigners subside.
All shall be Latium; Troy without a name;
And her lost sons forget from whence they came.
From blood so mix'd, a pious race shall flow,
Equal to gods, excelling all below.
No nation more respect to you shall pay,
Or greater off'rings on your altars lay."
Juno consents, well pleas'd that her desires
Had found success, and from the cloud retires.

The peace thus made, the Thund'rer next prepares
To force the wat'ry goddess from the wars.
Deep in the dismal regions void of light,
Three daughters at a birth were born to Night:
These their brown mother, brooding on her care,
Endued with windy wings to flit in air,
With serpents girt alike, and crown'd with
hissing hair.
In heav'n the Diræ call'd, and still at hand,
Before the throne of angry Jove they stand,
His ministers of wrath, and ready still
The minds of mortal men with fears to fill,
Whene'er the moody sire, to wreak his hate
On realms or towns deserving of their fate,
Hurls down diseases, death and deadly care,
And terrifies the guilty world with war.
One sister plague if these from heav'n he sent,
To fright Juturna with a dire portent.

The pest comes whirling down: by far more slow
Springs the swift arrow from the Parthian bow,
Or Cydon yew, when, traversing the skies,
And drench'd in pois'nous juice, the sure
destruction flies.
With such a sudden and unseen a flight
Shot thro' the clouds the daughter of the night.
Soon as the field enclos'd she had in view,
And from afar her destin'd quarry knew,
Contracted, to the boding bird she turns,
Which haunts the ruin'd piles and hallow'd urns,
And beats about the tombs with nightly wings,
Where songs obscene on sepulchers she sings.
Thus lessen'd in her form, with frightful cries
The Fury round unhappy Turnus flies,
Flaps on his shield, and flutters o'er his eyes.

A lazy chillness crept along his blood;
Chok'd was his voice; his hair with horror stood.
Juturna from afar beheld her fly,
And knew th' ill omen, by her screaming cry
And stridor of her wings. Amaz'd with fear,
Her beauteous breast she beat, and rent her
flowing hair.

"Ah me!" she cries, "in this unequal strife
What can thy sister more to save thy life?
Weak as I am, can I, alas! contend
In arms with that inexorable fiend?
Now, now, I quit the field! forbear to fright
My tender soul, ye baleful birds of night;
The lashing of your wings I know too well,
The sounding flight, and fun'ral screams of hell!
These are the gifts you bring from haughty Jove,
The worthy recompense of ravish'd love!
Did he for this exempt my life from fate?
O hard conditions of immortal state,

Tho' born to death, not privileg'd to die,
But forc'd to bear impos'd eternity!
Take back your envious bribes, and let me go
Companion to my brother's ghost below!
The joys are vanish'd: nothing now remains,
Of life immortal, but immortal pains.
What earth will open her devouring womb,
To rest a weary goddess in the tomb!"
She drew a length of sighs; nor more she said,
But in her azure mantle wrapp'd her head,
Then plung'd into her stream, with deep despair,
And her last sobs came bubbling up in air.

Now stern Æneas his weighty spear
Against his foe, and thus upbraids his fear:
"What farther subterfuge can Turnus find?
What empty hopes are harbor'd in his mind?
'Tis not thy swiftness can secure thy flight;
Not with their feet, but hands, the valiant fight.
Vary thy shape in thousand forms, and dare
What skill and courage can attempt in war;
Wish for the wings of winds, to mount the sky;
Or hid, within the hollow earth to lie!"
The champion shook his head, and made this short reply:
"No threats of thine my manly mind can move;
'Tis hostile heav'n I dread, and partial Jove."
He said no more, but, with a sigh, repress'd
The mighty sorrow in his swelling breast.

Then, as he roll'd his troubled eyes around,
An antique stone he saw, the common bound
Of neighb'ring fields, and barrier of the ground;
So vast, that twelve strong men of modern days
Th' enormous weight from earth could hardly raise.
He heav'd it at a lift, and, pois'd on high,

Ran stagg'ring on against his enemy,
But so disorder'd, that he scarcely knew
His way, or what unwieldy weight he threw.
His knocking knees are bent beneath the load,
And shiv'ring cold congeals his vital blood.
The stone drops from his arms, and, falling short
For want of vigor, mocks his vain effort.
And as, when heavy sleep has clos'd the sight,
The sickly fancy labors in the night;
We seem to run; and, destitute of force,
Our sinking limbs forsake us in the course:
In vain we heave for breath; in vain we cry;
The nerves, unbrac'd, their usual strength deny;
And on the tongue the falt'ring accents die:
So Turnus far'd; whatever means he tried,
All force of arms and points of art employ'd,
The Fury flew athwart, and made
  th' endeavor void.

A thousand various thoughts his soul confound;
He star'd about, nor aid nor issue found;
His own men stop the pass,
  and his own walls surround.
Once more he pauses, and looks out again,
And seeks the goddess charioteer in vain.
Trembling he views the thund'ring chief advance,
And brandishing aloft the deadly lance:
Amaz'd he cow'rs beneath his conqu'ring foe,
Forgets to ward, and waits the coming blow.
Astonish'd while he stands, and fix'd with fear,
Aim'd at his shield he sees th' impending spear.

The hero measur'd first, with narrow view,
The destin'd mark; and, rising as he threw,
With its full swing the fatal weapon flew.
Not with less rage the rattling thunder falls,
Or stones from batt'ring-engines break the walls:

Swift as a whirlwind, from an arm so strong,
The lance drove on, and bore the death along.
Naught could his sev'nfold shield the prince avail,
Nor aught, beneath his arms, the coat of mail:
It pierc'd thro' all, and with a grisly wound
Transfix'd his thigh, and doubled him to ground.
With groans the Latins rend the vaulted sky:
Woods, hills, and valleys, to the voice reply.

Now low on earth the lofty chief is laid,
With eyes cast upward, and with arms display'd,
And, recreant, thus to the proud victor pray'd:
"I know my death deserv'd, nor hope to live:
Use what the gods and thy good fortune give.
Yet think, O think, if mercy may be shown—
Thou hadst a father once, and hast a son—
Pity my sire, now sinking to the grave;
And for Anchises' sake old Daunus save!
Or, if thy vow'd revenge pursue my death,
Give to my friends my body void of breath!
The Latian chiefs have seen me beg my life;
Thine is the conquest, thine the royal wife:
Against a yielded man, 'tis mean ignoble strife."

In deep suspense the Trojan seem'd to stand,
And, just prepar'd to strike, repress'd his hand.
He roll'd his eyes, and ev'ry moment felt
His manly soul with more compassion melt;
When, casting down a casual glance, he spied
The golden belt that glitter'd on his side,
The fatal spoils which haughty Turnus tore
From dying Pallas, and in triumph wore.
Then, rous'd anew to wrath, he loudly cries
(Flames, while he spoke, came flashing from his eyes)
"Traitor, dost thou, dost thou to grace pretend,
Clad, as thou art, in trophies of my friend?
To his sad soul a grateful off'ring go!

'Tis Pallas, Pallas gives this deadly blow."
He rais'd his arm aloft, and, at the word,
Deep in his bosom drove the shining sword.
The streaming blood distain'd his arms around,
And the disdainful soul came rushing thro' the wound.

Metamorphoses

Ovid

Translated by John Dryden

Book I

The Creation of the World

Of bodies chang'd to various forms, I sing:
Ye Gods, from whom these miracles did spring,
Inspire my numbers with coelestial heat;
Till I my long laborious work complete:
And add perpetual tenour to my rhimes,
Deduc'd from Nature's birth, to Cæsar's times.
Before the seas, and this terrestrial ball,
And Heav'n's high canopy, that covers all,
One was the face of Nature; if a face:
Rather a rude and indigested mass:
A lifeless lump, unfashion'd, and unfram'd,
Of jarring seeds; and justly Chaos nam'd.
No sun was lighted up, the world to view;
No moon did yet her blunted horns renew:
Nor yet was Earth suspended in the sky,
Nor pois'd, did on her own foundations lye:
Nor seas about the shores their arms had thrown;
But earth, and air, and water, were in one.
Thus air was void of light, and earth unstable,
And water's dark abyss unnavigable.
No certain form on any was imprest;
All were confus'd, and each disturb'd the rest.
For hot and cold were in one body fixt;
And soft with hard, and light with heavy mixt.

But God, or Nature, while they thus contend,
To these intestine discords put an end:
Then earth from air, and seas from earth were driv'n,

And grosser air sunk from ætherial Heav'n.
Thus disembroil'd, they take their proper place;
The next of kin, contiguously embrace;
And foes are sunder'd, by a larger space.
The force of fire ascended first on high,
And took its dwelling in the vaulted sky:
Then air succeeds, in lightness next to fire;
Whose atoms from unactive earth retire.
Earth sinks beneath, and draws a num'rous throng
Of pond'rous, thick, unwieldy seeds along.
About her coasts, unruly waters roar;
And rising, on a ridge, insult the shore.
Thus when the God, whatever God was he,
Had form'd the whole, and made the parts agree,
That no unequal portions might be found,
He moulded Earth into a spacious round:
Then with a breath, he gave the winds to blow;
And bad the congregated waters flow.
He adds the running springs, and standing lakes;
And bounding banks for winding rivers makes.
Some part, in Earth are swallow'd up, the most
In ample oceans, disembogu'd, are lost.
He shades the woods, the vallies he restrains
With rocky mountains, and extends the plains.

And as five zones th' ætherial regions bind,
Five, correspondent, are to Earth assign'd:
The sun with rays, directly darting down,
Fires all beneath, and fries the middle zone:
The two beneath the distant poles, complain
Of endless winter, and perpetual rain.
Betwixt th' extremes, two happier climates hold
The temper that partakes of hot, and cold.
The fields of liquid air, enclosing all,
Surround the compass of this earthly ball:
The lighter parts lye next the fires above;
The grosser near the wat'ry surface move:

Thick clouds are spread, and storms engender there,
And thunder's voice, which wretched mortals fear,
And winds that on their wings cold winter bear.
Nor were those blust'ring brethren left at large,
On seas, and shores, their fury to discharge:
Bound as they are, and circumscrib'd in place,
They rend the world, resistless, where they pass;
And mighty marks of mischief leave behind;
Such is the rage of their tempestuous kind.
First Eurus to the rising morn is sent
(The regions of the balmy continent);
And Eastern realms, where early Persians run,
To greet the blest appearance of the sun.
Westward, the wanton Zephyr wings his flight;
Pleas'd with the remnants of departing light:
Fierce Boreas, with his off-spring, issues forth
T' invade the frozen wagon of the North.
While frowning Auster seeks the Southern sphere;
And rots, with endless rain, th' unwholesome year.

High o'er the clouds, and empty realms of wind,
The God a clearer space for Heav'n design'd;
Where fields of light, and liquid æther flow;
Purg'd from the pond'rous dregs of Earth below.

Scarce had the Pow'r distinguish'd these,
when straight
The stars, no longer overlaid with weight,
Exert their heads, from underneath the mass;
And upward shoot, and kindle as they pass,
And with diffusive light adorn their heav'nly place.
Then, every void of Nature to supply,
With forms of Gods he fills the vacant sky:
New herds of beasts he sends, the plains to share:
New colonies of birds, to people air:
And to their oozy beds, the finny fish repair.

A creature of a more exalted kind
Was wanting yet, and then was Man design'd:
Conscious of thought, of more capacious breast,
For empire form'd, and fit to rule the rest:
Whether with particles of heav'nly fire
The God of Nature did his soul inspire,
Or Earth, but new divided from the sky,
And, pliant, still retain'd th' ætherial energy:
Which wise Prometheus temper'd into paste,
And, mixt with living streams,
the godlike image cast.

Thus, while the mute creation downward bend
Their sight, and to their earthly mother tend,
Man looks aloft; and with erected eyes
Beholds his own hereditary skies.
From such rude principles our form began;
And earth was metamorphos'd into Man.

The Golden Age

The golden age was first; when Man yet new,
No rule but uncorrupted reason knew:
And, with a native bent, did good pursue.
Unforc'd by punishment, unaw'd by fear,
His words were simple, and his soul sincere;
Needless was written law, where none opprest:
The law of Man was written in his breast:
No suppliant crowds before the judge appear'd,
No court erected yet, nor cause was heard:
But all was safe, for conscience was their guard.
The mountain-trees in distant prospect please,
E're yet the pine descended to the seas:
E're sails were spread, new oceans to explore:
And happy mortals, unconcern'd for more,
Confin'd their wishes to their native shore.

No walls were yet; nor fence, nor mote, nor mound,
Nor drum was heard, nor trumpet's angry sound:
Nor swords were forg'd; but void of care and crime,
The soft creation slept away their time.
The teeming Earth, yet guiltless of the plough,
And unprovok'd, did fruitful stores allow:
Content with food, which Nature freely bred,
On wildings and on strawberries they fed;
Cornels and bramble-berries gave the rest,
And falling acorns furnish'd out a feast.
The flow'rs unsown, in fields and meadows reign'd:
And Western winds immortal spring maintain'd.
In following years, the bearded corn ensu'd
From Earth unask'd, nor was that Earth renew'd.
From veins of vallies, milk and nectar broke;
And honey sweating through the pores of oak.

The Silver Age

But when good Saturn, banish'd from above,
Was driv'n to Hell, the world was under Jove.
Succeeding times a silver age behold,
Excelling brass, but more excell'd by gold.
Then summer, autumn, winter did appear:
And spring was but a season of the year.
The sun his annual course obliquely made,
Good days contracted, and enlarg'd the bad.
Then air with sultry heats began to glow;
The wings of winds were clogg'd with ice and snow;
And shivering mortals, into houses driv'n,
Sought shelter from th' inclemency of Heav'n.
Those houses, then, were caves, or homely sheds;
With twining oziers fenc'd; and moss their beds.
Then ploughs, for seed, the fruitful furrows broke,
And oxen labour'd first beneath the yoke.

The Brazen Age

To this came next in course, the brazen age:
A warlike offspring, prompt to bloody rage,
Not impious yet...

The Iron Age

Hard steel succeeded then:
And stubborn as the metal, were the men.
Truth, modesty, and shame, the world forsook:
Fraud, avarice, and force, their places took.
Then sails were spread, to every wind that blew.
Raw were the sailors, and the depths were new:
Trees, rudely hollow'd, did the waves sustain;
E're ships in triumph plough'd the wat'ry plain.

Then land-marks limited to each his right:
For all before was common as the light.
Nor was the ground alone requir'd to bear
Her annual income to the crooked share,
But greedy mortals, rummaging her store,
Digg'd from her entrails first the precious oar;
Which next to Hell, the prudent Gods had laid;
And that alluring ill, to sight display'd.
Thus cursed steel, and more accursed gold,
Gave mischief birth, and made that mischief bold:
And double death did wretched Man invade,
By steel assaulted, and by gold betray'd,
Now (brandish'd weapons glittering in their hands)
Mankind is broken loose from moral bands;
No rights of hospitality remain:
The guest, by him who harbour'd him, is slain,
The son-in-law pursues the father's life;
The wife her husband murders, he the wife.

The step-dame poyson for the son prepares;
The son inquires into his father's years.
Faith flies, and piety in exile mourns;
And justice, here opprest, to Heav'n returns.

The Giants' War

Nor were the Gods themselves more safe above;
Against beleaguer'd Heav'n the giants move.
Hills pil'd on hills, on mountains mountains lie,
To make their mad approaches to the skie.
Till Jove, no longer patient, took his time
T' avenge with thunder their audacious crime:
Red light'ning plaid along the firmament,
And their demolish'd works to pieces rent.
Sing'd with the flames, and with the bolts transfixt,
With native Earth, their blood the monsters mixt;
The blood, endu'd with animating heat,
Did in th' impregnant Earth new sons beget:
They, like the seed from which they sprung, accurst,
Against the Gods immortal hatred nurst,
An impious, arrogant, and cruel brood;
Expressing their original from blood.

Which when the king of Gods beheld from high
(Withal revolving in his memory,
What he himself had found on Earth of late,
Lycaon's guilt, and his inhumane treat),
He sigh'd; nor longer with his pity strove;
But kindled to a wrath becoming Jove:

Then call'd a general council of the Gods;
Who summon'd, issue from their blest abodes,
And fill th' assembly with a shining train.
A way there is, in Heav'n's expanded plain,

Which, when the skies are clear, is seen below,
And mortals, by the name of Milky, know.
The ground-work is of stars;
    through which the road
Lyes open to the Thunderer's abode:
The Gods of greater nations dwell around,
And, on the right and left, the palace bound;
The commons where they can: the nobler sort
With winding-doors wide open, front the court.
This place, as far as Earth with Heav'n may vie,
I dare to call the Louvre of the skie.
When all were plac'd, in seats distinctly known,
And he, their father, had assum'd the throne,
Upon his iv'ry sceptre first he leant,
Then shook his head, that shook the firmament:
Air, Earth, and seas, obey'd th' almighty nod;
And, with a gen'ral fear, confess'd the God.
At length, with indignation, thus he broke
His awful silence, and the Pow'rs bespoke.

I was not more concern'd in that debate
Of empire, when our universal state
Was put to hazard, and the giant race
Our captive skies were ready to embrace:
For tho' the foe was fierce, the seeds of all
Rebellion, sprung from one original;
Now, wheresoever ambient waters glide,
All are corrupt, and all must be destroy'd.
Let me this holy protestation make,
By Hell, and Hell's inviolable lake,
I try'd whatever in the godhead lay:
But gangren'd members must be lopt away,
Before the nobler parts are tainted to decay.
There dwells below, a race of demi-gods,
Of nymphs in waters, and of fawns in woods:
Who, tho' not worthy yet, in Heav'n to live,
Let 'em, at least, enjoy that Earth we give.

Can these be thought securely lodg'd below,
When I my self, who no superior know,
I, who have Heav'n and Earth at my command,
Have been attempted by Lycaon's hand?

At this a murmur through the synod went,
And with one voice they vote his punishment.
Thus, when conspiring traitors dar'd to doom
The fall of Cæsar, and in him of Rome,
The nations trembled with a pious fear;
All anxious for their earthly Thunderer:
Nor was their care, o Cæsar, less esteem'd
By thee, than that of Heav'n for Jove was deem'd:
Who with his hand, and voice, did first restrain
Their murmurs, then resum'd his speech again.
The Gods to silence were compos'd, and sate
With reverence, due to his superior state.

Cancel your pious cares; already he
Has paid his debt to justice, and to me.
Yet what his crimes, and what my judgments were,
Remains for me thus briefly to declare.
The clamours of this vile degenerate age,
The cries of orphans, and th' oppressor's rage,
Had reach'd the stars: I will descend, said I,
In hope to prove this loud complaint a lye.
Disguis'd in humane shape, I travell'd round
The world, and more than what I heard, I found.
O'er Mænalus I took my steepy way,
By caverns infamous for beasts of prey:
Then cross'd Cyllene, and the piny shade
More infamous, by curst Lycaon made:
Dark night had cover'd Heaven, and Earth, before
I enter'd his unhospitable door.
Just at my entrance, I display'd the sign
That somewhat was approaching of divine.
The prostrate people pray; the tyrant grins;

And, adding profanation to his sins,
I'll try, said he, and if a God appear,
To prove his deity shall cost him dear.
'Twas late; the graceless wretch my death prepares,
When I shou'd soundly sleep, opprest with cares:
This dire experiment he chose, to prove
If I were mortal, or undoubted Jove:
But first he had resolv'd to taste my pow'r;
Not long before, but in a luckless hour,
Some legates, sent from the Molossian state,
Were on a peaceful errand come to treat:
Of these he murders one, he boils the flesh;
And lays the mangled morsels in a dish:
Some part he roasts; then serves it up, so drest,
And bids me welcome to this humane feast.
Mov'd with disdain, the table I o'er-turn'd;
And with avenging flames, the palace burn'd.
The tyrant in a fright, for shelter gains
The neighb'ring fields, and scours along the plains.
Howling he fled, and fain he wou'd have spoke;
But humane voice his brutal tongue forsook.
About his lips the gather'd foam he churns,
And, breathing slaughters, still with rage he burns,
But on the bleating flock his fury turns.
His mantle, now his hide, with rugged hairs
Cleaves to his back; a famish'd face he bears;
His arms descend, his shoulders sink away
To multiply his legs for chase of prey.
He grows a wolf, his hoariness remains,
And the same rage in other members reigns.
His eyes still sparkle in a narr'wer space:
His jaws retain the grin, and violence of his face.

This was a single ruin, but not one
Deserves so just a punishment alone.
Mankind's a monster, and th' ungodly times
Confed'rate into guilt, are sworn to crimes.

All are alike involv'd in ill, and all
Must by the same relentless fury fall.
Thus ended he; the greater Gods assent;
By clamours urging his severe intent;
The less fill up the cry for punishment.
Yet still with pity they remember Man;
And mourn as much as heav'nly spirits can.
They ask, when those were lost of humane birth,
What he wou'd do with all this waste of Earth:
If his dispeopl'd world he would resign
To beasts, a mute, and more ignoble line;
Neglected altars must no longer smoke,
If none were left to worship, and invoke.
To whom the Father of the Gods reply'd,
Lay that unnecessary fear aside:
Mine be the care, new people to provide.
I will from wondrous principles ordain
A race unlike the first, and try my skill again.

Already had he toss'd the flaming brand;
And roll'd the thunder in his spacious hand;
Preparing to discharge on seas and land:
But stopt, for fear, thus violently driv'n,
The sparks should catch his axle-tree of Heav'n.
Rememb'ring in the fates, a time when fire
Shou'd to the battlements of Heaven aspire,
And all his blazing worlds above shou'd burn;
And all th' inferior globe to cinders turn.
His dire artill'ry thus dismist, he bent
His thoughts to some securer punishment:
Concludes to pour a wat'ry deluge down;
And what he durst not burn, resolves to drown.

The northern breath, that freezes floods, he binds;
With all the race of cloud-dispelling winds:
The south he loos'd, who night and horror brings;
And foggs are shaken from his flaggy wings.

From his divided beard two streams he pours,
His head, and rheumy eyes distill in show'rs,
With rain his robe, and heavy mantle flow:
And lazy mists are low'ring on his brow;
Still as he swept along, with his clench'd fist
He squeez'd the clouds, th' imprison'd clouds resist:
The skies, from pole to pole, with peals resound;
And show'rs enlarg'd, come pouring on the ground.
Then, clad in colours of a various dye,
Junonian Iris breeds a new supply
To feed the clouds: impetuous rain descends;
The bearded corn beneath the burden bends:
Defrauded clowns deplore their perish'd grain;
And the long labours of the year are vain.

Nor from his patrimonial Heaven alone
Is Jove content to pour his vengeance down;
Aid from his brother of the seas he craves,
To help him with auxiliary waves.
The wat'ry tyrant calls his brooks and floods,
Who roll from mossy caves (their moist abodes);
And with perpetual urns his palace fill:
To whom in brief, he thus imparts his will.

Small exhortation needs; your pow'rs employ:
And this bad world, so Jove requires, destroy.
Let loose the reins to all your wat'ry store:
Bear down the damms, and open ev'ry door.

The floods, by Nature enemies to land,
And proudly swelling with their new command,
Remove the living stones, that stopt their way,
And gushing from their source, augment the sea.
Then, with his mace, their monarch struck
the ground;
With inward trembling Earth receiv'd the wound;
And rising streams a ready passage found.

Th' expanded waters gather on the plain:
They float the fields, and over-top the grain;
Then rushing onwards, with a sweepy sway,
Bear flocks, and folds, and lab'ring hinds away.
Nor safe their dwellings were, for, sap'd by floods,
Their houses fell upon their household Gods.
The solid piles, too strongly built to fall,
High o'er their heads, behold a wat'ry wall:
Now seas and Earth were in confusion lost;
A world of waters, and without a coast.

One climbs a cliff; one in his boat is born:
And ploughs above, where late he sow'd his corn.
Others o'er chimney-tops and turrets row,
And drop their anchors on the meads below:
Or downward driv'n, they bruise the tender vine,
Or tost aloft, are knock'd against a pine.
And where of late the kids had cropt the grass,
The monsters of the deep now take their place.
Insulting Nereids on the cities ride,
And wond'ring dolphins o'er the palace glide.
On leaves, and masts of mighty oaks they brouze;
And their broad fins entangle in the boughs.
The frighted wolf now swims amongst the sheep;
The yellow lion wanders in the deep:
His rapid force no longer helps the boar:
The stag swims faster, than he ran before.
The fowls, long beating on their wings in vain,
Despair of land, and drop into the main.
Now hills, and vales no more distinction know;
And levell'd Nature lies oppress'd below.
The most of mortals perish in the flood:
The small remainder dies for want of food.

A mountain of stupendous height there stands
Betwixt th' Athenian and Boeotian lands,
The bound of fruitful fields, while fields they were,

But then a field of waters did appear:
Parnassus is its name; whose forky rise
Mounts thro' the clouds, and mates the lofty skies.
High on the summit of this dubious cliff,
Deucalion wafting, moor'd his little skiff.
He with his wife were only left behind
Of perish'd Man; they two were human kind.
The mountain nymphs, and Themis they adore,
And from her oracles relief implore.
The most upright of mortal men was he;
The most sincere, and holy woman, she.

When Jupiter, surveying Earth from high,
Beheld it in a lake of water lie,
That where so many millions lately liv'd,
But two, the best of either sex, surviv'd;
He loos'd the northern wind; fierce Boreas flies
To puff away the clouds, and purge the skies:
Serenely, while he blows, the vapours driv'n,
Discover Heav'n to Earth, and Earth to Heav'n.
The billows fall, while Neptune lays his mace
On the rough sea, and smooths its furrow'd face.
Already Triton, at his call, appears
Above the waves; a Tyrian robe he wears;
And in his hand a crooked trumpet bears.
The sovereign bids him peaceful sounds inspire,
And give the waves the signal to retire.
His writhen shell he takes; whose narrow vent
Grows by degrees into a large extent,
Then gives it breath; the blast with doubling sound,
Runs the wide circuit of the world around:
The sun first heard it, in his early east,
And met the rattling echoes in the west.
The waters, list'ning to the trumpet's roar,
Obey the summons, and forsake the shore.

A thin circumference of land appears;
And Earth, but not at once, her visage rears,

And peeps upon the seas from upper grounds;
The streams, but just contain'd within their bounds,
By slow degrees into their channels crawl;
And Earth increases, as the waters fall.
In longer time the tops of trees appear,
Which mud on their dishonour'd branches bear.

At length the world was all restor'd to view;
But desolate, and of a sickly hue:
Nature beheld her self, and stood aghast,
A dismal desert, and a silent waste.

Which when Deucalion, with a piteous look
Beheld, he wept, and thus to Pyrrha spoke:
Oh wife, oh sister, oh of all thy kind
The best, and only creature left behind,
By kindred, love, and now by dangers joyn'd;
Of multitudes, who breath'd the common air,
We two remain; a species in a pair:
The rest the seas have swallow'd; nor have we
Ev'n of this wretched life a certainty.
The clouds are still above; and, while I speak,
A second deluge o'er our heads may break.
Shou'd I be snatcht from hence, and thou remain,
Without relief, or partner of thy pain,
How cou'dst thou such a wretched life sustain?
Shou'd I be left, and thou be lost, the sea
That bury'd her I lov'd, shou'd bury me.
Oh cou'd our father his old arts inspire,
And make me heir of his informing fire,
That so I might abolisht Man retrieve,
And perisht people in new souls might live.
But Heav'n is pleas'd, nor ought we to complain,
That we, th' examples of mankind, remain.
He said; the careful couple join their tears:
And then invoke the Gods, with pious prayers.
Thus, in devotion having eas'd their grief,

From sacred oracles they seek relief;
And to Cephysus' brook their way pursue:
The stream was troubled, but the ford they knew;
With living waters, in the fountain bred,
They sprinkle first their garments, and their head,
Then took the way, which to the temple led.
The roofs were all defil'd with moss, and mire,
The desert altars void of solemn fire.
Before the gradual, prostrate they ador'd;
The pavement kiss'd; and thus the saint implor'd.

O righteous Themis, if the Pow'rs above
By pray'rs are bent to pity, and to love;
If humane miseries can move their mind;
If yet they can forgive, and yet be kind;
Tell how we may restore, by second birth,
Mankind, and people desolated Earth.
Then thus the gracious Goddess, nodding, said;
Depart, and with your vestments veil your head:
And stooping lowly down, with losen'd zones,
Throw each behind your backs, your mighty
    mother's bones.
Amaz'd the pair, and mute with wonder stand,
Till Pyrrha first refus'd the dire command.
Forbid it Heav'n, said she, that I shou'd tear
Those holy relics from the sepulcher.
They ponder'd the mysterious words again,
For some new sense; and long they sought in vain:
At length Deucalion clear'd his cloudy brow,
And said, the dark Ænigma will allow
A meaning, which, if well I understand,
From sacrilege will free the God's command:
This Earth our mighty mother is, the stones
In her capacious body, are her bones:
These we must cast behind. With hope, and fear,
The woman did the new solution hear:
The man diffides in his own augury,

And doubts the Gods; yet both resolve to try.
Descending from the mount, they first unbind
Their vests, and veil'd, they cast the stones behind:
The stones (a miracle to mortal view,
But long tradition makes it pass for true)
Did first the rigour of their kind expel,
And suppled into softness, as they fell;
Then swell'd, and swelling, by degrees grew warm;
And took the rudiments of human form.
Imperfect shapes: in marble such are seen,
When the rude chizzel does the man begin;
While yet the roughness of the stone remains,
Without the rising muscles, and the veins.
The sappy parts, and next resembling juice,
Were turn'd to moisture, for the body's use:
Supplying humours, blood, and nourishment;
The rest, too solid to receive a bent,
Converts to bones; and what was once a vein,
Its former name and Nature did retain.
By help of pow'r divine, in little space,
What the man threw, assum'd a manly face;
And what the wife, renew'd the female race.
Hence we derive our nature; born to bear
Laborious life; and harden'd into care.

The rest of animals, from teeming Earth
Produc'd, in various forms receiv'd their birth.
The native moisture, in its close retreat,
Digested by the sun's ætherial heat,
As in a kindly womb, began to breed:
Then swell'd, and quicken'd by the vital seed.
And some in less, and some in longer space,
Were ripen'd into form, and took a sev'ral face.
Thus when the Nile from Pharian fields is fled,
And seeks, with ebbing tides, his ancient bed,
The fat manure with heav'nly fire is warm'd;
And crusted creatures, as in wombs, are form'd;

These, when they turn the glebe, the peasants find;
Some rude, and yet unfinish'd in their kind:
Short of their limbs, a lame imperfect birth:
One half alive; and one of lifeless earth.

For heat, and moisture, when in bodies join'd,
The temper that results from either kind
Conception makes; and fighting till they mix,
Their mingled atoms in each other fix.
Thus Nature's hand the genial bed prepares
With friendly discord, and with fruitful wars.

From hence the surface of the ground, with mud
And slime besmear'd (the fæces of the flood),
Receiv'd the rays of Heav'n: and sucking in
The seeds of heat, new creatures did begin:
Some were of sev'ral sorts produc'd before,
But of new monsters, Earth created more.
Unwillingly, but yet she brought to light
Thee, Python too, the wond'ring world to fright,
And the new nations, with so dire a sight:
So monstrous was his bulk, so large a space
Did his vast body, and long train embrace.
Whom Phœbus basking on a bank espy'd;
E're now the God his arrows had not try'd
But on the trembling deer, or mountain goat;
At this new quarry he prepares to shoot.
Though ev'ry shaft took place, he spent the store
Of his full quiver; and 'twas long before
Th' expiring serpent wallow'd in his gore.
Then, to preserve the fame of such a deed,
For Python slain, he Pythian games decred.
Where noble youths for mastership shou'd strive,
To quoit, to run, and steeds, and chariots drive.
The prize was fame: in witness of renown
An oaken garland did the victor crown.
The laurel was not yet for triumphs born;

But every green alike by Phœbus worn,
Did, with promiscuous grace, his flowing locks adorn.

The Transformation of Daphne into a Lawrel

The first and fairest of his loves, was she
Whom not blind fortune, but the dire decree
Of angry Cupid forc'd him to desire:
Daphne her name, and Peneus was her sire.
Swell'd with the pride, that new success attends,
He sees the stripling, while his bow he bends,
And thus insults him: Thou lascivious boy,
Are arms like these for children to employ?
Know, such achievements are my proper claim;
Due to my vigour, and unerring aim:
Resistless are my shafts, and Python late
In such a feather'd death, has found his fate.
Take up the torch (and lay my weapons by),
With that the feeble souls of lovers fry.
To whom the son of Venus thus reply'd,
Phœbus, thy shafts are sure on all beside,
But mine of Phœbus, mine the fame shall be
Of all thy conquests, when I conquer thee.

He said, and soaring, swiftly wing'd his flight:
Nor stopt but on Parnassus' airy height.
Two diff'rent shafts he from his quiver draws;
One to repel desire, and one to cause.
One shaft is pointed with refulgent gold:
To bribe the love, and make the lover bold:
One blunt, and tipt with lead, whose base allay
Provokes disdain, and drives desire away.
The blunted bolt against the nymph he drest:
But with the sharp transfixt Apollo's breast.

Th' enamour'd deity pursues the chase;
The scornful damsel shuns his loath'd embrace:
In hunting beasts of prey, her youth employs;
And Phœbe rivals in her rural joys.
With naked neck she goes, and shoulders bare;
And with a fillet binds her flowing hair.
By many suitors sought, she mocks their pains,
And still her vow'd virginity maintains.
Impatient of a yoke, the name of bride
She shuns, and hates the joys, she never try'd.
On wilds, and woods, she fixes her desire:
Nor knows what youth, and kindly love, inspire.
Her father chides her oft: Thou ow'st, says he,
A husband to thy self, a son to me.
She, like a crime, abhors the nuptial bed:
She glows with blushes, and she hangs her head.
Then casting round his neck her tender arms,
Sooths him with blandishments, and filial charms:
Give me, my Lord, she said, to live, and die,
A spotless maid, without the marriage tie.
'Tis but a small request; I beg no more
Than what Diana's father gave before.
The good old sire was soften'd to consent;
But said her wish wou'd prove her punishment:
For so much youth, and so much beauty join'd,
Oppos'd the state, which her desires design'd.

The God of light, aspiring to her bed,
Hopes what he seeks, with flattering fancies fed;
And is, by his own oracles, misled.
And as in empty fields the stubble burns,
Or nightly travelers, when day returns,
Their useless torches on dry hedges throw,
That catch the flames, and kindle all the row;
So burns the God, consuming in desire,
And feeding in his breast a fruitless fire:
Her well-turn'd neck he view'd (her neck was bare)

And on her shoulders her dishevel'd hair;
Oh were it comb'd, said he, with what a grace
Wou'd every waving curl become her face!
He view'd her eyes, like heav'nly lamps that shone,
He view'd her lips, too sweet to view alone,
Her taper fingers, and her panting breast;
He praises all he sees, and for the rest
Believes the beauties yet unseen are best:
Swift as the wind, the damsel fled away,
Nor did for these alluring speeches stay:
Stay Nymph, he cry'd, I follow, not a foe.
Thus from the lion trips the trembling doe;
Thus from the wolf the frighten'd lamb removes,
And, from pursuing falcons, fearful doves;
Thou shunn'st a God, and shunn'st a God, that loves.
Ah, lest some thorn shou'd pierce thy tender foot,
Or thou shou'dst fall in flying my pursuit!
To sharp uneven ways thy steps decline;
Abate thy speed, and I will bate of mine.
Yet think from whom thou dost so rashly fly;
Nor basely born, nor shepherd's swain am I.
Perhaps thou know'st not my superior state;
And from that ignorance proceeds thy hate.
Me Claros, Delphi, Tenedos obey;
These hands the Patareian scepter sway.
The King of Gods begot me: what shall be,
Or is, or ever was, in Fate, I see.
Mine is th' invention of the charming lyre;
Sweet notes, and heav'nly numbers, I inspire.
Sure is my bow, unerring is my dart;
But ah! more deadly his, who pierc'd my heart.
Med'cine is mine; what herbs and simples grow
In fields, and forests, all their pow'rs I know;
And am the great physician call'd, below.
Alas that fields and forests can afford.

No remedies to heal their love-sick lord!
To cure the pains of love, no plant avails:
And his own physic, the physician falls.

She heard not half; so furiously she flies;
And on her ear th' imperfect accent dies,
Fear gave her wings; and as she fled, the wind
Increasing, spread her flowing hair behind;
And left her legs and thighs expos'd to view:
Which made the God more eager to pursue.
The God was young, and was too hotly bent
To lose his time in empty compliment:
But led by love, and fir'd with such a sight,
Impetuously pursu'd his near delight.

As when th' impatient greyhound slipt from far,
Bounds o'er the glebe to course the fearful hare,
She in her speed does all her safety lay;
And he with double speed pursues the prey;
O'er-runs her at the sitting turn, and licks
His chaps in vain, and blows upon the flix:
She 'scapes, and for the neighb'ring covert strives,
And gaining shelter, doubts if yet she lives:
If little things with great we may compare,
Such was the God, and such the flying fair,
She urg'd by fear, her feet did swiftly move,
But he more swiftly, who was urg'd by love.
He gathers ground upon her in the chase:
Now breathes upon her hair, with nearer pace;
And just is fast'ning on the wish'd embrace.
The nymph grew pale, and in a mortal fright,
Spent with the labour of so long a flight;
And now despairing, cast a mournful look
Upon the streams of her paternal brook;
Oh help, she cry'd, in this extremest need!
If water Gods are deities indeed:
Gape Earth, and this unhappy wretch entomb;

Or change my form, whence all my sorrows come.
Scarce had she finish'd, when her feet she found
Benumb'd with cold, and fasten'd to the ground:
A filmy rind about her body grows;
Her hair to leaves, her arms extend to boughs:
The nymph is all into a lawrel gone;
The smoothness of her skin remains alone.
Yet Phœbus loves her still, and casting round
Her bole, his arms, some little warmth he found.
The tree still panted in th' unfinish'd part:
Not wholly vegetive, and heav'd her heart.
He fixt his lips upon the trembling rind;
It swerv'd aside, and his embrace declin'd.
To whom the God, Because thou canst not be
My mistress, I espouse thee for my tree:
Be thou the prize of honour, and renown;
The deathless poet, and the poem, crown.
Thou shalt the Roman festivals adorn,
And, after poets, be by victors worn.
Thou shalt returning Cæsar's triumph grace;
When pomps shall in a long procession pass.
Wreath'd on the posts before his palace wait;
And be the sacred guardian of the gate.
Secure from thunder, and unharm'd by Jove,
Unfading as th' immortal Pow'rs above:
And as the locks of Phœbus are unshorn,
So shall perpetual green thy boughs adorn.
The grateful tree was pleas'd with what he said;
And shook the shady honours of her head.

The Transformation of Io into a Heifer

An ancient forest in Thessalia grows;
Which Tempe's pleasing valley does enclose:
Through this the rapid Peneus take his course;

From Pindus rolling with impetuous force;
Mists from the river's mighty fall arise:
And deadly damps enclose the cloudy skies:
Perpetual fogs are hanging o'er the wood;
And sounds of waters deaf the neighbourhood.
Deep, in a rocky cave, he makes abode
(A mansion proper for a mourning God).
Here he gives audience; issuing out decrees
To rivers, his dependent deities.
On this occasion hither they resort;
To pay their homage, and to make their court.
All doubtful, whether to congratulate
His daughter's honour, or lament her fate.
Sperchæus, crown'd with poplar, first appears;
Then old Apidanus came crown'd with years:
Enipeus turbulent, Amphrysos tame;
And Æas last with lagging waters came.
Then, of his kindred brooks, a num'rous throng
Condole his loss; and bring their urns along.
Not one was wanting of the wat'ry train,
That fill'd his flood, or mingled with the main:
But Inachus, who in his cave, alone,
Wept not another's losses, but his own,
For his dear Io, whether stray'd, or dead,
To him uncertain, doubtful tears he shed.
He sought her through the world;
but sought in vain;
And no where finding, rather fear'd her slain.

Her, just returning from her father's brook,
Jove had beheld, with a desiring look:
And, Oh fair daughter of the flood, he said,
Worthy alone of Jove's imperial bed,
Happy whoever shall those charms possess;
The king of Gods (nor is thy lover less)
Invites thee to yon cooler shades; to shun
The scorching rays of the meridian sun.

Nor shalt thou tempt the dangers of the grove
Alone, without a guide; thy guide is Jove.
No puny Pow'r, but he whose high command
Is unconfin'd, who rules the seas and land;
And tempers thunder in his awful hand,
Oh fly not: for she fled from his embrace
O'er Lerna's pastures: he pursu'd the chase
Along the shades of the Lyrcæan plain;
At length the God, who never asks in vain,
Involv'd with vapours, imitating night,
Both Air, and Earth; and then suppress'd her flight,
And mingling force with love, enjoy'd the full delight.
Mean-time the jealous Juno, from on high,
Survey'd the fruitful fields of Arcady;
And wonder'd that the mist shou'd over-run
The face of day-light, and obscure the sun.
No nat'ral cause she found, from brooks, or bogs,
Or marshy lowlands, to produce the fogs;
Then round the skies she sought for Jupiter,
Her faithless husband; but no Jove was there:
Suspecting now the worst, Or I, she said,
Am much mistaken, or am much betray'd.
With fury she precipitates her flight:
Dispels the shadows of dissembled night;
And to the day restores his native light.
Th' Almighty Leacher, careful to prevent
The consequence, foreseeing her descent,
Transforms his mistress in a trice; and now
In Io's place appears a lovely cow.
So sleek her skin, so faultless was her make,
Ev'n Juno did unwilling pleasure take
To see so fair a rival of her love;
And what she was, and whence, inquir'd of Jove:
Of what fair herd, and from what pedigree?
The God, half caught, was forc'd upon a lye:

And said she sprung from Earth. She took the word,
And begg'd the beauteous heyfer of her lord.
What should he do? 'twas equal shame to Jove
Or to relinquish, or betray his love:
Yet to refuse so slight a gift, wou'd be
But more t' increase his consort's jealousy:
Thus fear, and love, by turns, his heart assail'd;
And stronger love had sure, at length, prevail'd:
But some faint hope remain'd, his jealous queen
Had not the mistress through the heifer seen.
The cautious Goddess, of her gift possest,
Yet harbour'd anxious thoughts within her breast;
As she who knew the falsehood of her Jove;
And justly fear'd some new relapse of love.
Which to prevent, and to secure her care,
To trusty Argus she commits the fair.

The head of Argus (as with stars the skies)
Was compass'd round, and wore an hundred eyes.
But two by turns their lids in slumber steep;
The rest on duty still their station keep;
Nor cou'd the total constellation sleep.
Thus, ever present, to his eyes, and mind,
His charge was still before him, tho' behind.
In fields he suffer'd her to feed by Day,
But when the setting sun to night gave way,
The captive cow he summon'd with a call;
And drove her back, and ty'd her to the stall.
On leaves of trees, and bitter herbs she fed,
Heav'n was her canopy, bare earth her bed:
So hardly lodg'd, and to digest her food,
She drank from troubled streams, defil'd with mud.
Her woeful story fain she wou'd have told,
With hands upheld, but had no hands to hold.
Her head to her ungentle keeper bow'd,
She strove to speak, she spoke not, but she low'd:
Affrighted with the noise, she look'd around,
And seem'd t' inquire the author of the sound.

Once on the banks where often she had play'd
(Her father's banks), she came, and there survey'd
Her alter'd visage, and her branching head;
And starting, from her self she wou'd have fled.
Her fellow nymphs, familiar to her eyes,
Beheld, but knew her not in this disguise.
Ev'n Inachus himself was ignorant;
And in his daughter, did his daughter want.
She follow'd where her fellows went, as she
Were still a partner of the company:
They stroke her neck; the gentle heifer stands,
And her neck offers to their stroking hands.
Her father gave her grass; the grass she took;
And lick'd his palms, and cast a piteous look;
And in the language of her eyes, she spoke.
She wou'd have told her name, and ask'd relief,
But wanting words, in tears she tells her grief.
Which, with her foot she makes him understand;
And prints the name of Io in the sand.

Ah wretched me! her mournful father cry'd;
She, with a sigh, to wretched me reply'd:
About her milk-white neck, his arms he threw;
And wept, and then these tender words ensue.
And art thou she, whom I have sought around
The world, and have at length so sadly found?
So found, is worse than lost: with mutual words
Thou answer'st not, no voice thy tongue affords:
But sighs are deeply drawn from out thy breast;
And speech deny'd, by lowing is express'd.
Unknowing, I prepar'd thy bridal bed;
With empty hopes of happy issue fed.
But now the husband of a herd must be
Thy mate, and bell'wing sons thy progeny.
Oh, were I mortal, death might bring relief:
But now my God-head but extends my grief:
Prolongs my woes, of which no end I see,

And makes me curse my immortality!
More had he said, but fearful of her stay,
The starry guardian drove his charge away,
To some fresh pasture; on a hilly height
He sate himself, and kept her still in sight.

The Eyes of Argus Transform'd into a Peacock's Train

Now Jove no longer cou'd her suff'rings bear;
But call'd in haste his airy messenger,
The son of Maia, with severe decree
To kill the keeper, and to set her free.
With all his harness soon the God was sped,
His flying hat was fastened on his head,
Wings on his heels were hung, and in his hand
He holds the virtue of the snaky wand.
The liquid air his moving pinions wound,
And, in the moment, shoot him on the ground.
Before he came in sight, the crafty God
His wings dismiss'd, but still retain'd his rod:
That sleep-procuring wand wise Hermes took,
But made it seem to sight a shepherd's hook.
With this, he did a herd of goats control;
Which by the way he met, and slyly stole.
Clad like a country swain, he pip'd, and sung;
And playing, drove his jolly troop along.

With pleasure, Argus the musician heeds;
But wonders much at those new vocal reeds.
And whosoe'er thou art, my friend, said he,
Up hither drive thy goats, and play by me:
This hill has browz for them, and shade for thee.
The God, who was with ease induc'd to climb,
Began discourse to pass away the time;
And still betwixt, his tuneful pipe he plies;

And watch'd his hour, to close the keeper's eyes.
With much ado, he partly kept awake;
Not suff'ring all his eyes repose to take:
And ask'd the stranger, who did reeds invent,
And whence began so rare an instrument?

The Transformation of Syrinx into Reeds

Then Hermes thus: A nymph of late there was
Whose heav'nly form her fellows did surpass.
The pride and joy of fair Arcadia's plains,
Belov'd by deities, ador'd by swains:
Syrinx her name, by Sylvans oft pursu'd,
As oft she did the lustful Gods delude:
The rural, and the woodland Pow'rs disdain'd;
With Cynthia hunted, and her rites maintain'd:
Like Phœbe clad, even Phœbe's self she seems,
So tall, so straight, such well-proportion'd limbs:
The nicest eye did no distinction know,
But that the goddess bore a golden bow:
Distinguish'd thus, the sight she cheated too.
Descending from Lycæus, Pan admires
The matchless nymph, and burns with new desires.
A crown of pine upon his head he wore;
And thus began her pity to implore.
But e'er he thus began, she took her flight
So swift, she was already out of sight.
Nor stay'd to hear the courtship of the God;
But bent her course to Ladon's gentle flood:
There by the river stopt, and tir'd before;
Relief from water nymphs her pray'rs implore.

Now while the lustful God, with speedy pace,
Just thought to strain her in a strict embrace,
He fill'd his arms with reeds, new rising on the place.

And while he sighs, his ill success to find,
The tender canes were shaken by the wind;
And breath'd a mournful air, unheard before;
That much surprising Pan, yet pleas'd him more.
Admiring this new music, Thou, he said,
Who canst not be the partner of my bed,
At least shall be the comfort of my mind:
And often, often to my lips be joyn'd.
He form'd the reeds, proportion'd as they are,
Unequal in their length, and wax'd with care,
They still retain the name of his ungrateful fair.

While Hermes pip'd, and sung, and told his tale,
The keeper's winking eyes began to fail,
And drowsy slumber on the lids to creep;
Till all the watchman was at length asleep.
Then soon the God his voice, and song suppress;
And with his pow'rful rod confirm'd his rest:
Without delay his crooked faulchion drew,
And at one fatal stroke the keeper slew.
Down from the rock fell the dissever'd head,
Opening its eyes in death; and falling, bled;
And mark'd the passage with a crimson trail:
Thus Argus lies in pieces, cold, and pale;
And all his hundred eyes, with all their light,
Are clos'd at once, in one perpetual night.
These Juno takes, that they no more may fail,
And spreads them in her peacock's gaudy tail.

Impatient to revenge her injur'd bed,
She wreaks her anger on her rival's head;
With Furies frights her from her native home;
And drives her gadding, round the world to roam:
Nor ceas'd her madness, and her flight, before
She touch'd the limits of the Pharian shore.
At length, arriving on the banks of Nile,
Wearied with length of ways, and worn with toil,

She laid her down; and leaning on her knees,
Invok'd the cause of all her miseries:
And cast her languishing regards above,
For help from Heav'n, and her ungrateful Jove.
She sigh'd, she wept, she low'd; 'twas all she cou'd;
And with unkindness seem'd to tax the God.
Last, with an humble pray'r, she beg'd repose,
Or death at least, to finish all her woes.
Jove heard her vows, and with a flatt'ring look,
In her behalf to jealous Juno spoke,
He cast his arms about her neck, and said,
Dame, rest secure; no more thy nuptial bed
This nymph shall violate; by Styx I swear,
And every oath that binds the Thunderer.
The Goddess was appeas'd; and at the word
Was Io to her former shape restor'd.
The rugged hair began to fall away;
The sweetness of her eyes did only stay,
Tho' not so large; her crooked horns decrease;
The wideness of her jaws and nostrils cease:
Her hoofs to hands return, in little space:
The five long taper fingers take their place,
And nothing of the heifer now is seen,
Beside the native whiteness of the skin.
Erected on her feet she walks again:
And two the duty of the four sustain.
She tries her tongue; her silence softly breaks,
And fears her former lowings when she speaks:
A Goddess now, through all th' Ægyptian State:
And serv'd by priests, who in white linen wait.

Her son was Epaphus, at length believ'd
The son of Jove, and as a God receiv'd;
With sacrifice ador'd, and public pray'rs,
He common temples with his mother shares.
Equal in years, and rival in renown
With Epaphus, the youthful Phæton

Like honour claims; and boasts his sire the sun.
His haughty looks, and his assuming air,
The son of Isis could no longer bear:
Thou tak'st thy mother's word too far, said he,
And hast usurp'd thy boasted pedigree.
Go, base pretender to a borrow'd name.
Thus tax'd, he blush'd with anger, and with shame;
But shame repress'd his rage: the daunted youth
Soon seeks his mother, and inquires the truth:
Mother, said he, this infamy was thrown
By Epaphus on you, and me your son.
He spoke in public, told it to my face;
Nor durst I vindicate the dire disgrace:
Even I, the bold, the sensible of wrong,
Restrain'd by shame, was forc'd to hold my tongue.
To hear an open slander, is a curse:
But not to find an answer, is a worse.
If I am Heav'n-begot, assert your son
By some sure sign; and make my father known,
To right my honour, and redeem your own.
He said, and saying cast his arms about
Her neck, and beg'd her to resolve the doubt.

'Tis hard to judge if Clymene were mov'd
More by his pray'r, whom she so dearly lov'd,
Or more with fury fir'd, to find her name
Traduc'd, and made the sport of common fame.
She stretch'd her arms to Heav'n, and fix'd her eyes
On that fair planet that adorns the skies;
Now by those beams, said she, whose holy fires
Consume my breast, and kindle my desires;
By him, who sees us both, and clears our sight,
By him, the public minister of light,
I swear that Sun begot thee; if I lye,
Let him his cheerful influence deny:
Let him no more this perjur'd creature see;
And shine on all the world but only me.

If still you doubt your mother's innocence,
His eastern mansion is not far from hence;
With little pains you to his Leve go,
And from himself your parentage may know.
With joy th' ambitious youth his mother heard,
And eager, for the journey soon prepar'd.
He longs the world beneath him to survey;
To guide the chariot; and to give the day:
From Meroe's burning sands he bends his course,
Nor less in India feels his father's force:
His travel urging, till he came in sight;
And saw the palace by the purple light.

Book VIII

The Story of Nisus and Scylla

Now shone the morning star in bright array,
To vanquish night, and usher in the day:
The wind veers southward, and moist clouds arise,
That blot with shades the blue meridian skies.
Cephalus feels with joy the kindly gales,
His new allies unfurl the swelling sails;
Steady their course, they cleave the yielding main,
And, with a wish, th' intended harbour gain.
Mean-while King Minos, on the Attick strand,
Displays his martial skill, and wastes the land.
His army lies encamped upon the plains,
Before Alcathoe's walls, where Nisus reigns;
On whose grey head a lock of purple hue,
The strength, and fortune of his kingdom, grew.

Six moons were gone, and past, when still from far
Victoria hover'd o'er the doubtful war.
So long, to both inclin'd, th' impartial maid
Between 'em both her equal wings display'd.
High on the walls, by Phœbus vocal made,
A turret of the palace rais'd its head;
And where the God his tuneful harp resign'd.
The sound within the stones still lay enshrin'd:
Hither the daughter of the purple king
Ascended oft, to hear its music ring;
And, striking with a pebble, wou'd release
Th' enchanted notes, in times of happy peace.
But now, from thence, the curious maid beheld

Rough feats of arms, and combats of the field:
And, since the siege was long, had learnt the name
Of ev'ry chief, his character, and fame;
Their arms, their horse, and quiver she descry'd,
Nor cou'd the dress of war the warrior hide.

Europa's son she knew above the rest,
And more, than well became a virgin breast:
In vain the crested morion veils his face,
She thinks it adds a more peculiar grace:
His ample shield, embost with burnish'd gold,
Still makes the bearer lovelier to behold:
When the tough jav'lin, with a whirl, he sends,
His strength and skill the sighing maid commends;
Or, when he strains to draw the circling bow,
And his fine limbs a manly posture show,
Compar'd with Phœbus, he performs so well,
Let her be judge, and Minos shall excel.

But when the helm put off, display'd to sight,
And set his features in an open light;
When, vaulting to his seat, his steed he prest,
Caparison'd in gold, and richly drest;
Himself in scarlet sumptuously array'd,
New passions rise, and fire the frantick maid.
O happy spear! she cries, that feels his touch;
Nay, ev'n the reins he holds are blest too much.
Oh! were it lawful, she cou'd wing her way
Thro' the stern hostile troops without dismay;
Or throw her body to the distant ground,
And in the Cretans happy camp be found.
Wou'd Minos but desire it! she'd expose
Her native country to her country's foes;
Unbar the gates, the town with flames infest,
Or any thing that Minos shou'd request.

And as she sate, and pleas'd her longing sight,
Viewing the king's pavilion veil'd with white,

Shou'd joy, or grief, she said, possess my breast,
To see my country by a war opprest?
I'm in suspense! For, tho' 'tis grief to know
I love a man that is declar'd my foe;
Yet, in my own despite, I must approve
That lucky war, which brought the man I love.
Yet, were I tender'd as a pledge of peace,
The cruelties of war might quickly cease.
Oh! with what joy I'd wear the chains he gave!
A patient hostage, and a willing slave.
Thou lovely object! if the nymph that bare
Thy charming person, were but half so fair;
Well might a God her virgin bloom desire,
And with a rape indulge his amorous fire.
Oh! had I wings to glide along the air,
To his dear tent I'd fly, and settle there:
There tell my quality, confess my flame,
And grant him any dowry that he'd name.
All, all I'd give; only my native land,
My dearest country, shou'd excepted stand,
For, perish love, and all expected joys,
E're, with so base a thought, my soul complies.
Yet, oft the vanquish'd some advantage find,
When conquer'd by a noble, gen'rous mind.
Brave Minos justly has the war begun,
Fir'd with resentment for his murder'd son:
The righteous Gods a righteous cause regard,
And will, with victory, his arms reward:
We must be conquer'd; and the captive's fate
Will surely seize us, tho' it seize us late.
Why then shou'd love be idle, and neglect
What Mars, by arms and perils, will effect?
Oh! Prince, I dye, with anxious fear opprest,
Lest some rash hand shou'd wound my charmer's breast:
For, if they saw, no barb'rous mind cou'd dare
Against that lovely form to raise a spear.

But I'm resolv'd, and fix'd in this decree,
My father's country shall my dowry be.
Thus I prevent the loss of life and blood,
And, in effect, the action must be good.
Vain resolution! for, at ev'ry gate
The trusty sentinels, successive, wait:
The keys my father keeps; ah! there's my grief;
'Tis he obstructs all hopes of my relief.
Gods! that this hated light I'd never seen!
Or, all my life, without a father been!
But Gods we all may be; for those that dare,
Are Gods, and Fortune's chiefest favours share.
The ruling Pow'rs a lazy pray'r detest,
The bold adventurer succeeds the best.
What other maid, inspir'd with such a flame,
But wou'd take courage, and abandon shame?
But wou'd, tho' ruin shou'd ensue, remove
Whate'er oppos'd, and clear the way to love?
This, shall another's feeble passion dare?
While I sit tame, and languish in despair:
No; for tho' fire and sword before me lay,
Impatient love thro' both shou'd force its way.
Yet I have no such enemies to fear,
My sole obstruction is my father's hair;
His purple lock my sanguine hope destroys,
And clouds the prospect of my rising joys.

Whilst thus she spoke, amid the thick'ning air
Night supervenes, the greatest nurse of care:
And, as the Goddess spreads her sable wings,
The virgin's fears decay, and courage springs.
The hour was come, when Man's o'er-labour'd breast
Surceas'd its care, by downy sleep possest:
All things now hush'd, Scylla with silent tread
Urg'd her approach to Nisus' royal bed:
There, of the fatal lock (accursed theft!)
She her unwitting father's head bereft.

In safe possession of her impious prey,
Out at a postern gate she takes her way.
Embolden'd, by the merit of the deed
She traverses the adverse camp with speed,
Till Minos' tent she reach'd: the righteous king
She thus bespoke, who shiver'd at the thing.

Behold th' effect of love's resistless sway!
I, Nisus' royal seed, to thee betray
My country, and my Gods. For this strange task,
Minos, no other boon but thee I ask.
This purple lock, a pledge of love, receive;
No worthless present, since in it I give
My father's head. Mov'd at a crime so new,
And with abhorrence fill'd, back Minos drew,
Nor touch'd th' unhallow'd gift;
but thus exclaim'd
(With mein indignant, and with eyes inflam'd),
Perdition seize thee, thou, thy kind's disgrace!
May thy devoted carcass find no place
In earth, or air, or sea, by all out-cast!
Shall Minos, with so foul a monster, blast
His Cretan world, where cradled Jove was nurst?
Forbid it Heav'n! away, thou most accurst!

And now Alcathoe, its lord exchang'd,
Was under Minos' domination rang'd.
While the most equal king his care applies
To curb the conquer'd, and new laws devise,
The fleet, by his command, with hoisted sails,
And ready oars, invites the murm'ring gales.
At length the Cretan hero anchor weigh'd,
Repaying, with neglect, th' abandon'd maid.
Deaf to her cries, he furrows up the main:
In vain she prays, solicits him in vain.

And now she furious grows in wild despair,
She wrings her hands, and throws aloft her hair.

Where run'st thou? (thus she vents her deep distress)
Why shun'st thou her that crown'd thee with success?
Her, whose fond love to thee cou'd sacrifice
Her country, and her parent, sacred ties!
Can nor my love, nor proffer'd presents find
A passage to thy heart, and make thee kind?
Can nothing move thy pity? O ingrate,
Can'st thou behold my lost, forlorn estate,
And not be soften'd? Can'st thou throw off one
Who has no refuge left but thee alone?
Where shall I seek for comfort? whither fly?
My native country does in ashes lye:
Or were't not so, my treason bars me there,
And bids me wander. Shall I next repair
To a wrong'd father, by my guilt undone?
Me all Mankind deservedly will shun.
I, out of all the world, my self have thrown,
To purchase an access to Crete alone;
Which, since refus'd, ungen'rous man, give o'er
To boast thy race; Europa never bore
A thing so savage. Thee some tigress bred,
On the bleak Syrt's inhospitable bed;
Or where Charybdis pours its rapid tide
Tempestuous. Thou art not to Jove ally'd;
Nor did the king of Gods thy mother meet
Beneath a bull's forg'd shape, and bear to Crete.
That fable of thy glorious birth is feign'd;
Some wild outrageous bull thy dam sustain'd.
O father Nisus, now my death behold;
Exult, o city, by my baseness sold:
Minos, obdurate, has aveng'd ye all;
But 'twere more just by those I wrong'd to fall:
For why shou'dst thou, who only didst subdue
By my offending, my offence pursue?
Well art thou matcht to one whose am'rous flame
Too fiercely rag'd, for human-kind to tame;
One who, within a wooden heifer thrust,

Courted a low'ring bull's mistaken lust;
And, from whose monster-teeming womb, the Earth
Receiv'd, what much it mourn'd, a bi-form birth.
But what avails my plaints? the whistling wind,
Which bears him far away, leaves them behind.
Well weigh'd Pasiphæ, when she prefer'd
A bull to thee, more brutish than the herd.
But ah! Time presses, and the labour'd oars
To distance drive the fleet, and lose
the less'ning shores.
Think not, ungrateful man, the liquid way
And threat'ning billows shall enforce my stay.
I'll follow thee in spite: My arms I'll throw
Around thy oars, or grasp thy crooked prow,
And drag thro' drenching seas.
Her eager tongue
Had hardly clos'd the speech,
when forth she sprung
And prov'd the deep. Cupid with added force
Recruits each nerve, and aids her wat'ry course.
Soon she the ship attains, unwelcome guest;
And, as with close embrace its sides she prest,
A hawk from upper air came pouring down
('Twas Nisus cleft the sky with wings new grown).
At Scylla's head his horny bill he aims;
She, fearful of the blow, the ship disclaims,
Quitting her hold: and yet she fell not far,
But wond'ring, finds her self sustain'd in air.
Chang'd to a lark, she mottled pinions shook,
And, from the ravish'd lock, the name of Ciris took.

The Labyrinth

Now Minos, landed on the Cretan shore,
Performs his vows to Jove's protecting pow'r;
A hundred bullocks of the largest breed,

With flow'rets crown'd, before his altar bleed:
While trophies of the vanquish'd, brought from far
Adorn the palace with the spoils of war.

Mean-while the monster of a human-beast,
His family's reproach, and stain, increas'd.
His double kind the rumour swiftly spread,
And evidenc'd the mother's beastly deed.
When Minos, willing to conceal the shame
That sprung from the reports of tat'ling Fame,
Resolves a dark enclosure to provide,
And, far from sight, the two-form'd creature hide.

Great Dædalus of Athens was the man
That made the draught, and form'd the wondrous plan;
Where rooms within themselves encircled lye,
With various windings, to deceive the eye.
As soft Mæander's wanton current plays,
When thro' the Phrygian fields it loosely strays;
Backward and forward rolls the dimpl'd tide,
Seeming, at once, two different ways to glide:
While circling streams their former banks survey,
And waters past succeeding waters see:
Now floating to the sea with downward course,
Now pointing upward to its ancient source,
Such was the work, so intricate the place,
That scarce the workman all its turns cou'd trace;
And Dædalus was puzzled how to find
The secret ways of what himself design'd.

These private walls the Minotaur include,
Who twice was glutted with Athenian blood:
But the third tribute more successful prov'd,
Slew the foul monster, and the plague remov'd.
When Theseus, aided by the virgin's art,
Had trac'd the guiding thread thro' ev'ry part,
He took the gentle maid, that set him free,

And, bound for Dias, cut the briny sea.
There, quickly cloy'd, ungrateful, and unkind,
Left his fair consort in the isle behind,
Whom Bacchus saw, and straining in his arms
Her rifled bloom, and violated charms,
Resolves, for this, the dear engaging dame
Shou'd shine for ever in the rolls of Fame;
And bids her crown among the stars be plac'd,
With an eternal constellation grac'd.
The golden circlet mounts; and, as it flies,
Its diamonds twinkle in the distant skies;
There, in their pristine form, the gemmy rays
Between Alcides, and the dragon blaze.

The Story of Dædalus and Icarus

In tedious exile now too long detain'd,
Dædalus languish'd for his native land:
The sea foreclos'd his flight; yet thus he said:
Tho' Earth and water in subjection laid,
O cruel Minos, thy dominion be,
We'll go thro' air; for sure the air is free.
Then to new arts his cunning thought applies,
And to improve the work of Nature tries.
A row of quills in gradual order plac'd,
Rise by degrees in length from first to last;
As on a cliff th' ascending thicket grows,
Or, different reeds the rural pipe compose.
Along the middle runs a twine of flax,
The bottom stems are joyn'd by pliant wax.
Thus, well compact, a hollow bending brings
The fine composure into real wings.

His boy, young Icarus, that near him stood,
Unthinking of his fate, with smiles pursu'd

The floating feathers, which the moving air
Bore loosely from the ground,
    and wasted here and there.
Or with the wax impertinently play'd,
And with his childish tricks the great
    design delay'd.

The final master-stroke at last impos'd,
And now, the neat machine compleatly clos'd;
Fitting his pinions on, a flight he tries,
And hung self-balanc'd in the beaten skies.
Then thus instructs his child: My boy, take care
To wing your course along the middle air;
If low, the surges wet your flagging plumes;
If high, the sun the melting wax consumes:
Steer between both: nor to the northern skies,
Nor south Orion turn your giddy eyes;
But follow me: let me before you lay
Rules for the flight, and mark the pathless way.
Then teaching, with a fond concern, his son,
He took the untry'd wings, and fix'd 'em on;
But fix'd with trembling hands; and as he speaks,
The tears roll gently down his aged cheeks.
Then kiss'd, and in his arms embrac'd him fast,
But knew not this embrace must be the last.
And mounting upward, as he wings his flight,
Back on his charge he turns his aking sight;
As parent birds, when first their callow care
Leave the high nest to tempt the liquid air.
Then cheers him on, and oft, with fatal art,
Reminds the stripling to perform his part.

These, as the angler at the silent brook,
Or mountain-shepherd leaning on his crook,
Or gaping plowman, from the vale descries,
They stare, and view 'em with religious eyes,
And strait conclude 'em Gods; since none, but they,
Thro' their own azure skies cou'd find a way.

Now Delos, Paros on the left are seen,
And Samos, favour'd by Jove's haughty queen;
Upon the right, the isle Lebynthos nam'd,
And fair Calymne for its honey fam'd.
When now the boy, whose childish thoughts aspire
To loftier aims, and make him ramble high'r,
Grown wild, and wanton, more embolden'd flies
Far from his guide, and soars among the skies.
The soft'ning wax, that felt a nearer sun,
Dissolv'd apace, and soon began to run.
The youth in vain his melting pinions shakes,
His feathers gone, no longer air he takes:
Oh! Father, father, as he strove to cry,
Down to the sea he tumbled from on high,
And found his Fate; yet still subsists by fame,
Among those waters that retain his name.

The father, now no more a father, cries,
Ho Icarus! where are you? as he flies;
Where shall I seek my boy? he cries again,
And saw his feathers scatter'd on the main.
Then curs'd his art; and fun'ral rites confer'd,
Naming the country from the youth interr'd.

A partridge, from a neighb'ring stump, beheld
The sire his monumental marble build;
Who, with peculiar call, and flutt'ring wing,
Chirpt joyful, and malicious seem'd to sing:
The only bird of all its kind, and late
Transform'd in pity to a feather'd state:
From whence, O Dædalus, thy guilt we date.

His sister's son, when now twelve years were past,
Was, with his uncle, as a scholar plac'd;
The unsuspecting mother saw his parts,
And genius fitted for the finest arts.
This soon appear'd; for when the spiny bone

In fishes' backs was by the stripling known,
A rare invention thence he learnt to draw,
Fil'd teeth in ir'n, and made the grating saw.
He was the first, that from a knob of brass
Made two strait arms with widening stretch to pass;
That, while one stood upon the center's place,
The other round it drew a circling space.
Dædalus envy'd this, and from the top
Of fair Minerva's temple let him drop;
Feigning, that, as he lean'd upon the tow'r,
Careless he stoop'd too much, and tumbled o'er.

The Goddess, who th' ingenious still befriends,
On this occasion her assistance lends;
His arms with feathers, as he fell, she veils,
And in the air a new made bird he sails.
The quickness of his genius, once so fleet,
Still in his wings remains, and in his feet:
Still, tho' transform'd, his ancient name he keeps,
And with low flight the new-shorn stubble sweeps,
Declines the lofty trees, and thinks it best
To brood in hedge-rows o'er its humble nest;
And, in remembrance of the former ill,
Avoids the heights, and precipices still.

At length, fatigu'd with long laborious flights,
On fair Sicilia's plains the artist lights;
Where Cocalus the king, that gave him aid,
Was, for his kindness, with esteem repaid.
Athens no more her doleful tribute sent,
That hardship gallant Theseus did prevent;
Their temples hung with garlands, they adore
Each friendly God, but most Minerva's pow'r:
To her, to Jove, to all, their altars smoke,
They each with victims, and perfumes invoke.

Now talking Fame, thro' every Grecian town,
Had spread, immortal Theseus, thy renown.

From him the neighb'ring nations in distress,
In suppliant terms implore a kind redress.

The Story of Meleager and Atalanta

From him the Caledonians sought relief;
Though valiant Meleagros was their chief.
The cause, a boar, who ravag'd far and near:
Of Cynthia's wrath, th' avenging minister.
For Œneus with autumnal plenty bless'd,
By gifts to Heav'n his gratitude express'd:
Cull'd sheafs, to Ceres; to Lyæus, wine;
To Pan, and Pales, offer'd sheep and kine;
And fat of olives, to Minerva's shrine.
Beginning from the rural Gods, his hand
Was lib'ral to the Pow'rs of high command:
Each deity in ev'ry kind was bless'd,
Till at Diana's fane th' invidious honour ceas'd.

Wrath touches ev'n the Gods; the Queen of Night,
Fir'd with disdain, and jealous of her right,
Unhonour'd though I am, at least, said she,
Not unreveng'd that impious act shall be.
Swift as the word, she sped the boar away,
With charge on those devoted fields to prey.
No larger bulls th' Ægyptian pastures feed,
And none so large Sicilian meadows breed:
His eye-balls glare with fire suffus'd with blood;
His neck shoots up a thick-set thorny wood;
His bristled back a trench impal'd appears,
And stands erected, like a field of spears;
Froth fills his chaps, he sends a grunting sound,
And part he churns, and part befoams the ground,
For tusks with Indian elephants he strove,
And Jove's own thunder from his mouth he drove.

He burns the leaves; the scorching blast invades
The tender corn, and shrivels up the blades:
Or suff'ring not their yellow beards to rear,
He tramples down the spikes, and intercepts the year:
In vain the barns expect their promis'd load,
Nor barns at home, nor recks are heap'd abroad:
In vain the hinds the threshing-floor prepare,
And exercise their flail in empty air.
With olives ever-green the ground is strow'd,
And grapes ungather'd shed their gen'rous blood.
Amid the fold he rages, nor the sheep
Their shepherds, nor the grooms their bulls can keep.

From fields to walls the frighted rabble run,
Nor think themselves secure within the town:
Till Meleagros, and his chosen crew,
Contemn the danger, and the praise pursue.
Fair Leda's twins (in time to stars decreed)
One fought on foot, one curb'd the fiery steed;
Then issu'd forth fam'd Jason after these,
Who mann'd the foremost ship that sail'd the seas;
Then Theseus join'd with bold Perithous came;
A single concord in a double name:
The Thestian sons, Idas who swiftly ran,
And Ceneus, once a woman, now a man.
Lynceus, with eagle's eyes, and lion's heart;
Leucippus, with his never-erring dart;
Acastus, Phileus, Phœnix, Telamon,
Echion, Lelix, and Eurytion,
Achilles' father, and great Phocus' son;
Dryas the fierce, and Hippasus the strong;
With twice old Iolas, and Nestor then but young.
Lærtes active, and Ancæus bold;
Mopsus the sage, who future things foretold;
And t' other seer, yet by his wife unsold.
A thousand others of immortal fame;
Among the rest, fair Atalanta came,

Grace of the woods: a diamond buckle bound
Her vest behind, that else had flow'd
upon the ground,
And shew'd her buskin'd legs; her head was bare,
But for her native ornament of hair;
Which in a simple knot was ty'd above,
Sweet negligence! unheeded bait of love!
Her sounding quiver, on her shoulder ty'd,
One hand a dart, and one a bow supply'd.
Such was her face, as in a nymph display'd
A fair fierce boy, or in a boy betray'd
The blushing beauties of a modest maid.
The Caledonian chief at once the dame
Beheld, at once his heart receiv'd the flame,
With Heav'ns averse. O happy youth, he cry'd;
For whom thy fates reserve so fair a bride!
He sigh'd, and had no leisure more to say;
His honour call'd his eyes another way,
And forc'd him to pursue the now-neglected prey.

There stood a forest on a mountain's brow,
Which over-look'd the shaded plains below.
No sounding ax presum'd those trees to bite;
Coeval with the world, a venerable sight.
The heroes there arriv'd, some spread around
The toils; some search the footsteps on the ground:
Some from the chains the faithful dogs unbound.
Of action eager, and intent in thought,
The chiefs their honourable danger sought:
A valley stood below; the common drain
Of waters from above, and falling rain:
The bottom was a moist, and marshy ground,
Whose edges were with bending oziers crown'd:
The knotty bulrush next in order stood,
And all within of reeds a trembling wood.

From hence the boar was rous'd, and sprung amain,
Like lightning sudden, on the warrior train;

Beats down the trees before him, shakes the ground.
The forest echoes to the crackling sound;
Shout the fierce youth, and clamours ring around.
All stood with their protended spears prepar'd,
With broad steel heads the brandish'd
weapons glar'd.
The beast impetuous with his tusks aside
Deals glancing wounds; the fearful dogs divide:
All spend their mouths aloof, but none abide.
Echion threw the first, but miss'd his mark,
And stuck his boar-spear on a maple's bark.
Then Jason; and his javelin seem'd to take,
But fail'd with over-force, and whiz'd
above his back.
Mopsus was next; but e'er he threw, address'd
To Phœbus, thus: O patron, help thy priest:
If I adore, and ever have ador'd
Thy pow'r divine, thy present aid afford;
That I may reach the beast. The God allow'd
His pray'r, and smiling, gave him what he cou'd:
He reach'd the savage, but no blood he drew:
Dian unarm'd the javelin, as it flew.

This chaf'd the boar, his nostrils flames expire,
And his red eye-balls roll with living fire.
Whirl'd from a sling, or from an engine thrown,
Amid the foes, so flies a mighty stone,
As flew the beast: the left wing put to flight,
The chiefs o'er-born, he rushes on the right.
Eupalamos and Pelagon he laid
In dust, and next to death, but for their fellows' aid.
Onesimus far'd worse, prepar'd to fly,
The fatal fang drove deep within his thigh,
And cut the nerves: the nerves no more sustain
The bulk; the bulk unprop'd, falls headlong
on the plain.

Nestor had fail'd the fall of Troy to see,
But leaning on his lance, he vaulted on a tree;
Then gath'ring up his feet, look'd down with fear,
And thought his monstrous foe was still too near.
Against a stump his tusk the monster grinds,
And in the sharpen'd edge new vigour finds;
Then, trusting to his arms, young Othrys found,
And ranch'd his hips with one continu'd wound.

Now Leda's twins, the future stars, appear;
White were their habits, white their horses were:
Conspicuous both, and both in act to throw,
Their trembling lances brandish'd at the foe:
Nor had they miss'd; but he to thickets fled,
Conceal'd from aiming spears, not pervious
to the steed.
But Telamon rush'd in, and happ'd to meet
A rising root, that held his fastened feet;
So down he fell, whom, sprawling on the ground,
His brother from the wooden gyves unbound.

Mean-time the virgin-huntress was not slow
T' expel the shaft from her contracted bow:
Beneath his ear the fast'ned arrow stood,
And from the wound appear'd the trickling blood.
She blush'd for joy: but Meleagros rais'd
His voice with loud applause, and the fair
archer prais'd.
He was the first to see, and first to show
His friends the marks of the successful blow.
Nor shall thy valour want the praises due,
He said; a virtuous envy seiz'd the crew.
They shout; the shouting animates their hearts,
And all at once employ their thronging darts:
But out of order thrown, in air they joyn,
And multitude makes frustrate the design.
With both his hands the proud Ancæus takes,

And flourishes his double-biting ax:
Then, forward to his fate, he took a stride
Before the rest, and to his fellows cry'd,
Give place, and mark the diff'rence, if you can,
Between a woman warrior, and a man,
The boar is doom'd; nor though Diana lend
Her aid, Diana can her beast defend.
Thus boasted he; then stretch'd, on tiptoe stood,
Secure to make his empty promise good.
But the more wary beast prevents the blow,
And upward rips the groin of his audacious foe.
Ancæus falls; his bowels from the wound
Rush out, and clotted blood disdains the ground.

Perithous, no small portion of the war,
Press'd on, and shook his lance: to whom from far
Thus Theseus cry'd; O stay, my better part,
My more than mistress; of my heart, the heart.
The strong may fight aloof; Ancæus try'd
His force too near, and by presuming dy'd:
He said, and while he spake his javelin threw,
Hissing in air th' unerring weapon flew;
But on an arm of oak, that stood betwixt
The marks-man and the mark, his lance he fixt.

Once more bold Jason threw, but fail'd to wound
The boar, and slew an undeserving hound,
And thro' the dog the dart was nail'd to ground.

Two spears from Meleager's hand were sent,
With equal force, but various in th' event:
The first was fix'd in earth, the second stood
On the boar's bristled back, and deeply
drank his blood.
Now while the tortur'd savage turns around,
And flings about his foam, impatient of the wound,
The wound's great author close at hand provokes
His rage, and plies him with redoubled strokes;

Wheels, as he wheels; and with his pointed dart
Explores the nearest passage to his heart.
Quick, and more quick he spins in giddy gires,
Then falls, and in much foam his soul expires.
This act with shouts heav'n-high the friendly band
Applaud, and strain in theirs the victor's hand.
Then all approach the slain with vast surprise,
Admire on what a breadth of earth he lies,
And scarce secure, reach out their spears afar,
And blood their points, to prove their
partnership of war.

But he, the conqu'ring chief, his foot impress'd
On the strong neck of that destructive beast;
And gazing on the nymph with ardent eyes,
Accept, said he, fair Nonacrine, my prize,
And, though inferior, suffer me to join
My labours, and my part of praise, with thine:
At this presents her with the tusky head
And chine, with rising bristles roughly spread.
Glad she receiv'd the gift; and seem'd to take
With double pleasure, for the giver's sake.
The rest were seiz'd with sullen discontent,
And a deaf murmur through the squadron went:
All envy'd; but the Thestyan brethren show'd
The least respect, and thus they vent
their spleen aloud:
Lay down those honour'd spoils,
nor think to share,
Weak woman as thou art, the prize of war:
Ours is the title, thine a foreign claim,
Since Meleagrus from our lineage came.
Trust not thy beauty; but restore the prize,
Which he, besotted on that face, and eyes,
Would rend from us: at this, inflam'd with spite,
From her they snatch the gift,
from him the giver's right.

But soon th' impatient prince his fauchion drew,
And cry'd, Ye robbers of another's due,
Now learn the diff'rence, at your proper cost,
Betwixt true valour, and an empty boast.
At this advanc'd, and sudden as the word,
In proud Plexippus' bosom plung'd the sword:
Toxeus amaz'd, and with amazement slow,
Or to revenge, or ward the coming blow,
Stood doubting; and while doubting thus he stood,
Receiv'd the steel bath'd in his brother's blood.

Pleas'd with the first, unknown the second news;
Althæa to the temples pays their dues
For her son's conquest; when at length appear
Her grisly brethren stretch'd upon the bier:
Pale at the sudden sight, she chang'd her cheer,
And with her cheer her robes; but hearing tell
The cause, the manner, and by whom they fell,
'Twas grief no more, or grief and rage were one
Within her soul; at last 'twas rage alone;
Which burning upwards in succession, dries
The tears, that stood consid'ring in her eyes.

There lay a log unlighted on the hearth,
When she was lab'ring in the throws of birth
For th' unborn chief; the fatal sisters came,
And rais'd it up, and toss'd it on the flame:
Then on the rock a scanty measure place
Of vital flax, and turn'd the wheel apace;
And turning sung, To this red brand and thee,
O new born babe, we give an equal destiny;
So vanish'd out of view. The frighted dame
Sprung hasty from her bed, and quench'd the flame:
The log, in secret lock'd, she kept with care,
And that, while thus preserv'd, preserv'd her heir.
This brand she now produc'd; and first she strows
The hearth with heaps of chips, and after blows;

Thrice heav'd her hand, and heav'd,
she thrice repress'd:
The sister and the mother long contest,
Two doubtful titles, in one tender breast:
And now her eyes, and cheeks with fury glow,
Now pale her cheeks, her eyes with pity flow:
Now low'ring looks presage approaching storms,
And now prevailing love her face reforms:
Resolv'd, she doubts again; the tears she dry'd
With burning rage, are by new tears supply'd;
And as a ship, which winds and waves assail
Now with the current drives, now with the gale,
Both opposite, and neither long prevail:
She feels a double force, by turns obeys
Th' imperious tempest, and th' impetuous seas:
So fares Althæa's mind, she first relents
With pity, of that pity then repents:
Sister, and mother long the scales divide,
But the beam nodded on the sister's side.
Sometimes she softly sigh'd, then roar'd aloud;
But sighs were stifled in the cries of blood.

The pious, impious wretch at length decreed,
To please her brothers' ghost, her son
should bleed:
And when the fun'ral flames began to rise,
Receive, she said, a sister's sacrifice;
A mother's bowels burn: high in her hand,
Thus while she spoke, she held the fatal brand;
Then thrice before the kindled pile she bow'd,
And the three Furies thrice invok'd aloud:
Come, come, revenging sisters, come, and view
A sister paying her dead brothers due:
A crime I punish, and a crime commit;
But blood for blood, and death for death is fit:
Great crimes must be with greater crimes repaid,
And second fun'rals on the former laid.
Let the whole houshold in one ruin fall,

And may Diana's curse o'ertake us all.
Shall Fate to happy Oenus still allow
One son, while Thestius stands depriv'd of two?
Better three lost, than one unpunish'd go.
Take then, dear ghosts (while yet admitted new
In Hell you wait my duty), take your due:
A costly off'ring on your tomb is laid,
When with my blood the price of yours is paid.

Ah! whither am I hurry'd? Ah! forgive,
Ye shades, and let your sister's issue live;
A mother cannot give him death; tho' he
Deserves it, he deserves it not from me.

Then shall th' unpunish'd wretch insult the slain,
Triumphant live, nor only live, but reign?
While you, thin shades, the sport of winds, are tost
O'er dreary plains, or tread the burning coast.
I cannot, cannot bear; 'tis past, 'tis done;
Perish this impious, this detested son:
Perish his sire, and perish I withal;
And let the house's heir, and the hop'd kingdom fall.

Where is the mother fled, her pious love,
And where the pains with which ten months I strove!
Ah! had'st thou dy'd, my son, in infant years,
Thy little hearse had been bedew'd with tears.

Thou liv'st by me; to me thy breath resign;
Mine is the merit, the demerit thine.
Thy life by double title I require;
Once giv'n at birth, and once preserv'd from fire:
One murder pay, or add one murder more,
And me to them who fell by thee restore.

I would, but cannot: my son's image stands
Before my sight; and now their angry hands

My brothers hold, and vengeance these exact;
This pleads compassion, and repents the fact.

He pleads in vain, and I pronounce his doom:
My brothers, though unjustly, shall o'ercome.
But having paid their injur'd ghosts their due,
My son requires my death, and mine shall his pursue.

At this, for the last time, she lifts her hand,
Averts her eyes, and, half unwilling, drops the brand.
The brand, amid the flaming fuel thrown,
Or drew, or seem'd to draw, a dying groan;
The fires themselves but faintly lick'd their prey,
Then loath'd their impious food, and would
have shrunk away.

Just then the hero cast a doleful cry,
And in those absent flames began to fry:
The blind contagion rag'd within his veins;
But he with manly patience bore his pains:
He fear'd not Fate, but only griev'd to die
Without an honest wound, and by a death so dry.
Happy Ancæus, thrice aloud he cry'd,
With what becoming fate in arms he dy'd!
Then call'd his brothers, sisters, sire around,
And, her to whom his nuptial vows were bound,
Perhaps his mother; a long sigh she drew,
And his voice failing, took his last adieu.
For as the flames augment, and as they stay
At their full height, then languish to decay,
They rise and sink by fits; at last they soar
In one bright blaze, and then descend no more:
Just so his inward heats, at height, impair,
Till the last burning breath shoots out the soul in air.

Now lofty Calidon in ruins lies;
All ages, all degrees unsluice their eyes,

And Heav'n, and Earth resound with murmurs,
groans, and cries.
Matrons and maidens beat their breasts, and tear
Their habits, and root up their scatter'd hair:
The wretched father, father now no more,
With sorrow sunk, lies prostrate on the floor,
Deforms his hoary locks with dust obscene,
And curses age, and loathes a life prolong'd with pain.
By steel her stubborn soul his mother freed,
And punish'd on her self her impious deed.

Had I a hundred tongues, a wit so large
As could their hundred offices discharge;
Had Phœbus all his Helicon bestow'd
In all the streams, inspiring all the God;
Those tongues, that wit, those streams,
that God in vain
Would offer to describe his sisters' pain:
They beat their breasts with many a bruising blow,
Till they turn livid, and corrupt the snow.
The corps they cherish, while the corps remains,
And exercise, and rub with fruitless pains;
And when to fun'ral flames 'tis born away,
They kiss the bed on which the body lay:
And when those fun'ral flames no longer burn
(The dust compos'd within a pious urn),
Ev'n in that urn their brother they confess,
And hug it in their arms, and to their bosoms press.

His tomb is rais'd; then, stretch'd along the ground,
Those living monuments his tomb surround:
Ev'n to his name, inscrib'd, their tears they pay,
Till tears, and kisses wear his name away.

But Cynthia now had all her fury spent,
Not with less ruin than a race content:
Excepting Gorge, perish'd all the seed,

And her whom Heav'n for Hercules decreed.
Satiate at last, no longer she pursu'd
The weeping sisters; but with wings endu'd,
And horny beaks, and sent to flit in air;
Who yearly round the tomb in feather'd flocks repair.

The Transformation of the Naiads

Theseus mean-while acquitting well his share
In the bold chace confed'rate like a war,
To Athens' lofty tow'rs his march ordain'd,
By Pallas lov'd, and where Erectheus reign'd.
But Achelous stop'd him on the way,
By rains a deluge, and constrain'd his stay.

O fam'd for glorious deeds, and great by blood,
Rest here, says he, nor trust the rapid flood;
It solid oaks has from its margin tore,
And rocky fragments down its current bore,
The murmur hoarse, and terrible the roar.
Oft have I seen herds with their shelt'ring fold
Forc'd from the banks, and in the torrent roll'd;
Nor strength the bulky steer from ruin freed,
Nor matchless swiftness sav'd the racing steed.
In cataracts when the dissolving snow
Falls from the hills, and floods the plains below;
Toss'd by the eddies with a giddy round,
Strong youths are in the sucking whirlpools drown'd.
'Tis best with me in safety to abide,
Till usual bounds restrain the ebbing tide,
And the low waters in their channel glide.

Theseus perswaded, in compliance bow'd:
So kind an offer, and advice so good,
O Achelous, cannot be refus'd;
I'll use them both, said he; and both he us'd.

The grot he enter'd, pumice built the hall,
And tophi made the rustic of the wall;
The floor, soft moss, an humid carpet spread,
And various shells the chequer'd roof inlaid.
'Twas now the hour when the declining sun
Two thirds had of his daily journey run;
At the spread table Theseus took his place,
Next his companions in the daring chase;
Perithous here, there elder Lelex lay,
His locks betraying age with sprinkled grey.
Acharnia's river-God dispos'd the rest,
Grac'd with the equal honour of the feast,
Elate with joy, and proud of such a guest.
The nymphs were waiters, and with naked feet
In order serv'd the courses of the meat.
The banquet done, delicious wine they brought,
Of one transparent gem the cup was wrought.

Then the great hero of this gallant train,
Surveying far the prospect of the main:
What is that land, says he, the waves embrace?
(And with his finger pointed at the place);
Is it one parted isle which stands alone?
How nam'd? and yet methinks it seems not one.
To whom the watery God made this reply;
'Tis not one isle, but five; distinct they lye;
'Tis distance which deceives the cheated eye.
But that Diana's act may seem less strange,
These once proud Naiads were,
before their change.
'Twas on a day more solemn than the rest,
Ten bullocks slain, a sacrificial feast:
The rural Gods of all the region near
They bid to dance, and taste the hallow'd cheer.
Me they forgot: affronted with the slight,
My rage, and stream swell'd to the greatest height;
And with the torrent of my flooding store,

Large woods from woods, and fields from
fields I tore.
The guilty nymphs, oh! then, remembering me,
I, with their country, wash'd into the sea;
And joining waters with the social main,
Rent the gross land, and split the firm champagne.
Since, the Echinades, remote from shore
Are view'd as many isles, as nymphs before.

Perimele turn'd into an Island

But yonder far, lo, yonder does appear
An isle, a part to me for ever dear.
From that (it sailors Perimele name)
I doting, forc'd by rape a virgin's fame.
Hippodamas's passion grew so strong,
Gall'd with th' abuse, and fretted at the wrong,
He cast his pregnant daughter from a rock;
I spread my waves beneath, and broke the shock;
And as her swimming weight my stream convey'd,
I su'd for help divine, and thus I pray'd:
O pow'rful thou, whose trident does command
The realm of waters, which surround the land;
We sacred rivers, wheresoe'er begun,
End in thy lot, and to thy empire run.
With favour hear, and help with present aid;
Her whom I bear 'twas guilty I betray'd.
Yet if her father had been just, or mild,
He would have been less impious to his child;
In her, have pity'd force in the abuse;
In me, admitted love for my excuse.
O let relief for her hard case be found,
Her, whom paternal rage expell'd from ground,
Her, whom paternal rage relentless drown'd.
Grant her some place, or change her to a place,
Which I may ever clasp with my embrace.

His nodding head the sea's great ruler bent,
And all his waters shook with his assent.
The nymph still swam, tho' with the fright distrest,
I felt her heart leap trembling in her breast;
But hardening soon, whilst I her pulse explore,
A crusting Earth cas'd her stiff body o'er;
And as accretions of new-cleaving soil
Enlarg'd the mass, the nymph became an isle.

The Story of Baucis and Philemon

Thus Achelous ends: his audience hear
With admiration, and admiring, fear
The Pow'rs of Heav'n; except Ixion's Son,
Who laugh'd at all the Gods, believ'd in none:
He shook his impious head, and thus replies.
These legends are no more than pious lies:
You attribute too much to heav'nly sway,
To think they give us forms, and take away.

The rest of better minds, their sense declar'd
Against this doctrine, and with horror heard.
Then Lelex rose, an old experienc'd man,
And thus with sober gravity began;
Heav'n's pow'r is infinite: Earth, Air, and Sea,
The manufacture mass, the making Pow'r obey:
By proof to clear your doubt; in Phrygian ground
Two neighb'ring trees, with walls encompass'd round,
Stand on a mod'rate rise, with wonder shown,
One a hard oak, a softer linden one:
I saw the place, and them, by Pittheus sent
To Phrygian realms, my grandsire's government.
Not far from thence is seen a lake, the haunt
Of coots, and of the fishing cormorant:
Here Jove with Hermes came; but in disguise

Of mortal men conceal'd their deities;
One laid aside his thunder, one his rod;
And many toilsome steps together trod:
For harbour at a thousand doors they knock'd,
Not one of all the thousand but was lock'd.
At last an hospitable house they found,
A homely shed; the roof, not far from ground,
Was thatch'd with reeds, and straw,
together bound.
There Baucis and Philemon liv'd, and there
Had liv'd long marry'd, and a happy pair:
Now old in love, though little was their store,
Inur'd to want, their poverty they bore,
Nor aim'd at wealth, professing to be poor.
For master, or for servant here to call,
Was all alike, where only two were all.
Command was none, where equal love was paid,
Or rather both commanded, both obey'd.

From lofty roofs the Gods repuls'd before,
Now stooping, enter'd through the little door:
The man (their hearty welcome first express'd)
A common settle drew for either guest,
Inviting each his weary limbs to rest.
But ere they sate, officious Baucis lays
Two cushions stuff'd with straw, the seat to raise;
Coarse, but the best she had; then rakes the load
Of ashes from the hearth, and spreads abroad
The living coals; and, lest they should expire,
With leaves, and bark she feeds her infant fire:
It smokes; and then with trembling breath
she blows,
Till in a cheerful blaze the flames arose.
With brush-wood, and with chips she
strengthens these,
And adds at last the boughs of rotten trees.
The fire thus form'd, she sets the kettle on

(Like burnish'd gold the little seether shone),
Next took the coleworts which her husband got
From his own ground (a small well-water'd spot);
She stripp'd the stalks of all their leaves; the best
She cull'd, and them with handy care she drest.
High o'er the hearth a chine of bacon hung;
Good old Philemon seiz'd it with a prong,
And from the sooty rafter drew it down,
Then cut a slice, but scarce enough for one;
Yet a large portion of a little store,
Which for their sakes alone he wish'd were more.
This in the pot he plung'd without delay,
To tame the flesh, and drain the salt away.
The time between, before the fire they sat,
And shorten'd the delay by pleasing chat.

A beam there was, on which a beechen pail
Hung by the handle, on a driven nail:
This fill'd with water, gently warm'd, they set
Before their guests; in this they bath'd their feet,
And after with clean towels dry'd their sweat.
This done, the host produc'd the genial bed,
Sallow the feet, the borders, and the sted,
Which with no costly coverlet they spread,
But coarse old garments; yet such robes as these
They laid alone, at feasts, on holidays.
The good old housewife, tucking up her gown,
The table sets; th' invited Gods lie down.
The trivet-table of a foot was lame,
A blot which prudent Baucis overcame,
Who thrusts beneath the limping leg a sherd,
So was the mended board exactly rear'd:
Then rubb'd it o'er with newly gather'd mint,
A wholesome herb, that breath'd a grateful scent.
Pallas began the feast, where first was seen
The party-colour'd olive, black, and green:
Autumnal cornels next in order serv'd,

In lees of wine well pickled, and preserv'd.
A garden-salad was the third supply,
Of endive, radishes, and succory:
Then curds, and cream, the flow'r of country fare,
And new-laid eggs, which Baucis' busie care
Turn'd by a gentle fire, and roasted rare.
All these in earthen ware were serv'd to board;
And next in place, an earthen pitcher stor'd,
With liquor of the best the cottage could afford.
This was the table's ornament and pride,
With figures wrought: like pages at his side
Stood beechen bowls; and these were shining clean,
Varnish'd with wax without, and lin'd within.
By this the boiling kettle had prepar'd,
And to the table sent the smoking lard;
On which with eager appetite they dine,
A sav'ry bit, that serv'd to relish wine:
The wine itself was suiting to the rest,
Still working in the must, and lately press'd.
The second course succeeds like that before,
Plums, apples, nuts, and of their wintry store
Dry figs, and grapes, and wrinkled dates were set
In canisters, t' enlarge the little treat:
All these a milk-white honey-comb surround,
Which in the midst the country-banquet crown'd:
But the kind hosts their entertainment grace
With hearty welcome, and an open face:
In all they did, you might discern with ease,
A willing mind, and a desire to please.

Mean-time the beechen bowls went round,
and still,
Though often empty'd, were observ'd to fill;
Fill'd without hands, and of their own accord
Ran without feet, and danc'd about the board.
Devotion seiz'd the pair, to see the feast
With wine, and of no common grape, increas'd;

And up they held their hands, and fell to pray'r,
Excusing, as they could, their country fare.

One goose they had ('twas all they could allow),
A wakeful sentry, and on duty now,
Whom to the Gods for sacrifice they vow:
Her with malicious zeal the couple view'd;
She ran for life, and limping they pursu'd:
Full well the fowl perceiv'd their bad intent,
And would not make her master's compliment;
But persecuted, to the Pow'rs she flies,
And close between the legs of Jove she lies:
He with a gracious ear the suppliant heard,
And sav'd her life; then what he has declar'd,
And own'd the God. The neighbourhood, said he,
Shall justly perish for impiety:
You stand alone exempted; but obey
With speed, and follow where we lead the way:
Leave these accurs'd; and to the mountain's height
Ascend; nor once look backward in your flight.

They haste, and what their tardy feet deny'd,
The trusty staff (their better leg) supply'd.
An arrow's flight they wanted to the top,
And there secure, but spent with travel, stop;
Then turn their now no more forbidden eyes;
Lost in a lake the floated level lies:
A watery desert covers all the plains,
Their cot alone, as in an isle, remains.
Wondering, with weeping eyes, while they deplore
Their neighbours' fate, and country now no more,
Their little shed, scarce large enough for two,
Seems, from the ground increas'd, in height
    and bulk to grow.
A stately temple shoots within the skies,
The crotches of their cot in columns rise:
The pavement polish'd marble they behold,

The gates with sculpture grac'd, the spires
and tiles of gold.

Then thus the sire of Gods, with looks serene,
Speak thy desire, thou only just of men;
And thou, o woman, only worthy found
To be with such a man in marriage bound.

A-while they whisper; then, to Jove address'd,
Philemon thus prefers their joint request:
We crave to serve before your sacred shrine,
And offer at your altars rites divine:
And since not any action of our life
Has been polluted with domestic strife;
We beg one hour of death, that neither she
With widow's tears may live to bury me,
Nor weeping I, with wither'd arms may bear
My breathless Baucis to the sepulcher.

The Godheads sign their suit. They run their race
In the same tenour all th' appointed space:
Then, when their hour was come, while they relate
These past adventures at the temple gate,
Old Baucis is by old Philemon seen
Sprouting with sudden leaves of spritely green:
Old Baucis look'd where old Philemon stood,
And saw his lengthen'd arms a sprouting wood:
New roots their fasten'd feet begin to bind,
Their bodies stiffen in a rising rind:
Then, ere the bark above their shoulders grew,
They give, and take at once their last adieu.
At once, Farewell, o faithful spouse, they said;
At once th' encroaching rinds their
closing lips invade.
Ev'n yet, an ancient Tyanæan shows
A spreading oak, that near a linden grows;
The neighbourhood confirm the prodigy,

Grave men, not vain of tongue, or like to lie.
I saw my self the garlands on their boughs,
And tablets hung for gifts of granted vows;
And off'ring fresher up, with pious pray'r,
The good, said I, are God's peculiar care,
And such as honour Heav'n, shall heav'nly
honour share.

The Changes of Proteus

He ceas'd in his relation to proceed,
Whilst all admir'd the author, and the deed;
But Theseus most, inquisitive to know
From Gods what wondrous alterations grow.
Whom thus the Calydonian stream address'd,
Rais'd high to speak, the couch his elbow press'd.
Some, when transform'd, fix in the lasting change;
Some with more right, thro' various figures range.
Proteus, thus large thy privilege was found,
Thou inmate of the seas, which Earth surround.
Sometimes a blooming youth you grac'd the shore;
Oft a fierce lion, or a furious boar:
With glist'ning spires now seem'd an hissing snake,
The bold would tremble in his hands to take:
With horns assum'd a bull; sometimes you prov'd
A tree by roots, a stone by weight unmov'd:
Sometimes two wav'ring contraries became,
Flow'd down in water, or aspir'd in flame.

The Story of Erisichthon

In various shapes thus to deceive the eyes,
Without a settled stint of her disguise,
Rash Erisichthon's daughter had the pow'r,

And brought it to Autolicus in dow'r.
Her atheist sire the slighted Gods defy'd,
And ritual honours to their shrines deny'd.
As fame reports, his hand an ax sustain'd,
Which Ceres' consecrated grove profan'd;
Which durst the venerable gloom invade,
And violate with light the awful shade.
An ancient oak in the dark center stood,
The covert's glory, and itself a wood:
Garlands embrac'd its shaft, and from the boughs
Hung tablets, monuments of prosp'rous vows.
In the cool dusk its unpierc'd verdure spread,
The Dryads oft their hallow'd dances led;
And oft, when round their gaging arms they cast,
Full fifteen ells it measu'rd in the waste:
Its height all under standards did surpass,
As they aspir'd above the humbler grass.

These motives, which would gentler minds restrain,
Could not make Triope's bold son abstain;
He sternly charg'd his slaves with strict decree,
To fell with gashing steel the sacred tree.
But whilst they, ling'ring, his commands delay'd,
He snatch'd an Ax, and thus blaspheming said:
Was this no oak, nor Ceres' favourite care,
But Ceres' self, this arm, unaw'd, shou'd dare
Its leafy honours in the dust to spread,
And level with the earth its airy head.
He spoke, and as he poiz'd a slanting stroke,
Sighs heav'd, and tremblings shook the frighted oak;
Its leaves look'd sickly, pale its acorns grew,
And its long branches sweat a chilly dew.
But when his impious hand a wound bestow'd,
Blood from the mangled bark in currents flow'd.
When a devoted bull of mighty size,
A sinning nation's grand atonement, dies;
With such a plenty from the spouting veins,
A crimson stream the turfy altars stains.

The wonder all amaz'd; yet one more bold,
The fact dissuading, strove his ax to hold.
But the Thessalian, obstinately bent,
Too proud to change, too harden'd to repent,
On his kind monitor, his eyes, which burn'd
With rage, and with his eyes his weapon turn'd;
Take the reward, says he, of pious dread:
Then with a blow lopp'd off his parted head.
No longer check'd, the wretch his crime pursu'd,
Doubled his strokes, and sacrilege renew'd;
When from the groaning trunk a voice was heard,
A Dryad I, by Ceres' love preferr'd,
Within the circle of this clasping rind
Coeval grew, and now in ruin join'd;
But instant vengeance shall thy sin pursue,
And death is cheer'd with this prophetic view.

At last the oak with cords enforc'd to bow,
Strain'd from the top, and sap'd with wounds below,
The humbler wood, partaker of its fate,
Crush'd with its fall, and shiver'd with its weight.

The grove destroy'd, the sister Dryads moan,
Griev'd at its loss, and frighted at their own.
Strait, suppliants for revenge to Ceres go,
In sable weeds, expressive of their woe.

The beauteous Goddess with a graceful air
Bow'd in consent, and nodded to their pray'r.
The awful motion shook the fruitful ground,
And wav'd the fields with golden harvests crown'd.
Soon she contriv'd in her projecting mind
A plague severe, and piteous in its kind
(If plagues for crimes of such presumptuous height
Could pity in the softest breast create).
With pinching want, and hunger's keenest smart,
To tear his vitals, and corrode his heart.

But since her near approach by Fate's deny'd
To famine, and broad climes their pow'rs divide,
A nymph, the mountain's ranger, she address'd,
And thus resolv'd, her high commands express'd.

The Description of Famine

Where frozen Scythia's utmost bound is plac'd,
A desert lies, a melancholy waste:
In yellow crops there Nature never smil'd,
No fruitful tree to shade the barren wild.
There sluggish cold its icy station makes,
There paleness, frights, and anguish
trembling shakes,
Of pining famine this the fated seat,
To whom my orders in these words repeat:
Bid her this miscreant with her sharpest pain
Chastise, and sheath herself into his veins;
Be unsubdu'd by plenty's baffled store,
Reject my empire, and defeat my pow'r.
And lest the distance, and the tedious way,
Should with the toil, and long fatigue dismay,
Ascend my chariot, and convey'd on high,
Guide the rein'd dragons thro' the parting sky.

The nymph, accepting of the granted carr,
Sprung to the seat, and posted thro' the air;
Nor stop'd till she to a bleak mountain came
Of wondrous height, and Caucasus its name.
There in a stony field the fiend she found,
Herbs gnawing, and roots scratching from the ground.
Her elfelock hair in matted tresses grew,
Sunk were her eyes, and pale her ghastly hue,
Wan were her lips, and foul with clammy glew.
Her throat was furr'd, her guts appear'd within

With snaky crawlings thro' her parchment skin.
Her jutting hips seem'd starting from their place,
And for a belly was a belly's space,
Her dugs hung dangling from her craggy spine,
Loose to her breast, and fasten'd to her chine.
Her joints protuberant by leanness grown,
Consumption sunk the flesh, and rais'd the bone.
Her knees large orbits bunch'd to monstrous size,
And ankles to undue proportion rise.

This plague the nymph, not daring to draw near,
At distance hail'd, and greeted from afar.
And tho' she told her charge without delay,
Tho' her arrival late, and short her stay,
She felt keen famine, or she seem'd to feel,
Invade her blood, and on her vitals steal.
She turn'd, from the infection to remove,
And back to Thessaly the serpents drove.

The fiend obey'd the Goddess' command
(Tho' their effects in opposition stand),
She cut her way, supported by the wind,
And reach'd the mansion by the nymph assign'd.

'Twas night, when entering Erisichthon's room,
Dissolv'd in sleep, and thoughtless of his doom,
She clasp'd his limbs, by impious labour tir'd,
With battish wings, but her whole self inspir'd;
Breath'd on his throat and chest a tainting blast,
And in his veins infus'd an endless fast.

The task dispatch'd, away the Fury flies
From plenteous regions, and from rip'ning skies;
To her old barren north she wings her speed,
And cottages distress'd with pinching need.

Still slumbers Erisichthon's senses drown,
And sooth his fancy with their softest down.

He dreams of viands delicate to eat,
And revels on imaginary meat,
Chaws with his working mouth, but chaws in vain,
And tires his grinding teeth with fruitless pain;
Deludes his throat with visionary fare,
Feasts on the wind, and banquets on the air.

The morning came, the night, and slumbers past,
But still the furious pangs of hunger last;
The cank'rous rage still gnaws with griping pains,
Stings in his throat, and in his bowels reigns.

Strait he requires, impatient in demand,
Provisions from the air, the seas, the land.
But tho' the land, air, seas, provisions grant,
Starves at full tables, and complains of want.
What to a people might in dole be paid,
Or victual cities for a long blockade,
Could not one wolfish appetite assuage;
For glutting nourishment increas'd its rage.
As rivers pour'd from ev'ry distant shore,
The sea insatiate drinks, and thirsts for more;
Or as the fire, which all materials burns,
And wasted forests into ashes turns,
Grows more voracious, as the more it preys,
Recruits dilate the flame, and spread the blaze:
So impious Erisichthon's hunger raves,
Receives refreshments, and refreshments craves.
Food raises a desire for food, and meat
Is but a new provocative to eat.
He grows more empty, as the more supply'd,
And endless cramming but extends the void.

The Transformations of Erisichthon's Daughter

Now riches hoarded by paternal care
Were sunk, the glutton swallowing up the heir.
Yet the devouring flame no stores abate,
Nor less his hunger grew with his estate.
One daughter left, as left his keen desire,
A daughter worthy of a better sire:
Her too he sold, spent Nature to sustain;
She scorn'd a lord with generous disdain,
And flying, spread her hand upon the main.
Then pray'd: Grant, thou, I bondage may escape,
And with my liberty reward thy rape;
Repay my virgin treasure with thy aid
('Twas Neptune who deflower'd the beauteous maid).

The God was mov'd, at what the fair had su'd,
When she so lately by her master view'd
In her known figure, on a sudden took
A fisher's habit, and a manly look.
To whom her owner hasted to inquire;
O thou, said he, whose baits hide treach'rous wire;
Whose art can manage, and experienc'd skill
The taper angle, and the bobbing quill,
So may the sea be ruffled with no storm,
But smooth with calms, as you the truth inform;
So your deceit may no shy fishes feel,
Till struck, and fasten'd on the bearded steel.
Did not you standing view upon the strand,
A wand'ring maid? I'm sure I saw her stand;
Her hair disorder'd, and her homely dress
Betray'd her want, and witness'd her distress.

Me heedless, she reply'd, whoe'er you are,
Excuse, attentive to another care.
I settled on the deep my steady eye;
Fix'd on my float, and bent on my employ.

And that you may not doubt what I impart,
So may the ocean's God assist my art,
If on the beach since I my sport pursu'd,
Or man, or woman but my self I view'd.
Back o'er the sands, deluded, he withdrew,
Whilst she for her old form put off her new.

Her sire her shifting pow'r to change perceiv'd;
And various chapmen by her sale deceiv'd.
A fowl with spangled plumes, a brinded steer,
Sometimes a crested mare, or antler'd deer:
Sold for a price, she parted, to maintain
Her starving parent with dishonest gain.

At last all means, as all provisions, fail'd;
For the disease by remedies prevail'd;
His muscles with a furious bite he tore,
Gorg'd his own tatter'd flesh, and gulph'd his gore.
Wounds were his feast, his life to life a prey,
Supporting Nature by its own decay.

But foreign stories why shou'd I relate?
I too my self can to new forms translate,
Tho' the variety's not unconfin'd,
But fix'd, in number, and restrain'd in kind:
For often I this present shape retain,
Oft curl a snake the volumes of my train.
Sometimes my strength into my horns transfer'd,
A bull I march, the captain of the herd.
But whilst I once those goring weapons wore,
Vast wresting force one from my forehead tore.
Lo, my maim'd brows the injury still own;
He ceas'd; his words concluding with a groan.

Book X

The Story of Orpheus and Eurydice

Thence, in his saffron robe, for distant Thrace,
Hymen departs, thro' air's unmeasur'd space;
By Orpheus call'd, the nuptial Pow'r attends,
But with ill-omen'd augury descends;
Nor cheerful look'd the God, nor prosp'rous spoke,
Nor blaz'd his torch, but wept in hissing smoke.
In vain they whirl it round, in vain they shake,
No rapid motion can its flames awake.
With dread these inauspicious signs were view'd,
And soon a more disastrous end ensu'd;
For as the bride, amid the Naiad train,
Ran joyful, sporting o'er the flow'ry plain,
A venom'd viper bit her as she pass'd;
Instant she fell, and sudden breath'd her last.

When long his loss the Thracian had deplor'd,
Not by superior Pow'rs to be restor'd;
Inflam'd by love, and urg'd by deep despair,
He leaves the realms of light, and upper air;
Daring to tread the dark Tenarian road,
And tempt the shades in their obscure abode;
Thro' gliding spectres of th' interr'd to go,
And phantom people of the world below:
Persephone he seeks, and him who reigns
O'er ghosts, and Hell's uncomfortable plains.
Arriv'd, he, tuning to his voice his strings,
Thus to the king and queen of shadows sings.

Ye Pow'rs, who under Earth your realms extend,
To whom all mortals must one day descend;
If here 'tis granted sacred truth to tell:
I come not curious to explore your Hell;
Nor come to boast (by vain ambition fir'd)
How Cerberus at my approach retir'd.
My wife alone I seek; for her lov'd sake
These terrors I support, this journey take.
She, luckless wandering, or by fate misled,
Chanc'd on a lurking viper's crest to tread;
The vengeful beast, enflam'd with fury, starts,
And thro' her heel his deathful venom darts.
Thus was she snatch'd untimely to her tomb;
Her growing years cut short, and springing bloom.
Long I my loss endeavour'd to sustain,
And strongly strove, but strove, alas, in vain:
At length I yielded, won by mighty love;
Well known is that omnipotence above!
But here, I doubt, his unfelt influence fails;
And yet a hope within my heart prevails.
That here, ev'n here, he has been known of old;
At least if truth be by tradition told;
If fame of former rapes belief may find,
You both by love, and love alone, were join'd.
Now, by the horrors which these realms surround;
By the vast chaos of these depths profound;
By the sad silence which eternal reigns
O'er all the waste of these wide-stretching plains;
Let me again Eurydice receive,
Let Fate her quick-spun thread of life re-weave.
All our possessions are but loans from you,
And soon, or late, you must be paid your due;
Hither we haste to human-kind's last seat,
Your endless empire, and our sure retreat.
She too, when ripen'd years she shall attain,
Must, of avoidless right, be yours again:
I but the transient use of that require,

Which soon, too soon, I must resign entire.
But if the destinies refuse my vow,
And no remission of her doom allow;
Know, I'm determin'd to return no more;
So both retain, or both to life restore.

Thus, while the bard melodiously complains,
And to his lyre accords his vocal strains,
The very bloodless shades attention keep,
And silent, seem compassionate to weep;
Ev'n Tantalus his flood unthirsty views,
Nor flies the stream, nor he the stream pursues;
Ixion's wond'ring wheel its whirl suspends,
And the voracious vulture, charm'd, attends;
No more the Belides their toil bemoan,
And Sisiphus reclin'd, sits list'ning on his stone.

Then first ('tis said) by sacred verse subdu'd,
The Furies felt their cheeks with tears bedew'd:
Nor could the rigid king, or queen of Hell,
Th' impulse of pity in their hearts repel.

Now, from a troop of shades that last arriv'd,
Eurydice was call'd, and stood reviv'd:
Slow she advanc'd, and halting seem to feel
The fatal wound, yet painful in her heel.
Thus he obtains the suit so much desir'd,
On strict observance of the terms requir'd:
For if, before he reach the realms of air,
He backward cast his eyes to view the fair,
The forfeit grant, that instant, void is made,
And she for ever left a lifeless shade.

Now thro' the noiseless throng their way they bend,
And both with pain the rugged road ascend;
Dark was the path, and difficult, and steep,
And thick with vapours from the smoky deep.
They well-nigh now had pass'd the bounds of night,

And just approach'd the margin of the light,
When he, mistrusting lest her steps might stray,
And gladsome of the glimpse of dawning day,
His longing eyes, impatient, backward cast
To catch a lover's look, but look'd his last;
For, instant dying, she again descends,
While he to empty air his arms extends.
Again she dy'd, nor yet her lord reprov'd;
What could she say, but that too well he lov'd?
One last farewell she spoke, which scarce he heard;
So soon she drop'd, so sudden disappear'd.

All stunn'd he stood, when thus his wife he view'd
By second Fate, and double death subdu'd:
Not more amazement by that wretch was shown,
Whom Cerberus beholding, turn'd to stone;
Nor Olenus cou'd more astonish'd look,
When on himself Lethæa's fault he took,
His beauteous wife, who too secure had dar'd
Her face to vye with Goddesses compar'd:
Once join'd by love, they stand united still,
Turn'd to contiguous rocks on Ida's hill.

Now to repass the Styx in vain he tries,
Charon averse, his pressing suit denies.
Sev'n days entire, along th' infernal shores,
Disconsolate, the bard Eurydice deplores;
Defil'd with filth his robe, with tears his cheeks,
No sustenance but grief, and cares, he seeks:
Of rigid Fate incessant he complains,
And Hell's inexorable Gods arraigns.
This ended, to high Rhodope he hastes,
And Hæmus' mountain, bleak with northern blasts.

And now his yearly race the circling sun
Had thrice complete thro' wat'ry Pisces run,
Since Orpheus fled the face of womankind,

And all soft union with the sex declin'd.
Whether his ill success this change had bred,
Or binding vows made to his former bed;
Whate'er the cause, in vain the nymphs contest,
With rival eyes to warm his frozen breast:
For ev'ry nymph with love his lays inspir'd,
But ev'ry nymph repuls'd, with grief retir'd.

A hill there was, and on that hill a mead,
With verdure thick, but destitute of shade.
Where, now, the Muse's son no sooner sings,
No sooner strikes his sweet resounding strings.
But distant groves the flying sounds receive,
And list'ning trees their rooted stations leave;
Themselves transplanting, all around they grow,
And various shades their various kinds bestow.
Here, tall Chaonian oaks their branches spread,
While weeping poplars there erect their head.
The foodful Esculus here shoots his leaves,
That turf soft lime-tree, this, fat beach receives;
Here, brittle hazels, laurels here advance,
And there tough ash to form the hero's lance;
Here silver firs with knotless trunks ascend,
There, scarlet oaks beneath their acorns bend.
That spot admits the hospitable plane,
On this, the maple grows with clouded grain;
Here, wat'ry willows are with Lotus seen;
There, tamarisk, and box for ever green.
With double hue here myrtles grace the ground,
And laurestines, with purple berries crown'd.
With pliant feet, now, ivies this way wind,
Vines yonder rise, and elms with vines entwin'd.
Wild Ornus now, the pitch-tree next takes root,
And Arbutus adorn'd with blushing fruit.
Then easy-bending palms, the victor's prize,
And pines erect with bristly tops arise.
For Rhea grateful still the pine remains,

For Atys still some favour she retains;
He once in human shape her breast had warm'd,
And now is cherish'd, to a tree transform'd.

The Fable of Cyparissus

Amid the throng of this promiscuous wood,
With pointed top, the taper cypress stood;
A tree, which once a youth, and heav'nly fair,
Was of that deity the darling care,
Whose hand adapts, with equal skill, the strings
To bows with which he kills, and harps
to which he sings.

For heretofore, a mighty stag was bred,
Which on the fertile fields of Cæa fed;
In shape and size he all his kind excell'd,
And to Carthæan nymphs was sacred held.
His beamy head, with branches high display'd,
Afforded to itself an ample shade;
His horns were gilt, and his smooth neck
was grac'd
With silver collars thick with gems encas'd:
A silver boss upon his forehead hung,
And brazen pendants in his ear-rings rung.
Frequenting houses, he familiar grew,
And learnt by custom, Nature to subdue;
Till by degrees, of fear, and wildness, broke,
Ev'n stranger hands his proffer'd neck
might stroke.

Much was the beast by Cæa's youth caress'd,
But thou, sweet Cyparissus, lov'dst him best:
By thee, to pastures fresh, he oft was led,
By thee oft water'd at the fountain's head:
His horns with garlands, now, by thee were ty'd,

And, now, thou on his back wou'dst wanton ride;
Now here, now there wou'dst bound along the plains,
Ruling his tender mouth with purple reins.

'Twas when the summer sun, at noon of day,
Thro' glowing Cancer shot his burning ray,
'Twas then, the fav'rite stag, in cool retreat,
Had sought a shelter from the scorching heat;
Along the grass his weary limbs he laid,
Inhaling freshness from the breezy shade:
When Cyparissus with his pointed dart,
Unknowing, pierc'd him to the panting heart.
But when the youth, surpris'd, his error found,
And saw him dying of the cruel wound,
Himself he would have slain thro' desp'rate grief:
What said not Phœbus, that might yield relief!
To cease his mourning, he the boy desir'd,
Or mourn no more than such a loss requir'd.
But he, incessant griev'd: at length address'd
To the superior Pow'rs a last request;
Praying, in expiation of his crime,
Thenceforth to mourn to all succeeding time.

And now, of blood exhausted he appears,
Drain'd by a torrent of continual tears;
The fleshy colour in his body fades,
And a green tincture all his limbs invades;
From his fair head, where curling locks late hung,
A horrid bush with bristled branches sprung,
Which stiffening by degrees, its stem extends,
Till to the starry skies the spire ascends.

Apollo sad look'd on, and sighing, cry'd,
Then, be for ever, what thy pray'r imply'd:
Bemoan'd by me, in others grief excite;
And still preside at ev'ry fun'ral rite.

Thus the sweet artist in a wondrous shade

Of verdant trees, which harmony had made,
Encircled sate, with his own triumphs crown'd,
Of listening birds, and savages around.
Again the trembling strings he dext'rous tries,
Again from discord makes soft music rise.
Then tunes his voice: O Muse, from whom I sprung,
Jove be my theme, and thou inspire my song.
To Jove my grateful voice I oft have rais'd,
Oft his almighty pow'r with pleasure prais'd.
I sung the giants in a solemn strain,
Blasted, and thunder-struck on Phlegra's plain.
Now be my lyre in softer accents mov'd,
To sing of blooming boys by Gods belov'd;
And to relate what virgins, void of shame,
Have suffer'd vengeance for a lawless flame.

The King of Gods once felt the burning joy,
And sigh'd for lovely Ganimede of Troy:
Long was he puzzled to assume a shape
Most fit, and expeditious for the rape;
A bird's was proper, yet he scorns to wear
Any but that which might his thunder bear.
Down with his masquerading wings he flies,
And bears the little Trojan to the skies;
Where now, in robes of heav'nly purple drest,
He serves the nectar at th' Almighty's feast,
To slighted Juno an unwelcome guest.

Hyacinthus Transform'd into a Flower

Phœbus for thee too, Hyacinth, design'd
A place among the Gods, had Fate been kind:
Yet this he gave; as oft as wintry rains
Are past, and vernal breezes sooth the plains,
From the green turf a purple flow'r you rise,
And with your fragrant breath perfume the skies.

You when alive were Phœbus' darling boy;
In you he plac'd his Heav'n, and fix'd his joy:
Their God the Delphic priests consult in vain;
Eurotas now he loves, and Sparta's plain:
His hands the use of bow and harp forget,
And hold the dogs, or bear the corded net;
O'er hanging cliffs swift he pursues the game;
Each hour his pleasure, each augments his flame.

The mid-day sun now shone with equal light
Between the past, and the succeeding night;
They strip, then, smooth'd with suppling oil, essay
To pitch the rounded quoit, their wonted play:
A well-pois'd disk first hasty Phœbus threw,
It cleft the air, and whistled as it flew;
It reach'd the mark, a most surprising length;
Which spoke an equal share of art, and strength.
Scarce was it fall'n, when with too eager hand
Young Hyacinth ran to snatch it from the sand;
But the curst orb, which met a stony soil,
Flew in his face with violent recoil.
Both faint, both pale, and breathless now appear,
The boy with pain, the am'rous God with fear.
He ran, and rais'd him bleeding from the ground,
Chafes his cold limbs, and wipes the fatal wound:
Then herbs of noblest juice in vain applies;
The wound is mortal, and his skill defies.

As in a water'd garden's blooming walk,
When some rude hand has bruis'd its tender stalk,
A fading lily droops its languid head,
And bends to earth, its life, and beauty fled:
So Hyacinth, with head reclin'd, decays,
And, sickening, now no more his charms displays.

O thou art gone, my boy, Apollo cry'd,
Defrauded of thy youth in all its pride!
Thou, once my joy, art all my sorrow now;

And to my guilty hand my grief I owe.
Yet from my self I might the fault remove,
Unless to sport, and play, a fault should prove,
Unless it too were call'd a fault to love.
Oh cou'd I for thee, or but with thee, dye!
But cruel Fates to me that pow'r deny.
Yet on my tongue thou shalt for ever dwell;
Thy name my lyre shall sound, my verse shall tell;
And to a flow'r transform'd, unheard-of yet,
Stamp'd on thy leaves my cries thou shalt repeat.
The time shall come, prophetic I foreknow,
When, joyn'd to thee, a mighty chief shall grow,
And with my plaints his name thy leaf shall show.

While Phœbus thus the laws of Fate reveal'd,
Behold, the blood which stain'd the verdant field,
Is blood no longer; but a flow'r full blown,
Far brighter than the Tyrian scarlet shone.
A lily's form it took; its purple hue
Was all that made a diff'rence to the view,
Nor stop'd he here; the God upon its leaves
The sad expression of his sorrow weaves;
And to this hour the mournful purple wears
Ai, Ai, inscrib'd in funeral characters.
Nor are the Spartans, who so much are fam'd
For virtue, of their Hyacinth asham'd;
But still with pompous woe, and solemn state,
The Hyacinthian feasts they yearly celebrate.

The Transformations of the Cerastæ and Propœtides

Inquire of Amathus, whose wealthy ground
With veins of every metal does abound,
If she to her Propœtides wou'd show,
The honour Sparta does to him allow?

Nor more, she'd say, such wretches wou'd
we grace,
Than those whose crooked horns deform'd
their face,
From thence Cerastæ call'd, an impious race:
Before whose gates a rev'rend altar stood,
To Jove inscrib'd, the hospitable God:
This had some stranger seen with gore besmear'd,
The blood of lambs, and bulls it had appear'd:
Their slaughter'd guests it was; nor flock nor herd.

Venus these barb'rous sacrifices view'd
With just abhorrence, and with wrath pursu'd:
At first, to punish such nefarious crimes,
Their towns she meant to leave, her
once-lov'd climes:
But why, said she, for their offence shou'd I
My dear delightful plains, and cities fly?
No, let the impious people, who have sinn'd,
A punishment in death, or exile, find:
If death, or exile too severe be thought,
Let them in some vile shape bemoan their fault.
While next her mind a proper form employs,
Admonish'd by their horns, she fix'd her choice.
Their former crest remains upon their heads,
And their strong limbs an ox's shape invades.

The blasphemous Propœtides deny'd
Worship of Venus, and her pow'r defy'd:
But soon that pow'r they felt, the first that sold
Their lewd embraces to the world for gold.
Unknowing how to blush, and shameless grown,
A small transition changes them to stone.

The Story of Pygmalion and the Statue

Pygmalion loathing their lascivious life,
Abhorr'd all womankind, but most a wife:
So single chose to live, and shunn'd to wed,
Well pleas'd to want a consort of his bed.
Yet fearing idleness, the nurse of ill,
In sculpture exercis'd his happy skill;
And carv'd in iv'ry such a maid, so fair,
As Nature could not with his art compare,
Were she to work; but in her own defense
Must take her pattern here, and copy hence.
Pleas'd with his idol, he commends, admires,
Adores; and last, the thing ador'd, desires.
A very virgin in her face was seen,
And had she mov'd, a living maid had been:
One wou'd have thought she cou'd have stirr'd, but strove
With modesty, and was asham'd to move.
Art hid with art, so well perform'd the cheat,
It caught the carver with his own deceit:
He knows 'tis madness, yet he must adore,
And still the more he knows it, loves the more:
The flesh, or what so seems, he touches oft,
Which feels so smooth, that he believes it soft.
Fir'd with this thought, at once he strain'd the breast,
And on the lips a burning kiss impress'd.
'Tis true, the harden'd breast resists the gripe,
And the cold lips return a kiss unripe:
But when, retiring back, he look'd again,
To think it iv'ry, was a thought too mean:
So wou'd believe she kiss'd, and courting more,
Again embrac'd her naked body o'er;
And straining hard the statue, was afraid
His hands had made a dint, and hurt his maid:

Explor'd her limb by limb, and fear'd to find
So rude a gripe had left a livid mark behind:
With flatt'ry now he seeks her mind to move,
And now with gifts (the pow'rful bribes of love),
He furnishes her closet first; and fills
The crowded shelves with rarities of shells;
Adds orient pearls, which from the conchs he drew,
And all the sparkling stones of various hue:
And parrots, imitating human tongue,
And singing-birds in silver cages hung:
And ev'ry fragrant flow'r, and od'rous green,
Were sorted well, with lumps of amber laid between:
Rich fashionable robes her person deck,
Pendants her ears, and pearls adorn her neck:
Her taper'd fingers too with rings are grac'd,
And an embroider'd zone surrounds her slender waste.
Thus like a queen array'd, so richly dress'd,
Beauteous she shew'd, but naked shew'd the best.
Then, from the floor, he rais'd a royal bed,
With cov'rings of Sydonian purple spread:
The solemn rites perform'd, he calls her bride,
With blandishments invites her to his side;
And as she were with vital sense possess'd,
Her head did on a plumy pillow rest.

The feast of Venus came, a solemn day,
To which the Cypriots due devotion pay;
With gilded horns the milk-white heifers led,
Slaughter'd before the sacred altars, bled.

Pygmalion off'ring, first approach'd the shrine,
And then with pray'rs implor'd the Pow'rs divine:
Almighty Gods, if all we mortals want,
If all we can require, be yours to grant;
Make this fair statue mine, he wou'd have said,
But chang'd his words for shame; and only pray'd,
Give me the likeness of my iv'ry maid.

The golden Goddess, present at the pray'r,
Well knew he meant th' inanimated fair,
And gave the sign of granting his desire;
For thrice in cheerful flames ascends the fire.
The youth, returning to his mistress, hies,
And impudent in hope, with ardent eyes,
And beating breast, by the dear statue lies.
He kisses her white lips, renews the bliss,
And looks, and thinks they redden at the kiss;
He thought them warm before: nor longer stays,
But next his hand on her hard bosom lays:
Hard as it was, beginning to relent,
It seem'd, the breast beneath his fingers bent;
He felt again, his fingers made a print;
'Twas flesh, but flesh so firm, it rose against the dint:
The pleasing task he fails not to renew;
Soft, and more soft at ev'ry touch it grew;
Like pliant wax, when chasing hands reduce
The former mass to form, and frame for use.
He would believe, but yet is still in pain,
And tries his argument of sense again,
Presses the pulse, and feels the leaping vein.
Convinc'd, o'erjoy'd, his studied thanks, and praise,
To her, who made the miracle, he pays:
Then lips to lips he join'd; now freed from fear,
He found the savour of the kiss sincere:
At this the waken'd image op'd her eyes,
And view'd at once the light, and lover with surprise.
The Goddess, present at the match she made,
So bless'd the bed, such fruitfulness convey'd,
That ere ten months had sharpen'd either horn,
To crown their bliss, a lovely boy was born;
Paphos his name, who grown to manhood, wall'd
The city Paphos, from the founder call'd.

The Story of Cinyras and Myrrha

Nor him alone produc'd the fruitful queen;
But Cinyras, who like his sire had been
A happy prince, had he not been a sire.
Daughters, and fathers, from my song retire;
I sing of horror; and could I prevail,
You shou'd not hear, or not believe my tale.
Yet if the pleasure of my song be such,
That you will hear, and credit me too much,
Attentive listen to the last event,
And, with the sin, believe the punishment:
Since Nature cou'd behold so dire a crime,
I gratulate at least my native clime,
That such a land, which such a monster bore,
So far is distant from our Thracian shore.
Let Araby extol her happy coast,
Her cinnamon, and sweet Amomum boast,
Her fragrant flow'rs, her trees with precious tears,
Her second harvests, and her double years;
How can the land be call'd so bless'd,
that Myrrha bears?
Nor all her od'rous tears can cleanse her crime;
Her Plant alone deforms the happy clime:
Cupid denies to have inflam'd thy heart,
Disowns thy love, and vindicates his dart:
Some Fury gave thee those infernal pains,
And shot her venom'd vipers in thy veins.
To hate thy sire, had merited a curse;
But such an impious love deserv'd a worse.
The neighb'ring monarchs, by thy beauty led,
Contend in crowds, ambitious of thy bed:
The world is at thy choice; except but one,
Except but him, thou canst not choose, alone.
She knew it too, the miserable maid,
Ere impious love her better thoughts betray'd,

And thus within her secret soul she said:
Ah Myrrha! whither wou'd thy wishes tend?
Ye Gods, ye sacred laws, my soul defend
From such a crime as all mankind detest,
And never lodg'd before in human breast!
But is it sin? Or makes my mind alone
Th' imagin'd sin? For Nature makes it none.
What tyrant then these envious laws began,
Made not for any other beast, but Man!
The father-bull his daughter may bestride,
The horse may make his mother-mare a bride;
What piety forbids the lusty ram,
Or more salacious goat, to rut their dam?
The hen is free to wed the chick she bore,
And make a husband, whom she hatch'd before.
All creatures else are of a happier kind,
Whom nor ill-natur'd laws from pleasure bind,
Nor thoughts of sin disturb their peace of mind.
But Man a slave of his own making lives;
The fool denies himself what Nature gives:
Too-busy senates, with an over-care,
To make us better than our kind can bear,
Have dash'd a spice of envy in the laws,
And straining up too high, have spoil'd the cause.
Yet some wise nations break their cruel chains,
And own no laws, but those which love ordains;
Where happy daughters with their sires are join'd,
And piety is doubly paid in kind.
O that I had been born in such a clime,
Not here, where 'tis the country makes the crime!
But whither wou'd my impious fancy stray?
Hence hopes, and ye forbidden thoughts away!
His worth deserves to kindle my desires,
But with the love, that daughters bear to sires.
Then had not Cinyras my father been,
What hinder'd Myrrha's hopes to be his queen?
But the perverseness of my fate is such,

That he's not mine, because he's mine too much:
Our kindred-blood debars a better tie;
He might be nearer, were he not so nigh.
Eyes, and their objects, never must unite;
Some distance is requir'd to help the sight:
Fain wou'd I travel to some foreign shore,
Never to see my native country more,
So might I to my self my self restore;
So might my mind these impious thoughts remove,
And ceasing to behold, might cease to love.
But stay I must, to feed my famish'd sight,
To talk, to kiss, and more, if more I might:
More, impious maid! What more canst thou design?
To make a monstrous mixture in thy line,
And break all statutes human and divine!
Can'st thou be call'd (to save thy wretched life)
Thy mother's rival, and thy father's wife?
Confound so many sacred names in one,
Thy brother's mother! Sister to thy son!
And fear'st thou not to see th' infernal bands,
Their heads with snakes; with torches arm'd
their hands
Full at thy face th' avenging brands to bear,
And shake the serpents from their hissing hair;
But thou in time th' increasing ill control,
Nor first debauch the body by the soul;
Secure the sacred quiet of thy mind,
And keep the sanctions Nature has design'd.
Suppose I shou'd attempt, th' attempt were vain,
No thoughts like mine, his sinless soul profane;
Observant of the right: and o that he
Cou'd cure my madness, or be mad like me!
Thus she: but Cinyras, who daily sees
A crowd of noble suitors at his knees,
Among so many, knew not whom to choose,
Irresolute to grant, or to refuse.
But having told their names, inquir'd of her

Who pleas'd her best, and whom she would prefer.
The blushing maid stood silent with surprise,
And on her father fix'd her ardent eyes,
And looking sigh'd, and as she sigh'd, began
Round tears to shed, that scalded as they ran.
The tender sire, who saw her blush, and cry,
Ascrib'd it all to maiden modesty,
And dry'd the falling drops, and yet more kind,
He stroak'd her cheeks, and holy kisses join'd.
She felt a secret venom fire her blood,
And found more pleasure, than a daughter shou'd;
And, ask'd again what lover of the crew
She lik'd the best, she answer'd, One like you.
Mistaking what she meant, her pious will
He prais'd, and bid her so continue still:
The word of pious heard, she blush'd with shame
Of secret guilt, and cou'd not bear the name.

'Twas now the mid of night, when slumbers close
Our eyes, and sooth our cares with soft repose;
But no repose cou'd wretched Myrrha find,
Her body rolling, as she roll'd her mind:
Mad with desire, she ruminates her sin,
And wishes all her wishes o'er again:
Now she despairs, and now resolves to try;
Wou'd not, and wou'd again, she knows not why;
Stops, and returns; makes, and retracts the vow;
Fain wou'd begin, but understands not how.
As when a pine is hew'd upon the plains,
And the last mortal stroke alone remains,
Lab'ring in pangs of death, and threatening all,
This way, and that she nods,
consid'ring where to fall:
So Myrrha's mind, impell'd on either side,
Takes ev'ry bent, but cannot long abide;
Irresolute on which she shou'd rely,
At last, unfix'd in all, is only fix'd to die.

On that sad thought she rests, resolv'd on death,
She rises, and prepares to choke her breath:
Then while about the beam her zone she ties,
Dear Cinyras farewell, she softly cries;
For thee I die, and only wish to be
Not hated, when thou know'st die I for thee:
Pardon the crime, in pity to the cause:
This said, about her neck the noose she draws.
The nurse, who lay without, her faithful guard,
Though not the words, the murmurs over-heard;
And sighs, and hollow sounds: surpris'd with fright,
She starts, and leaves her bed, and springs a light;
Unlocks the door, and entering out of breath,
The dying saw, and instruments of death;
She shrieks, she cuts the zone with trembling haste,
And in her arms her fainting charge embrac'd:
Next (for she now had leisure for her tears),
She weeping ask'd, in these her blooming years,
What unforeseen misfortune caus'd her care,
To loath her life, and languish in despair!
The maid, with down-cast eyes, and mute with grief
For death unfinish'd, and ill-tim'd relief,
Stood sullen to her suit: the beldame press'd
The more to know, and bar'd her wither'd breast,
Adjur'd her by the kindly food she drew
From those dry founts, her secret ill to shew.
Sad Myrrha sigh'd, and turn'd her eyes aside:
The nurse still urg'd, and wou'd not be deny'd:
Nor only promis'd secrecy, but pray'd
She might have leave to give her offer'd aid.
Good-will, she said, my want of strength supplies,
And diligence shall give what age denies:
If strong desires thy mind to fury move,
With charms and med'cines I can cure thy love:
If envious eyes their hurtful rays have cast,
More pow'rful verse shall free thee from the blast:
If Heav'n offended sends thee this disease,

Offended Heav'n with pray'rs we can appease.
What then remains, that can these cares procure?
Thy house is flourishing, thy fortune sure:
Thy careful mother yet in health survives,
And, to thy comfort, thy kind father lives.
The virgin started at her father's name,
And sigh'd profoundly, conscious of the shame
Nor yet the nurse her impious love divin'd,
But yet surmis'd that love disturb'd her mind:
Thus thinking, she pursu'd her point, and laid,
And lull'd within her lap the mourning maid;
Then softly sooth'd her thus; I guess your grief:
You love, my child; your love shall find relief.
My long-experienc'd age shall be your guide;
Rely on that, and lay distrust aside.
No breath of air shall on the secret blow,
Nor shall (what most you fear) your father know.
Struck once again, as with a thunder-clap,
The guilty virgin bounded from her lap,
And threw her body prostrate on the bed.
And, to conceal her blushes, hid her head;
There silent lay, and warn'd her with her hand
To go: but she receiv'd not the command;
Remaining still importunate to know:
Then Myrrha thus: Or ask no more, or go;
I pr'ythee go, or staying spare my shame;
What thou would'st hear, is impious ev'n to name.
At this, on high the beldame holds her hands,
And trembling both with age, and terror stands;
Adjures, and falling at her feet entreats,
Sooths her with blandishments, and frights
 with threats,
To tell the crime intended, or disclose
What part of it she knew, if she no farther knows.
And last, if conscious to her counsel made,
Confirms anew the promise of her aid.
Now Myrrha rais'd her head; but soon oppress'd

With shame, reclin'd it on her nurse's breast;
Bath'd it with tears, and strove to have confess'd:
Twice she began, and stopp'd; again she try'd;
The falt'ring tongue its office still deny'd.
At last her veil before her face she spread,
And drew a long preluding sigh, and said,
O happy mother, in thy marriage-bed!
Then groan'd, and ceas'd. The good old
 woman shook,
Stiff were her eyes, and ghastly was her look:
Her hoary hair upright with horror stood,
Made (to her grief) more knowing than she wou'd.
Much she reproach'd, and many things she said,
To cure the madness of th' unhappy maid,
In vain: for Myrrha stood convict of ill;
Her reason vanquish'd, but unchang'd her will:
Perverse of mind, unable to reply;
She stood resolv'd, or to possess, or die.
At length the fondness of a nurse prevail'd
Against her better sense, and virtue fail'd:
Enjoy, my child, since such is thy desire,
Thy love, she said; she durst not say, thy sire:
Live, though unhappy, live on any terms;
Then with a second oath her faith confirms.

The solemn feast of Ceres now was near,
When long white linen stoles the matrons wear;
Rank'd in procession walk the pious train,
Off'ring first-fruits, and spikes of yellow grain:
For nine long nights the nuptial-bed they shun,
And sanctifying harvest, lie alone.

Mix'd with the crowd, the queen forsook her lord,
And Ceres' pow'r with secret rites ador'd:
The royal couch, now vacant for a time,
The crafty crone, officious in her crime,
The first occasion took: the king she found

Easy with wine, and deep in pleasures drown'd,
Prepar'd for love: the beldame blew the flame,
Confess'd the passion, but conceal'd the name.
Her form she prais'd; the monarch ask'd her years;
And she reply'd, The same thy Myrrha bears.
Wine, and commended beauty fir'd his thought;
Impatient, he commands her to be brought.
Pleas'd with her charge perform'd, she hies her home,
And gratulates the nymph, the task was overcome.
Myrrha was joy'd the welcome news to hear;
But clog'd with guilt, the joy was insincere:
So various, so discordant is the mind,
That in our will a diff'rent will we find.
Ill she presag'd, and yet pursu'd her lust;
For guilty pleasures give a double gust.

'Twas depth of night: Arctophylax had driv'n
His lazy wain half round the northern Heav'n,
When Myrrha hasten'd to the crime desir'd:
The moon beheld her first, and first retir'd:
The stars amaz'd, ran backward from the sight,
And (shrunk within their sockets) lost their light.
Icarius first withdraws his holy flame:
The virgin sign, in Heav'n the second name,
Slides down the belt, and from her station flies,
And night with sable clouds involves the skies.
Bold Myrrha still pursues her black intent;
She stumbled thrice (an omen of th' event);
Thrice shriek'd the fun'ral owl, yet on she went,
Secure of shame, because secure of sight;
Ev'n bashful sins are impudent by night.
Link'd hand in hand, th' accomplice, and the dame,
Their way exploring, to the chamber came:
The door was ope; they blindly grope their way,
Where dark in bed th' expecting monarch lay.
Thus far her courage held, but here forsakes;
Her faint knees knock at ev'ry step she makes.

The nearer to her crime, the more within
She feels remorse, and horror of her sin;
Repents too late her criminal desire,
And wishes, that unknown she could retire.
Her lingering thus, the nurse (who fear'd delay
The fatal secret might at length betray)
Pull'd forward, to complete the work begun,
And said to Cinyras, Receive thy own.
Thus saying, she deliver'd kind to kind,
Accurs'd, and their devoted bodies join'd.
The sire, unknowing of the crime, admits
His bowels, and profanes the hallow'd sheets;
He found she trembled, but believ'd she strove
With maiden modesty against her love,
And sought with flatt'ring words
vain fancies to remove.
Perhaps he said, My daughter, cease thy fears
(Because the title suited with her years);
And, Father, she might whisper him again,
That names might not be wanting to the sin.

Full of her sire, she left th' incestuous bed,
And carry'd in her womb the crime she bred.
Another, and another night she came;
For frequent sin had left no sense of shame:
Till Cinyras desir'd to see her face,
Whose body he had held in close embrace,
And brought a taper; the revealer, light,
Expos'd both crime, and criminal to sight.
Grief, rage, amazement, could no speech afford,
But from the sheath he drew th' avenging sword:
The guilty fled: the benefit of night,
That favour'd first the sin, secur'd the flight.
Long wand'ring thro' the spacious fields, she bent
Her voyage to th' Arabian continent;
Then pass'd the region which Panchæa join'd,
And flying, left the palmy plains behind.

Nine times the moon had mew'd her horns; at length
With travel weary, unsupply'd with strength,
And with the burden of her womb oppress'd,
Sabæan fields afford her needful rest:
There, loathing life, and yet of death afraid,
In anguish of her spirit, thus she pray'd:
Ye Pow'rs, if any so propitious are
T' accept my penitence, and hear my pray'r;
Your judgments, I confess, are justly sent;
Great sins deserve as great a punishment:
Yet since my life the living will profane,
And since my death the happy dead will stain,
A middle state your mercy may bestow,
Betwixt the realms above, and those below:
Some other form to wretched Myrrha give,
Nor let her wholly die, nor wholly live.

The pray'rs of penitents are never vain;
At least she did her last request obtain:
For while she spoke, the ground began to rise,
And gather'd round her feet, her legs, and thighs;
Her toes in roots descend, and spreading wide,
A firm foundation for the trunk provide:
Her solid bones convert to solid wood,
To pith her marrow, and to sap her blood:
Her arms are boughs, her fingers change their kind,
Her tender skin is harden'd into rind.
And now the rising tree her womb invests,
Now shooting upwards still, invades her breasts,
And shades the neck; when weary with delay,
She sunk her head within, and met it half the way.
And tho' with outward shape she lost her sense,
With bitter tears she wept her last offence;
And still she weeps, nor sheds her tears in vain;
For still the precious drops her name retain.
Mean-time the mis-begotten infant grows,

And ripe for birth, distends with deadly throes
The swelling rind, with unavailing strife,
To leave the wooden womb, and pushes into life.
The mother-tree, as if oppress'd with pain,
Writhes here, and there, to break the bark, in vain;
And, like a lab'ring woman, wou'd have pray'd,
But wants a voice to call Lucina's aid:
The bending bole sends out a hollow sound,
And trickling tears fall thicker on the ground.
The mild Lucina came uncall'd, and stood
Beside the struggling boughs, and heard the groaning wood;
Then reach'd her midwife-hand to speed the throes,
And spoke the pow'rful spells, that babes to birth disclose.
The bark divides, the living load to free,
And safe delivers the convulsive tree.
The ready nymphs receive the crying child,
And wash him in the tears the parent plant distill'd.
They swath'd him with their scarfs; beneath him spread
The ground with herbs; with roses rais'd his head.
The lovely babe was born with ev'ry grace,
Ev'n envy must have prais'd so fair a face:
Such was his form, as painters when they show
Their utmost art, on naked loves bestow:
And that their arms no diff'rence might betray,
Give him a bow, or his from Cupid take away.
Time glides along with undiscover'd haste,
The future but a length behind the past;
So swift are years. The babe, whom just before
His grandsire got, and whom his sister bore;
The drop, the thing, which late the tree enclos'd,
And late the yawning bark to life expos'd;
A babe, a boy, a beauteous youth appears,

And lovelier than himself at riper years.
Now to the queen of love he gave desires,
And, with her pains, reveng'd his mother's fires.

The Story of Venus and Adonis

For Cytherea's lips while Cupid prest,
He with a heedless arrow raz'd her breast,
The Goddess felt it, and with fury stung,
The wanton mischief from her bosom flung:
Yet thought at first the danger slight, but found
The dart too faithful, and too deep the wound.
Fir'd with a mortal beauty, she disdains
To haunt th' Idalian mount, or Phrygian plains.
She seeks not Cnidos, nor her Paphian shrines,
Nor Amathus, that teems with brazen mines:
Ev'n Heav'n itself with all its sweets unsought,
Adonis far a sweeter Heav'n is thought.
On him she hangs, and fonds with ev'ry art,
And never, never knows from him to part.
She, whose soft limbs had only been display'd
On rosie beds beneath the myrtle shade,
Whose pleasing care was to improve each grace,
And add more charms to an unrival'd face,
Now buskin'd, like the virgin huntress, goes
Thro' woods, and pathless wilds,
 and mountain-snows
With her own tuneful voice she joys to cheer
The panting hounds, that chase the flying deer.
She runs the labyrinth of fearful hares,
But fearless beasts, and dang'rous prey forbears,
Hunts not the grinning wolf, or foamy boar,
And trembles at the lion's hungry roar.
Thee too, Adonis, with a lover's care
She warns, if warn'd thou wou'dst
 avoid the snare,

To furious animals advance not nigh,
Fly those that follow, follow those that fly;
'Tis chance alone must the survivors save,
Whene'er brave spirits will attempt the brave.
O! lovely youth! in harmless sports delight;
Provoke not beasts, which, arm'd by Nature, fight.
For me, if not thy self, vouchsafe to fear;
Let not thy thirst of glory cost me dear.
Boars know not bow to spare a blooming age;
No sparkling eyes can sooth the lion's rage.
Not all thy charms a savage breast can move,
Which have so deeply touch'd the queen of love.
When bristled boars from beaten thickets spring,
In grinded tusks a thunderbolt they bring.
The daring hunters lions rouz'd devour,
Vast is their fury, and as vast their pow'r:
Curst be their tawny race! If thou would'st hear
What kindled thus my hate, then lend an ear:
The wond'rous tale I will to thee unfold,
How the fell monsters rose from crimes of old.
But by long toils I faint: see! wide-display'd,
A grateful poplar courts us with a shade.
The grassy turf, beneath, so verdant shows,
We may secure delightfully repose.
With her Adonis here be Venus blest;
And swift at once the grass and him she prest.
Then sweetly smiling, with a raptur'd mind,
On his lov'd bosom she her head reclin'd,
And thus began; but mindful still of bliss,
Seal'd the soft accents with a softer kiss.

Perhaps thou may'st have heard a virgin's name,
Who still in swiftness swiftest youths o'ercame.
Wondrous! that female weakness should outdo
A manly strength; the wonder yet is true.
'Twas doubtful, if her triumphs in the field
Did to her form's triumphant glories yield;

Whether her face could with more ease decoy
A crowd of lovers, or her feet destroy.
For once Apollo she implor'd to show
If courteous Fates a consort would allow:
A consort brings thy ruin, he reply'd;
O! learn to want the pleasures of a bride!
Nor shalt thou want them to thy wretched cost,
And Atalanta living shall be lost.
With such a rueful Fate th' affrighted maid
Sought green recesses in the wood-land glade.
Nor sighing suiters her resolves could move,
She bad them show their speed, to show their love.
He only, who could conquer in the race,
Might hope the conquer'd virgin to embrace;
While he, whose tardy feet had lagg'd behind,
Was doom'd the sad reward of death to find.
Tho' great the prize, yet rigid the decree,
But blind with beauty, who can rigor see?
Ev'n on these laws the fair they rashly sought,
And danger in excess of love forgot.

There sat Hippomenes, prepar'd to blame
In lovers such extravagance of flame.
And must, he said, the blessing of a wife
Be dearly purchas'd by a risk of life?
But when he saw the wonders of her face,
And her limbs naked, springing to the race,
Her limbs, as exquisitely turn'd, as mine,
Or if a woman thou, might vie with thine,
With lifted hands, he cry'd, forgive the tongue
Which durst, ye youths, your well-tim'd
    courage wrong.
I knew not that the nymph, for whom you strove,
Deserv'd th' unbounded transports of your love.
He saw, admir'd, and thus her spotless frame
He prais'd, and praising, kindled his own flame.
A rival now to all the youths who run,

Envious, he fears they should not be undone.
But why (reflects he) idly thus is shown
The fate of others, yet untry'd my own?
The coward must not on love's aid depend;
The God was ever to the bold a friend.
Mean-time the virgin flies, or seems to fly,
Swift as a Scythian arrow cleaves the sky:
Still more and more the youth her charms admires.
The race itself t' exalt her charms conspires.
The golden pinions, which her feet adorn,
In wanton flutt'rings by the winds are born.
Down from her head, the long, fair tresses flow,
And sport with lovely negligence below.
The waving ribbands, which her buskins tie,
Her snowy skin with waving purple die;
As crimson veils in palaces display'd,
To the white marble lend a blushing shade.
Nor long he gaz'd, yet while he gaz'd, she gain'd
The goal, and the victorious wreath obtain'd.
The vanquish'd sigh, and, as the law decreed,
Pay the dire forfeit, and prepare to bleed.

Then rose Hippomenes, not yet afraid,
And fix'd his eyes full on the beauteous maid.
Where is (he cry'd) the mighty conquest won,
To distance those, who want the nerves to run?
Here prove superior strength, nor shall it be
Thy loss of glory, if excell'd by me.
High my descent, near Neptune I aspire,
For Neptune was grand-parent to my sire.
From that great God the fourth my self I trace,
Nor sink my virtues yet beneath my race.
Thou from Hippomenes, o'ercome, may'st claim
An envy'd triumph, and a deathless fame.

While thus the youth the virgin pow'r defies,
Silent she views him still with softer eyes.

Thoughts in her breast a doubtful strife begin,
If 'tis not happier now to lose, than win.
What God, a foe to beauty, would destroy
The promis'd ripeness of this blooming boy?
With his life's danger does he seek my bed?
Scarce am I half so greatly worth, she said.
Nor has his beauty mov'd my breast to love,
And yet, I own, such beauty well might move:
'Tis not his charms, 'tis pity would engage
My soul to spare the greenness of his age.
What, that heroic courage fires his breast,
And shines thro' brave disdain of Fate confest?
What, that his patronage by close degrees
Springs from th' imperial ruler of the seas?
Then add the love, which bids him undertake
The race, and dare to perish for my sake.
Of bloody nuptials, heedless youth, beware!
Fly, timely fly from a too barb'rous fair.
At pleasure choose; thy love will be repaid
By a less foolish, and more beauteous maid.
But why this tenderness, before unknown?
Why beats, and pants my breast for him alone?
His eyes have seen his num'rous rivals yield;
Let him too share the rigor of the field,
Since, by their fates untaught, his own he courts,
And thus with ruin insolently sports.
Yet for what crime shall he his death receive?
Is it a crime with me to wish to live?
Shall his kind passion his destruction prove?
Is this the fatal recompense of love?
So fair a youth, destroy'd, would conquest shame,
And nymphs eternally detest my fame.
Still why should nymphs my guiltless fame upbraid?
Did I the fond adventurer persuade?
Alas! I wish thou would'st the course decline,
Or that my swiftness was excell'd by thine.
See! what a virgin's bloom adorns the boy!

Why wilt thou run, and why thy self destroy?
Hippomenes! O that I ne'er had been
By those bright eyes unfortunately seen!
Ah! tempt not thus a swift, untimely Fate;
Thy life is worthy of the longest date.
Were I less wretched, did the galling chain
Of rigid Gods not my free choice restrain,
By thee alone I could with joy be led
To taste the raptures of a nuptial bed.

Thus she disclos'd the woman's secret heart,
Young, innocent, and new to Cupid's dart.
Her thoughts, her words, her actions wildly rove,
With love she burns, yet knows not that 'tis love.

Her royal sire now with the murm'ring crowd
Demands the race impatiently aloud.
Hippomenes then with true fervour pray'd,
My bold attempt let Venus kindly aid.
By her sweet pow'r I felt this am'rous fire,
Still may she succour, whom she did inspire.
A soft, unenvious wind, with speedy care,
Wafted to Heav'n the lover's tender pray'r.
Pity, I own, soon gain'd the wish'd consent,
And all th' assistance he implor'd I lent.
The Cyprian lands, tho' rich, in richness yield
To that, surnam'd the Tamasenian field.
That field of old was added to my shrine,
And its choice products consecrated mine.
A tree there stands, full glorious to behold,
Gold are the leafs, the crackling branches gold.
It chanc'd, three apples in my hand I bore,
Which newly from the tree I sportive tore;
Seen by the youth alone, to him I brought
The fruit, and when, and how to use it, taught.
The signal sounding by the king's command,
Both start at once, and sweep th' imprinted sand.

So swiftly mov'd their feet, they might with ease,
Scarce moisten'd, skim along the glassy seas;
Or with a wondrous levity be born
O'er yellow harvests of unbending corn.
Now fav'ring peals resound from ev'ry part,
Spirit the youth, and fire his fainting heart.
Hippomenes! (they cry'd) thy life preserve,
Intensely labour, and stretch ev'ry nerve.
Base fear alone can baffle thy design,
Shoot boldly onward, and the goal is thine.
'Tis doubtful whether shouts, like these, convey'd
More pleasures to the youth, or to the maid.
When a long distance oft she could have gain'd,
She check'd her swiftness, and her feet restrain'd:
She sigh'd, and dwelt, and languish'd on his face,
Then with unwilling speed pursu'd the race.
O'er-spent with heat, his breath he faintly drew,
Parch'd was his mouth, nor yet the goal in view,
And the first apple on the plain he threw.
The nymph stop'd sudden at th' unusual sight,
Struck with the fruit so beautifully bright.
Aside she starts, the wonder to behold,
And eager stoops to catch the rolling gold.
Th' observant youth past by, and scour'd along,
While peals of joy rung from th' applauding throng.
Unkindly she corrects the short delay,
And to redeem the time fleets swift away,
Swift, as the lightning, or the northern wind,
And far she leaves the panting youth behind.
Again he strives the flying nymph to hold
With the temptation of the second gold:
The bright temptation fruitlessly was tossed,
So soon, alas! she won the distance lost.
Now but a little interval of space
Remain'd for the decision of the race.
Fair author of the precious gift, he said,
Be thou, O Goddess, author of my aid!

Then of the shining fruit the last he drew,
And with his full-collected vigor threw:
The virgin still the longer to detain,
Threw not directly, but a-cross the plain.
She seem'd a-while perplex'd in dubious thought,
If the far-distant apple should be sought:
I lur'd her backward mind to seize the bait,
And to the massie gold gave double weight.
My favour to my votary was show'd,
Her speed I lessen'd, and increas'd her load.
But lest, tho' long, the rapid race be run,
Before my longer, tedious tale is done,
The youth the goal, and so the virgin won.

Might I, Adonis, now not hope to see
His grateful thanks pour'd out for victory?
His pious incense on my altars laid?
But he nor grateful thanks, nor incense paid.
Enrag'd I vow'd, that with the youth the fair,
For his contempt, should my keen vengeance share;
That future lovers might my pow'r revere,
And, from their sad examples, learn to fear.
The silent fanes, the sanctify'd abodes,
Of Cybele, great mother of the Gods,
Rais'd by Echion in a lonely wood,
And full of brown, religious horror stood.
By a long painful journey faint, they chose!
Their weary limbs here secret to repose.
But soon my pow'r inflam'd the lustful boy,
Careless of rest he sought untimely joy.
A hallow'd gloomy cave, with moss o'er-grown,
The temple join'd, of native pumice-stone,
Where antique images by priests were kept.
And wooden deities securely slept.
Thither the rash Hippomenes retires,
And gives a loose to all his wild desires,
And the chaste cell pollutes with wanton fires.

The sacred statues trembled with surprise,
The tow'ry Goddess, blushing, veil'd her eyes;
And the lewd pair to Stygian sounds had sent,
But unrevengeful seem'd that punishment,
A heavier doom such black profaneness draws,
Their taper figures turn to crooked paws.
No more their necks the smoothness can retain,
Now cover'd sudden with a yellow mane.
Arms change to legs: each finds the hard'ning breast
Of rage unknown, and wond'rous strength possest.
Their alter'd looks with fury grim appear,
And on the ground their brushing tails they hear.
They haunt the woods: their voices, which before
Were musically sweet, now hoarsely roar.
Hence lions, dreadful to the lab'ring swains,
Are tam'd by Cybele, and curb'd with reins,
And humbly draw her car along the plains.
But thou, Adonis, my delightful care,
Of these, and beasts, as fierce as these, beware!
The savage, which not shuns thee, timely shun,
For by rash prowess should'st thou be undone,
A double ruin is contain'd in one.
Thus cautious Venus school'd her fav'rite boy;
But youthful heat all cautions will destroy.
His sprightly soul beyond grave counsels flies,
While with yok'd swans the Goddess
cuts the skies.
His faithful hounds, led by the tainted wind,
Lodg'd in thick coverts chanc'd a boar to find.
The callow hero show'd a manly heart,
And pierc'd the savage with a side-long dart.
The flying savage, wounded, turn'd again,
Wrench'd out the gory dart, and foam'd with pain.
The trembling boy by flight his safety sought,
And now recall'd the lore, which Venus taught;
But now too late to fly the boar he strove,
Who in the groin his tusks impetuous drove,

On the discolour'd grass Adonis lay,
The monster trampling o'er his beauteous prey.

Fair Cytherea, Cyprus scarce in view,
Heard from afar his groans, and own'd them true,
And turn'd her snowy swans, and backward flew.
But as she saw him gasp his latest breath,
And quiv'ring agonize in pangs of death,
Down with swift flight she plung'd, nor rage forbore,
At once her garments, and her hair she tore.
With cruel blows she beat her guiltless breast,
The Fates upbraided, and her love confest.
Nor shall they yet (she cry'd) the whole devour
With uncontroll'd, inexorable pow'r:
For thee, lost youth, my tears, and restless pain
Shall in immortal monuments remain,
With solemn pomp in annual rites return'd,
Be thou for ever, my Adonis, mourn'd,
Could Pluto's queen with jealous fury storm,
And Menthe to a fragrant herb transform?
Yet dares not Venus with a change surprise,
And in a flow'r bid her fall'n hero rise?
Then on the blood sweet nectar she bestows,
The scented blood in little bubbles rose:
Little as rainy drops, which flutt'ring fly,
Born by the winds, along a low'ring sky.
Short time ensu'd, till where the blood was shed,
A flow'r began to rear its purple head:
Such, as on Punick apples is reveal'd,
Or in the filmy rind but half conceal'd.
Still here the Fate of lovely forms we see,
So sudden fades the sweet Anemonie.
The feeble stems, to stormy blasts a prey,
Their sickly beauties droop, and pine away.
The winds forbid the flow'rs to flourish long,
Which owe to winds their names in Grecian song.

Book XI

The Death of Orpheus

Here, while the Thracian bard's enchanting strain
Sooths beasts, and woods, and all the listn'ing plain,
The female Bacchanals, devoutly mad,
In shaggy skins, like savage creatures, clad,
Warbling in air perceiv'd his lovely lay,
And from a rising ground beheld him play.
When one, the wildest, with dishevel'd hair,
That loosely stream'd, and ruffled in the air;
Soon as her frantic eye the lyrist spy'd,
See, see! the hater of our sex, she cry'd.
Then at his face her missive javelin sent,
Which whiz'd along, and brushed him as it went;
But the soft wreathes of ivy twisted round,
Prevent a deep impression of the wound.
Another, for a weapon, hurls a stone,
Which, by the sound subdu'd as soon as thrown,
Falls at his feet, and with a seeming sense
Implores his pardon for its late offence.
But now their frantic rage unbounded grows,
Turns all to madness, and no measure knows:
Yet this the charms of music might subdue,
But that, with all its charms, is conquer'd too;
In louder strains their hideous yellings rise,
And squeaking horn-pipes echo thro' the skies,
Which, in hoarse consort with the drum, confound
The moving lyre, and ev'ry gentle sound:
Then 'twas the deafen'd stones flew on with speed,
And saw, unsooth'd, their tuneful poet bleed.

The birds, the beasts, and all the savage crew
Which the sweet lyrist to attention drew,
Now, by the female mob's more furious rage,
Are driv'n, and forc'd to quit the shady stage.
Next their fierce hands the bard himself assail,
Nor can his song against their wrath prevail:
They flock, like birds, when in a clustering flight,
By day they chase the boding fowl of night.
So crowded amphitheatres survey
The stag, to greedy dogs a future prey.
Their steely javelins, which soft curls entwine
Of budding tendrils from the leafy vine,
For sacred rites of mild religion made,
Are flung promiscuous at the poet's head.
Those clods of earth or flints discharge, and these
Hurl prickly branches sliver'd from the trees.
And, lest their passion shou'd be unsupply'd,
The rabble crew, by chance, at distance spy'd
Where oxen, straining at the heavy yoke,
The fallow'd field with slow advances broke;
Nigh which the brawny peasants dug the soil,
Procuring food with long laborious toil.
These, when they saw the ranting throng draw near,
Quitted their tools, and fled, possest with fear.
Long spades, and rakes of mighty size were found,
Carelessly left upon the broken ground.
With these the furious lunatics engage,
And first the lab'ring oxen feel their rage;
Then to the poet they return with speed,
Whose fate was, past prevention, now decreed:
In vain he lifts his suppliant hands, in vain
He tries, before, his never-failing strain.
And, from those sacred lips, whose thrilling sound
Fierce tigers, and insensate rocks cou'd wound,
Ah Gods! how moving was the mournful sight!
To see the fleeting soul now take its flight.
Thee the soft warblers of the feather'd kind

Bewail'd; for thee thy savage audience pin'd;
Those rocks and woods that oft thy strain had led,
Mourn for their charmer, and lament him dead;
And drooping trees their leafy glories shed.
Naids and Dryads with dishevel'd hair
Promiscuous weep, and scarfs of sable wear;
Nor cou'd the river-Gods conceal their moan,
But with new floods of tears augment their own.
His mangled limbs lay scatter'd all around,
His head, and harp a better fortune found;
In Hebrus' streams they gently roll'd along,
And sooth'd the waters with a mournful song.
Soft deadly notes the lifeless tongue inspire,
A doleful tune sounds from the floating lyre;
The hollows banks in solemn consort mourn,
And the sad strain in echoing groans return.
Now with the current to the sea they glide,
Born by the billows of the briny tide;
And driv'n where waves round rocky
Lesbos roar,
They strand, and lodge upon
Methymna's shore.

But here, when landed on the foreign soil,
A venom'd snake, the product of the isle
Attempts the head, and sacred locks embru'd
With clotted gore, and still fresh-dropping blood.
Phœbus, at last, his kind protection gives,
And from the fact the greedy monster drives:
Whose marbled jaws his impious crime atone,
Still grinning ghastly, tho' transform'd to stone.

His ghost flies downward to the Stygian shore,
And knows the places it had seen before:
Among the shadows of the pious train
He finds Eurydice, and loves again;
With pleasure views the beauteous phantom's charms,

And clasps her in his unsubstantial arms.
There side by side they unmolested walk,
Or pass their blissful hours in pleasing talk;
Aft or before the bard securely goes,
And, without danger, can review his spouse.

The Thracian Women Transform'd to Trees

Bacchus, resolving to revenge the wrong,
Of Orpheus murder'd, on the madding throng,
Decreed that each accomplice dame should stand
Fix'd by the roots along the conscious land.
Their wicked feet, that late so nimbly ran
To wreak their malice on the guiltless man,
Sudden with twisted ligatures were bound,
Like trees, deep planted in the turfy ground.
And, as the fowler with his subtle gins,
His feather'd captives by the feet entwines,
That flutt'ring pant, and struggle to get loose,
Yet only closer draw the fatal noose;
So these were caught; and, as they strove in vain
To quit the place, they but increas'd their pain.
They flounce and toil, yet find
themselves controll'd;
The root, tho' pliant, toughly keeps its hold.
In vain their toes and feet they look to find,
For ev'n their shapely legs are cloth'd with rind.
One smites her thighs with a lamenting stroke,
And finds the flesh transform'd to solid oak;
Another, with surprise, and grief distrest,
Lays on above, but beats a wooden breast.
A rugged bark their softer neck invades,
Their branching arms shoot up delightful shades;
At once they seem, and are, a real grove,
With mossy trunks below, and verdant leaves above.

The Fable of Midas

Nor this suffic'd; the God's disgust remains,
And he resolves to quit their hated plains;
The vineyards of Tymole engross his care,
And, with a better choir, he fixes there;
Where the smooth streams of clear Pactolus roll'd,
Then undistinguish'd for its sands of gold.
The satyrs with the nymphs, his usual throng,
Come to salute their God, and jovial danc'd along.
Silenus only miss'd; for while he reel'd,
Feeble with age, and wine, about the field,
The hoary drunkard had forgot his way,
And to the Phrygian clowns became a prey;
Who to king Midas drag the captive God,
While on his totty pate the wreaths of ivy nod.

Midas from Orpheus had been taught his lore,
And knew the rites of Bacchus long before.
He, when he saw his venerable guest,
In honour of the God ordain'd a feast.
Ten days in course, with each continu'd night,
Were spent in genial mirth, and brisk delight:
Then on th' eleventh, when with brighter ray
Phosphor had chas'd the fading stars away,
The king thro' Lydia's fields young
Bacchus sought,
And to the God his foster-father brought.
Pleas'd with the welcome sight, he bids him soon
But name his wish, and swears to grant the boon.
A glorious offer! yet but ill bestow'd
On him whose choice so little judgment show'd.
Give me, says he (nor thought he ask'd too much),
That with my body whatsoe'er I touch,
Chang'd from the nature which it held of old,
May be converted into yellow gold.
He had his wish; but yet the God repin'd,
To think the fool no better wish could find.

But the brave king departed from the place,
With smiles of gladness sparkling in his face:
Nor could contain, but, as he took his way,
Impatient longs to make the first essay.
Down from a lowly branch a twig he drew,
The twig strait glitter'd with a golden hue:
He takes a stone, the stone was turn'd to gold;
A clod he touches, and the crumbling mold
Acknowledg'd soon the great transforming pow'r,
In weight and substance like a mass of ore.
He pluck'd the corn, and strait his grasp appears
Fill'd with a bending tuft of golden ears.
An apple next he takes, and seems to hold
The bright Hesperian vegetable gold.
His hand he careless on a pillar lays.
With shining gold the fluted pillars blaze:
And while he washes, as the servants pour,
His touch converts the stream to Danæ's show'r.

To see these miracles so finely wrought,
Fires with transporting joy his giddy thought.
The ready slaves prepare a sumptuous board,
Spread with rich dainties for their happy lord;
Whose pow'rful hands the bread no sooner hold,
But its whole substance is transform'd to gold:
Up to his mouth he lifts the sav'ry meat,
Which turns to gold as he attempts to eat:
His patron's noble juice of purple hue,
Touch'd by his lips, a gilded cordial grew;
Unfit for drink, and wondrous to behold,
It trickles from his jaws a fluid gold.

The rich poor fool, confounded with surprise,
Starving in all his various plenty lies:
Sick of his wish, he now detests the pow'r,
For which he ask'd so earnestly before;
Amidst his gold with pinching famine curst;

And justly tortur'd with an equal thirst.
At last his shining arms to Heav'n he rears,
And in distress, for refuge, flies to pray'rs.
O father Bacchus, I have sinn'd, he cry'd,
And foolishly thy gracious gift apply'd;
Thy pity now, repenting, I implore;
Oh! may I feel the golden plague no more.

The hungry wretch, his folly thus confest,
Touch'd the kind deity's good-natur'd breast;
The gentle God annull'd his first decree,
And from the cruel compact set him free.
But then, to cleanse him quite from further harm,
And to dilute the relics of the charm,
He bids him seek the stream that cuts the land
Nigh where the tow'rs of Lydian Sardis stand;
Then trace the river to the fountain head,
And meet it rising from its rocky bed;
There, as the bubbling tide pours forth amain,
To plunge his body in, and wash away the stain.
The king instructed to the fount retires,
But with the golden charm the stream inspires:
For while this quality the man forsakes,
An equal pow'r the limpid water takes;
Informs with veins of gold the neighb'ring land,
And glides along a bed of golden sand.

Now loathing wealth, th' occasion of his woes,
Far in the woods he sought a calm repose;
In caves and grottos, where the nymphs resort,
And keep with mountain Pan their sylvan court.
Ah! had he left his stupid soul behind!
But his condition alter'd not his mind.

For where high Tmolus rears his shady brow,
And from his cliffs surveys the seas below,
In his descent, by Sardis bounded here,

By the small confines of Hypæpa there,
Pan to the nymphs his frolic ditties play'd,
Tuning his reeds beneath the chequer'd shade.
The nymphs are pleas'd, the boasting sylvan plays,
And speaks with slight of great Apollo's lays.
Tmolus was arbiter; the boaster still
Accepts the trial with unequal skill.
The venerable judge was seated high
On his own hill, that seem'd to touch the sky.
Above the whisp'ring trees his head he rears,
From their encumbering boughs to free his ears;
A wreath of oak alone his temples bound,
The pendant acorns loosely dangled round.
In me your judge, says he, there's no delay:
Then bids the goatherd God begin, and play.
Pan tun'd the pipe, and with his rural song
Pleas'd the low taste of all the vulgar throng;
Such songs a vulgar judgment mostly please,
Midas was there, and Midas judg'd with these.

The mountain sire with grave deportment now
To Phœbus turns his venerable brow:
And, as he turns, with him the listening wood
In the same posture of attention stood.
The God his own Parnassian laurel crown'd,
And in a wreath his golden tresses bound,
Graceful his purple mantle swept the ground.
High on the left his iv'ry lute he rais'd,
The lute, emboss'd with glitt'ring jewels, blaz'd
In his right hand he nicely held the quill,
His easy posture spoke a master's skill.
The strings he touch'd with more than human art,
Which pleas'd the judge's ear, and sooth'd his heart;
Who soon judiciously the palm decreed,
And to the lute postpon'd the squeaking reed.

All, with applause, the rightful sentence heard,
Midas alone dissatisfy'd appear'd;

To him unjustly giv'n the judgment seems,
For Pan's barbaric notes he most esteems.
The lyric God, who thought his untun'd ear
Deserv'd but ill a human form to wear,
Of that deprives him, and supplies the place
With some more fit, and of an ampler space:
Fix'd on his noddle an unseemly pair,
Flagging, and large, and full of whitish hair;
Without a total change from what he was,
Still in the man preserves the simple ass.

He, to conceal the scandal of the deed,
A purple turban folds about his head;
Veils the reproach from public view, and fears
The laughing world would spy his monstrous ears.
One trusty barber-slave, that us'd to dress
His master's hair, when lengthen'd to excess,
The mighty secret knew, but knew alone,
And, tho' impatient, durst not make it known.
Restless, at last, a private place he found,
Then dug a hole, and told it to the ground;
In a low whisper he reveal'd the case,
And cover'd in the earth, and silent left the place.

In time, of trembling reeds a plenteous crop
From the confided furrow sprouted up;
Which, high advancing with the ripening year,
Made known the tiller, and his fruitless care:
For then the rustling blades, and whisp'ring wind,
To tell th' important secret, both combin'd.

The Building of Troy

Phœbus, with full revenge, from Tmolus flies,
Darts thro' the air, and cleaves the liquid skies;
Near Hellespont he lights, and treads the plains

Where great Laomedon sole monarch reigns;
Where, built between the two projecting strands,
To Panomphæan Jove an altar stands.
Here first aspiring thoughts the king employ,
To found the lofty tow'rs of future Troy.
The work, from schemes magnificent begun,
At vast expense was slowly carry'd on:
Which Phœbus seeing, with the trident God
Who rules the swelling surges with his nod,
Assuming each a mortal shape, combine
At a set price to finish his design.
The work was built; the king their price denies,
And his injustice backs with perjuries.
This Neptune cou'd not brook, but drove the main,
A mighty deluge, o'er the Phrygian plain:
'Twas all a sea; the waters of the deep
From ev'ry vale the copious harvest sweep;
The briny billows overflow the soil,
Ravage the fields, and mock the plowman's toil.

Nor this appeas'd the God's revengeful mind,
For still a greater plague remains behind;
A huge sea-monster lodges on the sands,
And the king's daughter for his prey demands.
To him that sav'd the damsel, was decreed
A set of horses of the Sun's fine breed:
But when Alcides from the rock unty'd
The trembling fair, the ransom was deny'd.
He, in revenge, the new-built walls attack'd,
And the twice-perjur'd city bravely sack'd.
Telamon aided, and in justice shar'd
Part of the plunder as his due reward:
The princess, rescu'd late, with all her charms,
Hesione, was yielded to his arms;
For Peleus, with a Goddess-bride, was more
Proud of his spouse, than of his birth before:
Grandsons to Jove there might be more than one,
But he the Goddess had enjoy'd alone.

The Story of Thetis and Peleus

For Proteus thus to virgin Thetis said,
Fair Goddess of the waves, consent to wed,
And take some spritely lover to your bed.
A son you'll have, the terror of the field,
To whom in fame, and pow'r his sire shall yield.

Jove, who ador'd the nymph with boundless love,
Did from his breast the dangerous flame remove.
He knew the Fates, nor car'd to raise up one,
Whose fame and greatness should eclipse his own,
On happy Peleus he bestow'd her charms,
And bless'd his grandson in the Goddess' arms:

A silent creek Thessalia's coast can show;
Two arms project, and shape it like a bow;
'Twould make a bay, but the transparent tide
Does scarce the yellow-gravel'd bottom hide;
For the quick eye may thro' the liquid wave
A firm unweedy level beach perceive.
A grove of fragrant myrtle near it grows,
Whose boughs, tho' thick, a beauteous
grot disclose;
The well-wrought fabric, to discerning eyes,
Rather by art than Nature seems to rise.
A bridled dolphin oft fair Thetis bore
To this her lov'd retreat, her fav'rite shore.
Here Peleus seiz'd her, slumbring while she lay,
And urg'd his suit with all that love could say:
But when he found her obstinately coy,
Resolv'd to force her, and command the joy;
The nymph, o'erpowr'd, to art for succour flies
And various shapes the eager youth surprise:
A bird she seems, but plies her wings in vain,
His hands the fleeting substance still detain:
A branchy tree high in the air she grew;

About its bark his nimble arms he threw:
A tiger next she glares with flaming eyes;
The frighten'd lover quits his hold, and flies:
The sea-Gods he with sacred rites adores,
Then a libation on the ocean pours;
While the fat entrails crackle in the fire,
And sheets of smoke in sweet perfume aspire;
Till Proteus rising from his oozy bed,
Thus to the poor desponding lover said:
No more in anxious thoughts your mind employ,
For yet you shall possess the dear expected joy.
You must once more th' unwary nymph surprise,
As in her coolly grot she slumbering lies;
Then bind her fast with unrelenting hands,
And strain her tender limbs with knotted bands.
Still hold her under ev'ry different shape,
Till tir'd she tries no longer to escape.
Thus he: then sunk beneath the glassy flood,
And broken accents flutter'd, where he stood.

Bright Sol had almost now his journey done,
And down the steepy western convex run;
When the fair Nereid left the briny wave,
And, as she us'd, retreated to her cave.
He scarce had bound her fast, when she arose,
And into various shapes her body throws:
She went to move her arms, and found 'em ty'd;
Then with a sigh, some God assists ye, cry'd,
And in her proper shape stood blushing by his side.
About her waist his longing arms he flung,
From which embrace the great Achilles sprung.

The Transformation of Dædalion

Peleus unmix'd felicity enjoy'd
(Blest in a valiant son, and virtuous bride),

Till Fortune did in blood his hands imbrue,
And his own brother by curst chance he slew:
Then driv'n from Thessaly, his native clime,
Trachinia first gave shelter to his crime;
Where peaceful Ceyx mildly fill'd the throne,
And like his sire, the morning planet, shone;
But now, unlike himself, bedew'd with tears,
Mourning a brother lost, his brow appears.
First to the town with travel spent, and care,
Peleus, and his small company repair:
His herds, and flocks the while at leisure feed,
On the rich pasture of a neighb'ring mead.
The prince before the royal presence brought,
Shew'd by the suppliant olive what he sought;
Then tells his name, and race, and country right,
But hides th' unhappy reason of his flight.
He begs the king some little town to give,
Where they may safe his faithful vassals live.
Ceyx reply'd: To all my bounty flows,
A hospitable realm your suit has chose.
Your glorious race, and far-resounding fame,
And grandsire Jove, peculiar favours claim.
All you can wish, I grant; entreaties spare;
My kingdom (would 'twere worth the sharing) share.

Tears stop'd his speech: astonish'd Peleus pleads
To know the cause from whence his grief proceeds.
The prince reply'd: There's none of ye but deems
This hawk was ever such as now it seems;
Know 'twas a hero once, Dædalion nam'd,
For warlike deeds, and haughty valour fam'd;
Like me to that bright luminary born,
Who wakes Aurora, and brings on the morn.
His fierceness still remains, and love of blood,
Now dread of birds, and tyrant of the wood.
My make was softer, peace my greatest care;

But this my brother wholly bent on war;
Late nations fear'd, and routed armies fled
That force, which now the tim'rous pigeons dread.
A daughter he possess'd, divinely fair,
And scarcely yet had seen her fifteenth year;
Young Chione: a thousand rivals strove
To win the maid, and teach her how to love.
Phœbus, and Mercury by chance one day
From Delphi, and Cyllene past this way;
Together they the virgin saw: desire
At once warm'd both their breasts with
    am'rous fire.
Phœbus resolv'd to wait till close of day;
But Mercury's hot love brook'd no delay;
With his entrancing rod the maid he charms,
And unresisted revels in her arms.
'Twas night, and Phœbus in a beldam's dress,
To the late rifled beauty got access.
Her time complete nine circling moons had run;
To either God she bore a lovely son:
To Mercury Autolycus she brought,
Who turn'd to thefts and tricks his
    subtle thought;
Possess'd he was of all his father's slight,
At will made white look black, and black
    look white.
Philammon born to Phœbus, like his sire,
The Muses lov'd, and finely struck the lyre,
And made his voice, and touch in
    harmony conspire.
In vain, fond maid, you boast this double birth,
The love of Gods, and royal father's worth,
And Jove among your ancestors rehearse!
Could blessings such as these e'er prove a curse?
To her they did, who with audacious pride,
Vain of her own, Diana's charms decry'd.
Her taunts the Goddess with resentment fill;

My face you like not, you shall try my skill.
She said; and strait her vengeful bow she strung,
And sent a shaft that pierc'd her guilty tongue:
The bleeding tongue in vain its accents tries;
In the red stream her soul reluctant flies.
With sorrow wild I ran to her relief,
And try'd to moderate my brother's grief.
He, deaf as rocks by stormy surges beat,
Loudly laments, and hears me not entreat.
When on the fun'ral pile he saw her laid,
Thrice he to rush into the flames assay'd,
Thrice with officious care by us was stay'd.
Now, mad with grief, away he fled amain,
Like a stung heifer that resents the pain,
And bellowing wildly bounds along the plain.
O'er the most rugged ways so fast he ran,
He seem'd a bird already, not a man:
He left us breathless all behind; and now
In quest of death had gain'd Parnassus' brow:
But when from thence headlong himself he threw,
He fell not, but with airy pinions flew.
Phœbus in pity chang'd him to a fowl,
Whose crooked beak and claws the birds control,
Little of bulk, but of a warlike soul.
A hawk become, the feather'd race's foe,
He tries to case his own by other's woe.

A Wolf Turn'd into Marble

While they astonish'd heard the king relate
These wonders of his hapless brother's fate;
The prince's herdsman at the court arrives,
And fresh surprise to all the audience gives.
O Peleus, Peleus! dreadful news I bear,
He said; and trembled as he spoke for fear.
The worst, affrighted Peleus bid him tell,

Whilst Ceyx too grew pale with friendly zeal.
Thus he began: When Sol mid-heav'n had gain'd,
And half his way was past, and half remain'd,
I to the level shore my cattle drove,
And let them freely in the meadows rove.
Some stretch'd at length admire the wat'ry plain,
Some crop'd the herb, some wanton swam
    the main.
A temple stands of antique make hard by,
Where no gilt domes, nor marble lure the eye;
Unpolish'd rafters bear its lowly height,
Hid by a grove, as ancient, from the sight.
Here Nereus, and the Nereids they adore;
I learnt it from the man who thither bore
His net, to dry it on the sunny shore.
Adjoyns a lake, enclos'd with willows round,
Where swelling waves have overflow'd
    the mound,
And, muddy, stagnate on the lower ground.
From thence a rustling noise increasing flies,
Strikes the still shore; and frights us
    with surprise,
Strait a huge wolf rush'd from the
    marshy wood,
His jaws besmear'd with mingled foam,
    and blood,
Tho' equally by hunger urg'd, and rage,
His appetite he minds not to assuage;
Nought that he meets, his rabid fury spares,
But the whole herd with mad disorder tears.
Some of our men who strove to drive him thence,
Torn by his teeth, have dy'd in their defense.
The echoing lakes, the sea, and fields, and shore,
Impurpled blush with streams of reeking gore.
Delay is loss, nor have we time for thought;
While yet some few remain alive, we ought
To seize our arms, and with confederate force

Try if we so can stop his bloody course.
But Peleus car'd not for his ruin'd herd;
His crime he call'd to mind, and thence inferr'd,
That Psamathe's revenge this havoc made,
In sacrifice to murder'd Phocus' shade.
The king commands his servants to their arms;
Resolv'd to go; but the loud noise alarms
His lovely queen, who from her chamber flew,
And her half-plaited hair behind her threw:
About his neck she hung with loving fears,
And now with words, and now with pleading tears,
Entreated that he'd send his men alone,
And stay himself, to save two lives in one.
Then Peleus: Your just fears, o queen, forget;
Too much the offer leaves me in your debt.
No arms against the monster I shall bear,
But the sea nymphs appease with humble pray'r.

The citadel's high turrets pierce the sky,
Which home-bound vessels, glad, from far descry;
This they ascend, and thence with sorrow ken
The mangled heifers lye, and bleeding men;
Th' inexorable ravager they view,
With blood discolour'd, still the rest pursue:
There Peleus pray'd submissive tow'rds the sea,
And deprecates the ire of injur'd Psamathe.
But deaf to all his pray'rs the nymph remain'd,
Till Thetis for her spouse the boon obtain'd.
Pleas'd with the luxury, the furious beast,
Unstop'd, continues still his bloody feast:
While yet upon a sturdy bull he flew,
Chang'd by the nymph, a marble block he grew.
No longer dreadful now the wolf appears,
Bury'd in stone, and vanish'd like their fears.
Yet still the Fates unhappy Peleus vex'd;
To the Magnesian shore he wanders next.
Acastus there, who rul'd the peaceful clime,
Grants his request, and expiates his crime.

The Story of Ceyx and Alcyone

These prodigies affect the pious prince,
But more perplex'd with those that happen'd since,
He purposes to seek the Clarian God,
Avoiding Delphi, his more fam'd abode,
Since Phlegyan robbers made unsafe the road.
Yet could he not from her he lov'd so well,
The fatal voyage, he resolv'd, conceal;
But when she saw her lord prepar'd to part,
A deadly cold ran shiv'ring to her heart;
Her faded cheeks are chang'd to boxen hue,
And in her eyes the tears are ever new.
She thrice essay'd to speak; her accents hung,
And falt'ring dy'd unfinish'd on her tongue,
And vanish'd into sighs: with long delay
Her voice return'd, and found the wonted way.

Tell me, my lord, she said, what fault unknown
Thy once belov'd Alcyone has done?
Whither, ah, whither, is thy kindness gone!
Can Ceyx then sustain to leave his wife,
And unconcern'd forsake the sweets of life?
What can thy mind to this long journey move?
Or need'st thou absence to renew thy love?
Yet, if thou go'st by land, tho' grief possess
My soul ev'n then, my fears will be the less.
But ah! be warn'd to shun the wat'ry way,
The face is frightful of the stormy sea:
For late I saw a-drift disjointed planks,
And empty tombs erected on the banks.
Nor let false hopes to trust betray thy mind,
Because my sire in caves constrains the wind,
Can with a breath their clam'rous rage appease,
They fear his whistle, and forsake the seas:
Not so; for once indulg'd, they sweep the main;
Deaf to the call, or hearing, hear in vain;

But bent on mischief bear the waves before,
And not content with seas, insult the shore,
When ocean, air, and Earth, at once engage,
And rooted forests fly before their rage:
At once the clashing clouds to battle move,
And lightnings run across the fields above:
I know them well, and mark'd their rude comport,
While yet a child within my father's court:
In times of tempest they command alone,
And he but sits precarious on the throne:
The more I know, the more my fears augment;
And fears are oft prophetic of th' event.
But if not fears, or reasons will prevail,
If Fate has fix'd thee obstinate to sail,
Go not without thy wife, but let me bear
My part of danger with an equal share,
And present, what I suffer only fear:
Then o'er the bounding billows shall we fly,
Secure to live together, or to die.

These reasons mov'd her warlike husband's heart,
But still he held his purpose to depart:
For as he lov'd her equal to his life,
He would not to the seas expose his wife;
Nor could be wrought his voyage to refrain,
But sought by arguments to sooth her pain:
Nor these avail'd; at length he lights on one,
With which so difficult a cause he won:
My love, so short an absence cease to fear,
For by my father's holy flame I swear,
Before two moons their orb with light adorn,
If Heav'n allow me life, I will return.

This promise of so short a stay prevails;
He soon equips the ship, supplies the sails,
And gives the word to launch; she trembling views
This pomp of death, and parting tears renews:

Last with a kiss, she took a long farewell,
Sigh'd with a sad presage, and swooning fell:
While Ceyx seeks delays, the lusty crew,
Rais'd on their banks, their oars in order drew
To their broad breasts, the ship with fury flew.

The queen recover'd, rears her humid eyes,
And first her husband on the poop espies,
Shaking his hand at distance on the main;
She took the sign, and shook her hand again.
Still as the ground recedes, contracts her view
With sharpen'd sight, till she no longer knew
The much-lov'd face; that comfort lost supplies
With less, and with the galley feeds her eyes;
The galley born from view by rising gales,
She follow'd with her sight the flying sails:
When ev'n the flying sails were seen no more,
Forsaken of all sight she left the shore.

Then on her bridal bed her body throws,
And sought in sleep her wearied eyes to close:
Her husband's pillow, and the widow'd part
Which once he press'd, renew'd the former smart.

And now a breeze from shore began to blow,
The sailors ship their oars, and cease to row;
Then hoist their yards a-trip, and all their sails
Let fall, to court the wind, and catch the gales:
By this the vessel half her course had run,
Both shores were lost to sight, when at the close
Of day a stiffer gale at east arose:
The sea grew white, the rolling waves from far,
Like heralds, first denounce the wat'ry war.

This seen, the master soon began to cry,
Strike, strike the top-sail; let the main-sheet fly,
And furl your sails: the winds repel the sound,
And in the speaker's mouth the speech is drown'd.

Yet of their own accord, as danger taught
Each in his way, officiously they wrought;
Some stow their oars, or stop the leaky sides,
Another bolder, yet the yard bestrides,
And folds the sails; a fourth with labour laves
Th' intruding seas, and waves ejects on waves.

In this confusion while their work they ply,
The winds augment the winter of the sky,
And wage intestine wars; the suff'ring seas
Are toss'd, and mingled, as their tyrants please.
The master would command, but in despair
Of safety, stands amaz'd with stupid care,
Nor what to bid, or what forbid he knows,
Th' ungovern'd tempest to such fury grows:
Vain is his force, and vainer is his skill;
With such a concourse comes the flood of ill;
The cries of men are mix'd with rattling shrowds;
Seas dash on seas, and clouds encounter clouds:
At once from east to west, from pole to pole,
The forky lightnings flash, the roaring thunders roll.

Now waves on waves ascending scale the skies,
And in the fires above the water fries:
When yellow sands are sifted from below,
The glittering billows give a golden show:
And when the fouler bottom spews the black
The Stygian dye the tainted waters take:
Then frothy white appear the flatted seas,
And change their colour, changing their disease,
Like various fits the Trachin vessel finds,
And now sublime, she rides upon the winds;
As from a lofty summit looks from high,
And from the clouds beholds the nether sky;
Now from the depth of Hell they lift their sight,
And at a distance see superior light;
The lashing billows make a loud report,

And beat her sides, as batt'ring rams a fort:
Or as a lion bounding in his way,
With force augmented, bears against his prey,
Sidelong to seize; or unapal'd with fear,
Springs on the toils, and rushes on the spear:
So seas impell'd by winds, with added pow'r
Assault the sides, and o'er the hatches tow'r.

The planks (their pitchy cov'ring wash'd away)
Now yield; and now a yawning breach display:
The roaring waters with a hostile tide
Rush through the ruins of her gaping side.
Mean-time in sheets of rain the sky descends,
And ocean swell'd with waters upwards tends;
One rising, falling one, the Heav'ns and sea
Meet at their confines, in the middle way:
The sails are drunk with show'rs,
and drop with rain,
Sweet waters mingle with the briny main.
No star appears to lend his friendly light;
Darkness, and tempest make a double night;
But flashing fires disclose the deep by turns,
And while the lightnings blaze, the water burns.

Now all the waves their scatter'd force unite,
And as a soldier foremost in the fight,
Makes way for others, and an host alone
Still presses on, and urging gains the town;
So while th' invading billows come a-breast,
The hero tenth advanc'd before the rest,
Sweeps all before him with impetuous sway,
And from the walls descends upon the prey;
Part following enter, part remain without,
With envy hear their fellows' conqu'ring shout,
And mount on others' backs, in hopes to share
The city, thus become the seat of war.

An universal cry resounds aloud,
The sailors run in heaps, a helpless crowd;
Art fails, and courage falls, no succour near;
As many waves, as many deaths appear.
One weeps, and yet despairs of late relief;
One cannot weep, his fears congeal his grief,
But stupid, with dry eyes expects his fate:
One with loud shrieks laments his lost estate,
And calls those happy whom their fun'rals wait.
This wretch with pray'rs and vows the
Gods implores,
And ev'n the skies he cannot see, adores.
That other on his friends his thoughts bestows,
His careful father, and his faithful spouse.
The covetous worldling in his anxious mind,
Thinks only on the wealth he left behind.

All Ceyx his Alcyone employs,
For her he grieves, yet in her absence joys:
His wife he wishes, and would still be near,
Not her with him, but wishes him with her:
Now with last looks he seeks his native shore,
Which Fate has destin'd him to see no more;
He sought, but in the dark tempestuous night
He knew not whither to direct his sight.
So whirl the seas, such darkness blinds the sky,
That the black night receives a deeper dye.

The giddy ship ran round; the tempest tore
Her mast, and over-board the rudder bore.
One billow mounts, and with a scornful brow,
Proud of her conquest gain'd, insults the
waves below;
Nor lighter falls, than if some giant tore
Pindus and Athos with the freight they bore,
And toss'd on seas; press'd with the pond'rous blow,
Down sinks the ship within th' abyss below:
Down with the vessel sink into the main

The many, never more to rise again.
Some few on scatter'd planks, with fruitless care,
Lay hold, and swim; but while they swim, despair.

Ev'n he who late a scepter did command,
Now grasps a floating fragment in his hand;
And while he struggles on the stormy main,
Invokes his father, and his wife's, in vain.
But yet his consort is his greatest care,
Alcyone he names amidst his pray'r;
Names as a charm against the waves and wind;
Most in his mouth, and ever in his mind.
Tir'd with his toil, all hopes of safety past,
From pray'rs to wishes he descends at last;
That his dead body, wafted to the sands,
Might have its burial from her friendly hands,
As oft as he can catch a gulp of air,
And peep above the seas, he names the fair;
And ev'n when plung'd beneath, on her he raves,
Murm'ring Alcyone below the waves:
At last a falling billow stops his breath,
Breaks o'er his head, and whelms him underneath.
That night, his heav'nly form obscur'd with tears,
And since he was forbid to leave the skies,
He muffled with a cloud his mournful eyes.

Mean-time Alcyone (his fate unknown)
Computes how many nights he had been gone.
Observes the waining moon with hourly view,
Numbers her age, and wishes for a new;
Against the promis'd time provides with care,
And hastens in the woof the robes he was to wear:
And for her self employs another loom,
New-dress'd to meet her lord returning home,
Flatt'ring her heart with joys, that never
were to come:
She fum'd the temples with an od'rous flame,

And oft before the sacred altars came,
To pray for him, who was an empty name.
All Pow'rs implor'd, but far above the rest
To Juno she her pious vows address'd,
Her much-lov'd lord from perils to protect,
And safe o'er seas his voyage to direct:
Then pray'd, that she might still possess his heart,
And no pretending rival share a part;
This last petition heard of all her pray'r,
The rest, dispers'd by winds, were lost in air.

But she, the Goddess of the nuptial bed,
Tir'd with her vain devotions for the dead,
Resolv'd the tainted hand should be repell'd,
Which incense offer'd, and her altar held:
Then Iris thus bespoke: Thou faithful maid,
By whom thy queen's commands are well convey'd,
Haste to the house of sleep, and bid the God
Who rules the night by visions with a nod,
Prepare a dream, in figure, and in form
Resembling him, who perish'd in the storm;
This form before Alcyone present,
To make her certain of the sad event.

Endu'd with robes of various hue she flies,
And flying draws an arch (a segment of the skies):
Then leaves her bending bow, and from the steep
Descends, to search the silent house of sleep.

The House of Sleep

Near the Cymmerians, in his dark abode,
Deep in a cavern, dwells the drowzy God;
Whose gloomy mansion nor the rising sun,
Nor setting, visits, nor the lightsome noon;

But lazy vapours round the region fly,
Perpetual twilight, and a doubtful sky:
No crowing cock does there his wings display,
Nor with his horny bill provoke the day;
Nor watchful dogs, nor the more wakeful geese,
Disturb with nightly noise the sacred peace;
Nor beast of Nature, nor the tame are nigh,
Nor trees with tempests rock'd, nor human cry;
But safe repose without an air of breath
Dwells here, and a dumb quiet next to death.

An arm of Lethe, with a gentle flow
Arising upwards from the rock below,
The palace moats, and o'er the pebbles creeps,
And with soft murmurs calls the coming sleeps.
Around its entry nodding poppies grow,
And all cool simples that sweet rest bestow;
Night from the plants their sleepy virtue drains,
And passing, sheds it on the silent plains:
No door there was th' unguarded house to keep,
On creaking hinges turn'd, to break his sleep.

But in the gloomy court was rais'd a bed,
Stuff'd with black plumes, and on an ebon-sted:
Black was the cov'ring too, where lay the God,
And slept supine, his limbs display'd abroad:
About his head fantastic visions fly,
Which various images of things supply,
And mock their forms; the leaves on trees
not more,
Nor bearded ears in fields, nor sands upon
the shore.

The virgin ent'ring bright, indulg'd the day
To the brown cave, and brush'd the dreams away:
The God disturb'd with this new glare of light,
Cast sudden on his face, unseal'd his sight,

And rais'd his tardy head, which sunk again,
And sinking, on his bosom knock'd his chin;
At length shook off himself, and ask'd the dame,
(And asking yawn'd) for what intent she came.

To whom the Goddess thus: O sacred rest,
Sweet pleasing sleep, of all the Pow'rs the best!
O peace of mind, repairer of decay,
Whose balms renew the limbs to labours
of the day,
Care shuns thy soft approach, and sullen
flies away!
Adorn a dream, expressing human form,
The shape of him who suffer'd in the storm,
And send it flitting to the Trachin court,
The wreck of wretched Ceyx to report:
Before his queen bid the pale spectre stand,
Who begs a vain relief at Juno's hand.
She said, and scarce awake her eyes could keep,
Unable to support the fumes of sleep;
But fled, returning by the way she went,
And swerv'd along her bow with swift ascent.

The God, uneasy till he slept again,
Resolv'd at once to rid himself of pain;
And, tho' against his custom, call'd aloud,
Exciting Morpheus from the sleepy crowd:
Morpheus, of all his numerous train, express'd
The shape of man, and imitated best;
The walk, the words, the gesture could supply,
The habit mimic, and the mein bely;
Plays well, but all his action is confin'd,
Extending not beyond our human kind.
Another, birds, and beasts, and dragons apes,
And dreadful images, and monster shapes:
This demon, Icelos, in Heav'n's high hall
The Gods have nam'd; but men Phobetor call.

A third is Phantasus, whose actions roll
On meaner thoughts, and things devoid of soul;
Earth, fruits, and flow'rs he represents in dreams,
And solid rocks unmov'd, and running streams.
These three to kings, and chiefs their scenes display,
The rest before th' ignoble commons play.
Of these the chosen Morpheus is dispatch'd;
Which done, the lazy monarch, over-watch'd,
Down from his propping elbow drops his head,
Dissolv'd in sleep, and shrinks within his bed.

Darkling the demon glides, for flight prepar'd,
So soft, that scarce his fanning wings are heard.
To Trachin, swift as thought, the flitting shade,
Thro' air his momentary journey made:
Then lays aside the steerage of his wings,
Forsakes his proper form, assumes the king's;
And pale, as death, despoil'd of his array,
Into the queen's apartment takes his way,
And stands before the bed at dawn of day:
Unmov'd his eyes, and wet his beard appears;
And shedding vain, but seeming real tears;
The briny waters dropping from his hairs.
Then staring on her with a ghastly look,
And hollow voice, he thus the queen bespoke.

Know'st thou not me? Not yet, unhappy wife?
Or are my features perish'd with my life?
Look once again, and for thy husband lost,
Lo all that's left of him, thy husband's ghost!
Thy vows for my return were all in vain,
The stormy south o'ertook us in the main,
And never shalt thou see thy living lord again.
Bear witness, Heav'n, I call'd on thee in death,
And while I call'd, a billow stop'd my breath.
Think not, that flying fame reports my fate;
I present, I appear, and my own wreck relate.

Rise, wretched widow, rise; nor undeplor'd
Permit my soul to pass the Stygian ford;
But rise, prepar'd in black, to mourn thy
perish'd lord.

Thus said the player-God; and adding art
Of voice and gesture, so perform'd his part,
She thought (so like her love the shade appears)
That Ceyx spake the words, and Ceyx shed
the tears;
She groan'd, her inward soul with grief opprest,
She sigh'd, she wept, and sleeping beat her breast;
Then stretch'd her arms t' embrace his body bare;
Her clasping arms enclose but empty air:
At this, not yet awake, she cry'd, O stay;
One is our fate, and common is our way!

So dreadful was the dream, so loud she spoke,
That starting sudden up, the slumber broke:
Then cast her eyes around, in hope to view
Her vanish'd lord, and find the vision true:
For now the maids, who waited her commands,
Ran in with lighted tapers in their hands.
Tir'd with the search, not finding what she seeks,
With cruel blows she pounds her blubber'd cheeks;
Then from her beaten breast the linen tare,
And cut the golden caul that bound her hair.
Her nurse demands the cause; with louder cries
She prosecutes her griefs, and thus replies.

No more Alcyone; she suffer'd death
With her lov'd lord, when Ceyx lost his breath:
No flatt'ry, no false comfort, give me none,
My shipwreck'd Ceyx is for ever gone:
I saw, I saw him manifest in view,
His voice, his figure, and his gestures knew:
His lustre lost, and ev'ry living grace,

Yet I retain'd the features of his face;
Tho' with pale cheeks, wet beard,
 and dropping hair,
None but my Ceyx could appear so fair:
I would have strain'd him with a strict embrace,
But thro' my arms he slipt, and vanish'd
 from the place:
There, ev'n just there he stood; and as she spoke,
Where last the spectre was she cast her look:
Fain would she hope, and gaz'd upon the ground,
If any printed footsteps might be found.

Then sigh'd, and said: This I too well foreknew,
And my prophetic fears presag'd too true:
'Twas what I begg'd, when with a bleeding heart
I took my leave, and suffer'd thee to part;
Or I to go along, or thou to stay,
Never, ah never to divide our way!
Happier for me, that all our hours assign'd
Together we had liv'd; ev'n not in death disjoin'd!
So had my Ceyx still been living here,
Or with my Ceyx I had perish'd there:
Now I die absent, in the vast profound;
And me, without my self, the seas have drown'd.
The storms were not so cruel: should I strive
To lengthen life, and such a grief survive;
But neither will I strive, nor wretched thee
In death forsake, but keep thee company.
If not one common sepulchre contains
Our bodies, or one urn our last remains,
Yet Ceyx and Alcyone shall join,
Their names remember'd in one common line.

No farther voice her mighty grief affords,
For sighs come rushing in betwixt her words,
And stop'd her tongue; but what her
 tongue deny'd,

Soft tears, and groans, and dumb
complaints supply'd.

'Twas morning; to the port she takes her way,
And stands upon the margin of the sea:
That place, that very spot of ground she sought,
Or thither by her destiny was brought,
Where last he stood: and while she sadly said,
'Twas here he left me, lingering here delay'd
His parting kiss, and there his anchors weigh'd.

Thus speaking, while her thoughts
past actions trace,
And call to mind, admonish'd by the place,
Sharp at her utmost ken she cast her eyes,
And somewhat floating from afar descries:
It seems a corps a-drift to distant sight,
But at a distance who could judge aright?
It wafted nearer yet, and then she knew,
That what before she but surmis'd, was true:
A corps it was, but whose it was, unknown,
Yet mov'd, howe'er, she made the cause her own.
Took the bad omen of a shipwreck'd man,
As for a stranger wept, and thus began.

Poor wretch, on stormy seas to lose thy life,
Unhappy thou, but more thy widow'd wife;
At this she paus'd: for now the flowing tide
Had brought the body nearer to the side:
The more she looks, the more her fears increase,
At nearer sight; and she's her self the less:
Now driv'n ashore, and at her feet it lies,
She knows too much in knowing whom she sees:
Her husband's corps; at this she loudly shrieks,
'Tis he, 'Tis he, she cries, and tears her cheeks,
Her hair, and vest; and stooping to the sands,
About his neck she cast her trembling hands.

And is it thus, o dearer than my life,
Thus, thus return'st thou to thy longing wife!
She said, and to the neighb'ring mole she strode,
(Rais'd there to break th' incursions of the flood).

Headlong from hence to plunge herself
she springs,
But shoots along, supported on her wings;
A bird new-made, about the banks she plies,
Not far from shore, and short excursions tries;
Nor seeks in air her humble flight to raise,
Content to skim the surface of the seas:
Her bill tho' slender, sends a creaking noise,
And imitates a lamentable voice.
Now lighting where the bloodless body lies,
She with a fun'ral note renews her cries:
At all her stretch, her little wings she spread,
And with her feather'd arms embrac'd the dead:
Then flick'ring to his pallid lips, she strove
To print a kiss, the last essay of love.
Whether the vital touch reviv'd the dead,
Or that the moving waters rais'd his head
To meet the kiss, the vulgar doubt alone;
For sure a present miracle was shown.
The Gods their shapes to winter-birds translate,
But both obnoxious to their former fate.
Their conjugal affection still is ty'd,
And still the mournful race is multiply'd:
They bill, they tread; Alcyone compress'd,
Sev'n days sits brooding on her floating nest:
A wintry queen: her sire at length is kind,
Calms ev'ry storm, and hushes ev'ry wind;
Prepares his empire for his daughter's ease,
And for his hatching nephews smooths the seas.

Æsacus Transform'd into a Cormorant

These some old man sees wanton in the air,
And praises the unhappy constant pair.
Then to his friend the long-neck'd
corm'rant shows,
The former tale reviving others' woes:
That sable bird, he cries, which cuts the flood
With slender legs, was once of royal blood;
His ancestors from mighty Tros proceed,
The brave Laomedon, and Ganymede
(Whose beauty tempted Jove to steal the boy),
And Priam, hapless prince! who fell with Troy:
Himself was Hector's brother, and (had Fate
But giv'n this hopeful youth a longer date)
Perhaps had rival'd warlike Hector's worth,
Tho' on the mother's side of meaner birth;
Fair Alyxothoe, a country maid,
Bare Æsacus by stealth in Ida's shade.
He fled the noisy town, and pompous court,
Lov'd the lone hills, and simple rural sport.
And seldom to the city would resort.
Yet he no rustic clownishness profest,
Nor was soft love a stranger to his breast:
The youth had long the nymph Hesperie woo'd,
Oft thro' the thicket, or the mead pursu'd:
Her haply on her father's bank he spy'd,
While fearless she her silver tresses dry'd;
Away she fled: not stags with half such speed,
Before the prowling wolf, scud o'er the mead;
Not ducks, when they the safer flood forsake,
Pursu'd by hawks, so swift regain the lake.
As fast he follow'd in the hot career;
Desire the lover wing'd, the virgin fear.
A snake unseen now pierc'd her heedless foot;
Quick thro' the veins the venom'd juices shoot:

She fell, and 'scap'd by death his fierce pursuit;
Her lifeless body, frighted, he embrac'd,
And cry'd, Not this I dreaded, but thy haste:
O had my love been less, or less thy fear!
The victory, thus bought, is far too dear.
Accursed snake! yet I more curs'd than he!
He gave the wound; the cause was given by me.
Yet none shall say, that unreveng'd you dy'd.
He spoke; then climb'd a cliff's o'er-hanging side,
And, resolute, leap'd on the foaming tide.
Tethys receiv'd him gently on the wave;
The death he sought deny'd, and feathers gave.
Debarr'd the surest remedy of grief,
And forc'd to live, he curst th' unask'd relief.
Then on his airy pinions upward flies,
And at a second fall successless tries;
The downy plume a quick descent denies.
Enrag'd, he often dives beneath the wave,
And there in vain expects to find a grave.
His ceaseless sorrow for th' unhappy maid,
Meager'd his look, and on his spirits prey'd.
Still near the sounding deep he lives; his name
From frequent diving and emerging came.

Book XV

The Pythagorean Philosophy

A king is sought to guide the growing state,
One able to support the public weight
And fill the throne where Romulus had sate.
Renown, which oft bespeaks the public voice,
Had recommended Numa to their choice:
A peaceful, pious prince; who not content
To know the Sabine rites, his study bent
To cultivate his mind; to learn the laws
Of Nature, and explore their hidden cause.
Urg'd by this care, his country he forsook,
And to Crotona thence his journey took.
Arriv'd, he first inquir'd the founder's name
Of this new colony; and whence he came.
Then thus a senior of the place replies
(Well read, and curious of antiquities):
'Tis said, Alcides hither took his way
From Spain, and drove along his conquer'd prey;
Then, leaving in the fields his grazing cows,
He sought himself some hospitable house:
Good Croton entertain'd his godlike guest;
While he repair'd his weary limbs with rest.
The hero, thence departing, bless'd the place;
And here, he said, in time's revolving race,
A rising town shall take his name from thee.
Revolving time fulfill'd the prophecy:
For Myscelos, the justest man on Earth,
Alemon's son, at Argos had his birth:
Him Hercules, arm'd with his club of oak,

O'ershadow'd in a dream, and thus bespoke:
Go, leave thy native soil, and make abode,
Where Æsaris rolls down his rapid flood:
He said; and sleep forsook him, and the God.
Trembling he wak'd, and rose with anxious heart;
His country laws forbad him to depart:
What shou'd he do? 'Twas death to go away,
And the God menac'd, if he dar'd to stay.
All day he doubted, and when night came on,
Sleep, and the same forewarning dream, begun:
Once more the God stood threatening o'er his head;
With added curses if he disobey'd.
Twice warn'd, he study'd flight; but wou'd convey,
At once, his person, and his wealth away:
Thus while he linger'd, his design was heard;
A speedy process form'd, and death declar'd.
Witness there needed none of his offence;
Against himself the wretch was evidence:
Condemn'd, and destitute of human aid,
To him, for whom he suffer'd, thus he pray'd.
O Pow'r, who hast deserv'd in Heav'n a throne,
Not giv'n, but by thy labours made thy own,
Pity thy suppliant, and protect his cause,
Whom thou hast made obnoxious to the laws.
A custom was of old, and still remains,
Which life, or death by suffrages ordains:
White stones, and black within an urn are cast;
The first absolve, but Fate is in the last.
The judges to the common urn bequeath
Their votes, and drop the sable signs of death;
The box receives all black, but, pour'd from thence,
The stones came candid forth; the hue of innocence.
Thus Alemonides his safety won,

Preserv'd from death by Alcumena's son:
Then to his kinsman-God his vows he pays,
And cuts with prosp'rous gales th' Ionian seas:
He leaves Tarentum favour'd by the wind,
And Thurine bays, and Ternises, behind;
Soft Sybaris, and all the capes that stand
Along the shore, he makes in sight of land;
Still doubling, and still coasting, till he found
The mouth of Æsaris, and promis'd ground;
Then saw, where, on the margin of the flood,
The tomb, that held the bones of Croton stood:
Here, by the Gods' command, he built, and wall'd
The place predicted; and Crotona call'd.
Thus Fame, from time to time, delivers down
The sure tradition of th' Italian town.
Here dwelt the man divine, whom Samos bore,
But now self-banish'd from his native shore,
Because he hated tyrants, nor cou'd bear
The chains, which none but servile souls will wear.
He, tho' from Heav'n remote, to Heav'n cou'd move,
With strength of mind, and tread th' abyss above;
And penetrate, with his interior light,
Those upper depths, which Nature hid from sight:
And what he had observ'd, and learnt from thence,
Lov'd in familiar language to dispense.
The crowd with silent admiration stand,
And heard him, as they heard their God's command;
While he discours'd of Heav'n's mysterious laws,
The world's original, and Nature's cause;
And what was God; and why the fleecy snows
In silence fell, and rattling winds arose;

What shook the steadfast Earth,
    and whence begun
The dance of planets round the radiant sun;
If thunder was the voice of angry Jove,
Or clouds, with nitre pregnant, burst above:
Of these, and things beyond the common reach,
He spoke, and charm'd his audience with
    his speech.
He first the taste of flesh from tables drove,
And argu'd well, if arguments cou'd move:
O mortals, from your fellows' blood abstain,
Nor taint your bodies with a food profane:
While corn, and pulse by Nature are bestow'd,
And planted orchards bend their willing load;
While labour'd gardens wholesome herbs produce,
And teeming vines afford their gen'rous juice;
Nor tardier fruits of cruder kind are lost,
But tam'd with fire, or mellow'd by the frost;
While kine to pails distended udders bring,
And bees their honey redolent of Spring;
While Earth not only can your needs supply,
But, lavish of her store, provides for luxury;
A guiltless feast administers with ease,
And without blood is prodigal to please.
Wild beasts their maws with their slain brethren fill;
And yet not all, for some refuse to kill;
Sheep, goats, and oxen, and the nobler steed,
On browz, and corn, and flow'ry meadows, feed.
Bears, tigers, wolves, the Lyon's angry brood,
Whom Heav'n endu'd with principles of blood,
He wisely sundered from the rest, to yell
In forests, and in lonely caves to dwell;
Where stronger beasts oppress the weak by might,
And all in prey, and purple feasts delight.
O impious use! to Nature's laws oppos'd,
Where bowels are in other bowels clos'd:
Where fatten'd by their fellow's fat, they thrive;

Maintain'd by murder, and by death they live.
'Tis then for nought, that Mother Earth provides
The stores of all she shows, and all she hides,
If men with fleshy morsels must be fed,
And chaw with bloody teeth the breathing bread:
What else is this, but to devour our guests,
And barb'rously renew Cyclopean feasts!
We, by destroying life, our life sustain;
And gorge th' ungodly maw with meats obscene.
Not so the Golden Age, who fed on fruit,
Nor durst with bloody meals their mouths pollute.
Then birds in airy space might safely move,
And tim'rous hares on heaths securely rove:
Nor needed fish the guileful hooks to fear,
For all was peaceful; and that peace sincere.
Whoever was the wretch (and curs'd be he)
That envy'd first our food's simplicity,
Th' essay of bloody feasts on brutes began,
And after forg'd the sword to murder Man.
Had he the sharpen'd steel alone employ'd
On beasts of prey; that other beasts destroy'd,
Or Man invaded with their fangs and paws,
This had been justify'd by Nature's laws,
And self-defense: but who did feasts begin
Of flesh, he stretch'd necessity to sin.
To kill man-killers, Man has lawful pow'r,
But not th' extended license, to devour.
Ill habits gather by unseen degrees,
As brooks make rivers, rivers run to seas.
The sow, with her broad snout, for rooting up
Th' entrusted seed, was judg'd to spoil the crop,
And intercept the sweating farmer's hope:
The covetous churl, of unforgiving kind,
Th' offender to the bloody priest resign'd:
Her hunger was no plea: for that she dy'd.
The goat came next in order to be try'd:
The goat had cropt the tendrils of the vine:

In vengeance laity, and clergy join,
Where one had lost his profit, one his wine.
Here was, at least, some shadow of offence;
The sheep was sacrific'd on no pretense,
But meek, and unresisting innocence.
A patient, useful creature, born to bear
The warm, and woolly fleece, that cloth'd
her murderer;
And daily to give down the milk she bred,
A tribute for the grass on which she fed.
Living, both food and raiment she supplies,
And is of least advantage, when she dies.
How did the toiling ox his death deserve,
A downright simple drudge, and born to serve?
O tyrant! with what justice canst thou hope
The promise of the year, a plenteous crop;
When thou destroy'st thy lab'ring steer, who till'd,
And plough'd with pains, thy else ungrateful field?
From his yet reeking neck, to draw the yoke,
That neck, with which the surly clods he broke;
And to the hatchet yield thy husbandman,
Who finish'd Autumn, and the Spring began!
Nor this alone! but Heav'n it self to bribe,
We to the Gods our impious acts ascribe:
First recompense with death their creatures' toil;
Then call the bless'd above to share the spoil:
The fairest victim must the Pow'rs appease
(So fatal 'tis sometimes too much to please!),
A purple fillet his broad brows adorns,
With flow'ry garlands crown'd, and gilded horns:
He hears the murd'rous pray'r the priest prefers,
But understands not, 'tis his doom he hears:
Beholds the meal betwixt his temples cast
(The fruit and product of his labours past);
And in the water views perhaps the knife
Uplifted, to deprive him of his life;
Then broken up alive, his entrails sees

Torn out, for priests t' inspect the Gods' decrees.
From whence, o mortal men, this gust of blood
Have you deriv'd, and interdicted food?
Be taught by me this dire delight to shun,
Warn'd by my precepts, by my practice won:
And when you eat the well-deserving beast,
Think, on the lab'rour of your field you feast!
Now since the God inspires me to proceed,
Be that, whate'er inspiring Pow'r, obey'd.
For I will sing of mighty mysteries,
Of truths conceal'd before, from human eyes,
Dark oracles unveil and open all the skies.
Pleas'd as I am to walk along the sphere
Of shining stars, and travel with the year,
To leave the heavy Earth, and scale the height
Of Atlas, who supports the heav'nly weight;
To look from upper light, and thence survey
Mistaken mortals wand'ring from the way,
And wanting wisdom, fearful for the state
Of future things, and trembling at their Fate!
Those I would teach; and by right reason bring
To think of death, as but an idle thing.
Why thus affrighted at an empty name,
A dream of darkness, and fictitious flame?
Vain themes of wit, which but in poems pass,
And fables of a world, that never was!
What feels the body, when the soul expires,
By time corrupted, or consum'd by fires?
Nor dies the spirit, but new life repeats
In other forms, and only changes seats.
Ev'n I, who these mysterious truths declare,
Was once Eupborbus in the Trojan war;
My name, and lineage I remember well,
And how in fight by Sparta's king I fell.
In Argive Juno's fane I late beheld
My buckler hung on high, and own'd my
former shield.

Then, death, so call'd, is but old matter dress'd
In some new figure, and a vary'd vest:
Thus all things are but alter'd, nothing dies;
And here, and there th' unbody'd spirit flies.
By time, or force, or sickness dispossest,
And lodges, where it lights, in man or beast;
Or hunts without, till ready limbs it find,
And actuates those according to their kind;
From tenement to tenement is toss'd,
The soul is still the same, the figure only lost:
And, as the soften'd wax new seals receives,
This face assumes, and that impression leaves;
Now call'd by one, now by another name;
The form is only chang'd, the wax is still
the same:
So death, so call'd, can but the form deface;
Th' immortal soul flies out in empty space,
To seek her fortune in some other place.
Then let not piety be put to flight,
To please the taste of glutton appetite;
But suffer inmate souls secure to dwell,
Lest from their seats your parents you expel;
With rabid hunger feed upon your kind,
Or from a beast dislodge a brother's mind.
And since, like Typhis parting from the shore,
In ample seas I sail, and depths untry'd before,
This let me further add, that Nature knows
No steadfast station, but, or ebbs, or flows:
Ever in motion; she destroys her old,
And casts new figures in another mold.
Ev'n times are in perpetual flux, and run,
Like rivers from their fountain, rolling on,
For time, no more than streams, is at a stay;
The flying hour is ever on her way:
And as the fountain still supplies her store,
The wave behind impels the wave before;
Thus in successive course the minutes run,

And urge their predecessor minutes on,
Till moving, ever new: for former things
Are set aside, like abdicated kings:
And every moment alters what is done,
And innovates some act, till then unknown.
Darkness we see emerges into light,
And shining suns descend to sable night;
Ev'n Heav'n it self receives another dye,
When weary'd animals in slumbers lie
Of midnight ease: another, when the gray
Of morn preludes the splendor of the day.
The disk of Phœbus, when he climbs on high,
Appears at first but as a bloodshot eye;
And when his chariot downwards drives to bed.
His ball is with the same suffusion red;
But mounted high in his meridian race
All bright he shines, and with a better face:
For there, pure particles of Æther flow,
Far from th' infection of the world below.
Nor equal light th' unequal Moon adorns,
Or in her waxing, or her waning horns,
For ev'ry day she wanes, her face is less;
But gath'ring into globe, she fattens at increase.
Perceiv'st thou not the process of the year,
How the four seasons in four forms appear,
Resembling human life in ev'ry shape they wear?
Spring first, like infancy, shoots out her head,
With milky juice requiring to be fed:
Helpless, tho' fresh, and wanting to be led.
The green stem grows in stature, and in size,
But only feeds with hope the farmer's eyes;
Then laughs the childish year with
flow'rets crown'd,
And lavishly perfumes the fields around,
But no substantial nourishment receives;
Infirm the stalks, unsolid are the leaves.
Proceeding onward whence the year began,

The Summer grows adult, and ripens into Man.
This season, as in men, is most replete
With kindly moisture, and prolific heat.
Autumn succeeds, a sober tepid age,
Not froze with fear, nor boiling into rage;
More than mature, and tending to decay,
When our brown locks repine to mix with
odious gray.
Last, Winter creeps along with tardy pace,
Sour is his front, and furrow'd is his face;
His scalp if not dishonour'd quite of hair,
The ragged fleece is thin; and thin is worse
than bare.
Ev'n our own bodies daily change receive,
Some part of what was theirs before, they leave;
Nor are to-day, what yesterday they were;
Nor the whole same to-morrow will appear.
Time was, when we were sow'd, and just began,
From some few fruitful drops,
the promise of a man:
Then Nature's hand (fermented as it was)
Moulded to shape the soft, coagulated mass;
And when the little man was fully form'd,
The breathless embryo with a spirit warm'd;
But when the mother's throws begin to come,
The creature, pent within the narrow room,
Breaks his blind prison, pushing to repair
His stifled breath, and draw the living air;
Cast on the margin of the world he lies,
A helpless babe, but by instinct he cries.
He next essays to walk, but downward press'd
On four feet imitates his brother beast:
By slow degrees he gathers from the ground
His legs, and to the rolling chair is bound;
Then walks alone; a horseman now become,
He rides a stick, and travels round the room.
In time he vaunts among his youthful peers,

Strong-bon'd, and strung with nerves, in pride of years,
He runs with mettle his first merry stage,
Maintains the next, abated of his rage,
But manages his strength, and spares his age.
Heavy the third, and stiff, he sinks apace,
And tho' tis down hill all, but creeps along the race.
Now sapless on the verge of death he stands,
Contemplating his former feet and hands;
And, Milo-like, his slacken'd sinews sees,
And wither'd arms, once fit to cope with Hercules,
Unable now to shake, much less to tear, the trees.
So Helen wept, when her too faithful glass
Reflected on her eyes the ruins of her face:
Wondering, what charms her ravishers cou'd spy,
To force her twice, or ev'n but once t' enjoy!
Thy teeth, devouring time, thine, envious age,
On things below still exercise your rage:
With venom'd grinders you corrupt your meat,
And then, at lingering meals, the morsels eat.
Nor those, which elements we call, abide,
Nor to this figure, nor to that are ty'd;
For this eternal world is said, of old,
But four prolific principles to hold,
Four different bodies; two to Heav'n ascend,
And other two down to the center tend:
Fire first with wings expanded mounts on high,
Pure, void of weight, and dwells in upper sky;
Then air, because unclog'd in empty space,
Flies after fire, and claims the second place:
But weighty water, as her nature guides,
Lies on the lap of Earth; and Mother
        Earth subsides.
All things are mix'd of these, which all contain,
And into these are all resolv'd again:
Earth rarifies to dew; expanded more,
The subtle dew in air begins to soar;
Spreads, as she flies, and weary of her name

Extenuates still, and changes into flame;
Thus having by degrees perfection won,
Restless they soon untwist the web, they spun,
And fire begins to lose her radiant hue,
Mix'd with gross air, and air descends to dew;
And dew condensing, does her form forego,
And sinks, a heavy lump of Earth below.
Thus are their figures never at a stand,
But chang'd by Nature's innovating hand;
All things are alter'd, nothing is destroy'd,
The shifted scene for some new show employ'd.
Then, to be born, is to begin to be
Some other thing we were not formerly:
And what we call to die, is not t' appear,
Or be the thing, that formerly we were.
Those very elements, which we partake
Alive, when dead some other bodies make:
Translated grow, have sense, or can discourse;
But death on deathless substance has no force.
That forms are chang'd, I grant; that nothing can
Continue in the figure it began:
The golden age, to silver was debas'd:
To copper that; our metal came at last.
The face of places, and their forms, decay;
And that is solid Earth, that once was sea:
Seas in their turn retreating from the shore,
Make solid land, what ocean was before;
And far from strands are shells of fishes found,
And rusty anchors fix'd on mountain-ground:
And what were fields before, now wash'd and worn
By falling floods from high, to valleys turn,
And crumbling still descend to level lands;
And lakes, and trembling bogs, are barren sands.
And the parch'd desert floats in streams unknown;
Wandering to drink of waters not her own.
Here Nature living fountains opes; and there
Seals up the wombs, where living fountains were;

Or earthquakes stop their ancient course, and bring
Diverted streams to feed a distant spring.
So Licus, swallow'd up, is seen no more,
But far from thence knocks out another door.
Thus Erasinus dives; and blind in Earth
Runs on, and gropes his way to second birth,
Starts up in Argos' meads, and shakes his locks
Around the fields, and fattens all the flocks.
So Mysus by another way is led,
And, grown a river, now disdains his head:
Forgets his humble birth, his name forsakes,
And the proud title of Caïcus takes.
Large Amenane, impure with yellow sands,
Runs rapid often, and as often stands,
And here he threats the drunken fields to drown;
And there his dugs deny to give their liquor down.
Anigros once did wholesome draughts afford,
But now his deadly waters are abhorr'd:
Since, hurt by Hercules, as Fame resounds,
The centaurs in his current wash'd their wounds.
The streams of Hypanis are sweet no more,
But brackish lose the taste they had before.
Antissa, Pharos, Tyre, in seas were pent,
Once isles, but now increase the continent;
While the Leucadian coast, main land before,
By rushing seas is sever'd from the shore.
So Zancle to th' Italian earth was ty'd,
And men once walk'd, where ships at anchor ride.
Till Neptune overlook'd the narrow way,
And in disdain pour'd in the conqu'ring sea.
Two cities that adorn'd th' Achaian ground,
Buris, and Helice, no more are found,
But whelm'd beneath a lake, are sunk and drown'd;
And boatsmen through the crystal water show,
To wondering passengers, the walls below.
Near Traten stands a hill, expos'd in air
To winter-winds, of leafy shadows bare:

This once was level ground: but (strange to tell)
Th' included vapours, that in caverns dwell,
Lab'ring with cholic pangs; and close confin'd,
In vain sought issue for the rumbling wind:
Yet still they heav'd for vent, and heaving still
Enlarg'd the concave, and shot up the hill;
As breath extends a bladder, or the skins
Of goats are blown t' enclose the hoarded wines:
The mountain yet retains a mountain's face,
And gather'd rubbish heals the hollow space.
Of many wonders, which I heard, or knew,
Retrenching most, I will relate but few:
What, are not springs with qualities oppos'd,
Endu'd at seasons, and at seasons lost?
Thrice in a day thine, Ammon, change their form,
Cold at high noon, at morn, and evening warm:
Thine, Athaman, will kindle wood, if thrown
On the pil'd earth, and in the waning moon.
The Thracians have a stream, if any try
The taste, his harden'd bowels petrify;
Whate'er it touches, it converts to stones,
And makes a marble pavement, where it runs.
Crathis, and Sybaris her sister flood,
That slide through our Calabrian
neighbour wood,
With gold, and amber dye the shining hair,
And thither youth resort (for who would
not be fair?).
But stranger virtues yet in streams we find,
Some change not only bodies, but the mind:
Who has not heard of Salmacis obscene,
Whose waters into women soften men?
Or Æthiopian lakes, which turn the brain
To madness, or in heavy sleep constrain?
Clytorian streams the love of wine expel
(Such is the virtue of th' abstemious well),
Whether the colder nymph that rules the flood

Extinguishes, and balks the drunken God;
Or that Melampus (so have some assur'd)
When the mad Prœtides with charms he cur'd,
And pow'rful herbs, both charms, and simples cast
Into the sober spring, where still their virtues last.
Unlike effects Lyncestis will produce;
Who drinks his waters, tho' with mod'rate use,
Reels as with wine, and sees with double sight:
His heels too heavy, and his head too light.
Ladon, once Pheneos, an Arcadian stream
(Ambiguous in th' effects, as in the name),
By day is wholesome bev'rage; but is thought
By night infected, and a deadly draught.
Thus running rivers, and the standing lake,
Now of these virtues, now of those partake:
Time was (and all things time, and Fate obey)
When fast Ortygia floated on the sea;
Such were Cyanean isles, when Typhis steer'd
Betwixt their straights, and their collision fear'd;
They swam, where now they sit; and firmly join'd
Secure of rooting up, resist the wind.
Nor Ætna vomiting sulphurous fire
Will ever belch; for sulphur will expire
(The veins exhausted of the liquid store):
Time was, she cast no flames;
in time will cast no more.
For whether Earth's an animal, and air
Imbibes; her lungs with coolness to repair,
And what she sucks remits; she still requires
Inlets for air, and outlets for her fires;
When tortur'd with convulsive fits she shakes,
That motion chokes the vent,
till other vent she makes:
Or when the winds in hollow caves are clos'd,
And subtle spirits find that way oppos'd,
They toss up flints in air; the flints that hide
The seeds of fire, thus toss'd in air, collide,

Kindling the sulphur, till the fuel spent
The cave is cool' d, and the fierce winds relent.
Or whether sulphur, catching fire, feeds on
Its unctuous parts, till all the matter gone
The flames no more ascend; for Earth supplies
The fat that feeds them; and when Earth denies
That food, by length of time consum'd, the fire
Famish'd for want of fuel must expire.
A race of men there are, as Fame has told,
Who shiv'ring suffer Hyperborean cold,
Till nine times bathing in Minerva's lake,
Soft feathers, to defend their naked sides, they take.
'Tis said, the Scythian wives (believe who will)
Transform themselves to birds by magic skill;
Smear'd over with an oil of wond'rous might,
That adds new pinions to their airy flight.
But this by sure experiment we know,
That living creatures from corruption grow:
Hide in a hollow pit a slaughter'd steer,
Bees from his putrid bowels will appear;
Who, like their parents, haunt the fields, and bring
Their honey-harvest home, and hope another Spring.
The warlike-steed is multiply'd, we find,
To wasps, and hornets of the warrior kind.
Cut from a crab his crooked claws, and hide
The rest in Earth, a scorpion thence will glide,
And shoot his sting, his tail in circles toss'd
Refers the limbs his backward father lost:
And worms, that stretch on leaves their filmy loom,
Crawl from their bags, and butterflies become.
Ev'n slime begets the frog's loquacious race:
Short of their feet at first, in little space
With arms, and legs endu'd, long leaps they take
Rais'd on their hinder part, and swim the lake,

And waves repel: for Nature gives their kind,
To that intent, a length of legs behind.
The cubs of bears a living lump appear,
When whelp'd, and no determin'd figure wear.
Their mother licks 'em into shape, and gives
As much of form, as she her self receives.
The grubs from their sexangular abode
Crawl out unfinish'd, like the maggot's brood:
Trunks without limbs; 'till time at leisure brings
The thighs they wanted, and their tardy wings.
The bird who draws the carr of Juno, vain
Of her crown'd head, and of her starry train;
And he that bears th' Artillery of Jove,
The strong-pounc'd eagle, and the billing dove;
And all the feather'd kind, who cou'd suppose
(But that from sight, the surest sense, he knows)
They from th' included yolk,
        not ambient white, arose.
There are, who think the marrow of a man,
Which in the spine, while he was living, ran;
When dead, the pith corrupted will become
A snake, and hiss within the hollow tomb.
All these receive their birth from other things;
But from himself the Phoenix only springs:
Self-born, begotten by the parent flame
In which he burn'd, another, and the same;
Who not by corn, or herbs his life sustains,
But the sweet essence of Amomum drains:
And watches the rich gums Arabia bears,
While yet in tender dew they drop their tears.
He (his five centuries of life fulfill'd)
His nest on oaken boughs begins to build,
Or trembling tops of palm, and first he draws
The plan with his broad bill, and crooked claws,
Nature's artificers; on this the pile
Is form'd, and rises round, then with the spoil
Of Casia, Cynamon, and stems of Nard

(For softness strew'd beneath) his fun'ral
bed is rear'd:
Fun'ral and bridal both; and all around
The borders with corruptless myrrh are crown'd,
On this incumbent; till ætherial flame
First catches, then consumes the costly frame:
Consumes him too, as on the pile he lies;
He liv'd on odours, and in odours dies.
An infant Phœnix from the former springs,
His father's heir, and from his tender wings
Shakes off his parent dust, his method
he pursues,
And the same lease of life on the
same terms renews.
When grown to manhood he begins his reign,
And with stiff pinions can his flight sustain,
He lightens of its load the tree that bore
His father's royal sepulcher before,
And his own cradle: this (with pious care
Plac'd on his back) he cuts the buxom air,
Seeks the Sun's city, and his sacred church,
And decently lays down his burden in the porch.
A wonder more amazing wou'd we find?
Th' Hyæna shows it, of a double kind,
Varying the sexes in alternate years,
In one begets, and in another bears.
The thin Camelion fed with air, receives
The colour of the thing, to which he cleaves.
India when conquer'd, on the conqu'ring God
For planted vines the sharp-ey'd Lynx bestow'd,
Whose urine, shed before it touches Earth,
Congeals in air, and gives to gems their birth.
So Coral soft, and white in ocean's bed,
Comes harden'd up in air, and glows with red.
All changing species should my song recite;
Before I ceas'd, wou'd change the day to night.
Nations, and empires flourish, and decay,

By turns command, and in their turns obey;
Time softens hardy people, time again
Hardens to war a soft, unwarlike train.
Thus Troy for ten long years her foes withstood,
And daily bleeding bore th' expense of blood:
Now for thick streets it shows an empty space,
Or only fill'd with tombs of her own perish'd race,
Her self becomes the sepulcher of what she was.
Mycené, Sparta, Thebes of mighty fame,
Are vanish'd out of substance into name.
And Dardan Rome that just begins to rise,
On Tiber's banks, in time shall mate the skies:
Widening her bounds, and working on her way;
Ev'n now she meditates imperial sway:
Yet this is change, but she by changing thrives,
Like moons new-born, and in her cradle strives
To fill her infant-horns; an hour shall come,
When the round world shall be contain'd in Rome.
For thus old saws foretell, and Helenus
Anchises' drooping son enliven'd thus:
When Ilium now was in a sinking state;
And he was doubtful of his future fate:
O Goddess-born, with thy hard fortune strive,
Troy never can be lost, and thou alive.
Thy passage thou shalt free through fire,
and sword,
And Troy in foreign lands shall be restor'd.
In happier fields a rising town I see
Greater, than what e'er was, or is, or e'er shall be:
And Heav'n yet owes the world a race
deriv'd from thee.
Sages, and chiefs, of other lineage born,
The city shall extend, extended shall adorn:
But from lulus he must draw his breath,
By whom thy Rome shall rule the
conquer'd Earth:
Whom Heav'n will lend Mankind on
Earth to reign,

And late require the precious pledge again.
This Helenus to great Æneas told,
Which I retain, e'er since in other mould
My soul was cloth'd; and now rejoice to view
My country walls rebuilt, and Troy reviv'd anew,
Rais'd by the fall, decreed by loss to gain;
Enslav'd but to be free, and conquer'd but to reign.
'Tis time my hard-mouth'd coursers to control,
Apt to run riot, and transgress the goal:
And therefore I conclude, Whatever lies,
In Earth, or flits in air, or fills the skies,
All suffer change; and we, that are of soul
And body mix'd, are members of the whole.
Then when our sires, or grandsires, shall forsake
The forms of men, and brutal figures take,
Thus hous'd, securely let their spirits rest,
Nor violate thy father in the beast,
Thy friend, thy brother, any of thy kin,
If none of these, yet there's a man within:
O spare to make a Thyestæan meal,
T' enclose his body, and his soul expel.
Ill customs by degrees to habits rise,
Ill habits soon become exalted vice:
What more advance can mortals make in sin
So near perfection, who with blood begin?
Deaf to the calf, that lyes beneath the knife,
Looks up, and from her butcher begs her life:
Deaf to the harmless kid, that ere he dies
All methods to procure thy mercy tries,
And imitates in vain thy children's cries.
Where will he stop, who feeds with household bread,
Then eats the poultry, which before he fed?
Let plough thy steers; that when they lose their breath,
To Nature, not to thee, they may impute their death.

Let goats for food their loaded udders lend,
And sheep from winter-cold thy sides defend;
But neither sprindges, nets, nor snares employ,
And be no more ingenious to destroy.
Free as in air, let birds on Earth remain,
Nor let insidious glue their wings constrain;
Nor opening hounds the trembling stag affright,
Nor purple feathers intercept his flight:
Nor hooks conceal'd in baits for fish prepare,
Nor lines to heave 'em twinkling up in air.
Take not away the life you cannot give,
For all things have an equal right to live.
Kill noxious creatures, where 'tis sin to save;
This only just prerogative we have:
But nourish life with vegetable food,
And shun the sacrilegious taste of blood.
These precepts by the Samian sage were taught,
Which God-like Numa to the Sabines brought,
And thence transferr'd to Rome, by gift his own:
A willing people, and an offer'd throne.
O happy monarch, sent by Heav'n to bless
A salvage nation with soft arts of peace,
To teach religion, rapine to restrain,
Give laws to lust, and sacrifice ordain:
Himself a saint, a Goddess was his bride,
And all the Muses o'er his acts preside.

The Story of Hippolytus

Advanc'd in years he dy'd; one common date
His reign concluded, and his mortal state.
Their tears plebeians, and patricians shed,
And pious matrons wept their monarch dead.
His mournful wife, her sorrows to bewail,
Withdrew from Rome, and sought th' Arician vale.

Hid in thick woods, she made incessant moans,
Disturbing Cinthia's sacred rites with groans.
How oft the nymphs, who rul'd the wood and lake,
Reprov'd her tears, and words of comfort spice!
How oft (in vain) the son of Theseus said,
Thy stormy sorrows be with patience laid;
Nor are thy fortunes to be wept alone,
Weigh others' woes, and learn to bear thine own,
Be mine an instance to assuage thy grief:
Would mine were none!—yet mine may bring relief.
You've heard, perhaps, in conversation told,
What once befell Hippolytus of old;
To death by Theseus' easy faith betray'd,
And caught in snares his wicked step-dame laid.
The wondrous tale your credit scarce may claim,
Yet (strange to say) in me behold the same,
Whom lustful Phædra oft had press'd in vain,
With impious joys, my father's bed to stain;
Till seiz'd with fear, or by revenge inspir'd,
She charg'd on me the crimes herself desir'd.
Expell'd by Theseus, from his home I fled
With heaps of curses on my guiltless head.
Forlorn, I sought Pitthëan Trœzen's land,
And drove my chariot o'er Corinthus' strand;
When from the surface of the level main
A billow rising, heav'd above the plain;
Rolling, and gath'ring, till so high it swell'd,
A mountain's height th' enormous mass excell'd;
Then bellowing, burst; when from the summit cleav'd,
A horned bull his ample chest upheav'd.
His mouth, and nostrils, storms of briny rain,
Expiring, blew. Dread horror seiz'd my train.
I stood unmov'd. My father's cruel doom

Claim'd all my soul, nor fear could find a room.
Amaz'd, awhile my trembling coursers stood
With prick'd up ears, contemplating the flood;
Then starting sudden, from the dreadful view,
At once, like lightning, from the seas they flew,
And o'er the craggy rocks the rattling
chariot drew.
In vain to stop the hot-mouth'd steeds I try'd,
And bending backward all my strength apply'd;
The frothy foam in driving flakes disdains
The bits, and bridles, and bedews the reins.
But tho', as yet untam'd they run, at length
Their heady rage had tir'd beneath my strength,
When in the spokes, a stump entangling, tore
The shatter'd wheel, and from its axle bore.
The shock impetuous tossed me from the seat,
Caught in the reins beneath my horse's feet.
My reeking guts drag'd out alive, around
The jagged strump, my trembling nerves
were wound,
Then stretch'd the well-knit limbs,
in pieces hal'd,
Part stuck behind, and part the chariot trail'd;
Till, midst my cracking joints, and breaking bones,
I breath'd away my weary'd soul in groans.
No part distinguish'd from the rest was found,
But all my parts an universal wound.
Now say, self-tortur'd nymph, can you compare
Our griefs as equal, or in justice dare?
I saw besides the darksome realms of woe,
And bath'd my wounds in smoking streams below.
There I had staid, nor second life enjoy'd,
But Pœan's son his wondrous art employ'd.
To light restor'd, by medicinal skill,
In spite of Fate, and rigid Pluto's will,
Th' invidious object to preserve from view,
A misty cloud around me Cynthia threw;

And lest my sight should stir my foes to rage,
She stamp'd my visage with the marks of age.
My former hue was chang'd, and for it shown
A set of features, and a face unknown.
A-while the Goddess stood in doubt, or Crete,
Or Delos' isle, to choose for my retreat.
Delos, and Crete refus'd, this wood she chose,
Bad me my former luckless name depose,
Which kept alive the mem'ry of my woes;
Then said, Immortal life be thine; and thou,
Hippolytus once call'd, be Virbius now.
Here then a God, but of th' inferior race,
I serve my Goddess, and attend her chase.

Egeria Transform'd to a Fountain

But others' woes were useless to appease
Egeria's grief, or set her mind at ease.
Beneath the hill, all comfortless she laid,
The dropping tears her eyes incessant shed,
Till pitying Phœbe eas'd her pious woe,
Thaw'd to a spring, whose streams for ever flow.
The nymphs, and Virbius, like amazement fill'd,
As seiz'd the swains, who Tyrrhene furrows till'd;
When heaving up, a clod was seen to roll,
Untouch'd, self-mov'd, and big with human soul.
The spreading mass in former shape depos'd,
Began to shoot, and arms and legs disclos'd,
Till form'd a perfect man, the living mold
Op'd its new mouth, and future truths foretold;
And Tages nam'd by natives of the place,
Taught arts prophetic to the Tuscan race.
Or such as once by Romulus was shown,
Who saw his lance with sprouting
leaves o'er-grown,

When fix'd in Earth the point began to shoot,
And growing downward turn'd a fibrous root;
While spread aloft the branching arms display'd,
O'er wondering crowds, an unexpected shade.

The Story of Cippus

Or as when Cippus in the current view'd
The shooting horns that on his forehead stood,
His temples first he feels, and with surprise
His touch confirms th' assurance of his eyes.
Straight to the skies his horned front he rears,
And to the Gods directs these pious pray'rs.
If this portent be prosp'rous, O decree
To Rome th' event; if otherwise, to me.
An altar then of turf he hastes to raise,
Rich gums in fragrant exhalations blaze;
The panting entrails crackle as they fry,
And boding fumes pronounce a mystery,
Soon as the augur saw the holy fire,
And victims with presaging signs expire,
To Cippus then he turns his eyes with speed,
And views the horny honours of his head:
Then cry'd, Hail conqueror! thy call obey,
Those omens I behold presage thy sway.
Rome waits thy nod, unwilling to be free,
And owns thy sov'reign pow'r as Fate's decree.
He said—and Cippus, starting at th' event,
Spoke in these words his pious discontent.
Far hence, ye Gods, this execration send,
And the great race of Romulus defend.
Better that I in exile live abhorr'd,
Than e'er the Capitol shou'd style me lord.
This spoke, he hides with leaves his omen'd head.
Then prays, the senate next convenes, and said:

If augurs can foresee, a wretch is come,
Design'd by destiny the bane of Rome.
Two horns (most strange to tell)
his temples crown;
If e'er he pass the walls, and gain the town,
Your laws are forfeit, that ill-fated hour;
And liberty must yield to lawless pow'r.
Your gates he might have enter'd; but this arm
Seiz'd the usurper, and with-held the harm.
Haste, find the monster out, and let him be
Condemn'd to all the senate can decree;
Or ty'd in chains, or into exile thrown;
Or by the tyrant's death prevent your own.
The crowd such murmurs utter as they stand,
As swelling surges breaking on the strand;
Or as when gath'ring gales sweep o'er the grove,
And their tall heads the bending cedars move.
Each with confusion gaz'd, and then began
To feel his fellow's brows, and find the man.
Cippus then shakes his garland off, and cries,
The wretch you want, I offer to your eyes.
The anxious throng look'd down,
and sad in thought,
All wish'd they had not found
the sign they sought:
In haste with laurel wreaths his head they bind;
Such honour to such virtue was assign'd.
Then thus the senate—Hear, o Cippus, hear;
So god-like is thy tutelary care,
That since in Rome thy self forbids thy stay,
For thy abode those acres we convey
The plough-share can surround,
the labour of a day.
In deathless records thou shalt stand enroll'd,
And Rome's rich posts shall shine
with horns of gold.

The Occasion of Æsulapius being brought to Rome

Melodious maids of Pindus, who inspire
The flowing strains, and tune the vocal lyre;
Tradition's secrets are unlock'd to you,
Old tales revive, and ages past renew;
You, who can hidden causes best expound,
Say, whence the isle, which Tiber flows around,
Its altars with a heav'nly stranger grac'd,
And in our shrines the God of physic plac'd.
A wasting plague infected Latium's skies;
Pale, bloodless looks were seen, with ghastly eyes;
The dire disease's marks each visage wore,
And the pure blood was chang'd to putrid gore:
In vain were human remedies apply'd;
In vain the pow'r of healing herbs was try'd:
Weary'd with death, they seek celestial aid,
And visit Phœbus in his Delphic shade;
In the world's centre sacred Delphos stands,
And gives its oracles to distant lands:
Here they implore the God, with fervent vows,
His salutary pow'r to interpose,
And end a great afflicted city's woes.
The holy temple sudden tremors prov'd;
The laurel grove and all its quivers mov'd;
In hollow sounds the priestess, thus, began,
And thro' each bosom thrilling horrors ran.
"Th' assistance, Roman, which you here implore,
Seek from another, and a nearer shore;
Relief must be implor'd, and succour won,
Not from Apollo, but Apollo's son;
My son, to Latium born, shall bring redress:
Go with good omens, and expect success."
When these clear oracles the senate knew;
The sacred tripod's counsels they pursue,
Depute a pious and a chosen band,

Who sail to Epidaurus' neighb'ring land:
Before the Græcian elders when they stood,
They pray 'em to bestow the healing God:
"Ordain'd was he to save Ausonia's state;
So promis'd Delphi, and unerring Fate."
Opinions various their debates enlarge:
Some plead to yield to Rome the sacred charge;
Others, tenacious of their country's wealth,
Refuse to grant the pow'r, who guards its health.
While dubious they remain'd, the wasting light
Withdrew before the growing shades of night;
Now, Roman, clos'd in sleep were mortal eyes,
When health's auspicious God appears to thee,
And thy glad dreams his form celestial see:
In his left hand, a rural staff preferr'd,
His right is seen to stroke his decent beard.
"Dismiss," said he, with mildness all divine,
"Dismiss your fears; I come, and leave my shrine;
This serpent view, that with ambitious play
My staff encircles, mark him ev'ry way;
His form, tho' larger, nobler, I'll assume,
And chang'd, as Gods should be,
bring aid to Rome."
Here fled the vision, and the vision's flight
Was follow'd by the cheerful dawn of light.
Now was the morn with blushing
streaks o'erspread,
And all the starry fires of Heav'n were fled;
The chiefs perplex'd, and fill'd with doubtful care,
To their protector's sumptuous roofs repair,
By genuine signs implore him to express,
What seats he deigns to choose, what land to bless:
Scarce their ascending pray'rs had reach'd the sky;
Lo, the serpentine God, erected high!
Forerunning hissings his approach confest;
Bright shone his golden scales,
and wav'd his lofty crest;

The trembling altar his appearance spoke;
The marble floor, and glittering ceiling shook;
The doors were rock'd; the statue seem'd to nod;
And all the fabric own'd the present God:
His radiant chest he taught aloft to rise,
And round the temple cast his flaming eyes:
Struck was th' astonish'd crowd; the holy priest,
His temples with white bands of ribbon drest,
With rev'rent awe the Power divine confest!
The God! the God! he cries; all tongues be still!
Each conscious breast devoutest ardour fill!
O beauteous! O divine! assist our cares,
And be propitious to thy vot'ries prayers!
All with consenting hearts, and pious fear,
The words repeat, the deity revere:
The Romans in their holy worship join'd,
With silent awe, and purity of mind:
Gracious to them, his crest is seen to nod,
And, as an earnest of his care, the God,
Thrice hissing, vibrates thrice his forked tongue;
And now the smooth descent he glides along:
Still on the ancient seats he bends his eyes,
In which his statue breaths, his altars rise;
His long-lov'd shrine with kind concern he leaves,
And to forsake th' accustom'd mansion grieves:
At length, his sweeping bulk in state is born
Thro' the throng'd streets, which scatter'd
flowers adorn;
Thro' many a fold he winds his mazy course,
And gains the port and moles, which break
the ocean's force.
'Twas here he made a stand, and having view'd
The pious train, who his last steps pursu'd,
Seem'd to dismiss their zeal with gracious eyes,
While gleams of pleasure in his aspect rise.
And now the Latian vessel he ascends;
Beneath the weighty God the vessel bends:

The Latins on the strand great Jove appease,
Their cables loose, and plough the yielding seas:
The high-rear'd serpent from the stern displays
His gorgeous form, and the blue deep surveys;
The ship is wafted on with gentle gales,
And o'er the calm Ionian smoothly sails;
On the sixth morn th' Italian coast they gain,
And touch Lacinia, grac'd with Juno's fane;
Now fair Calabria to the sight is lost,
And all the cities on her fruitful coast;
They pass at length the rough Sicilian shore,
The Brutian soil, rich with metallic ore,
The famous isles, where Æolus was king,
And Pæstum blooming with eternal Spring:
Minerva's cape they leave, and Capreæ's isle,
Campania, on whose hills the vineyards smile,
The city, which Alcides' spoils adorn,
Naples, for soft delight and pleasure born;
Fair Stabiæ, with Cumean Sibyl's seats,
And Baia's tepid baths, and green retreats;
Linternum next they reach, where balmy gums
Distill from mastic trees, and spread perfumes:
Caieta, from the nurse so nam'd, for whom
With pious care Æneas rais'd a tomb,
Vulturne, whose whirlpools suck the
numerous sands,
And Trachas, and Minturnea's marshy lands,
And Formia's coast is left, and Circe's plain,
Which yet remembers her enchanting reign;
To Antium, last, his côurse the pilot guides.
Here, while the anchor'd vessel safely rides
(For now the ruffled deep portends a storm),
The spiry God unfolds his spheric form,
Thro' large indentings draws his lubric train,
And seeks the refuge of Apollo's fane;
The fane is situate on the yellow shore:
When the sea smil'd, and the winds rag'd no more,

He leaves his father's hospitable lands,
And furrows, with his rattling scales, the sands
Along the coast; at length the ship regains,
And sails to Tibur, and Lavinum's plains.
Here mingling crowds to meet their patron came,
Ev'n the chaste guardians of the Vestal flame,
From every part tumultuous they repair,
And joyful acclamations rend the air:
Along the flowery banks, on either side,
Where the tall ship floats on the swelling tide,
Dispos'd in decent order altars rise,
And crackling incense, as it mounts the skies,
The air with sweets refreshes; while the knife,
Warm with the victim's blood, lets out the
streaming life.
The world's great mistress, Rome,
receives him now;
On the mast's top reclin'd he waves his brow,
And from that height surveys the great abodes,
And mansions, worthy of residing Gods.
The land, a narrow neck, it self extends,
Round which his course the stream divided bends;
The stream's two arms, on either side, are seen,
Stretch'd out in equal length; the land between.
The isle, so call'd from hence derives its name:
'Twas here the salutary serpent came;
Nor sooner has he left the Latian pine,
But he assumes again his form divine,
And now no more the drooping city mourns,
Joy is again restor'd, and health returns.

The Deification of Julius Cæsar

But Æsculapius was a foreign power:
In his own city Cæsar we adore:

Him arms, and arts alike renown'd beheld,
In peace conspicuous, dreadful in the field;
His rapid conquest, and swift-finish'd wars,
The hero justly fix'd among the stars;
Yet is his progeny his greatest fame:
The son immortal makes the father's name.
The sea-girt Britons, by his courage tam'd,
For their high rocky cliffs, and fierceness fam'd;
His dreadful navies, which victorious rode
O'er Nile's affrighted waves and seven-sourc'd flood;
Numidia, and the spacious realms regain'd;
Where Cinyphis or flows, or Juba reign'd;
The powers of titled Mithridates broke,
And Pontus added to the Roman yoke;
Triumphal shows decreed, for conquests won,
For conquests, which the triumphs still outshone;
These are great deeds; yet less, than to have giv'n
The world a lord, in whom, propitious Heav'n,
When you decreed the sov'reign rule to place,
You blest with lavish bounty human race.
Now lest so great a prince might seem to rise
Of mortal stem, his sire much reach the skies;
The beauteous Goddess, that Æneas bore,
Foresaw it, and foreseeing did deplore;
For well she knew her hero's fate was nigh,
Devoted by conspiring arms to die.
Trembling, and pale, to every God, she cry'd,
Behold, what deep and subtle arts are try'd,
To end the last, the only branch that springs
From my lulus, and the Dardan kings!
How bent they are! how desp'rate to destroy
All that is left me of unhappy Troy!
Am I alone by Fate ordain'd to know
Uninterrupted care, and endless woe!
Now from Tydides' spear I feel the wound:
Now Ilium's tow'rs the hostile flames surround:
Troy laid in dust, my exil'd son I mourn,

Thro' angry seas, and raging billows born;
O'er the wide deep his wandring course he bends;
Now to the sullen shades of Styx descends,
With Turnus driv'n at last fierce wars to wage,
Or rather with unpitying Juno's rage.
But why record I now my ancient woes?
Sense of past ills in present fears I lose;
On me their points the impious daggers throw;
Forbid it, Gods, repel the direful blow:
If by curs'd weapons Numa's priest expires,
No longer shall ye burn, ye Vestal fires.
While such complainings Cypria's grief disclose;
In each celestial breast compassion rose:
Not Gods can alter Fate's resistless will;
Yet they foretold by signs th' approaching ill.
Dreadful were heard, among the clouds, alarms
Of echoing trumpets, and of clashing arms;
The Sun's pale image gave so faint a light,
That the sad Earth was almost veil'd in night;
The Æther's face with fiery meteors glow'd;
With storms of hail were mingled drops of blood;
A dusky hue the morning star o'erspread,
And the Moon's orb was stain'd with spots of red;
In every place portentous shrieks were heard,
The fatal warnings of th' infernal bird;
In ev'ry place the marble melts to tears;
While in the groves, rever'd thro' length of years,
Boding, and awful sounds the ear invade;
And solemn music warbles thro' the shade;
No victim can atone the impious age,
No sacrifice the wrathful Gods assuage;
Dire wars and civil fury threat the state;
And every omen points out Cæsar's fate:
Around each hallow'd shrine, and sacred dome,
Night-howling dogs disturb the peaceful gloom;
Their silent seats the wandering shades forsake,
And fearful tremblings the rock'd city shake.

Yet could not, by these prodigies, be broke
The plotted charm, or staid the fatal stroke;
Their swords th' assassins in the temple draw;
Their murth'ring hands nor Gods nor temples awe;
This sacred place their bloody weapons stain,
And Virtue falls, before the altar slain.
'Twas now fair Cypria, with her woes opprest,
In raging anguish smote her heav'nly breast;
Wild with distracting fears, the Goddess try'd
Her hero in th' ethereal cloud to hide,
The cloud, which youthful Paris did conceal,
When Menelaus urg'd the threat'ning steel;
The cloud, which once deceiv'd Tydides' sight,
And sav'd Æneas in th' unequal fight.
When Jove—In vain, fair daughter, you assay
To o'er-rule destiny's unconquer'd sway:
Your doubts to banish, enter Fate's abode;
A privilege to heav'nly powers allow'd;
There shall you see the records grav'd,
in length,
On ir'n and solid brass, with mighty strength;
Which Heav'n's and Earth's concussion
shall endure,
Maugre all shocks, eternal, and secure:
There, on perennial adamant design'd,
The various fortunes of your race you'll find:
Well I have mark'd 'em, and will now relate
To thee the settled laws of future Fate.
He, Goddess, for whose death the Fates
you blame,
Has finish'd his determin'd course with Fame:
To thee 'tis giv'n at length, that he shall shine
Among the Gods, and grace the worship'd shrine:
His son to all his greatness shall be heir,
And worthily succeed to empire's care:
Our self will lead his wars, resolv'd to aid
The brave avenger of his father's shade:

To him its freedom Mutina shall owe,
And Decius his auspicious conduct know;
His dreadful powers shall shake Pharsalia's plain,
And drench in gore Philippi's fields again:
A mighty leader, in Sicilia's flood,
Great Pompey's warlike son, shall be subdu'd:
Ægypt's soft queen, adorn'd with fatal charms,
Shall mourn her soldier's unsuccessful arms:
Too late shall find her swelling hopes were vain,
And know, that Rome o'er Memphis still must reign:
What name I Afric, or Nile's hidden head?
Far as both oceans roll, his power shall spread:
All the known Earth to him shall homage pay,
And the seas own his universal sway:
When cruel war no more disturbs Mankind;
To civil studies shall he bend his mind,
With equal justice guardian laws ordain,
And by his great example vice restrain:
Where will his bounty or his goodness end?
To times unborn his gen'rous views extend;
The virtues of his heir our praise engage,
And promise blessings to the coming age:
Late shall he in his kindred orbs be placed,
With Pylian years, and crowded honours graced.
Mean-time, your hero's fleeting spirit bear,
Fresh from his wounds, and change it to a star:
So shall great Julius rites divine assume,
And from the skies eternal smile on Rome.
This spoke, the Goddess to the senate flew;
Where, her fair form conceal'd from mortal view,
Her Cæsar's heav'nly part she made her care,
Nor left the recent soul to waste to air;
But bore it upwards to its native skies:
Glowing with new-born fires she saw it rise;
Forth springing from her bosom up it flew,
And kindling, as it soar'd, a comet grew:
Above the lunar sphere it took its flight,
And shot behind it a long trail of light.

The Reign of Augustus, in which Ovid Flourish'd

Thus rais'd, his glorious off-spring Julius view'd,
Beneficently great, and scattering good,
Deeds, that his own surpass'd, with joy beheld,
And his large heart dilates to be excell'd.
What tho' this prince refuses to receive
The preference, which his juster subjects give;
Fame uncontroll'd, that no restraint obeys,
The homage, shunn'd by modest virtue, pays,
And proves disloyal only in his praise.
Tho' great his sire, him greater we proclaim:
So Atreus yields to Agamemnon's fame;
Achilles so superior honours won,
And Peleus must submit to Peleus' son;
Examples yet more noble to disclose,
So Saturn was eclips'd, when Jove to empire rose;
Jove rules the Heav'ns, the Earth Augustus sways;
Each claims a monarch's, and a father's praise.
Celestials, who for Rome your cares employ;
Ye Gods, who guarded the remains of Troy;
Ye native Gods, here born, and fix'd by Fate;
Quirinus, founder of the Roman state;
O parent Mars, from whom Quirinus sprung;
Chaste Vesta, Cæsar's household Gods among,
Most sacred held; domestic Phœbus, thou,
To whom with Vesta chaste alike we bow;
Great guardian of the high Tarpeian rock;
And all ye Pow'rs, whom poets may invoke;
O grant, that day may claim our sorrows late,
When lov'd Augustus shall submit to Fate.
Visit those seats, where Gods and heroes dwell,
And leave, in tears, the world he rul'd so well!

The poet concludes

The work is finish'd, which nor dreads the rage
Of tempests, fire, or war, or wasting age;
Come, soon or late, death's undetermin'd day,
This mortal being only can decay;
My nobler part, my fame, shall reach the skies,
And to late times with blooming honours rise:
Whate'er th' unbounded Roman power obeys,
All climes and nations shall record my praise:
If 'tis allow'd to poets to divine,
One half of round eternity is mine.

FINIS

On the Nature of Things

De Rerum Natura

Lucretius

Edited by William Ellery Leonard

On the Nature of Things

Proem

Mother of Rome, delight of Gods and men,
Dear Venus that beneath the gliding stars
Makest to teem the many-voyaged main
And fruitful lands—for all of living things
Through thee alone are evermore conceived,
Through thee are risen to visit the great sun—
Before thee, Goddess, and thy coming on,
Flee stormy wind and massy cloud away,
For thee the dædal Earth bears scented flowers,
For thee waters of the unvexed deep
Smile, and the hollows of the serene sky
Glow with diffused radiance for thee!
For soon as comes the springtime face of day,
And procreant gales blow from the West unbarred,
First fowls of air, smit to the heart by thee,
Foretoken thy approach, O thou Divine,
And leap the wild herds round the happy fields
Or swim the bounding torrents. Thus amain,
Seized with the spell, all creatures follow thee
Whithersoever thou walkest forth to lead,
And thence through seas and mountains
and swift streams,
Through leafy homes of birds and greening plains,
Kindling the lure of love in every breast,
Thou bringest the eternal generations forth,
Kind after kind. And since 'tis thou alone
Guidest the Cosmos, and without thee naught

Is risen to reach the shining shores of light,
Nor aught of joyful or of lovely born,
Thee do I crave co-partner in that verse
Which I presume on Nature to compose
For Memmius mine, whom thou hast willed to be
Peerless in every grace at every hour.
Wherefore indeed, Divine one, give my words
Immortal charm. Lull to a timely rest
O'er sea and land the savage works of war,
For thou alone hast power with public peace
To aid mortality; since he who rules
The savage works of battle, puissant Mars,
How often to thy bosom flings his strength
O'ermastered by the eternal wound of love,
And there, with eyes and full throat
backward thrown,
Gazing, my Goddess, open-mouthed at thee,
Pastures on love his greedy sight, his breath
Hanging upon thy lips. Him thus reclined
Fill with thy holy body, round, above!
Pour from those lips soft syllables to win
Peace for the Romans, glorious Lady, peace!
For in a season troublous to the state
Neither may I attend this task of mine
With thought untroubled, nor mid such events
The illustrious scion of the Memmian house
Neglect the civic cause.
And for the rest, summon to judgments true,
Unbusied ears and singleness of mind
Withdrawn from cares; lest these
my gifts, arranged
For thee with eager service, thou disdain
Before thou comprehendest: since for thee
I prove the supreme law of Gods and sky,
And the primordial germs of things unfold,
Whence Nature all creates, and multiplies
And fosters all, and whither she resolves

Each in the end when each is overthrown.
This ultimate stock we have devised to name
Procreant atoms, matter, seeds of things,
Or primal bodies, as primal to the world.
Whilst human kind
Throughout the lands lay miserably crushed
Before all eyes beneath Religion—who
Would show her head along the region skies,
Glowering on mortals with her hideous face—
A Greek it was who first opposing dared
Raise mortal eyes that terror to withstand,
Whom nor the fame of Gods nor lightning's stroke
Nor threatening thunder of the ominous sky
Abashed; but rather chafed to angry zest
His dauntless heart to be the first to rend
The crossbars at the gates of Nature old.
And thus his will and hardy wisdom won;
And forward thus he fared afar, beyond
The flaming ramparts of the world, until
He wandered the unmeasurable All.
Whence he to us, a conqueror, reports
What things can rise to being, what cannot,
And by what law to each its scope prescribed,
Its boundary stone that clings so deep in Time.
Wherefore Religion now is under foot,
And us his victory now exalts to heaven.
I fear perhaps thou deemest that we fare
An impious road to realms of thought profane;
But 'tis that same religion oftener far
Hath bred the foul impieties of men:
As once at Aulis, the elected chiefs,
Foremost of heroes, Danaan counselors,
Defiled Diana's altar, virgin queen,
With Agamemnon's daughter, foully slain.
She felt the chaplet round her maiden locks
And fillets, fluttering down on either cheek,
And at the altar marked her grieving sire,

The priests beside him who concealed the knife,
And all the folk in tears at sight of her.
With a dumb terror and a sinking knee
She dropped; nor might avail her now that first
'Twas she who gave the king a father's name.
They raised her up, they bore the trembling girl
On to the altar—hither led not now
With solemn rites and hymeneal choir,
But sinless woman, sinfully foredone,
A parent felled her on her bridal day,
Making his child a sacrificial beast
To give the ships auspicious winds for Troy:
Such are the crimes to which Religion leads.
And there shall come the time when even thou,
Forced by the soothsayer's terror-tales, shalt seek
To break from us. Ah, many a dream even now
Can they concoct to rout thy plans of life,
And trouble all thy fortunes with base fears.
I own with reason: for, if men but knew
Some fixed end to ills, they would be strong
By some device unconquered to withstand
Religions and the menacings of seers.
But now nor skill nor instrument is theirs,
Since men must dread eternal pains in death.
For what the soul may be they do not know,
Whether 'tis born, or enter in at birth,
And whether, snatched by death, it die with us,
Or visit the shadows and the vasty caves
Of Orcus, or by some divine decree
Enter the brute herds, as our Ennius sang,
Who first from lovely Helicon brought down
A laurel wreath of bright perennial leaves,
Renowned forever among the Italian clans.
Yet Ennius too in everlasting verse
Proclaims those vaults of Acheron to be,
Though thence, he said, nor souls nor bodies fare,
But only phantom figures, strangely wan,

And tells how once from out those regions rose
Old Homer's ghost to him and shed salt tears
And with his words unfolded Nature's source.
Then be it ours with steady mind to clasp
The purport of the skies—the law behind
The wandering courses of the sun and moon;
To scan the powers that speed all life below;
But most to see with reasonable eyes
Of what the mind, of what the soul is made,
And what it is so terrible that breaks
On us asleep, or waking in disease,
Until we seem to mark and hear at hand
Dead men whose bones earth bosomed long ago.
I know how hard it is in Latian verse
To tell the dark discoveries of the Greeks,
Chiefly because our pauper-speech must find
Strange terms to fit the strangeness of the thing;
Yet worth of thine and the expected joy
Of thy sweet friendship do persuade me on
To bear all toil and wake the clear nights through,
Seeking with what of words and what of song
I may at last most gloriously uncloud
For thee the light beyond, wherewith to view
The core of being at the centre hid.

PHARSALIA

ON THE CIVIL WAR

LUCAN

Edited by Sir Edward Ridley

Pharsalia

Wars worse than civil on Emathian plains,
And crime let loose we sing: how Rome's high race
Plunged in her vitals her victorious sword;
Armies akin embattled, with the force
Of all the shaken earth bent on the fray;
And burst asunder, to the common guilt,
A kingdom's compact; eagle with eagle met,
Standard to standard, spear opposed to spear.
Whence, citizens, this rage, this boundless lust
To sate barbarians with the blood of Rome?
Did not the shade of Crassus, wandering still,
Cry for his vengeance? Could ye not have spoiled,
To deck your trophies, haughty Babylon?
Why wage campaigns that send no laurels home?
What lands, what oceans might have been the prize
Of all the blood thus shed in civil strife!
Where Titan rises, where night hides the stars,
'Neath southern noons with fiery rays aflame,
Or where keen frost that never yields to spring
In icy fetters binds the Scythian main:
Long since barbarian Araxes' stream,
And all the distant East, and those who know
(If any such there be) the birth of Nile,
Had felt our yoke. Then, then, with all the world
Beneath thee, Rome, if for nefarious war
Such be thy passion, turn upon thyself:
Not yet was wanting for thy sword a foe.
That crumbled houses and half-ruined homes
Now mark our cities; that the ancient streets
Scarce hear the footfall of the passer-by;
That mighty fragments lie beside the walls;

That hearths are desolate; that far and wide
Fields thick with bramble and untilled for years
Demand the labours of the hind in vain:
All this nor Pyrrhus caused, nor Punic chief,
Nor sword thrust deep. 'Twas civil strife alone
That dealt the wound and left the death behind.
Yet if the fates could find no other way
For Nero's coming, nor the gods with ease
Gain thrones in heaven; and if the Thunderer
Prevailed not till the giants' war was done,
We plain no more, ye gods! for such a boon
All wickedness be welcome and all crime;
Thronged with our dead be dire Pharsalia's fields,
Be Punic ghosts avenged by Roman blood;
Add, Cæsar, to these ills the Mutin toils;
Perusia's dearth; on Munda's final field
The shock of battle joined; let Leucas' Cape
Shatter the routed navies; servile hands
Unsheath the sword on fiery Etna's slopes:
Still Rome is gainer by the civil war.
Thou, Cæsar, art her prize. When thou shalt choose,
Thy watch relieved, to seek at length the stars,
All heaven rejoicing; and shalt hold a throne,
Or else elect to govern Phœbus' car
And light a subject world that shall not dread
To owe her brightness to a different Sun;
All shall concede thy right: do what thou wilt,
Select thy Godhead, and the central clime
Whence thou shalt rule the world
with power divine.
And yet the Northern or the Southern Pole
We pray thee, choose not; but in rays direct
Vouchsafe thy radiance to thy city Rome.
Press thou on either side, the universe
Should lose its equipoise: take thou the midst,
And weight the scales, and let that part of heaven
Where Cæsar sits be evermore serene

And smile upon us with unclouded blue.
Then may all men lay down their arms, and peace
Through all the nations reign, and shut the gates
That close the temple of the God of War.
Be thou my help, to me e'en now divine!
Let Delphi's steep her own Apollo guard,
And Nysa keep her Bacchus, uninvoked.
Rome is my subject and my muse art thou!
First of such deeds I purpose to unfold
The causes task immense what drove to arms
A maddened nation and from all the world
Struck peace away.
By envious fate's decrees
Abide not long the mightiest lords of earth;
Too great the burden, great shall be the fall.
Thus Rome o'ergrew her strength.
So when that hour,
The last in all the centuries, shall sound
The world's disruption, all things shall revert
To that primæval chaos, stars on stars
Shall crash; and fiery meteors from the sky
Plunge in the ocean. Earth shall then no more
Front with her bulwark the encroaching sea:
The moon, indignant at her path oblique,
Shall drive her chariot 'gainst her brother Sun
And claim the day for hers; and discord huge
Shall rend the spheres asunder. On themselves
The great are dashed: such end the gods have set
To height of power: nor ever Fortune shares
With other lands the weapons of her spite
Against a nation lord of land and sea.
Thou, Rome, degraded, sold, the common prey
Of triple despots, of a tyrant rule
Partnered as ne'er before-thyself art cause
Of all the ills. Ye chiefs, with greed of power
Blind, leagued for evil, is your force conjoined
To hold the world in common as your prize?

So long as Sea on Earth and Earth on Air
Lean for support while Titan runs his course,
And night with day divides an equal sphere,
No king shall brook his fellow, nor shall rule
Endure a rival. Search no foreign lands:
These walls are proof that in their infant days
A hamlet, not the world, was prize enough
To cause the shedding of a brothers blood.
Concord, on discord based, brief time endured,
Unwelcome to the rivals; and alone
Crassus delayed the advent of the war.
Like to the slender neck that separates
The seas of Græcia: should it be engulfed
Then would th' Ionian and Ægean mains
Break each on other: thus when Crassus fell,
Who held apart the chiefs, in piteous death,
And stained Assyria's plains with Latian blood,
Defeat in Parthia loosed the war in Rome.
More in that victory than ye thought was won,
Ye sons of Arsaces; your conquered foes
Took at your hands the rage of civil strife.
By sword the realm is parted; and the state
Supreme o'er earth and sea, wide as the world,
Could not find space for two. For Julia bore,
Cut off by fate unpitying, the bond
Of that ill-omened marriage and the pledge
Of blood united, to the shades below.
Hadst thou but longer stayed, it had been thine
To keep the parent and the spouse apart,
Strike sword from grasp and join
the threatening hands;
As Sabine matrons in the days of old
Joined in the midst the bridegroom and the sire.
With thee all trust was buried, and the chiefs
Could give their courage vent, and rushed to war.
Lest newer glories triumphs past obscure,
Late conquered Gaul the bays from pirates won,

This, Magnus, is thy fear; thy roll of fame,
Of glorious deeds accomplished for the state
Allows no equal; nor will Cæsar's pride
A prior rival in his triumphs brook;
Which had the right 'twere impious to inquire;
Each for his cause can vouch a judge supreme;
The victor, heaven: the vanquished, Cato, thee.
Nor were they like to like: the one in years
Now verging towards decay, in times of peace
Had unlearned war; but thirsting for applause
Gave to the people much, and proud of fame
His former glory cared not to renew,
But joyed in plaudits of the theatre,
His gift to Rome: his triumphs in the past,
Himself the shadow of a mighty name.
As when some oak, in fruitful field sublime,
Adorned with venerable spoils, and gifts
Of bygone leaders, by its weight to earth
With feeble roots still clings; its naked arms
And hollow trunk, though leafless, give a shade;
And though condemned beneath
the tempest's shock
To speedy fall, amid the sturdier trees
In sacred grandeur rules the forest still.
No such repute had Cæsar won, nor fame;
But energy was his that could not rest—
The only shame he knew was not to win.
Keen and unvanquished, where revenge or hope
Might call, resistless would he strike the blow
With sword unpitying: every victory won
Reaped to the full; the favour of the gods
Pressed to the utmost; all that stayed his course
Aimed at the summit of power, was thrust aside:
Triumph his joy, though ruin marked his track.
As parts the clouds a bolt by winds compelled,
With crack of riven air and crash of worlds,
And veils the light of day, and on mankind,

Blasting their vision with its flames oblique,
Sheds deadly fright; then turning to its home,
Nought but the air opposing, through its path
Spreads havoc, and collects its scattered fires.

Thebaid

Statius

Translated by J. H. Mozley

Thebaid

Lines 1-87 of Book I.

My spirit is touched by Pierian fire to recount the strife of brethren, and the battle of the alternate reign fought out with impious hatred, and all the guilty tale of Thebes. Whence, O goddesses, do ye bid me begin?—Shall I sing the origins of the dreadful race, the Sidonian rape and the inexorable terms of Agenor's law, and Camus searching o'er the main? Far backward runs the story, should I tell of the anxious husbandman of hidden war, sowing battles in the unhallowed soil, and searching to the uttermost, relate with what song Amphion bade the Tyrian mountains move to form a city's walls, whence came Bacchus' grievous wrath against his kindred towers; what deed fierce Juno wrought; against whom unhappy Athamas caught up his bow, and why with Palæmon in her arms his mother quailed not to leap into the vast Ionian sea. Nay rather here and now I will suffer the sorrows and the joys of Cadmus to have gone by: let the troubled house of Oedipus set a limit to my song, since not yet may I venture to utter the theme of the standards of Italy and the triumphs of the North, or Rhine twice brought beneath our yoke and Ister twice subject to our law and the Dacians hurled down from their conspiring mount, or how in those days or scarce-approaching manhood Jove was forfended to attack, and of thee, O glory added to the Latian name, whom succeeding early to thy sire's latest exploits Rome longs to be her own for ever. Yea, though a closer bound confine the stars, and the shining quarter of the sky that knows nought of Pleiads or Boreas or rending thunderbolt tempt thee, though he who curbs the fiery-footed steeds set with his own hand upon thy locks the exalted radiance of his diadem, or Jupiter yield thee an equal portion of the great heaven, abide contented with the governance of men, thou lord of earth and sea, and give constellations to the sky. A time will come when emboldened by Pierian frenzy I shall recount thy deeds: now do I pitch my harp but to the singing of Aonian arms and the sceptre fatal to both tyrants; of their madness unchecked by death and the strife of flames in the dissension of the funeral pyre; of kings' bodies lacking burial and cities drained by mutual slaughter, when the dark-blue waters of Dirce blushed red with Lernæan gore, and Thetis stood aghast at Ismenos, once wont to graze arid banks, flowing down with mighty heaps of slain. Which hero first dost thou make my theme, O Clio? Tydeus, uncontrolled in wrath? the sudden chasm that gaped for the laurel-crowned prophet? Distraught Hippomedon, too, repelling his river-foe with corpses demands my song, and I must lament the gallant Arcadian and his wars, and sing with a yet fiercer thrill the fate of Capaneus.

Already had Oedipus with avenging hand probed deep his sinning eyes and sunk his guilty shame in eternal night, abiding in a long and living death. But while he hugs his darkness and the uttermost seclusion of his dwelling, and keeps his secret chamber which the sun's rays and heaven behold not, yet with unwearied wings the fierce daylight of the mind hovers around him, and the Avenging Furies of his crimes assail his heart. Then he displays to heaven those empty orbs, the cruel, pitiful punishment of his life, and with blood-stained hands beats upon the hollow earth, and in dire accents utters this prayer: "Gods who hold sway over guilty souls and over Tartarus crowded with the damned, and thou O Styx, whom I behold, ghastly in thy shadowy depths, and thou Tisiphone, so oft the object of my prayer, be favourable now, and further my unnatural wish: if in aught I have found favour; if thou didst cherish me in thy bosom when I fell from my mother's womb, and didst heal the wounds of my pierced feet; if I sought the lake of Cirrha where it winds between the two summits of the range, when I could have lived contented with the false Polybus, and in the Phocian strait where three ways meet grappled with the aged king and cleft the visage of the trembling dotard, searching for my true sire; if by wit of the foreshowing I solved the riddles of the cruel Sphinx; if I knew exulting the sweet ecstasy and fatal union of my mother's bed, and passed many an unhallowed night, and begot sons for thee, as well thou knowest, yet soon, greedy for punishment, did violence to myself with tearing fingers and left my eyes upon my wretched mother—hear me to the end, if my prayer be worthy and such as thou wouldest inspire my ranging heart withal. Sightless though I was and driven from my throne, my sons, on whatever couch begotten, attempted not to give me guidance or consolation in my grief; nay, haughtily (ah! the maddening sting!) and raised to royalty with me long dead, they mock my blindness and abhor their father's groans. Do these too hold me accursed? and the father of gods beholds it, and does naught? Do thou at least, my due defender, come hither, and begin a work of vengeance that will blast their seed for ever! Set on thy head the gore-drenched circlet that my bloody nails tore of, and inspired by their father's curses go thou between the brethren, and with the sword sunder the binding ties of kinship. Grant me, thou queen of Tartarus' abyss, grant me to see the evil that my soul desires, nor will the spirit of the youths be slow to follow; come thou but worthy of thyself, thou shalt know them to be true sons of mine."

FINIS

www.ingramcontent.com/pod-product-compliance
Lightning Source LLC
Chambersburg PA
CBHW070333170726
48291CB00001B/34

9781944482459